Where Are They Now?

Southampton

Jamie Spoor

Where are they now?

www.where-are-they-now.co.uk/club/southampton

First published in 2021 by
Media House Books

© Media House Books 2021

ISBN 978-1-912027-54-5

Original cover design by Marten Sealby

Adams, Micky
Full-back
Born: *1961 Sheffield*
Playing career: *Sheffield United, Gillingham, Coventry City, Leeds United, Southampton, Stoke City, Fulham, Swansea City, Brentford (1974-1998)*

Adams became a regular during Saints' debut season in the Premier League and went on to make over 150 appearances during his five year stay on the south coast. Adams holds the dubious honour of being the first Saints player to be sent off in the Premier League. He also played for Gillingham, Coventry, Leeds, Stoke, Fulham, Swansea and Brentford before hanging up his boots. Adams then had an eventful time in the dugout. He won four promotions as manager including one with former club Fulham. Overall though, he had mixed fortunes in management, being named 'Manager of the Season' twice', being sacked by three different clubs but oversaw four promotions. Since leaving the game, Adams has appeared on several radio shows and set up his own football consultancy business in 2015. He has also helped to mentor youth players in Kyrgystan and coached at Harborough Town, one of the clubs close to his home in Leicestershire.

Adams, William
Half-back
Born: *1902 Tynemouth*
Died: *1963*
Playing career: *Sunderland Colliery, Guildford United, Southampton, West Ham United , Southend United (1925-1937)*

North East native Williams went on to become Southampton captain upon the departure of Mike Keeping, despite the fact that his first two appearance for the club came three years apart. Adams played over 200 times at The Dell before he moved on to the Uniteds of first West Ham and later Southend. He scored on his Hammers debut.... against former club Saints. After retirement in 1937, Adams briefly returned to Saints in a coaching capacity before running the Half Way Inn at Chandler's Ford. Adams died in 1963 aged 61 whilst still landlord of the pub.

Affleck, David
Centre-half
Born: *1912 Coylton, Ayrshire*
Died: *1984*
Playing career: *Notts County, Bristol City, Clapton Orient, Southampton, Yeovil Town (1932-1946)*

Dave Affleck was following in his family's footsteps by working in the mines of Scotland before being spotted in the local leagues by Bristol City. He was later ecruited by Tom Parker in 1937 as part of the new Southampton manager's drive to strengthen his team for Second Division promotion. It took £600 - a mammoth fee at the time - to stop Sunderland taking him north, but it proved to be money well spent. A commanding presence at the back and noted for his incisive tackling and aerial prowess, Affleck quickly established himself at The Dell. The outbreak of war brought his career to a halt and, during the conflict, he turned out for the Police XI and guested for Saints in unofficial wartime games. Played for non league Yeovil and coached at non league level in Somerset before becoming a full-time policeman.

"DID YOU KNOW?"

"Rickie Lambert scored all 34 penalties he took for Saints."

Agboola, Reuben

Left-back or sweeper
Born: *1962 Camden, London*
Playing career: *Cheshunt, Southampton, Southampton, Sunderland, Charlton Athletic, Port Vale, Swansea City. (1973-1994)*

Reuben Agboola's Saints career is a story of a sudden arrival and even quicker departure. Made his debut at Old Trafford only weeks after signing, and left under a cloud after a late night incident when he was hit by a car. A versatile utility player equally adept at right back as he was in midfield, Agboola was known for his stylish speed and reading of the game. Arguably was at his best during the 1983/84 season when Saints were First Division runners up and FA Cup semi finalists. The Londoner moved on to Sunderland where regained his top form and earned the first of nine caps that he was to win for Nigeria. Stops at Charlton, Port Vale and Swansea would follow before returning to the area to run the Pub in the Park in Southampton between 1994 nd 2004. This catering experience allowed him to move to the island of Majorca where he ran a seafront bistro. Uponm returning home, he took up a job as an assessor for Parkway Cars in Eastleigh.

Allan, Derek

Defender
Born: *1974 Irvine, Scotland*
Playing career: *Ayr United, Southampton, Brighton & Hove Albion, Kingstonian, Queen of the South, Dumbarton (1992-2005)*

Allan arrived at Saints with his career still in its infancy, but touted by then Saints manager Ian Branfoot as a star of the future. A series of niggling injuries restricted the centre back to only a solitary Premier League appearance - against Manchester City in 1993. He would make more of a name for himself during his time at south coast rivals Brighton and retired at the relatively young age of 30 having made 80 appearances for the Seagulls. Allan dropped down into the non league game and worked part-time for a stationery company. He returned to Scotland and took up coaching at former club Ayr.

Allen, Paul

Midfielder
Born: *1962 Aveley*
Playing career: *West Ham United, Tottenham Hotspur, Southampton, Luton Town (loan), Stoke City (loan), Swindon Town, Bristol City, Millwall, Purfleet (1979-1998)*

Before his West Ham side had won the 1980 Final against Arsenal, Paul Allen had already made history by becoming the youngest player to appear in a Wembley showpiece - aged 17 years 256 days. He went on to win the trophy again with Spurs in 1991. Considered workmanlike when compared to his more illustrious team-mates, he was an ideal foil for Saints manager Ian Branfoot, and went on to play almost 50 times for Southampton in the Premier League - featuring in the "Great Escape" of 1994. To this day, he declines to talk about his time under Branfoot, nursing "not particularly happy memories." Went on to play for Luton, Stoke, Swindon, Bristol City and Millwall and earned three caps for England at Under 21 level. In retirement, he joined the PFA in 2001 to work on the PA Sport Football live project, The Masters of Britain seven-a-side Football series, and the Hong Kong Soccer Sevens Tournament to work before joining their as Delegate Liaison Department.

Allen, Thomas

Goalkeeper
Born: *1897 Moxley*
Died: *1968*
Playing career: *Wednesday Old Park Works, Bilston United, Hickman's Institute, Wolverhampton Wanderers, Sunderland, Southampton, Coventry City, Accrington Stanley, Northampton Town, Kidderminster Harriers, Cradley Heath (1919-1938)*

Sunderland's loss was certainly Southampton's gain when they swooped to sign thr ex-Wolves 'keeper on a free. A regular in the club's inaugural Football League season, he was an ever present in a side that kept 26 clean sheets in the Third Division (South), winning the title by a nose from Plymouth. Tall, slightly built and with "miraculous" agility, he still holds the goalkeeping club record of 845 minutes without conceding a goal and the most appearances by a keeper in both league (291) and FA Cup (32).

After eight years as a Saint, he returned to the Midlands to be nearer his family home, also playing for Accrington and Northampton before a spell in non league. Allen was the subject of much dressing room banter - players in the bath would shout: "Look out the plug's pulled, we don't want to lose Tom down the drain" (a reference to his slender build). Died in May 1968 a few days after his 71st birthday.

Almeida, Marco

Centre-back
Born: *1977 Barreiro, Portugal*
Playing career: *Sporting CP, Sporting CP, Casa Pia, Lourinhanense, Campomaiorense, Southampton, Campomaiorense, Alverca, Ciudad Murcia, Maia, Portimonense, Nea Salamis, Lourosa, Akritas Chlorakas (1988-2011)*

Signed by Dave Jones on a one year loan, Almeida's brief Saints career amounted to a solitary, 20 minute cameo. On his debut against Arsenal, Almedia found himself facing an unknown Frenchman and was given a torrid time. His opponent who scored his first Gunners goal that day? Thierry Henry. Almeida went on to have spells in Spain, Greece and Cyprus and also had a trial with Cardiff under his former manager Jones. He played for Portugal at Under 20 and Under 21 level.

Anderson, Alexander

Full-back
Born: *1921 Monifieth, Scotland*
Died: *1999*
Playing career: *St Johnstone, Forfar Athletic, Southampton, Exeter C, Dundee United (1946-1955)*

Anderson began his career in his native Scotland before he was scouted and signed by Southampton. Despite receiving much praise for his impressive start on the south coast, he slipped to third choice full-back behind Bill Ellerington and Norman Kirkman. The latter went on to become Exeter's player/manager and persuaded Anderson to join him there. After only a handful of games for the Grecians, he returned to his homeland - via a brief spell at non league Cheltenham. Having retired from the game Alex returned to his original employment as an engineer. Died in 1999 aged 78.

St Mary's

Andrews, Alfred "Arthur"

Half-back
Born: *1891 Sunderland*
Died: *1964*
Playing career: *Sunderland Rovers, Sunderland Rovers, Southampton, Harland & Wolff, General Post Office, Cowes, Lymington (1913-1922)*

A North-East native and a boilermaker by trade, Andrews moved south to take up work on Southampton Docks during WW1. He won the South Hants War League as part of the Harland & Wolff works side, an earned a trial at The Dell in 1919. Andrews forced his way into the first team at full back and went on to play 12 times for the Southern League Saints. A broken leg in an FA Cup tie prematurely ended his playing career. Leaving Saints after less than a year, Andrews was offered a job in the docks and which he accepted and settled in the area. He died in the city in 1964.

Andrews, Ian

Goalkeeper
Born: *1964 Nottingham*
Playing career: *Swindon Town (loan), Celtic, Leeds United (loan), Southampton, Bournemouth, Leicester City (1982-2002)*

Following in the footsteps of legendary contemporaries Gordon Banks and Peter Shilton, Andrews was only 16 when he was signed by Leicester. He soon became first choice and hardly missed a game before agreeing to move north of the border to Celtic. However, he quickly fell out of favour and Chris Nicholl signed him for Saints for a £200,000 fee. Never managed to hold down a regular place between the sticks, mainly due to the presence of Tim Flowers, and moved on again, this time on to AFC Bournemouth. Later returned to Leicester as goalkeeping coach and physiotherapist - a role he later reprised for university side Team Bath.

5

Andrews, Leonard

Inside-forward
Born: *1888 Reading, Berkshire*
Died: *1969*
Playing career: *Reading, Southampton, Reading, Southampton, Watford, (1909-1925)*

A "clever and versatile" forward, Andrews was renowned for his penalty taking prowess. Channelling his inner Matt Le Tissier, Andrews would miss only two out of 22 spot-kicks and was equally as adept with either foot. Started out at Reading, he moved south in 1912 to link up with new Saints coach Jimmy McIntyre at the cash-strapped club. Of the three new players brought in that year. McIntyre would describe Andrews' signing as the "best of his coaching career". Andrews became Saints most consistent forward in the last three pre-War seasons, finishing his debut campaign as joint top scorer as a virtual ever present. Joined the 5th Battalion Wiltshire Regiment during the War, serving in the Middle East, rising through the ranks to Sergeant Major. He went to Reading to resume his career, before returning to The Dell where he was a title-winning regular in 1922. Ended his playing days with a brief spell at Watford, before taking up a job as an insurance salesman in Southampton.

Andruszewski, Manny

Defender
Born: *1955 Eastleigh, Hampshire*
Playing career: *Holy Cross F.C., Southampton, Tampa Bay Rowdies, Aldershot, Andover, Houston Dynamos, Dallas Sidekicks (1970-1985)*

Born in Eastleigh of Polish parentage, Manny played everywhere across the defence during the late 1970s. Andruszewski rose through the Saints ranks alongside others including, Nick Holmes, David Walker and Malcolm Waldron. A regular squad member who was often used for a specialist man marking role against particularly tricky opponents. Missed out on the famous 1976 cup final due to the signing of Peter Rodrigues that season and also the Football League Cup Final in 1979 having played an important role earlier in that cup run. Apart from one season at Aldershot (1982-1983), he spent the rest of his career in the USA playing in the NASL and Indoor Leagues. Returning home to England he worked for Peter Green furniture stores in Chandlers Ford and more recently set up his own gardening business back in Eastleigh.

Location of the Dell, now residential accommodation.

Angell, James

Right-half

Born: *1883 Bitterne, Southampton*
Died: *1960*
Playing career: *Woolston Alma, Southampton, Bitterne Guild, Eastleigh Athletic (1902-1908)*

Angell played at junior level for several local clubs in Hampshire before he joined the Saints and rose through the ranks. Won the Hampshire Senior Cup three times and a first team bow followed in 1906. Angell only played four times in red and white before he hung up his boots. Angell went into coaching as manager of Woolson Thorneycrofts after the war. He then scouted for Arsenal and Norwich before he later returned to Southampton as boss of the Saints "A" team. Also worked at Romsey Town FC in a variety of different positions - including manager, chairman and president. He combined his football career with part time employment as a local builder and his name adorned the advertising hoardings at the Dell for many years. Angell died in 1960 aged 77

Angus, John

Forward

Born: *1868 Blythswood Hill, Glasgow, Scotland*
Died: *1933*
Playing career: *Third Lanark, Ardwick, Southampton St Mary's, Fulham (1892-1895)*

The Saints history books will remember John Angus as a man of contrasting fortunes. Having chanced his arm with several Football League clubs, the Scottish forward became one of the first professionals for the club then known as Southampton St Mary's. Angus had the dubious 'honour' of being the first Saint to be sent off. Scored in their inaugural tie in the Southern League. Angus became a first team regular but left in 1895. Had a brief stint at Fulham and then became a house-painter in London. Angus died in 1933 at the age of 65.

"DID YOU KNOW?"

"Terry Paine holds the record for the most Southampton appearances (816)"

Arias, Federico

Striker

Born: *1979 Rosario, Argentina*
Playing career: *Rosario Central, Velez SArsfield, Southampton, Velez SArsfield, Quilmes, Belgrano de CV£rdoba, Sporting Cristal, Coronel Bolognesi, Martina Franca, Deportes Melipilla, Yaracuyanos, Tiro Federal (1998-2009)*

Arias enjoyed a long career, and arrived on the south coast in 2003. He never made a first team appearance for the Saints, though. Gordon Strachan, Southampton manager at the time, described the new boy as a quick and pacy forward player with two excellent feet. The Argentine U20 international retired in 2009 as one of the more obscure players to be on the books at Saints in recent years. Was last heard of playing in the lower leagues back in Argentina.

Armstrong, David

Midfielder

Born: *1954 Durham*
Playing career: *Middlesbrough, Southampton, Bournemouth (1971-1987)*

Already a record holder having played 356 consecutive games for Middlesbrough, it was no surprise to see a clamour for Armstrong's services. Noted for his consistency and durability, eyebrows were nevertheless raised when he swapped the north east for the south coast for a hefty £600,000 - a record at the time for both clubs. Already capped three times for England, Armstrong would go on to become the string pulling heartbeat of Lawrie McMenemy's midfield for the best part of a decade. His six seasons at the club co-incided with the club's most successful era, finishing First Division runners up to Liverpool in 1984 (Saints best ever league finish), and reached three major cup semi finals. He went on to become Southampton captain and showed his versatility by also filling in across the defence. 272 games later, he went on to Bournemouth where injury ended his career. He remained involved in the game, albeit in the commercial and community development aspect. He has since combined a day job in office supplies with punditry work and radio commentary.

Armstrong, Kenneth

Centre-half
Born: *1959 Bridgnorth*
Playing career: *Beith Juniors, Beith Juniors, Kilmarnock, Southampton, Notts County, Birmingham City, Walsall (1977-1986)*

Armstrong was signed by Lawrie McMenemy for £25,000 and immediately struck up an eye catching double act pairing with Mark Wright at the heart of the defence. During his debut season, Saints conceded only two goals in their first ten league games, on the way to a runners up finish in Division One - their best ever league season. Saints were unlikely contenders for a shock league and cup double until the final furlong of Armstrong's first and only season at the club. Wright picked up an injury and McMenemy opted for a reshuffle that saw Armstrong fall out of favour. He was loaned to Notts County then joined newly relegated Birmingham City for £75,000. Armstrong went on to work as an M&S trainee and then as Director of Operations for the NHS north of the border.

Arnold, John

Outside-left
Born: *1907 Cowley, Oxfordshire*
Died: *1984*
Playing career: *Southampton, Fulham (1928-1933)*

A multi-talented sportsman, John Arnold became one of the elite few to represent England at two different sports. Already a Hampshire cricketer of some renown when he joined Saints, he created a club record in his debut season as he plundered 21 goals as a winger - the most by a man in his position. He played a single Test match for his country in 1931. One of only twelve "dual internationals", he was also capped once by England at outside-left in a 2-1 defeat to Scotland in 1933. Making his feat even more unique, he would never play again at international level in either sport. Played 40 times for Saints until the cash-strapped club sold him - along with Mike Keeping - to Fulham for £5,000. Served in the fire service throughout the war and briefly resumed his cricket career, becoming a first class umpire whilst running a pub in the Southampton area.

Ashford, Ryan

Defender
Born: *1981 Honiton, Devon*
Playing career: *Southampton, Torquay United, Weymouth, Eastleigh, Sholing (1996-2013)*

Ashford, by his own admission, found life tough at the Saints as managers came and went throughout a turbulent time. His Southampton career amounted to all of 20 minutes, when he injured his ankle on his debut. He subsequently recovered but never regained his place in the first team. Scored on his full bow for Torquay and had a season at Weymouth. Ashford - a defender - returned to the Southampton area where he combined playing part time with a job in sales.

Astlund, Jan

Right-back
Born: *1978 Akersberga, Sweden*
Playing career: *IF Brommapojkarna, AIK, Vitaria S.C., IFK Norrkoping, Hammarby IF, Feyenoord, Southampton, Esbjerg fB (1994-2010)*

A Swedish international and a full back with 22 caps for his country. Astlund became known as Jesus by the Southampton faithful due to his long hair and beard. Released by Saints in 2008 he moved to Denmark where recurring injuries brought his career to an end. Spent the majority of his playing days in the lower leagues and in Europe. After he retired, worked in the tourism industry in his native Sweden.

Bainbridge, John

Forward
Born: *1880 Seaham*
Died: *1960*
Playing career: *Reading, Portsmouth, Southampton, Hartlepools United (1903-1911)*

A forger by trade, started out at Reading, then played 25 times for Portsmouth before joining Saints, where he struck up a potent right-wing partnership with Frank Jefferis as a "reliable" performer. Bainbridge played over 100 times in the Southern League First Division. Illness ended his days at the Dell. Bainbridge returned to his native north-east, and briefly played for newly formed Hartlepools before working in the coal mines.

Baird, Chris

Defender/midfielder
Born: *1982 Rasharkin, Northern Ireland*
Playing career: *Ballymena United, Southampton, Walsall, Watford, Fulham, Reading, Burnley, WBA, Derby County, Fulham (1998-date)*

Baird docked at Southampton on his first port of call as he began his voyage around the Premier and Football Leagues. The ultimate utility man, he was capped 79 times by Northern Ireland and played at Euro 2016 for his nation. Played in two major finals during his club career - the surprise package at right-back in Saints 2003 FA Cup final defeat to Arsenal and an ever present during Fulham's historic, giant killing run to the 2010 showpiece in the Europa League. Saints' Player of the Season in 2006-07, he stated it was "difficult" decision to leave St Mary's. Capable of playing anywhere across the back and even in midfield, Baird last played for Derby County before announcing his retirement in February 2019. Has been back at St Mary's, working as a scout since July of that year.

Baird, Ian

Striker
Born: *1964 Rotherham*
Playing career: *Southampton, Cardiff City, Newcastle United, Leeds United, Portsmouth, Leeds United, Middlesbrough, Hearts, Bristol City, Plymouth A, Brighton, Instant-Dict FC (1978-1998)*

Born in Rotherham but started his career at Southampton which was to take in nine league clubs. Moved into coaching, initially in Hong Kong, where he had a spell in charge of the national side.

In 2003 he set up his own contract hire and leasing firm IBMH (Ian Baird Motor Holdings). Managed Havant & Waterlooville before taking over at Eastleigh in October 2007. His tenure at the Conference South side ended in 2013 and Baird has since gone on to manage Sutton United. He returned to Havant & Waterlooville and has been assistant manager to Paul Doswell since May 2019.

Baker, Charles

Inside-forward
Born: *1867 Stafford*
Died: *1924*
Playing career: *Stafford Rangers, Stoke, Wolverhampton Wanderers, Stoke, Southampton (1889-1896)*

Charlie Baker arrived at Saints just in time for their inaugural Southern League season. Appointed as Southampton skipper, he quickly became a fan favourite because of his "pace and penetrative surges." A neat dribbler, his spell at the club only held sway for two seasons before he hung up his boots. Also turned out for Stafford Rangers, Wolves and Stoke (twice). Returning to his native Stafford, he continued his career as an amateur player, combining his part-time status with a job as a shoe finisher.

Ian Baird

Baker, Graham

Midfielder

Born: *1958 Southampton*
Playing career: *Southampton, Manchester City, Southampton, Aldershot, Fulham (1976-1991).*

Local lad Baker rose through the ranks and scored within a minute of his senior Saints debut in November 1977. Capitalising on this spectacular start, Baker quickly became a first team regular and England U21 recognition followed - he earned two caps against Norway and Romania in 1980. Baker moved on to Manchester City and had a fluctuating career at Maine Road before coming back to play under Chris Nicholl. After three further seasons in which he never secured a regular place, Baker moved on again, this time to divisional rivals Fulham (via Aldershot). He later set up a driving school, which he ran whilst staying involved in football as manager of Petersfield Town and Woking. He took the "Cards" to the Conference South play-off final, but then returned to Aldershot where he worked with the youth teams. He drifted out of the game and took up employment as security officer at Southampton Docks.

Baker, Stephen

Full-back

Born: *1962 Wallsend*
Playing career: *Wallsend Boys Club, Southampton, Burnley, Leyton Orient, Bournemouth, Aldershot, Farnborough Town , Hayes, Aldershot Town, Basingstoke Town (1978-2002)*

A tenacious and tough-tackling full-back, Baker progressed through the world renowned Wallsend Boys Club, before starting an apprenticeship at Saints in 1978. He was in and out of the side throughout his eight years at the club as a back up to players such as Ivan Golac, Mick Mills and Gerry Forrest He transferred to Leyton Orient in March 1988 for £50,000, where he enjoyed his most productive time, making 112 appearances in three seasons including a promotion to the old Third Division in 1988-1989. At the culmination of his playing career he returned to Saints Academy to coach for a while, then held a number of positions within the game. Last believed to be working for the PFA as an analyst.

Ball, Alan

Midfielder

Born: *1945 Farnworth, Lancashire*
Died: *2007*
Playing career: *Blackpool, Everton, Arsenal, Southampton, Blackpool, Southampton, Bristol Rovers. (1962-1982)*

A true legend at both local and national level. Tenacious midfielder Ball made 72 appearances in the full England team, a record that includes his key performance as a member of the team that won the World Cup on home soil in 1966. He became player-manager to Blackpool and also tried his luck with Vancouver Whitecaps. His varied life as a coach included service with Bristol Rovers, Portsmouth, Stoke City, and Exeter City. Appointed first team manager at Southampton in 1994, but after only one season, accepted an offer from his old friend Frannie Lee to take over at Manchester City in July 1995. After only 13 months he decided to quit and moved back to Hampshire. 'Bally' sadly died in the early hours of 25 April 2007. He suffered a heart attack while trying to put out a fire in his garden. Ball is widely regarded as one of the finest players ever to don the famous red and white shirt of Saints.

Ballard, Edgar

Full-back
Born: *1920 Brentford*
Died: *2008*
Playing career: *Hayes, Brentford, Leyton Orient, Southampton, Leyton Orient, Snowdown Colliery Welfare (1943-1965)*

Born within spitting distance of Brentford's Griffin Park, Ballard signed for Southampton from Leyton Orient. Shared a pitch with Alf Ramsey and Bill Ellerington at The Dell under the outstanding and reputable captaincy of Joe Mallett. Later became a franchising officer for a stamp firm, also working as a double glazing salesman. He died in St Leonard's on Sea, East Sussex, in 2004 aged 88.

Bamford, Harold

Left-half
Born: *1886 Sculcoates, Yorkshire*
Died: *1915*
Playing career: *Bitterne Guild, Southampton, Glossop (1908-1914)*

Employed as a pay clerk on Southampton Docks, Bamford spent three years with the Saints, mainly at reserve team level. Enlisted with the First Battalion Light Infantry (Shropshire) during the Great War but Second Lieutenant Bamford died of septicaemia a few days after being injured on the front line.

Banger, Nicky

Striker
Born: *1971 Southampton*
Playing career: *Southampton, Oldham Athletic, Oxford United, Dundee, Scunthorpe United, Plymouth Argyle, Merthyr Tydfill, Torquay United (1989-2006)*

Since hanging his boots up in 2006, Nicky Banger has been employed as player-coach and corporate manager at Eastleigh, as well as player coach of Brockenhurst. Later became commercial manager of Romsey Town, before becoming corporate sales manager of Havant & Waterlooville. He now holds the same role at non league Aldershot Town. Scored a League Cup hat-trick on his debut for Saints as a teenager in 1990 and played for the club in the Premier League. He ended his league career at Torquay and went on to work in a variety of roles off the pitch at non league level.

Barinaga Alberdi, Sabino

Forward
Born: *1922 Durango, Spain* **Died:** *1988*
Playing career: *Southampton, Real Madrid, Valladolid, Real Sociedad, Betis (1936-1955)*

Alberdi Barinaga was sensationally scouted and signed by Southampton in 1938. He spent two years in the club's reserves but despite scoring 62 goals in that time he never played for the first team. Returning to his native Spain as World War Two began, Barinaga moved on to Real Madrid - probably the only player ever to move directly from the Saints to the Bernabeu? He later went on to embark on a 25-year career in football management. Barinaga died in Madrid in 1988 at the age of 65 having suffered a heart attack.

Barlow, Thomas

Inside-forward
Born: *1875 Bolton* **Died:** *1944*
Playing career: *Halliwell Rovers, Bolton Wanderers, Southampton, Bolton Wanderers, Millwall Athletic, Oldham Athletic (1898-1907)*

Barlow combined playing for Bolton with working at a bleach factory. He decided to try his luck with Southern League Southampton in 1902. He struggled to adapt to life on the south coast however and, homesick, he returned to his native Bolton after only a single season with the Saints. Barlow died in 1944 aged 69.

Barnes, Walley

Full-back
Born: *1920 Brecon, Wales* **Died:** *1975*
Playing career: *Portsmouth, Southampton, Arsenal (1941-1956)*

Barnes guested for Southampton as an inside forward during the war. He played 32 games between 1941 and 1943 scoring 14 goals before moving to Arsenal where he became more widely known. He earned 22 caps for Wales and went on to manage the country of his birth. Barnes was boss of Wales between 1954 and 1956 and then went in to broadcasting, joining the BBC. Working closely with Kenneth Wolstenholme, he covered the 1966 World Cup final and continued to serve the Corporation until his death in 1975 aged 55.

Barratt, Josiah

Right winger
Born: *1895 Bulkington, Warwickshire* **Died:** *1968*
Playing career: *Southampton, Birmingham,
Pontypridd, Lincoln City, Bristol Rovers, Nuneaton
Town, Coventry Colliery (1919-1930)*
Known as "Joe", Barratt guested in a
friendly for Saints and then signed pro
from Second Division Birmingham. He
went on to be a virtual ever present in
Southampton's last ever Southern League
season. He was part of the club's first ever
campaign as a Football League side. A
crowd pleaser, Barrett - for some bizarre
unknown reason - played with a piece of
straw in his mouth. He finished his league
career at Bristol Rovers and then dropped
into the non league game. After the war he
coached at Coventry where his son Harry
later played.

Barrett, Albert

Half-back
Born: *1903 Stratford, London* **Died:** *1989*
Playing career: *Fairburn House Lads, Middlesex
Wanderers, Leytonstone, West Ham United,
Southampton, Fulham (1921-1937)*
Albert Barrett won England Schoolboy
honours and was capped by England
at amateur level during his West Ham
days. Despite this early promise, he failed
to make a first team appearance for the
Hammers and fared little better in red and
white, being quickly allowed to leave to
return to London with Fulham. It was at
Craven Cottage that his career really took
off as he played over 300 games and earned
his only England cap at full senior level. He
chaired the PFA and coached at non league
Leytonstone. Later went on to work as a
secretary in a Romford wholesalers, before
moving to South Africa. Barrett died in
1989 aged 86.

Barrett, Uriah

Goalkeeper
Born: *1874 Wootton Bassett*
Died: *1934*
Playing career: *Alma, Southampton St. Mary's
(1894-1895)*
The third known 'Barrett' to have played
for the Saints, he been plucked from local
parks football to join the Saints as an
amateur.

Combining playing with a job as a stone
sawyer, he played in Southampton's
biggest ever competitive win - a 14-0
thrashing of Newbury in the FA Cup
in 1894. Barrett would quit football to
concentrate on an alternative sporting
career as a cricketer, also working as a
shoe maker. He died reputedly from blood
poisoning after being struck on the leg by a
cricket ball.

Barry Brown, Kevan

Full-back
Born: *1966 Andover*
Playing career: *Southampton, Brighton & Hove
Albion, Aldershot, Woking, Yeovil Town (1984-2001)*
Brown joined as a trainee in 1982 and
then signed as a professional two years
later. He remained at The Dell until the
spring of 1987, playing over 120 games
for the reserves without earning a first
team breakthrough. Having signed for
south coast rivals Brighton on loan, Brown
moved to the Seagulls permanently that
same year. Brown went on to play over
50 games from Brighton before turning
out for Aldershot, Yeovil and two spells at
Woking. He earned one cap for England 'C'
and, upon retirement, worked as officer for
sport at St Francis School in Wiltshire.

Barry Brown, Peter

Outside-forward
Born: *1934 Andover*
Died: *2011*
Playing career: *Southampton, Wrexham, Poole
Town, Dorchester Town , Andover (1952-1963)*
Initially a sign maker, this 50s and 60s
outside-forward signed professional terms
in 1952, completing his National Service
before getting a chance to play for the club.
Often in competition with John Flood for
the number seven shirt, he spent most of
his time at The Dell in the Reserves, top
scoring for the second string in consecutive
seasons. After 16 games at outside-right,
the arrival of Terry Paine pushed Brown
down the pecking order and he left for
Wrexham - going on also to play for Poole,
Dorchester Town and non league Andover.
Later worked as a timekeeper on the Docks
and as a repairs inspector for Test Valley
Borough Council.

Bartlett, Neal

Midfielder
Born: *1975 Southampton*
Playing career: *Southampton, Fareham Town, BK Hacken, Bashley, Hereford United, (1990-2008)*
A player regarded as having "the world at his feet" by manager Ian Branfoot, but the arrival of Alan Ball saw him fall out of favour and he moved to Sweden after only 15 Premier League games. He later enrolled in the army with the Princess of Wales Regiment after drifting out the game. A case of what might have been, Private Bartlett opted to remain a soldier despite receiving offers to reignite his career.

Barton, Victor

Goalkeeper
Born: *1867 Netley, Hampshire* **Died:** *1906*
Career: *Southampton St. Mary's (1893-1893)*
One of the elite few to reach the zenith of his profession across two sports, Barton was a gunner for the Royal Artillery when he began his sporting career. He played cricket at professional first-class level for Kent, joining his native Hampshire as an eye catching all rounder. He famously dismissed the great WG Grace for a duck (without scoring) and played in a Test match for England against South Africa.

His football career consisted only of nine friendly games and a single competitive match for Southampton. Upon retirement as both footballer and cricketer, Barton moved to London where he worked in a sports outfitters company. Later became a hotelier but died at the young age of 38.

Basham, Steve

Striker
Born: *1977 Southampton*
Playing career: *Southampton, Wrexham, Preston, Oxford Utd, Exeter City, Luton Town (1994-2014)*
Southampton-born Basham signed for Saints as an 18 year old under manager Graeme Souness. Only a week after signing, he made a Premier League debut against Chelsea as a sub. His first - and it turned out - only start for his hometown team came at Old Trafford, with Basham restricted to a paltry 18 further games, all of them as sub, in the top flight. Scored one goal for Saints which came at Ewood Park. Moved to Preston under David Moyes then went on to Oxford United, Exeter and Luton before dropping into the non league circuit. Basham later earned a degree in accountancy and set up his own business which he continues to run to this day.

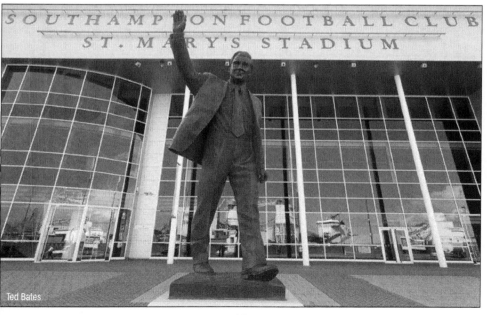

Ted Bates

Bates, Edric 'Ted' (MBE)

Forward
Born: *1918 Thetford* **Died:** *2003*
Playing career: *Norwich City, Folland Aircraft, Southampton (1935-1953)*

A Southampton legend both on the pitch and in the dugout, Ted Bates MBE served his beloved Saints in six capacities during his lifelong association with the club. Signed for Southampton by Tom Parker at 19, Bates would remain unbroken and unbowed on the south coast until his death 66 years later. He played over 200 wartime games for Saints and, by the time he had stopped playing, he had already begun his coaching career. Put in charge of the Reserves the Board turned to "Mr Southampton" as their new first team manager in 1955. Building a club with kindred spirit, Bates took Southampton into the First Division for the first time ever as he led them into Europe and blooded several emerging talents along the way. By the time he handed over to Lawrie McMenemy, Bates had become Southampton's longest serving manager - a record that still stands today. Bates then joined the Saints board where he would serve as director, chairman and president. He received the freedom of the city and an MBE in 2001. He died aged 85 in 2003 and remains immortalised in bronze as his statue adorns the forecourt of the club's St Mary's Stadium.

Beare, George

Inside-forward
Born: *1885 Southampton* **Died:** *1970*
Playing career: *Southampton, Blackpool, Everton, Bristol City, Cardiff City (1906-1923)*

The defender turned inside-forward was discovered by Saints when playing for his works team in Shirley, whilst also working as a bicycle maker. Beare's diminutive size worked against him and he didn't make his debut until his second season at the club, It would prove to be his one and only game in the red and white, as he then moved north to another coastal club, Blackpool. He went on to enjoy a 16-year career including with Division One Everton. When he hung up his boots he returned to his native Southampton to work on the Docks.

Beasant, Dave

Goalkeeper
Born: *1959 Willesden, London*
Playing career: *Wimbledon, Newcastle United, Chelsea, Grimsby Town, Wolverhampton Wanderers, Southampton, Nottingham Forest, Portsmouth, Tottenham Hotspur, Bradford City, Wigan Athletic, Brighton & Hove Albion, Fulham*

Even though he played over 800 professional games for 14 different clubs, 'Lurch' is best known for being the first goalkeeper to save a penalty in the FA Cup final. Capped twice by England, Beasant spent much of his early career with the Crazy Gang of Wimbledon, the ultimate "yo yo" club of the 80s. His save from John Aldridge in the 88' Cup final paved the way for one of the most famous FA Cup underdog wins of all time. Beasant broke the transfer record for a goalkeeper when he signed for Newcastle, then on to Chelsea and Saints via loan spells at Grimsby and Wolves. Having taken over from Ian Branfoot, Alan Ball quickly made Beasant his first choice keeper but he lost his place upon the signing of Bruce Grobbelaar. Saints Player of the Year in the Premier League 1995-96. Later, Beasant graduated from player to a wider coaching role via stints as goalkeeping coach and player coach. He played for Fulham into his 40s before taking up a role in Glenn Hoddle's football academy in Spain until it closed a decade ago. Now works at former Saint Steve Wood's Midas Sports Management.

Beattie, George

Inside-forward

Born: *1925 Aberdeen, Scotland* **Died:** *2012*
Playing career: *Southampton, Gloucester City, Newport County, Bradford Park Avenue (1947-1955)*

A fisherman by trade, Beattie was offered the chance of a step up to England's Second Division when Saints manager Bill Dodgin brought him south of the border to the south coast. His debut turned out to be his first and last game for the club. Managed at non league level then moved back to Newport to start a coal haulage business.

Beattie, James

Striker

Born: *1978 Lancaster*
Playing career: *Blackburn Rovers, Southampton, Everton, Sheffield U, Stoke City, Rangers, Blackpool, Sheffield U, Accrington Stanley (1995-2013)*

Known for his tenacity, aggression and ability with both feet, Beattie was the top English scorer with 23 goals in 2002-03 as Saints reached the FA Cup final, form that saw Beattie earn full England recognition (five caps). Scored 76 goals in 233 league games and still holds the record as Southampton's highest scoring Premier League player. Was appointed as manager of Accrington Stanley in 2013-14.

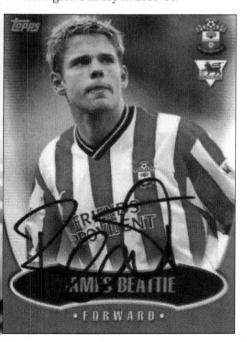

He then worked with fellow ex-Saint Garry Monk as a coach at Swansea, Leeds, Middlesbrough, Birmingham City and Sheffield Wednesday. Now living back in Southampton, Beattie and his wife Sarah have long been associated with Eastleigh-based charity Sophie's Appeal, raising £700,000 through donations, going on to become patrons. The charity - set up to support the social, emotional and educational welfare of ill children and their families - is in memory of six-year Sophie Barringer, a cancer victim and Saints fan. In 2019, Beattie auctioned off his 2003 FA Cup final boots, with the iconic footwear going on to make almost £1,000 for charity.

Beaumont, William

Half-back

Born: *1883 Ashton-in-Makerfield* **Died:** *1911*
Playing career: *Swindon Town, Portsmouth, Southampton (1906-1911)*

One of the few men to have bridged both sides of the bitter south coast divide. He played for Pompey for three years part time whilst working as a motor engineer. A consistent performer, he joined Southampton as a way of staying in the game and once again played on a part time basis, training at Fratton Park and only meeting up with his team-mates on match days. He missed only three games during his solitary season at The Dell, playing 27 times. He retired from the game in 1911 having contracted pneumonia.

Bedford, Brian

Centre-forward

Born: *1933 Ferndale, Rhondda Cynon Taf, Wales*
Playing career: *Reading, Southampton, Bournemouth, QPR, Brentford. (1954-1966)*

Had a terrific goal scoring rate throughout a career that took in six clubs. Upon retiring from the game, took up tennis, becoming a registered professional, and qualifying as an L.T.A. coach in 1972. Coached at I.L.E.A. sports centre and was pro at Richmond Lawn Tennis Club. A knee injury forced him to give up in 1986, when he became Stadium Manager at Q.P.R.'s Loftus Road until he was made redundant in 1992. Retired in 1995 and settled back in Llandaff, South Glamorgan.

Bell, Edward

Outside-forward
Born: *1886 Gibraltar* **Died:** *1918*
Playing career: *South Farnborough, Crystal Palace, Southampton (1907-1911)*

His achievements off the field as Captain Edward Bell during WW1 significantly outshone a low key football existence. Bell played a handful of games in the Southern League for Saints, and also turned out for Portsmouth and Crystal Palace as an amateur. Eight games at the Dell in total. In the war, he served in the 17th Middlesex as Captain Bell the adjutant to Major Frank Buckley - an England international who used his military title during his 32 years as a manager in the Football League. Bell took charge of his battalion when the Major was stricken by the enemy and would later be awarded a Military Cross for Gallantry. Bell was killed by a German shell on the Western Front in France, in 1918.

Bell, Mark

Outside-right
Born: *1881 Edinburgh, Scotland* **Died:** *1961*
Playing career: *Heart of Midlothian, Southampton, Heart of Midlothian, Fulham (1900-1919)*

Recruited by the Saints as part of a squad overhaul, he was one of six new signings having left his native Edinburgh to move south of the border.

Djamel Belmadi

Won the League Cup with Hearts in 1901. Injuries prevented him from making regular headway but he contributed six goals - including a brace in an 11-0 thrashing of Watford (Saints joint highest winning margin in the League) - in nine games, helping the club to the Southern League title in the process. After a season back at Hearts, he returned to the Southern League with Fulham, winning the title twice in successive seasons and then played for several different London clubs including Clapton, Leyton and New Brompton. After the War he emigrated to Australia where he worked as a railway porter.

Belmadi, Djamel

Midfielder
Born: *1976 Champigny-sur-Marne, France*
Playing career: *Al-Duhail, Paris Saint-Germain, Martigues, Marseille, Cannes, Celta Vigo, Marseille, Manchester City, Al-Ittihad, Al-Kharitiyath, Southampton, Valenciennes (1995-2009)*

Djamel Belmadi had jet-setted to four different countries with ten different sides by the time he arrived at Southampton - via Qatar, Spain and France. French born but of Algerian descent, he earned 20 caps for the north African nation. Despite struggling with injury, he was a player renowned for his vision, distribution and surging runs from midfield. Having initially joined on a one month loan after a trial, Saints manager Harry Redknapp and then his successor George Burley combined to re-sign Belmadi for the 2006-07 season. When Southampton failed to gain promotion back to the Premier League, he returned to France when he retired in 2009. He then embarked on a coaching career in Qatar and had a brief spell as manager of the country in 2014. Now in charge of his native Algeria, Belmadi led his nation to their second AFCON title in 2019.

"DID YOU KNOW?"

"Shane Long scored the Premier League's quickest ever goal, only seven seconds into Southampton's game at Watford in April 2019"

Hi, it's Franny Benali here, and as an ambassador of Saints Foundation...

Donate £10 to Saints Foundation
southamptonfc.com

Benali, Francis

Full-back
Born: *1968 Southampton*
Career: *Southampton, Nottingham F, (1988-2008)*
In recent years, Benali has remained a prominent local figure thanks to his off the field efforts. He has completed three "ultra endurance" challenges, running to every Premier League ground on 21 consecutive days in 2014, a distance of over 1,000 miles. Two years on, the former Saints full-back ran a marathon and cycled 75 miles each day to every stadium in England's top two tiers. If that wasn't enough, in 2019, he complete his "IronFran" challenges, doing seven triathlons in seven days - a 2.5 mile swim, 112-mile bike ride and a run of full marathon length, all in aid of Cancer Research UK. Benali raised over £2m in the process, earning an MBE in the process for services to charity. He was made an Honorary Graduate of Solent University in 2016 and is a Doctor of Sport for contribution to the community. He has also proved an unstinting servant to The Saints Foundation and Cancer Research UK. Benali earned the Freedom of the city of Southampton in 2016 as a result of his outstanding work. Benali has become a regular on Five Live, Soccer Saturday and BT Sport. Benali Twitter: *https://twitter. com/FrannyBenali?* Website: *http://www. francisbenali.com*

Bennett, Alan

Centre-back
Born: *1981 Cork, Ireland*
Playing career: *Reading, Southampton, Brentford, Wycombe Wanderers, Cheltenham Town, AFC Wimbledon (2000-date)*
Played in Europe for Cork City and capped twice by the Republic of Ireland before his six-month loan spell at St Mary's. Despite being championed by George Burley, Bennett was sent back to his former club before several other loan spells elsewhere. Went on to win promotion with Wycombe and captain Cheltenham Town.

Bennett, Frank

Forward
Born: *1969 Birmingham*
Playing career: *Southampton, Bristol Rovers, Exeter City (1992-2004)*
Bennett was combining a part-time football career with non league Halesowen with a job as a hotel porter and waiter, when Ian Branfoot signed him. Played 23 times, with 17 of those coming as a sub but he did score in one Premier League game against Chelsea. A skillful, nippy winger, Bennett was signed as replacement for the recently sold Rod Wallace but never convinced the manager's immediate successors Alan Ball and Dave Merrington, subsequently being loaned out to Shrewsbury. Eventually ending up in Bristol and working as a delivery driver for UPS.

Bennett, Paul

Centre-back
Born: *1952 Southampton*
Playing career: *Southampton, Reading, Aldershot (1968-1982)*
A rugged, no nonsense centre-half in the mould of John McGrath - ironically the man he followed into the first team - his strength in the tackle made him a fearsome proposition for opposition strikers. Made the number 5 shirt his own at the heart of the defence alongside Jim Steele, and will remembered as one of the "Boys of 76" even though he did not play in the final - but his appearance in the quarter final means he is still always a part of events commemorating Southampton's finest hour.

After the Cup was won, Lawrie McMenemy began to build a youthful squad tasked with winning promotion and Bennett was no longer part of the manager's plans. After 137 matches, he left the Dell to move to Reading, going on to play over 100 games for Aldershot. After retirement, he went on to become a director at a leisure centre, and is an Associate Lecturer at Solent University on several degree programmes including Football Studies.

Benson, Bob

Full-back
Born: *1883 Whitehaven, Cumbria* **Died:** *1916*
Playing career: *Dunston Villa, Shankhouse, , Swalwell, Newcastle United, Southampton, Sheffield United, Woolwich Arsenal (1902-1916)*

When Saints ever-present right-back Tom Robertson - a back-to-back title winner in 1903 and 1904 - left for pastures new, it seemed unlikely that the board would turn to pre-eminent Newcastle as the source of Robertson's kindred spirit. But there they would find their man in Bob Benson, an ex miner who'd started only once in his two seasons at St James Park. Big, bold and known for his strange penalty-taking technique (Benson have the ball placed on the spot by s team mate and then run half the length one the pitch to belt it in). He would only have one season at the Dell, going on to Sheffield United and Woolwich Arsenal, where he also worked in the munitions factory. Capped once by England in 1913. Having attended a game against Reading in 1915, Benson discovered Arsenal were a man short and so stepped in at the eleventh hour. He collapsed on the pitch and died in the changing room during the game of a burst blood vessel.

Beresford, John

Left-back
Born: *1966 Sheffield*
Playing career: *Manchester City, Finn Harps, Barnsley, Portsmouth, Newcastle United, Southampton, Birmingham City (1983-2000)*
From stopping attacks to keeping out racism, it's been quite the journey for former Saints defender turned pundit and campaigner Beresford.

John Beresford

Best known for his time with Portsmouth and Newcastle (where he won the First Division and twice finished Premier league runners up under Kevin Keegan), Beresford played 17 times in the Premier League for Saints and was capped twice at 'B' team level for England. Since then, Beresford has worked for BBC Radio Solent as a match summariser, also doing punditry work on ESPN and BT Sport. Beresford has been involved in a number of business ventures since retirement, including interior design and today runs a joinery and shopfitting business, BBJ Northern Ltd based in his hometown of Sheffield. In 2017, Beresford was awarded an MBE for his services to Show Racism the Red Card, taking anti-discrimination workshops into schools and regularly lecturing on the subject. Ironically, Beresford admitted to being one of those he now tries to educate having been guilty of racist abuse as a fan on the Bramall Lane terraces, only to change his outlook having met and played with black players.

Berkovic, Eyal

Midfielder
Born: *1972 Regba, Israel*
Playing career: *Maccabi Haifa, Southampton, West Ham United, Celtic, Blackburn Rovers, Manchester City, Portsmouth, Maccabi Tel Aviv (1982-2006)*
Having long kept an eye on the progress of Israeli schemer Eyal Berkovic, Graeme

Souness swooped to bring the talented if temperamental tyro to the south coast of England. Having begun his career with Maccabi Haifa in his homeland, Berkovic dazzled in the Premier League pressure cooker with his vision, distribution and quick feet - the most dazzling ever seen at The Dell according to former Saints boss Lawrie McMenemy. He scored twice in the famous 6-3 rout of Sir Alex Ferguson's all conquering Man United, but would only add two more goals to his tally in red and white. At times he had a seemingly telepathic understanding of fellow new signing and striker Egil Ostenstad. When Souness left, Harry Redknapp swooped to bring the Israeli to Upton Park. Eyal kept ground hopping, never staying at any one club longer than three years. Known for his fiery temper as much as his ability, Berkovic was noted for his run ins with managers and players alike, notably Kevin Keegan, his manager at Man City, and Hammers team mate John Hartson, General manager of Maccabi Haifa in 2014-15, Berkovic ended his playing career back where it started with that club in his native country. Earned 78 caps for Israel.

Eyal Berkovic

Bernard, Eugene
Goalkeeper
Born: *1914 Southampton* **Died:** *1973*
Playing career: *Southampton, Winchester City, Ryde Sports (1933-1942)*
Joined Southampton as an amateur in 1933 and uested for the club in wartime, before a serious hand injury prematurely ended his career. Later worked at Saints as reserve team coach, before going into the insurance business.

Bernard, Olivier
Defender
Born: *1979 Paris, France*
Playing career: *Lyon, Newcastle United, Darlington, Southampton, Rangers (1998-2007)*
Bernard left Lyon for Newcastle without having made the first team, and went on to have most of his career on Tyneside. But soon after he clocked up his century of appearances in the north east, he moved south to Saints on a five month loan deal. Played 15 times for Southampton but was unable to prevent their relegation to the Championship. Moved to Scotland for a brief stint with Rangers and retired in 2008. Since he hung up his boots, he has worked as an ambassador for *Kick it Out*, being inducted into their Hall of Fame in 2011. He is currently the owner and CEO of Northern League side Durham City.

Bevan, Scott
Goalkeeper
Born: *1979 Southampton*
Playing career: *Portsmouth, Southampton, Ayr United, Stoke City, Woking, Huddersfield Town, Wycombe Wanderers, Milton Keynes Dons, Tamworth, Kidderminster Harriers, Shrewsbury Town, Torquay United, Bristol Rovers (1996-2014)*
Bevan began his career at hometown club Southampton as an amateur schoolboy player. He turned pro in 1997 but never made the grade at The Dell. Goalkeeper Bevan would have better success elsewhere, though, as he played for Stoke, Woking, Huddersfield, AFC Wimbledon, Kidderminster, Shrewsbury and Bristol Rovers. Having retired at the end of 2017 after almost 300 domestic games, Bevan was appointed as Birmingham City's first ever Under 23 goalkeeping coach.

Bevis, William

Outside-forward
Born: *1918 Warsash* **Died:** *1994*
Playing career: *Gosport Borough, Portsmouth, Southampton, Winchester City, Cowes Sports, Warsash (1934-1953)*

With Southampton manager Tom Parker building a new-look side to bid for Third Division promotion, he did not have took for for the outside forward he was after. Bevis had failed to break through at Fratton Park and moved up the Solent to The Dell in 1937. In tandem with partner in crime Ted Bates, the pair laid on a glut of goals for free-scoring forwards Reg Tomlinson and Fred Briggs, before Bevis' football career was interrupted by the outbreak of war. He joined the merchant Navy as a gunner, and Petty Officer Bevis would later be adrift in the Atlantic after the sinking of his ship. Seven days later, he was rescued with former Saints keeper Alec Warnock one of his saviours. Earned the distinguished Service Medal from King George VI and returned to the Dell having been demobbed. He made another handful of appearances before retirement, returning to sea full time.

Bidewell, Sid

Inside-forward
Born: *1918 Watford* **Died:** *2003*
Playing career: *St Albans City, Wealdstone, Chelsea, Wrexham (guest), Southampton (guest), Colchester United (guest), Gravesend & Northfleet, Chelmsford City (1937-1951)*

A full-back, his career - like that of so many of his contemporaries - was cut short by the outbreak of the World War having started out with Chelsea. A lance corporal in the British Army, he also served in the RAF and played 18 wartime league and cup games for Chelsea before going on to guest with Wrexham, Southampton and Colchester United. Bidewell served in the RAF during the conflict, and returned to football at non league level with Gravesend&Northfleet and Chelmsford. After retiring, he moved into coaching with Chelsea's Reserves and was later appointed manager at Hemel Hempstead. Bidewell died aged 85 in 2003.

Binder, Thomas

Outside-right
Born: *1889 Weldon, Northamptonshire*
Died: *1969*
Playing career: *Kettering, Southampton (1912-1914)*

An amatuer-turned-pro outside right in the 1910s, Binder signed for the Southern League Saints from non league Kettering. Made his debut in the penultimate game of the 1912-13 season, a 3-0 league loss at Norwich in place of the unavailable Len Andrews. He failed to hold on to the shirt, however, and soon had to be content with regular appearances in Saints Reserve Alliance League side. Southampton offered him to newly promoted Luton, but only made two further appearances before returning to Kettering. Later ran a 17th century inn in Northamptonshire until his retirement. Died in 1969.

Birch, Ken

Right-half
Born: *1933 Birkenhead*
Died: *2015*
Playing career: *Birkenhead Boys, Bebington Hawks, Everton, Southampton, Chelmsford City, Bangor City, Benoni (1951-1963)*

A prolific striker at schoolboy level, Birch began his career at Everton in his native Merseyside but moved to Saints after 43 games at the top level for the Toffees. He inherited a place at the heart of the defence in a Saints team pushing for promotion from Division Three (South). They duly did so, with seven wins and three draws from the last ten games to earn a spot in the new nationalised Division III. His time at Saints came to an end when first Terry Simpson and then Dick Conner arrived to usurp him in the team. Birch went on to turn out for Chelmsford and Bangor at non league level, playing in the Cup Winners Cup against Napoli whilst at the Welsh club, having captained them to domestic cup glory. Scored in the home leg and got an assist in the second. Moved to South Africa where he represented Benoni, whom he later served as player-manager.

Bishop, Alfred

Inside-forward

Born: *1902 Aston* **Died:** *1944*
Playing career: *Royal Air Force, St Albans City, Southampton, Cradley Heath St Luke's, Barrow, Cradley Heath, Wellington Town, Leamington Town (1925-1930)*

The Saints manager Arthur Chadwick had started to oversee a rebuilding job when Alf Bishop - playing for the RAF - came to his attention. With Dick Rowley and Sammy Taylor, both of whom could play in the inside-forward positions, newly signed, Chadwick persuaded Bishop to sign for him upon his demobbing in the RAF. He was first choice inside-forward for the first seven games of the 1926-27 seasons but the form of Rowley and Taylor meant Bishop's days as a Saint were numbered. He played 23 games in the Southampton reserves before becoming a non league itinerant where he played for several clubs in the Midlands area. Briefly returned to the Football League with Barrow, he was called up to the war effort and served as an aircraft gunner pre-Dunkirk. He also held a job at the Birmingham Small Arms (BSA) factories in Birmingham and Stoke-on-Trent. Discharged from the RAF on compassionate grounds to be with his ill wife, and the two died four years apart, bot from tuberculosis.

Black, Ian

Goalkeeper

Born: *1924 Aberdeen, Scotland*
Died: *2012*
Playing career: *Aberdeen Boys Brigade, St Clement's, Southampton, Fulham, Bath City, Canterbury City (1946-1964)*

The only Scot to play for Saints in the 20th century, he was also the only goalkeeper to concede fewer League goals (95) than games he played in (97). Serving in REME, he guested for Chelsea in the 1945 League South Cup Final. Initially he joined as a guest for Southampton and made his debut in an unofficial game, before signing as a pro and making his 'proper' Saints bow in 1947. Before that season was out, Black had made his Scotland debut against England but despite a "confident and authoritative" performance, was unable to prevent a 0-2 defeat.

It proved the only cap he would get for his country. Black went on to play 104 times for the south coast side. Missing out on promotion three seasons running, Black left for Fulham after three years at Saints. Went on to make another 263 league appearances for Fulham and even scored when pressed into service as an outfield player. In his poet-playing days retirement, he was manager and owner of a sports shop in Tolworth, Kingston and represented Surrey at crown green bowls both indoors and out. He later worked as a secretary for the large bowls club in Tolworth and continued to play the sport until his late 80s. He died at the age of 88 in 2012.

Blackburn, Arthur

Full-back

Born: *1877 Blackburn* **Died:** *1938*
Playing career: *Mellor, Blackburn Rovers, Wellingborough, Blackburn Rovers, Southampton, Blackburn Rovers (1895-1902)*

His one season at The Dell came sandwiched between three separate spells at Blackburn Rovers. Blackburn-born Blackburn (if you get me) arrived at Southampton in good shape, he had been a notable distance runner in Lancashire. He maintained his fitness by working on the renovation of a church whilst also turning out for Saints on a Saturday. Despite his skill, a succession of ankle injuries thwarted his progress and soon dropped out of the Southern League side. A right-back, he never regained his place and returned home that summer. Went on to only play twice more in the Football League and after he retired, Blackburn coached in Rotterdam, Holland before he ran a tobacco shop on the outskirts of Blackburn. He died aged 62 in the town. Elder brother of England international Fred.

"DID YOU KNOW?"

"The club's nickname - the Saints - came as a result of Southampton being formed in 1885 by members of St Mary's church "

Blackmore, William
Outside-right
Born: 1891, *Southampton* **Died:** *1966*
Playing career: *Adelaide, Southampton, Woolston, Harland & Wolff, (1912-1920)*
Blackmore made an instant impression at The Dell having joined Saints as an amateur player. Scored twice on his Reserve team debut and was catapulted into the first team. In a sporadic career in red and white, Blackmore played at outside right (a winger in today's parlance), in a struggling side. He left Southampton but returned to The Dell in 1915 before the official league programme was abandoned a year into World War One. After the War he stayed at the club, helping to coach the reserves. He later worked in the docks and died in 1966 at the age of 75.

Blackstock, Dexter
Outside-right
Born: 1986, *Oxford*
Playing career: *Southampton, QPR, Nottingham Forest, Rotherham United (2003-2017)*
Rose through the ranks at Saints and made his debut as an 18-year-old in the midst of a striker crisis. No sooner had he burst on to the scene as Saints next big thing, that a "perfect" League Cup hat-trick - left-foot, right-foot, header - against Colchester in the League Cup followed. His stock only continued to rise with the winner in the south coast derby in 2004 but when Harry Redknapp arrived he was loaned out and went on to play for Plymouth, Derby, QPR, Nottingham Forest, Leeds and Rotherham. Blackstock was capped six times by the Caribbean nation Antigua and Barbuda.

Dexter Blackstock

Has since become distant from the game but has found himself much in demand throughout the Covid-19 pandemic due to his work with online pharmacy UK Meds and the CEO of MediConnect. Blackstock has also dabbled in the property business and was fined £24,000 in 2019 after several properties owned by him had fallen into disrepair

Blake, Joe
Outside-forward
Born: *1882 Belchamp Walter* **Died:** *1931*
Playing career: *Tottenham Hotspur, Cowes, Southampton, Thornycrofts (Woolston) (1905-1920)*
Taking up a job as a marine draughtsman at Cowes, Blake moved to the shipyards of Thorneycrofts and it was there that his Southampton career began. Equally at home on either flank, Blake scored on his debut but would not see the first team again for almost two and a half years, as manager Ernest Armfield deployed nine different players on the right wing. Upon the outbreak of war, he was retired to double his efforts at Thorneycrofts although he still played for the club during the war. Upon retirement he took up a full time job with Thornycrofts shipping merchants in Woolston.

Blake, Mark
Defender
Born: *1967 Portsmouth*
Playing career: *Southampton, Colchester United, Shrewsbury Town, Fulham, AS Cannes, Aldershot Town, Winchester City (1984-2003)*
A Portsmouth born defender, he started his career at Southampton in 1985. Blake was thrust into the Saints first team only days after signing due to an injury crisis at the back. He had a loan spell with Colchester United, before a transfer to Shrewsbury Town in 1990. After further spells with Fulham, AS Cannes and Aldershot he became player manager of Wessex League Winchester City where he led the club to a treble of League, League Cup and FA Vase. He joined Eastleigh as Head Coach in 2005 a position he held for 18 months. He still turns out for the Ex Saints team and is currently working in the IT industry as a sales director.

Blayney, Alan
Goalkeeper
Born: *1981 Belfast, Northern Ireland*
Playing career: *Southampton, Stockport County, Bournemouth, Rushden , Brighton & Hove Albion, Doncaster Rovers, Oldham Athletic, (1997-date)*
Capped five times by his country, Blayney was whisked away from Belfast to England. He joined Southampton aged 16 but, like George Best, became homesick. A goalkeeper with a natural ability, Blayney stepped in for the injured Paul Smith and ill Antti Niemi at the end of the 2003-04 season. Yet following a catastrophic 5-2 League Cup defeat to Watford the following season, he was dropped and replaced by the on loan Kasey Keller. He left Saints and played for a handful of clubs before returning to Northern Ireland. He remained in the game aworking at Larne FC as goalkeeping coach.

Bleidelis, Imants
Midfielder
Born: *1975 Riga*
Playing career: *Skonto, Southampton, Viborg FF, Grazer AK, Metalurgs (1992-2008)*
A 100-cap Latvian international, Bleidelis was unknown outside of his homeland when he signed for Saints in 2000. Despite joining on a three-and-a-half year contract, he would play only four times for the club. Three of those were as a sub including the infamous Prenton Park debacle, when Saints squandered a 3-0 lead against Tranmere in the FA Cup. Bleidelis had replaced compatriot and friend Marian Pahars but was then subbed himself as Hoddle tried - ultimately in vain - to rescue the tie. Bleidelis left the club by mutual consent in 2003 and returned to Latvia.

Blochel, Jozef
Forward
Born: *1962 Chalfont St Giles*
Playing career: *Southampton, Wimbledon, IK Arvika, Karlstad BK, Wycombe W (1980-1991)*
Blochel joined Southampton as an amateur schoolboy in September 1975, signing as a professional five years later. Despite becoming a reliable regular at Reserve team level, he never made the step up into the first team.

Joined Wimbledon on loan before he was released by Southampton. Blochel went on to an unremarkable career in the lower leagues before settling in Scandinavia. He worked as a tourism officer in Sweden and then took up a job as a council worker.

Bluff, Edgar
Inside-forward
Born: *1882 Attercliffe, Sheffield*
Died: *1952*
Playing career: *Yorkshire Light Infantry, First Army Corps, Southampton, Sheffield United, Birmingham, St Helens Town (1904-1908)*
Bluff had spent four years with the Yorkshire Light Infantry when he was plucked from works team obscurity to join Southern League Southampton - for the princely sum of £25. In tandem with Fred Harrison, he caught the eye of the England selectors and earned a call up as reserve for the match with Ireland in 1905. He was offloaded by Southampton the following year and later became a miner in Lancashire. Scored 18 goals in 39 games for Saints. Died 1952.

Blyth, Mel
Centre-back
Born: *1944 Norwich*
Playing career: *Norwich City, Scunthorpe United, Crystal Palace, Southampton, Cape Town City, Margate, Millwall, Houston Hurricane, Bulova SA, Andover (1967-1982)*
Voted Player of the Season in his debut campaign at the Dell, he formed the bedrock of Saints famous 76' Cup win with the Blyth/Steele pairing the mainstay of Saints run to Wembley and eventual victory. As Lawrie McMenemy's cup winners broke up, Blyth became the seventh member of the side to leave the club, and the arrival of Chris Nicholl as manager signalled the end of the now 33 year old's time on the south coast. Returned to Palace on loan and also played for Cape Town, Margate, Millwall, Houston Hurricanes and Andover. Later coached at Palace's Academy and acquired a match day role at the PFA. Also worked as a builder, a driving instructor and a coach in schools.

Blyth, Robert

Forward
Born: *1900 Muirkirk, Scotland*
Died: *1956*
Playing career: *Portsmouth, Southampton , Boston Wonder Workers (1921-1925)*

Followed in his father's footsteps by joining Portsmouth from the amateur leagues in his native Scotland. Blyth played eight times for 'Pompey' before he joined divisional rivals and champions elect Saints in 1922. With Charlie Brown firmly established as Southampton's right sided forward, Blyth's debut for the club was a year in the making. A dearth of games followed, again eight in total, before he was released by the club and moved abroad. He joined Boston Wonder Workers, a side for expats with many Scottish players. Returning back north of the border, Blyth became involved in his family's hotel business. When his father died in 1941, Blyth took over the management of the *Pompey* hotel, adjoining Fratton Park. His dad was also called Bob and played for Portsmouth, also serving as player-manager. He too moved to The Dell but never made the grade at Southampton. His cousins included Bill Shankly. Blyth Jr. died in 1956 aged 56.

Boa Morte, Luis

Winger/Midfielder
Born: *1977 Lisbon, Portugal*
Playing career: *Sporting CP, Lourinhanense (loan), Arsenal, Southampton, Fulham (loan), West Ham United, AEL, Orlando Pirates, Chesterfield, Four Marks (1994-2013)*

In his solitary season, Boa Morte played 17 times for the club, with ten of those as a sub. Playing mainly as a left winger, he scored once against Watford with a screamer before loaned out to second tier Fulham. It was his time with the Cottagers that earned Boa Morte his reputation and the first of his 28 caps for Portugal. A popular figure, he was voted Player of the Season by Fulham fans in 2005 and again in 2007 when he had moved to London rivals West Ham. Went to Greece and Larissa with former manager Chris Coleman in 2011 before he joined Orlando Pirates and later Toronto.

Luís Boa Morte

Returned to England where he played a dozen games for League Two Chesterfield then turned out for non league side Four Marks in the Hampshire Premier League. Since retiring, he has worked as a scout for Arsenal, and also as assistant manager of Portimonense U23s as well as being number two to compatriot Marco Silva at Everton until the pair were sacked in 2019.

Bogan, Tommy

Outside-right
Born: *1920 Glasgow, Scotland* **Died:** *1993*
Playing career: *Strathclyde, Blantyre Celtic, Renfrew, Hibernian, Celtic, Preston North End, Manchester United, Aberdeen, Southampton, Blackburn Rovers, Macclesfield Town (1943-1955)*

Bogan was the partner for another former Celtic player, Jimmy Delaney, on the right wing for Manchester United, but he was never assured of his place having to battle it out with Harry McShane and Cliff Birkett towards the end of his days at Old Trafford. Settled in Alderley Edge, Cheshire, after marrying Sir Matt Busby's niece, he was employed in the newspaper industry by the Daily Express and the Manchester Evening News after leaving the game. He died in September 1993, aged 73. Played nine times for Saints between 1951 and 1953.

Bond, Kevin

Central defender
Born: *1957 West Ham, London*
Playing career: *Bournemouth, Norwich City, Seattle Sounders, Manchester City, Southampton, Bournemouth, Exeter City, Sittingbourne, Dover Athletic (1972-1996)*

One of two famous footballing Bonds, Kevin's father John played in the mighty

Kevin Bond

West Ham side of the 1960s and 70s along with Geoff Hurst, Martin Peters and a certain Harry Redknapp. Kevin Bond would spend the first 12 years of his career playing with his father for Bournemouth, Norwich and Manchester City. With Saints struggling near the foot of the First Division, Lawrie McMeneny signed Bond Jr to slot into central defence alongside Mark Wright. Saints surged up the table and would have made it into Europe if not for UEFA's ban on English clubs. Continued to go from strength to strength with Wright next to him as Southampton made two successive semi finals in both domestic cups, losing on both occasions to Liverpool. After stints with Bournemouth and Alan Ball's Exeter, he ran a cafe in Southampton before turning out for Kent clubs Sittingbourne and Dover. Later moved into coaching and went on to manage Stafford Rangers, AFC Bournemouth, and QPR as number two to Redknapp, Hong Kong Pegasus and, most recently, Southend United. He also worked as assistant manager at Portsmouth under Ball, Spurs (again with Redknapp), Saints, Newcastle and West Ham.

Boruc, Artur

Goalkeeper
Born: *1980 Siedlce, Poland*
Playing career: *Bournemouth, Legia Warsaw, Celtic, Fiorentina, Southampton (1998-)*

Capped 65 times by Poland, Boruc began his career in his native homeland before signing for Celtic under Gordon Strachan on loan. He joined Southampton in 2012 and went on to play 49 times for the club. Known for his ability to play out from the back and start attacks with his distribution, he was a fan favourite at St Mary's. Picked up the nickname of the "Holy Goalie" for an incident at Celtic when he received a police caution for breaching the peace having made less than complimentary gestures to Rangers fans during an Old Firm game. He was first choice for his country during the 2006 World Cup finals and 2008 Euros. Boruc was still playing at Premier League level for Eddie Howe's AFC Bournemouth at the age of 39 before moving back to Poland in 2020.

Bosbury, Charles
Outside-right
Born: *1897 Newhaven* **Died:** *1929*
Playing career: *Southampton, Birmingham, Preston North End , Lincoln City (1914-1929)*
A tall, strong and pacy player, East Sussex-born Bosbury represented his county in athletics and had trials for Britain. His heart was always set on becoming a footballer, though, and he signed for Saints in 1921. Despite several Reserve team appearances, Bosbury never played for the senior side and moved to Birmingham only a year after joining. He went on to play for Preston and Lincoln City before his death from tuberculosis at the age of only 31.

Boulton, Colin
Goalkeeper
Born: *1945 Cheltenham*
Playing career: *Charlton Kings, Gloucester Police, Derby County, Southampton (1964-1981)*
A goalkeeper who played for Derby County between 1964-78 although he only played regulary for them when he took over from Les Green at the start of 1971. Whilst not usually the first name to come out when asked to name players from Derby County's two championship winning squads he was in fact the only player to appear in all 84 league games. He went on to make 344 appearances for them. When his playing career finished he rejoined the police force where he had been a cadet & then worked for Mitre the Sports Company. He still plays golf & plays in Derby's ex Rams annual golf day. He lives in Walton on Trent. Had a six match loan spell at Southampton in 1976 as cover for the injured Ian Turner and unconvincing Steve Middleton.

Bound, Matthew
Central defender
Born: *1972 Melksham*
Playing career: *Southampton, Hull City, Stockport County, Lincoln City, Swansea City, Oxford United, Weymouth, Eastleigh (1986-2009)*
His handful of Southampton games spanned three seasons, three different bosses - Chris Nicholl, Ian Branfoot and Alan Ball - and the inception of the Premiership.

His path to the first team was blocked by the likes of Neil 'Razor' Ruddock, Richard Hall, Kevin Moore and Ken Monkou. Had a loan spell at Hull, before he helped Southampton to their Premiership Great Escape in the 1993-94 season. That proved his final red and white flourish as he moved on to Stockport, paving the way for a lower league career which included a brief flirtation with Eastleigh FC. In his life after football, Bound combined running a holiday cottage, another eating enterprise and *Team Tours,* a business organising national and overseas trips for a variety of ages across several different sports. Currently lives in retirement in Weymouth.

Bowden, James
Centre-half
Born: *1880 Chorlton* **Died:** *1951*
Playing career: *Yardley Methodists, Erdington, Aston Villa, West Bromwich Albion, Southampton, Grimsby Town, Hyde, Stourbridge (1903-1916)*
Manchester born shell turner James Bowden had failed to make the grade at Aston Villa and saw game time further limited at local rivals West Bromwich Albion, progress hindered by sharing the number five shirt with Ted Pheasant. Having got injured in a shooting accident, he left the Midlands and moved south to Saints where his time at the Dell couldn't have been in starker contrast to his earlier days at West Brom. Bowden soon became Southampton's first choice - taking over from Bert Lee - and played 42 times in the 1906-07 season, impressing the fans with his "stylish neatness when in possession" despite his lack of height. For reasons unknown, he would leave Southampton despite his popularity to return to the Second Division with Grimsby. Later played in non league with Hyde and Stourbridge, going on to work on the railways in retirement.

"DID YOU KNOW?"

"Ted Bates "Mr Southampton" served as a player, manager, coach, director, president and chairman during his 36 years with the club"

Bowden, Oswald

Inside-forward
Born: *1912 Byker* **Died:** *1977*
Playing career: *Newcastle United Swifts, Newcastle United, Derby County, Nottingham Forest, Brighton & Hove Albion , Southampton (1929-1939)*

A pattern which followed throughout his 28-match career: he became something of a Reserve team specialist with senior chances few and far between. The final pre-War season, 1938-39 was spent at The Dell where he featured twice at outside-left before giving way to Arthur Holt. 25 Reserve team games later, he dropped into the Hampshire League with Cowes. Saints retained his registration but he would never play League football again, therefore ending the Oswald Bowden story. Died in 1977 back in his home town Newcastle.

Bowen, Jason

Striker
Born: *1972 Merthyr Tydfil, Wales*
Playing career: *Swansea City, Birmingham City, Southampton, Reading, Cardiff City, Newport County, Llanelli (1990-2013)*

Capped twice by Wales, Bowen made three Premiership appearances whilst on loan with Dave Jones' Saints side in 1997. The then Southampton manager wanted to make the move permanent but the two clubs failed to agree a fee and so he moved to Reading. More recently, he played for Cardiff in the legendary "Masters" tournament and now lives in Neath after a time in the building trade.

Bowen, Lionel

Left-back
Born: *1915, Sholing* **Died:** *1996*
Playing career: *Crystal Palace, Southampton, Winchester City (1934-1937)*

A product of local schools football and an uncompromising defender, he played twice for Southampton in the mid 30s, despite staying at The Dell for three seasons. He replaced Donovan Browning for the final two matches of the 1936-37 season. He was more well known for his role in the police, reaching the rank of Chief Superintendent with Hampshire Constabulary, receiving the Queen's Palace Medal for valour in 1977.

Bowles, Paul

Central defender
Born: *1957 Crumpsall* **Died:** *2017*
Playing career: *Manchester United, Crewe Alexandra, Port Vale, Southampton, Stockport County, Barrow (1975-1984)*

Spent time as a youth player at Manchester United, before he began his career with Crewe, where he went on to play over 200 times. Joined divisional rivals Port Vale for £30,000 in October 1979. He was sent out on loan to Southampton a few months later but never played first team football for "The Saints", instead having to make do with only three games for the Reserves. He returned to the Valiants almost as quickly as he had left, going on to become club captain but left for Stockport on a free transfer. After he hung up his boots, Bowles returned to Vale as a coach and also took up employment as a teacher. He died in 2017 at the age of 60.

Bowman, Tommy

Half-back
Born: *1873 Tarbolton, Scotland* **Died:** *1958*
Playing career: *Annbank, Blackpool, Aston Villa, Southampton, Portsmouth (1891-1912)*

A serial winner, Bowman brought his considerable ability to four different Football League clubs. A commanding and "hard to beat" defender, he was part of the Aston Villa side to win the First Division in 1900 and 1901, going on to lift the Southern League title in successive years at The Dell. Saints swept to back-to-back league championships in 1903 and 1904, with an FA Cup Final with the Saints in 1902 thrown in for good measure - this time ending up on the losing side. He trod the south coast divide and jumped ship to Portsmouth, where he went on to play another 80-odd league games in five years at Fratton Park, linking up with ex-Saint and former team mate Arthur Chadwick. Bowman drifted out of the game to work on the railway at Eastleigh. Played for the works side Eastleigh Athletic before he retired to work on the Docks and take up employment as a a boiler scaler. He turned out regularly for the ex Saints in reunion matches until the 1930s. Bowman died in the city in 1958.

Boyd, William

Centre-forward
Born: *1905 Cambuslang, Glasgow*
Died: *1967*
Playing career: *Sheffield United, Manchester Utd, Workington, Luton Town, Southampton (1930-1937)*
Plucked from local football, this son of a customs officer became a member of Saints exclusive "one game men" before returning to his previous job as engine maker's apprentice, then becoming an iron moulder.

Boyer, Phil

Striker
Born: *1949 Nottingham*
Playing career: *Derby County, York City, AFC Bournemouth, Norwich City, Southampton, Manchester City, Bulova SA, Grantham Town, Stamford AFC, Shepshed Charterhouse , (1965-1987)*
Synonymous for his strike partnership with Ted McDougall, the duo spearheaded the attacking fulcrum at four clubs - York, AFC Bournemouth, Norwich and Saints. He arrived at Norwich in a bid to save the Carrow Road club from relegation - although he proved unsuccessful as they went down with Manchester United and, ironically, his future employers Saints.

Shared half of the Canaries goals with McDougall as they went straight back up in 1974-75, losing to Aston Villa in the League Cup Final. Became the first ever Norwich player to be capped by England, his only cap coming against Wales in a 2-1 win in 1976. Lawrie McMenemy brought Boyer to The Dell, and McDougall swiftly followed. Although the pair missed out on the Saints Cup win by merely a month, they fired Southampton into the First Division the following 1976-77 season, losing in the League Cup final again. He was top scorer in the 1979-80 First Division campaign with 23 goals, including a run of eleven consecutive home games, three hat-tricks and a double in the downing of Brian Clough's Nottingham Forest. Boyer holds the rare distinction of making over 100 appearances for four different clubs. He scored 61 goals in 162 games but despite this return he was on his way out of the club following the arrival of Kevin Keegan. Moved on to Manchester City before a brief flirtation at non league level. Upon retirement he worked as a bank clerk and then as a courier. He continues to live in Nottingham.

Boyes, Kenneth

Outside-left

Born: *1895 Southampton* **Died:** *1963*
Playing career: *Southampton, Bristol Rovers, Poole, Weymouth (1914-1940)*

A talented multi sportsman of some acclaim, Boyes represented his battalion in both football and cricket during the war and was also the regimental sprint champion. He only played eight times in as many years at the Dell and left for Bristol Rovers where he also struggled for game time, playing two games in as many seasons. Nor did he have success as a cricketer - unlike his brother Jack who went onto play 500 times for Hampshire and the MCC. Boyes went on to work at Pirelli General in Eastleigh where he became the groundsman for their works team, until 1960. Died 3 years later.

Boyle, Jack

Winger

Born: *1990, Jersey*
Playing career: *Southampton, Salisbury City, Jersey Scottish , Airdrie United (2008-2013)*

A little known winger from the Channel Island of Jersey, he had a trial with Oldham before he joined Southampton in November 2008. He never made the grade and left after two injury hit years. Moved on to Salisbury in 2011 and then returned to regional football on the island.

Bradburn, George

Centre-half

Born: *1894 Wolverhampton* **Died:** *1975*
Playing career: *Walsall, Southampton (1914-1923)*

Working at the Whitehead Torpedo Works in Weymouth, George Bradburn had guested for Southampton. After hostilities had ceased, he return to his native Midlands for a season with Walsall in the first post-War campaign before signing for Southampton. An ex miner, he was a tall man with the ideal stature for a centre-half - a "strong and rugged defender". He made 28 appearances before eventually returning to former side Walsall on a free transfer, before his career came to an end. Bradburn ied in the West Midland town in 1975.

Bradford, James

Half-back

Born: *1902 Walsall* **Died:** *1944*
Playing career: *Bloxwich All Saints, Talbot Stead Tubeworks, Southampton, Cowes Sports (1922-1937)*

A one club man and a loyal Saint, Bradford had been playing for the Talbot Stead Tube Works when he scouted by Southampton and offered a trial. Bradford had the ideal attributes for a centre half - coming as he did from the mining community in Staffordshire. He went on to make the left-half position his own alongside Alec Campbell as Southampton reached the FA Cup semi final in 1925 and then when they became a selling club. Bradford survived the cull and went on to play 334 times at the Dell, scoring six times. After more than a decade at Saints, he retired at the end of the 1935-36 season. His loyalty and longevity earned him two benefit matches. Bradford went on to become mine host at the *Plume & Feathers* pub in St Mary's.

Bradley, Jack

Inside-forward

Born: *1916 Hemsworth* **Died:** *2002*
Playing career: *South Kirkby Colliery, Huddersfield Town, Swindon Town, Chelsea, Southampton, Bolton Wanderers, Norwich City (1935-1955)*

Joined Southampton from Chelsea (where he failed to make a first team appearance) but, as with many of his contemporaries, missed out a large chunk of his career due to the War. As the conflict broke out, Yorkshire born Bradley joined the Police Reserves and remained in Southampton playing in the southern war leagues. Bradley was deployed in the RAF. Returning to The Dell, he established himself as Saints first choice inside left half in tandem with Doug McGibbon at centre-forward. Bradley finished his debut season as joint top scorer along with George Lewis on 15 goals. Fell out with manager Bill Dodgin and was transferred to Bolton, going on to Norwich and finishing in non league with Yarmouth Town as player-manager. After football, he remained in Norfolk and became the licensee of the Jolly Farmers pub in Ormesby near Great Yarmouth. Bradley died in 2002 at the age of 86.

Bradley, Shayne

Striker
Born: *1979 Gloucester*
Playing career: *Southampton, Swindon Town, Exeter City, Mansfield Town, Eastwood Town, Chesterfield, Lincoln City (1998-2003)*

A powerfully built striker born in Gloucester, he signed for Saints when still at school. Bradley worked his way through the ranks to become a regular scorer in the reserves. Played up front with Michael Owen for England at youth level. In 2003 having made just four first team appearances with loan spells with Swindon and Exeter, he moved onto Mansfield Town but his playing career was finally ended that same year by recurring ankle injuries. After several surgeries, he returned to football as a youth coach with hometown club Gloucester City, before also becoming manager of Tufley Rovers. He also worked for Eon and as contract manager for utilities company Enserve.

Bradshaw, Joe

Outside-right
Born: *1884 Burnley, Lancashire*
Playing career: *Woolwich Polytechnic, Woolwich Arsenal, West Norwood, Southampton, Fulham, Chelsea, QPR , Southend United (1904-1915)*

Burnley born Bradshaw started out in the amateur London leagues before playing for a works team in Woolwich. Had a brief spell at Woolwich Arsenal where his father Harry was the manager - however Bradshaw Jr. never played for the first team. After another brief stint at West Norwood he moved to Southampton before again linking up with his father in London, this time at Fulham. Bradshaw never played for Saints at any level but went on to win the Southern League twice with the Cottagers as they went up into the Football League in 1907. Also played for Chelsea, QPR and Southend United before he retired as a player. Bradshaw's post-playing career saw him take the step into management - where he took charge of two of his former clubs in Fulham and Southend (the latter as player-manager), following in the footsteps of his dad. He also managed Swansea Town and Bristol City.

Brennan, James

Defender
Born: *1977 East York, Ontario, Canada*
Playing career: *Bristol City, Nottingham Forest, Huddersfield Town, Norwich City, Southampton, Toronto FC (1994-2010)*

A 49-cap Canadian international, Brennan made England his home for 12 years. Equally as adept as left-back as he was on the left side of midfield, he made the bulk of his Football League appearances for Nottingham Forest. Brennan joined Saints under George Burley in 2006 but left the club the following May and returned to his native Canada to play for newly formed Toronto. Brennan later managed the first team and has also coached at Aurora in his native country. As of 2019, Brennan is the boss of York9 FC in the Canadian Premier League. Won the First Division with Norwich in 2004 and the CONCACAF Gold Cup at international level in 2000. He was inducted into the Canadian football Hall of Fame in 2015.

Brewis, John

Inside-forward
Born: *1907 Tynemouth* **Died:** *1975*
Playing career: *Preston Colliery, West Stanley, Newark Town, York City, Southampton, Newport (IOW) (1928-1939)*

North East native Brewis started out in non league before moving into the Football League with York City. Cash strapped Southampton - having sold the likes of Bill Fraser, John Arnold and Arthur Wilson- still needed a loan from one of their directors to bring Brewis to the Dell as new manager George Kay searched for re-inforcements. Brewis quickly became first choice at inside-right, hitting a hat-trick against newly relegated Manchester United and ending the season with double figures. A "scientific" player, his diminutive stature did not hinder him as he earned a reputation as a man good in the air with a knack for scoring difficult headers. Brewis kept his place for much of the next two seasons until Fred Tully replaced him. He was eventually released and spent a bit of time with Newport on the Isle of Wight before joining the Navy, surviving the War and going on to become a hotelier.

Bridge, Wayne

Left-back

Born: *1980 Southampton*
Playing career: *Southampton, Chelsea, Fulham (loan), Manchester City, West Ham United (loan), Sunderland (loan), Brighton & Hove Albion (loan), Reading (1996-2014)*

A Premier League title winner with Chelsea, Bridge also won both domestic cups with Jose Mourinho's all-conquering side at Stamford Bridge. Played 161 games for Saints, earning a runners up medal in the 2003 FA Cup final, as a consistent and stylish presence at left-back. Bridge was capped 36 times for England and featured in three major tournaments, but despite these achievements, Bridge's off-the-field shenanigans have overshadowed his playing career.

Wayne Bridge

He famously fell out with former Blues team-mate John Terry after the latter had an affair with Bridge's partner Vanessa Peroncell. The pair refused to shake hands during a match between Chelsea and City and haven't spoken to each other since. Bridge has appeared on *I'm a Celebrity Get Me out of Here*, *Celebrity SAS: Who Dares Wins* and has participated in boxing bouts for Sport Relief and Sport Aid. Bridge is currently keeping busy with various media engagements, including podcasts, radio commentary and television punditry. He rarely stays out of the public eye during to his marriage to *The Saturdays* singer Frankie Sandford. Bridge jointly runs a London-based recruitment talent agency, *10TEN Talent,* and you can follow him on Twitter here: https://twitter.com/WayneBridge

Briggs, Fred

Centre-forward

Born: *1908 Wombwell* **Died:** *1998*
Playing career: *Wombwell, Rotherham United , Reading, Southampton (1932-1939)*

A winger turned centre-forward, Fred Briggs was Saints top scorer in his one full season at The Dell. Capable of playing anywhere across the front line, he played in the opening three games of the 1939-40 season but war was declared and his career stuttered to an early end. Dropping out of the game completely, Briggs became involved with the war effort as a worker at Supermarine Aviation in Southampton. The achievements of the Spitfire made the factory an obvious target for Germany's Luftwaffe, so the Woolston works factory duly dispersed. So Briggs returned to Reading and remained there once hostilities still working in the aviation industry. Employed by Pressed Steel, Miles Aircraft and Adwest Air, he retired in 1976 and died in the town in 1998.

"DID YOU KNOW?"

"In 1904, Saints became the first side from these shores to go on an overseas tour. They travelled to South America by boat and won 5 matches (scored 29, let in only 4!)."

Brittleton, Samuel
Inside-forward
Born: *1885 Wharton, Cheshire* **Died:** *1951*
Playing career: *Winsford United, Stockport County, Preston North End, Chorley, Southampton, Accrington Stanley (1905-1914)*

Brother of the more well known England international John Brittleton, Sam worked as a salt labourer before becoming a footballer. Played for Chorley at non league level before Southampton signed him despite the clamour from Second Division Manchester City. Described as "sometimes brilliant, sometimes less so", he was in and out of the side at inside left, scoring only four goals in a handful of appearances at the Dell. Brittleton went on to work in a factory as an engineer during the War

Broad, Thomas
Outside-right
Born: *1887 Stalybridge*
Died: *1966*
Playing career: *West Bromwich Albion, Chesterfield, Oldham Athletic, Bristol City, Manchester City, Stoke, Southampton, Weymouth, Rhyl (1905-1926)*

Broad was in the twilight of his playing days when he arrived at The Dell and, to this day, holds the distinction of being Southampton's oldest ever player at 37 years of age. He spent his solitary season on the south coast as cover for Bill "Tishy" Henderson and played nine games in total. Broad later worked for his local council.

Brookes, Richard
Full-back
Born: *1882 Reading, Berkshire*
Died: *1961*
Playing career: *Reading, Southampton (1908-1920)*

After a career in the army in which Brookes served in the 4th Battalion Kings Royal Rifles, he took up a job in Eastleigh as a railway worker before signing for Reading, and then Saints. A "strong, burly full-back with an inclination to be over exuberant" he played 19 matches in two seasons at full-back before losing his place in the team to veteran fans favourite Bert Lee. Brookes left the Dell in 1914 to recon the Army, only to return for a second time without ever adding to his first team career, spending a season with the side's second string.

Brophy, Henry
Half-back
Born: *1916 Leicester* **Died:** *1996*
Playing career: *Arsenal, Canterbury Waverley (loan), Margate (loan), Southampton, Corinthian Club (1933-1952)*

Harry "Henry" Brophy scored in each of his first four games having been drafted in at centre forward with regular striker Reg Tomlinson injured. After reverting to a more familiar left-half role, he remained a regular for the rest of the 1938-39 campaign, in what would be the final pre-War season. Brophy would see his career - fortunately not his life - ended by the outbreak of WW2 which brought his days as a Saint to a premature end. He joined the police and then the Merchant Navy during the War and served on a hospital ship during Dunkirk. Played for several clubs - including Chelsea and Fulham - as a guest - before emigrating to Australia. There, he moved into coaching and briefly took charge of the national team for two games in 1954 and 1955.

Brown, Albert
Striker
Born: *1879 Austrey, Warwickshire* **Died:** *1955*
Playing career: *Aston Villa, Southampton, QPR, Preston North End, Blackpool (1898-1906)*

Nicknamed the "Tamworth Sprinter", it was clear what Albert Brown's most valuable asset was. Hailed as the "fastest man in the kingdom", he possessed a powerful shot and made a lightning start to life at Saints. His 25 goals in 26 Southern League games - including seven in one game in an 11-0 trouncing of Northampton— shattered all records. Thanks in no small part to the efforts of Brown, Saints made it to the FA Cup final in 1902 but despite scoring in the replay against Sheffield United, Brown was unable to prevent the Blades winning the trophy. Hit by injury, he moved on to divisional rivals QPR for £96 where he was unable to recapture his goalscoring form. Later worked for Dunlop in his native Midlands and then reverted to pre-football job as a house painter. In all, he notched 35 goals in 46 outings for the Saints. Albert died in 1955.

Brown, Arthur

Goalkeeper
Born: *1888 Cowes*
Playing career: *Southampton, Cowes, Portsmouth, Southampton, Wanderers (1906-1912)*
An amateur player and part time engineer, he signed for Southampton but went on to hometown club Cowes and then Portsmouth. A string of outstanding performances turned the heads of the national selectors but - although he was never capped for England - he did represent Great Britain in the 1912 Olympic Games football tournament in Stockholm. Later worked as a civil engineer on the docks at Nova Scotia, Canada.

Brown, Charlie

Outside-right
Born: *1898 Stakeford* **Died:** *1979*
Playing career: *Southampton, QPR (1920-1927)*
A quick and crafty winger with a strange tendency to struggle in front of his home fans at the Dell, Brown joined the club in time for their first ever Football League seasonIn and was a crowd pleaser who managed to play almost 100 games for the club before losing his place to Sam Meston and moving to QPR. Also played for Poole Town before returning to Southampton to work for Supermarine at Wooston.

Brown, Eddy

Centre-forward
Born: *1926 Preston, Lancashire* **Died:** *2012*
Playing career: *Preston North End, Southampton, Coventry C, Birmingham C, Leyton O, (1948-1964)*
Eddy Brown moved south to The Dell in a swap deal with Charlie Wayman. Boasted a decent ratio of 34 in 59 for Southampton. Earned an FA Cup runners up medal at Birmingham City and scored against Barcelona in the Inter Cities Fairs Cup. Having finished his League career at Leyton Orient, he spent time as player-manager of Scarborough before retiring to Preston and fulfil his ambition of becoming a teacher. Taught French and sport. He also managed a local amateur team and was involved in charity projects. Also worked as a sales rep for a carpet firm.

Brown, George

Left-back
Born: *1883 Poole* **Died:** *1959*
Playing career: *Southampton (1910-1910)*
A one game wonder for the Saints, Brown made his solitary appearance for the club in a Hampshire Junior Cup tie vs Bournemouth in 1910. He deputised for Charlie Deacon at left-back before returning to Netley Hospital where he worked. He then became a victualler, providing supplies for crews of marine vessels going to sea. Died in 1959.

Brown, Gordon

Inside-forward
Born: *1933 Eastham* **Died:** *2005*
Playing career: *Wolverhampton Wanderers, Scunthorpe United, Derby County, Southampton, Barrow, Southport, Morecambe (1949-1965)*
Brown's stint at the Dell was brief but impactful. He scored an equaliser on his debut and then the winner the following week - a small but significant contribution as Saints became Third Division champions in 1960. Had averaged a goal every two games at Scunthorpe before moving to Saints after three years at Derby. He would spend most of his second season in the Reserves. Played for Barrow and Southport in the lower echelons of the Football League before retiring and working in Ellesmere Port for oil firm *Burma Castrol*.

Brown, Harry

Inside-forward
Born: *1883 Northampton* **Died:** *1934*
Playing career: *Northampton Town, West Bromwich Albion, Southampton, Newcastle United, Bradford PA, Fulham, Southampton (1902-1914)*

Armed with a deceptive style of play, Harry Brown played 100 games for the Saints across two spells and hit 43 goals. His first stint at The Dell, arriving from West Brom, attracted the attention of Newcastle. Moving to the North East in time for their title winning season of 1906-07, he was soon back in the more familiar surroundings of the Southern League. By the time he was at Fulham, he was actually back living in Southampton. This allowed him to combine playing for the Cottagers with a job in the fruit business. By the time he had left Fulham he had moved into the pub trade, latterly running the *Kingsland Tavern* in St Mary's Street. Served as a transport driver in the Army during WW2 and ran a greengrocer's after the conflict. Died at the age of 50 from a virus that had caused him to lose his sight.

Brown, Robert

Outside-forward
Born: *1869 Liverpool* **Died:** *1929*
Playing career: *Burton Wanderers, Southampton, Bristol Rovers, QPR , Swindon Town (1894-1901)*

Brown played 25 games for Saints in all competitions and before moving on to Bristol Rovers. After a stint with Swindon he retired to become a house decorator in his native Liverpool. Died in 1929.

Brown, William

Forward
Born: *1943 Croydon*
Playing career: *Southampton, Charlton Athletic, Romford, Chelmsford City , Bedford Town, Gillingham, Portsmouth, Brentford, (1960-1970)*

Bill Brown had earned a reputation as a deadly striker in non-league football and had scored 33 goals in 100 odd games for Gillingham. He began on schoolboy terms at Southampton but never made the grade. An ankle injury ended his career and he went back to work on the family's pig farm. He later bought a lorry and started his own conservatory company.

Browning, Donovan

Right-back
Born: *1916 Ashley, Hampshire* **Died:** *1997*
Playing career: *Southampton (1935-1939)*

'Don' Browning joined as an amateur but signed as a pro for after one season. A debut at right-back soon followed, but then he suffered a serious knee injury and never really recovered. He retired in 1939 and, whilst staying active in the farming world in Blandford, Dorset, he was a season ticket holder at The Dell. Died in 1997.

Browning, Robert

Inside-forward
Born: *1888 Kettering* **Died:** *1949*
Playing career: *Kettering Town, QPR , Southampton, Brentford (1910-1914)*

Bob Browning was nicknamed 'Lightning'. It was a moniker he had earned at the start of his career with his hometown team - due to his blistering pace - and it duly stuck. Stepping up to Southern League QPR, he had hit 20 goals in 54 games for The Hoops when divisional rivals Southampton came sniffing. A "clever forward with an accurate shot" was tasked with reviving a struggling Saints side, but his career on the south coast would be short lived. Serious cartilage damage just six games into his Southampton spell ended his time at The Dell before it had even begun. He did return to football with Brentford but never really recovered and became a window cleaner. After the war he moved to the Forest of Dean to work in the coalmines and turned out for amateur side Bream.

Bruton, Les

Centre-forward
Born: *1903 Foleshill*
Died: *1989*
Playing career: *Bell End Wesleyans, Foleshill, Southampton, Peterborough & Fletton United, Raith Rovers, Blackburn Rovers, Liverpool, Leamington Town (1922-1933)*

Les Bruton had trials with several Football League clubs - Arsenal and West Brom among them - when he was signed by Southampton from local football for the princely sum of £15. He boasted an impressive Reserve team record for the Saints, but proved not quite good enough for senior professional first team football - described as "not bad but needs to be quicker on and off the ball." In four seasons at the club he only played seven times and then moved to fellow Southern League side Peterborough. Spent a season in Scotland with Raith Rovers before he finally got his chance in Division One with Blackburn Rovers and Liverpool. Dropped into the non league game and then joined his hometown team Coventry as assistant coach. Became a motor mechanic in West Bromwich.

Buchanan, Robert

Forward
Born: *1867 Edinburgh, Scotland*
Died: *1909*
Playing career: *Johnstone, Abercorn, Sunderland Albion , Burnley, Woolwich Arsenal, Southampton, Sheppey United (1887-1899)*

Due to a penchant for the spectacular and ability to chase lost causes, he was given the nickname "Death or Glory Bob." By the time he arrived at The Dell he had already earned his one and only Scotland cap in 1891 (a 4-3 victory over Wales). A relative Football League veteran for Burnley and Arsenal, Buchanan was a virtual ever present for the Saints, missing only one Southern League tie in his first two seasons, winning the title on both occasions. 74 games later, he dropped into non league with Sheppey United, settling on the Kent coast and plying his post-football trade as an engine fitter. Died in Southwark, South London at the age of 41 in 1909.

Buckenham, Bill

Centre-forward
Born: *1888 Exeter* **Died:** *1954*
Playing career: *Woolwich Arsenal, Southampton, 12th Royal Field Artillery (1909-1910)*

Bombadier Bucknenham held the unprecedented feat of being registered for two clubs simultaneously. When he joined Southampton, he was still signed on as a Woolwich Arsenal player whilst turning out for the Royal Artillery at Aldershot. Scored in his first two games at The Dell but that would be as good as it got as he was dropped in favour of Frank Jefferis after four further games. His army career then took precedence, serving in the Great War in India with the Royal Field Artillery. Later reached the rank of Quarter-Master Sergeant before becoming a lift operator.

Bull, Gary

Striker
Born: *1966 West Bromwich*
Playing career: *Southampton, Cambridge United, Barnet, Nottingham F, Birmingham City, Brighton, York City, Scunthorpe United (1986-2012)*

Having been a trainee at Southampton, Bull never played for the Saints and joined Cambridge in March 1988. Enjoyed an extensive career in the lower echelons of the game and at non league level, his clubs included Brighton, York, Scunthorpe and Boston Town. It was at the latter where he became the club's all time top goalscorer, with over 200 goals despite not joining them until he 39. Played until he was 45 before finally retiring in 2012. Cousin of Wolves legend Steve Bull. After he hung up his boots he became a financial adviser and player agent.

Bullock, James

Inside-left/Centre-forward
Born: *1902 Gorton* **Died:** *1977*
Playing career: *Man City, Crewe A, Southampton, Chesterfield, Manchester United, (1922-1933)*

Bullock's arrival at The Dell saw the irresistible force meet the immovable object. Bill Rawlings was firmly established as Southampton's first choice centre-forward when Bullock came to the club from Crewe, where he had failed to shine across two spells at Gresty Road.

A small but deadly striker, he was forced into the Reserves during three and a half years of his five season stay at the Saints. He plundered a record-breaking 163 goals in 209 games at second string level, a staggering statistic that still stands today. He eventually got his first team chance and hit a further 14 goals in 37 games before falling out with the club and moving to Third Division (North) side Chesterfield. Finally got his yearned for move to the top flight with hometown team Manchester United, it ended in ignominy as United went down - although Bullock played only sporadically. He had a season in Ireland and one more in Wales before winding down at Cheshire League Hyde. Having retired he coached briefly at that club before becoming a railway worker.

Bundy, William

Centre-forward
Born: *1883 Eastleigh* **Died:** *1945*
Playing career: *Eastleigh Guild, Southampton, Eastleigh Athletic (1898-1922)*

A one match wonder at the Dell, Bundy was thrust into the limelight at centre-forward during a match against Reading with regular forwards Tom Barlow, Joe Turner and Harry Wood all injured. Despite a goal on his debut, Bundy would make no headway as the injured men returned and had to watch from the Reserves team as Saints swept to the Southern League title. Bundy soon left the Dell, going on to play for Eastleigh Athletic in the Hampshire League before taking up a job on the railways.

Burley, Benjamin

Outside-forward
Born: *1907 Sheffield* **Died:** *2003*
Playing career: *Darnall School, Netherhope Institute, Woodhouse Mill United, Sheffield United, Southampton, Grimsby Town, Norwich City, Darlington, Chelmsford City (1931-1940)*

Joined hometown club Sheffield United but never made a first team appearance for the Blades. His affinity with red and white continued when Burley joined Southampton but the 'thrustful' left winger would spend most of his days at the Dell with the Reserve team.

Used as cover for Fred Tully and Bill Luckett, he played two first team games in the dying embers of the 1933-34 season before leaving Saints and embarking on a nomadic journey through the lower leagues. Guested for various clubs - including Saints - during the war. Burley later ran a post office in Essex. Died in 2003.

Burns, Francis

Left-back
Born: *1948 Glenboig, North Lanarkshire, Scotland*
Playing career: *Manchester United, Southampton, Preston North End, Shamrock Rovers (1964-1982)*

Francis moved south of the border in 1965 and his six years at United would have been more productive had it not been for repeated injury problems. Ironically, he came to the attention of the Saints during a game at Old Trafford in which the visitors were beaten 4-1. Burns kept Terry Paine and John Sydenham quiet, persuading the club to part with £50,000 for him.

He was a regular starter until losing his place to Shay Brennan. He played the first seven games in United's European Cup winning campaign, he was a cultured defender and played 23 games for Saints and earned one cap for Scotland in 1969. Francis emigrated to Australia in 1987 where he coached in Perth and went on to run dry cleaning and industrial cleaning businesses in the Australia city. He now works for a local radio station.

Burnside, David

Attacking midfielder
Born: *1939 Kingswood* **Died:** *2009*
Playing career: *Bristol City, West Bromwich Albion, West Bromwich Albion, Southampton, Crystal Palace, Wolverhampton Wanderers, Los Angeles Wolves, Plymouth Argyle, Bristol City, Colchester United, Bath City (1955-1973)*

Twice capped by England at U21 level, David Burnside served notice of his blistering potential early on when he almost set a world record of keeping the ball up for 500 headers in a Sunday dispatch competition. Ted Bates signed him for Southampton for £18,000 and he instantly became a hit in the Saints side, dovetailing alongside Terry Paine and John Sydenham on the wings with fellow new arrivals George Kirby and George O'Brien in attack. Noted for his terrific range of passing and his ability to find space, Burnside had two burning ambitions - to win silverware and a full cap for England. He would achieve neither, but his stay at the Dell was a memorable one with 70 appearances (26 goals). Went on to play for Crystal Palace, Wolves, Plymouth, Bristol City and Colchester before retirement. After a spell at Bath City as player/manager, he managed England's U20 side and had a stint as joint caretaker boss at former club Bristol City. Burnside died at 69 in 2009.

John Burridge

@TheBudgieTweets

The greatest goalkeeper the world has never seen. I should still be playing.

Burridge, John

Goalkeeper
Born: *1951 Workington*
Playing career: *Workington, Blackpool, Aston Villa, Southend United, Crystal Palace, QPR, Wolverhampton Wanderers, Derby County, Sheffield United, Southampton, + lots! (1969-1997)*

In his senior career he played for 29 clubs in a career that last almost 30 years. Overall, 'Budgie' featured 771 times in the English and Scottish leagues and several more at non league level. Won the League Cup with Aston Villa in 1977 and was the oldest player to appear in the Premier League, for Manchester City aged 43. Southampton was his tenth club in 1987, signed by then manager Chris Nicholl. Moved to Newcastle two years later. He became a regular in the two seasons he spent at The Dell, going to make 75 appearance in red and white. He finished his playing days at Blyth Spartans in 1997 as player-manager, following a return to Newcastle as goalkeeping coach. Since then, he has worked in the same role for the Oman national side and currently works in India as goalkeeping coach for the Kerala Blasters. Has also done television punditry work.

Burrows, Thomas

Goalkeeper
Born: *1886 Portsmouth* **Died:** *1964*
Playing career: *Southampton (1904-1915)*

Burrows worked in the shipyards in Weston, missing Southampton's 1903 Southern League title win by a year. With George Clawley and Michael Byrne ahead of him in the pecking order, the goalkeeper finally got his chance until injury struck. Regaining possession of the keeper's jersey in 1909, Burrows would go on to make 48 successive appearances for Saints in the Southern League. An error strewn start to the 1910-11 season saw him dropped and replaced once more before moving on that summer. Went on to play for Merthyr Town during their promotion winning campaign and became a virtual ever present for the next few years, until war broke out. Following war time work on submarines in Portsmouth, Burrows had a job with Esso after the conflict.

Bushby, Thomas

Half-back
Born: *1914 Shildon* **Died:** *1997*
Playing career: *Southend United , Portsmouth, Folland Aircraft , Southampton (1934-1954)*

Guested for Saints and Chelsea during the War, but mainly turned out for the Folland Aircraft works team, where he and his wife worked. Several prominent players of the day - Southampton's Bill Dodgin and Ted Bates among them - also turned out for a formidable, all conquering side. Dodgin was manager of Saints by the time hostilities ceased and wasted no time in signing Bushby. He would get only two games at the Dell, turning down Aldershot's advances to work on the Docks while with Cowes. He would make over 250 successive appearances for the island side, before retiring in 1954.

Butt, Len

Left-half
Born: *1893 Freemantle, Southampton* **Died:** *1993*
Playing career: *Southampton, Bournemouth & Boscombe Athletic (1912-1927)*

At the time of his death in 1993, hwas the last surviving former Saint who signed for the club whilst still in the Southern League. With the outbreak of war, he joined the 5th Hampshire Regiment and served in India for four years. After the end of the war, he worked at Thornycrofts and played for their works team in the Hampshire League. Invited for a trial by work colleague and Saint Bert Lee, Butt joined the club in time for their first ever Southern League season and rose through the ranks from amateur to pro terms. With his sharpness in the tackle and crowd pleasing temerity, he earned the nickname "Badger Butt" and and went on to play 26 times for the club. He joined Boscombe (the club that would later become AFC Bournemouth) and helped them into the Football League as captain. Chalked up over 100 games, then returned to the Hampshire League with Cowes. When he retired in 1927, Butt stayed local and ran the Sailors Home pub in Eastleigh for a decade and later the *Edinburgh Arms* in Boscombe. He died in 2003, just 17 days shy of his 100th birthday.

Butterfield, Daniel

Defender
Born: *1979 Boston*
Playing career: *Southampton, Grimsby Town, Crystal Palace, Charlton Athletic, Southampton, Bolton Wanderers, Carlisle United, Exeter City (1993-2016)*

Saints manager Nigel Adkins had signed Frazer Richardson ahead of the 2010-11 season, but the new signing promptly dislocated a shoulder and Butterfield was brought in as a replacement. Played a key role in Saints promotion to the Championship - and then the Premier League the following year - before he fell out of favour following the arrival of Butterfield's former Palace team mate Nathaniel Clyne. He played over 500 career games in all four professional divisions of English football and is perhaps best known for what's known as a "perfect" hat-trick when on the books at Crystal Palace. Coming in the space of six minutes in a replayed FA Cup tie with Wolves, Butterfield - a right-back turned makeshift striker in an injury crisis - scored with his left foot, then his right and completed his treble with a header for the club's fastest ever such feat. Most recently, Butterfield worked as a first team coach for MK Dons.

Byrne, Michael

Goalkeeper
Born: *1880 Bristol*
Died: *1931*
Playing career: *Bristol Rovers, Southampton, Chelsea, Glossop (1902-1908)*

A Grenadier Guardsman in his pre-football days, Byrne joined Saints from Bristol Rovers as back up to first choice 'keeper George Clawley. Six games and two years later, he joined Second Division newcomers Chelsea - again as cover, this time for the infamous William "Fatty" Foulke, making four appearances in the 1905-06 season. Injury ended his career in west London, and he moved to Eastleigh via a brief spell at Glossop. Byrne returned to his native Bristol where he worked for *Imperial Tobacco* and later in a ware operator for a printing firm. Served in the Royal Defence Corps as a private during the War. Died in 1931 aged 51.

Byrne, Tony

Left-back
Born: *1946 Rathdowney, Ireland*
Died: *2016*
Playing career: *Millwall, Southampton, Hereford United, Newport County, Trowbridge (1963-1979)*

Capped 14 times by the Republic of Ireland, Byrne played for Millwall, Southampton, Hereford United and Newport during his career. After only a single game for Millwall he was signed by Saints manager Ted Bates for £8,000 despite still being 18. Broke his leg in a Reserve team game and had to wait a year for his Saints debut at Old Trafford, a 3-0 defeat to Man United. He played 114 times during his ten years at The Dell and earned all of his international caps whilst a Saints player. Later linked up with former Southampton colleague Terry Paine at Hereford for three seasons before moving across the border to Newport where he would finish his playing days. Having retired from football he worked as a foreman at Hereford gold course before taking up a job as a builder. He died in 2016 aged 70.

Caceres, Claudio

Left Winger/Attacking Midfielder
Born: *1982 Buenos Aires, Argentina*
Playing career: *Perth SC, Southampton, Brentford, Hull City, Perth Glory, Yeovil Town, Wycombe Wanderers, Aldershot Town, Perth Glory, Melbourne Victory, Central Coast Mariners, Wellington Phoenix, Inglewood United, Heidelberg United, Real Mataram, Chiangrai United, Bayswater City, Balcatta FC (1998-2015)*

Caceres was a much travelled player with a reputation as a journeyman during his playing days. After a stint in Australia with Perth, he moved to England and was signed by Southampton after a trial. His days at The Dell never came to fruition, though, and he left the club in 2001 after eight months without ever playing for the club in any capacity. Spent a few years dotted around the Football League with Yeovil, Hull City, Wycombe Wanderers, Brentford and Aldershot. Moved back to Australia where he won the A League with Melbourne and also later played in Thailand. Now 38, Caceres was jailed for 18 months in 2019 after being found guilty of dealing Class A drug methamphetamine.

Cain, Tom

Goalkeeper
Born: *1872 Sunderland* **Died:** *1952*
Playing career: *Stoke, Everton, Southampton St. Mary's, Grimsby Town (1893-1897)*

Played for Stoke and Everton before his arrival at a Saints side in their second Southern League season. Replacing Arthur Cox on his Southampton debut, he suffered a goalkeeping nightmare - conceding seven goals away to Clapton. He could have been discarded there and then but recovered from the setback to retain his place between the sticks before being replaced either by Cox or the on-loan "Gunner" Matt Reilly. George Clawley arrived and that was the end of Cain's time at Saints, going to Grimsby and then ending his playing days. In retirement he ran the *Royal Oak* pub in his native Sunderland and worked as a labourer on the docks at Gateshead.

Callagher, John

Centre-half
Born: *1898 Glasgow, Scotland* **Died:** *1980*
Playing career: *Southampton, Wigan Borough, Norwich City, Horwich RMI, Mossley (1921-1926)*

Centre-half Callagher became the apple of Southampton's eye when playing against them for Bury in the twice replayed FA Cup tie of 1923. A "class player", Callagher joined the Saints at the end of that season despite the Shakers rise to First Division prominence. He arrived at The Dell with John Woodhouse in a deal that saw Bill Turner go the other way to Gigg Lane. Despite his hype, he failed to settle in the south and played only game for Saints in a marathon season spanning nearly 50 games. Southampton offered to retain him but he asked for a move away and returned north to Wigan. After a brief liaison with the non league game, Callagher retired and became a fireman in Blackpool, earning a medal for bravery in 1938.

"DID YOU KNOW?"

"Matt Le Tissier scored 101 Premiership goals - a record that will be hard to beat. James Beattie's total of 68 is the closest so far."

Camara, Henri

Striker
Born: *1977 Dakar, Senegal*
Playing career: *Ionikos FC, ASC Diaraf, RC Strasbourg, Neuchatel Xamax, Grasshopper Club Z urich, Sedan, Wolverhampton Wanderers, Celtic, Southampton, Wigan Athletic, West Ham United, Stoke City, Sheffield United, Atromitos, Panetolikos, Kalloni, Lamia, Panetolikos, Apollon Smyrni (1998-Still playing)*

A net busting Senegalese striker who arrived at Saints on loan from relegated Wolves, straight into another bottom of the table dogfight. A "feisty, quality player with finishing power", Camara lived up to his billing with three goals in his first four games. At his most dangerous and exciting when direct and one-on-one, despite his best efforts, he was unable to prevent Saints going into the Championship - a third successive demotion for the player. Stayed in the Premier League with newly promoted Wigan and then led a nomadic life around England, Greece and Cyprus. He most recently played for Fostiras in Greece. Earned 99 caps for Senegal and played at the 2002 World Cup finals for his nation. A short but impactful spell for this ground hopper, with six goals in 12 games for Southampton.

Campbell, Alistair

Centre-half
Born: *1890 Southampton*
Died: *1943*
Playing career: *King Edward VI School, Southampton, Glossop North End, Southampton, Poole Town (1908-1927)*

Not to be confused with the former Downing Street spin doctor, Alec Campbell remains the only player in history to play for England at amateur level whilst still a schoolboy. He played seven games for Hampshire County Cricket Club as an opening batsman before focusing on his football career. Spotted and signed by Southampton in 1908 he quickly became one of the club's "brightest ever prospects." Played over 200 games for Saints in two spells at The Del during which he became "undoubtedly one of the club's best ever centre halves", captaining the club and cutting a distinctive figure at 6ft 2. He helped Jimmy McIntyre's men into the Football League for the first time ever before, now aged 36, he joined Poole and played a part as they reached the FA Cup third round for the first, and so far, only time in their history. After retirement, he managed Chesterfield and served in the Royal Artillery during WW2.

Campbell, Francis

Half-back
Born: *1907 Camlachie, Scotland*
Died: *1985*
Playing career: *Irvine Meadow, Southampton, Newport, Dumbarton (1931-1939)*

A relatively late bloomer, Campbell was detected by Southampton's radar aged 24, whilst playing in the backwaters of Scotland. Moving to the Dell in 1931, he initially shared the number 4 shirt with Bert Shelley and Stan Woodhouse in Saints well-stocked half back line. He soon developed into a "strong, agile and forceful player", quickly adapting to the step up to life in England's second tier. A versatile player, Campbell slotted in anywhere across the back line and was a virtual ever present until a knee injury hindered his progress. After making a total of 93 appearances for Saints, scoring five goals, he retired through arthritis before working for Folland aircraft.

Carnaby, Thomas

Half-back
Born: *1913 Newsham, Northumberland*
Died: *1971*
Playing career: *New Delaval United, Blyth Spartans, Southampton, Andover (1933-1947)*

Carnaby, from a mining family in the North east, played 16 games for Southampton in the final pre-War season. Described as a "brawny" centre back, he was used as cover for the dependable Dave Affleck. Had a run of games in the team until the end of the season but war soon broke out and - like so many of his contemporaries - Carnaby joined the efforts of the country. First in the local War Reserve Police, then transferred to the Southampton Borough force. Played war time football for a formidable police side, before returning to his native north east to play for South Shields after the conflict.

Carr, Jimmy

Outside-left
Born: *1893 Maryhill, Glasgow, Scotland*
Died: *1980*
Playing career: *Watford Orient, Watford,West Ham United, Reading, Southampton, Swansea Town, Southall, QPR (1908-1928)*

No relation to the modern day comedian of the same name. Although Scottish born, Carr made his name through Home Counties football to the the Southern League with Watford and West Ham. Guested for Portsmouth, Norwich and Kilmarnock during the War before signing for Reading, where he formed a potent wing partnership with Len Andrews. Had two more years with the Royals before he moved to Southampton along with Andrews. The two of them only had seven games together but, after Andrews left in 1924, Carr recovered from injury to spearhead their charge to the FA Cup final the following year. Released by the club, he eventually combined the running of a pub - *The Red Lion Hotel* - with playing for Southall, via a brief spell at Saints divisional rivals Swansea. He remained at the pub for many a year, and excelled at bowls to such an extent that he represented England at the 1954 Empire (later Commonwealth) Games in Vancouver... at the age of 60!

Carroll, Robert

Right winger/forward
Born: *1968 Greenford*
Playing career: *Southampton, Gosport Borough, Brentford, Fareham Town, Yeovil Town, Woking, Crawley Town, Salisbury City, Basingstoke Town, Worthing, Bashley (1986-1997)*

Played in the Football League for Brentford, before later embarking on a length career as a non league player. Made 140 appearances for Yeovil and is currently first team coach at Wessex Premier side Christchurch. A winger, Carroll began his youth career at Southampton but never played a first team game for the club before dropping into non league. Won the Hampshire Senior Cup with Basingstoke. Played for Fareham, Woking, Crawley, Salisbury City, Basingstoke, Worthing and Bashley.

Carter, George

Full-back
Born: *1866 Hereford*
Died: *1945*
Playing career: *Nil Desperandum, Southampton St. Mary's (1887-1894)*

Carter was employed as an engraver at Ordnance Survey at their offices in Southampton when Dr Russell Bencroft - a committee man at Southampton St Mary's - came to his attention. Having represented Herefordshire at both football and cricket, he captained Saints for six games of their first FA Cup campaign in 1891, in which the team reached the semi finals. His "playing from the back" was a "distinctive" feature of the cup run. A stalwart of a Cup-football only era, he captained the team to three successive Hampshire Junior Cup victories and two further Senior Cup wins. Earned a commemorative gold watch from the club for his services and he continued to work for the club in retirement, as manager of the Reserves team before becoming a life member. Represented Hampshire at water polo and continued in his role at Ordnance Survey until 1927.

Carter, Robert

Outside-right
Born: *1880 Hendon, County Durham* **Died:** *1928*
Playing career: *Sunderland Royal Rovers, Selbourne, Burslem Port Vale, Stockport County, Fulham, Southampton (1904-1910)*

Nicknamed "Toddler" because of his small feet, what Bob Carter lacked in size he made up for in stature. Played for Burslem Port Vale, Stockport and Fulham before joining Southampton in 1909. He took Jack Foster's first team place at The Dell, and became a regular at outside right, going on to play almost 50 times for the club. A nippy, elusive forward, Carter retired at the end of his first - and only - season at the club due to injury. He left Southampton and returned to Sunderland to become licensee of the *Ocean Queen* public house in the docklands area of the town. He died because of complications brought about by the head injury and died at the age of 47. 45 games and 14 goals for Saints, he is the father of the legendary footballing figure Horatio "Raich" Carter.

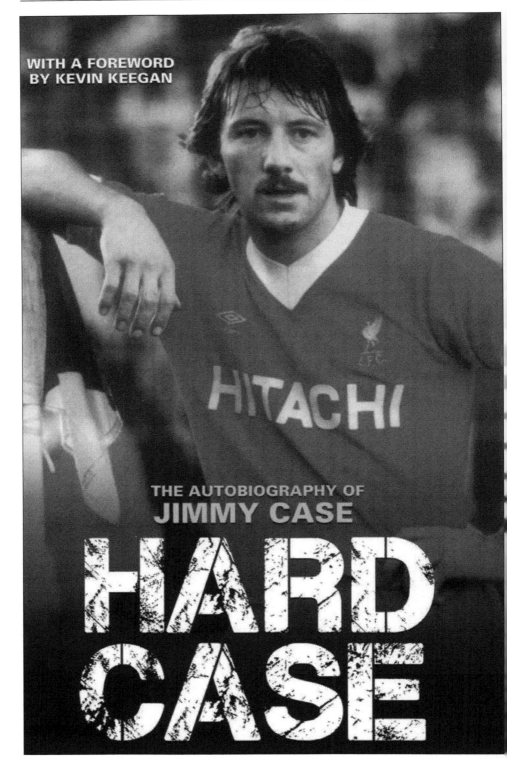

WITH A FOREWORD
BY KEVIN KEEGAN

THE AUTOBIOGRAPHY OF
JIMMY CASE

HARD
CASE

Case, Jimmy

Midfielder
Born: *1954 Liverpool*
Playing career: *Liverpool, Brighton, Southampton, Bournemouth, Halifax Town, Wrexham, Wanneroo British, Darlington, Brighton. (1985-1991)*

Case rose to fame playing for home town Liverpool before moving to Brighton who were playing top flight football at the time. The likeable Scouser moved along the south coast in 1985 to join Saints. Was transferred to Bournemouth by Ian Branfoot as one of his first acts after succeeding Chris Nicholl as manager. After a long and distinguished playing career, which saw him win four League titles, four Charity Shields and four European Cup and Super Cup victories, Case then managed Brighton for a short while and then Bashley in the New Forest. He continued to play in veteran teams for many years while also working in the media as a match summariser and more recently for his first love Liverpool FC as a pre match host and LFC TV. Case has also worked for BBC Radio Hampshire and "The Saint" - Southampton's in house radio station and BBC Radio Merseyside. He released his autobiography "Jimmy Case: My Story" in 2015.

Cassells, Keith

Forward/right winger
Born: *1957 Islington*
Playing career: *Watford, Peterborough United, Oxford U, Southampton. Brentford, Mansfield Town.*

Cassells made the jump from the Third Division to the First when Southampton - in need of attacking reinforcements - came calling. Signed as a replacement for the injured Steve Moran for £80,000, he failed to make a breakthrough at The Dell and made only 27 appearances, scoring five goals in the 1982-83 season under Lawrie McMenemy. Cassells later dropped back into the third tier when he joined Brentford, then moved further down the pyramid to Fourth Division Mansfield. His career was ended by injury in 1989 and later took up work as a postman, also going on to employment with the Hertfordshire Police Force, rising to the rank of detective sergeant.

Cassidy, Daniel

Right-half/forward
Born: *Heworth, Tyne and Wear 1907* **Died:** *1995*
Playing career: *Hebburn, Southampton, Darlington (1926-1937)*

Cassidy spent ten of his eleven years as a professional with Darlington in his native north east. Despite his association with "The Quakers", A right half or out-and-out forward, he also spent a season on the south coast at The Dell although he never played for Southampton at any level. Scored the winning goal for 'Darlo' against Stockport in the Third Division (North) Cup final at Old Trafford in 1934. After he retired Cassidy became a labourer and builder in Ireland. He died aged 88 in 1995.

Catlin, Norman

Outside-right
Born: *1918 Liverpool* **Died:** *1941*
Playing career: *Bitterne Boys Club, Arsenal, Southampton, Ryde Sports (1932-1939)*

Liverpool born Catlin catapulted himself into the national spotlight with his 17 goals in just one game of a 13-match run in which he hit 62 goals for Southampton Schoolboys. Turning out for England at amateur schoolboy level, he soon signed for Saints but never fulfilled the potential his dazzling start had promised. Catlin only made six appearances for the Saints at senior level. He quit League football at the age of 19 having promised much but delivered little. With a day job as a clerk for White Star Line, he continued to play part time at non league level for Andover and Ryde Sports before a second - brief - stint back at The Dell in the 1938-39 season. He joined the Royal Navy upon the outbreak of War and soon signed to play and had a spell at Bitterne when on leave. This arrangement did not last long as he went down with HMS Gloucester in action off Crete, Greece, in 1941 aged only 23.

"DID YOU KNOW?"

"Only three players have been Player of the Year in consecutive seasons - Peter Shilton, Tim Flowers and Matt Le Tiss."

Cavendish, Sidney

Inside-forward
Born: *1876 Burton-on-Trent* **Died:** *1954*
Playing career: *Overseal Town, Southampton, Freemantle, Clapton Orient (1898-1906)*

Arriving at the Dell as a prolific net-busting striker, Cavendish lived up to his burgeoning reputation with 14 goals in 12 games for the second string and scored on his Southern League debut - an 8-0 thumping of Gravesend. He would later also score Clapton Orient's first ever hat-trick at Reserve team level. The opposition? Southampton at the Dell. Served Salisbury as a player, then trainer and then as assistant manager. Later worked as a painter and decorator for the council.

Chadwick, Arthur

Centre-half
Born: *1875 Church, Lancashire* **Died:** *1936*
Playing career: *Southampton, Portsmouth, Northampton Town , Accrington Stanley , Exeter City, Exeter City, Reading (1895-1931)*

Chadwick moved to Saints from Burton Albion and became a virtual ever-present at centre half during his four years at The Dell, only once missing more than three games in a row. He played in the title-winning teams of 1898, 1899 and 1901 and the club's first FA Cup final - which they lost to Bury - sandwiched in between the second and third of those league triumphs, securing his place as an early Southampton great. Twice capped by England, he made a slice of unwanted history as the first ever Southampton player to be sent off in a League match. Chadwick moved on to fierce rivals Portsmouth, winning the league again, before he turned out for Northampton, Accrington Stanley and Exeter City. Having retired in 1910, he became the Devon club's first manager and took them into the Football League during his 14 years in charge - their longest serving boss and a record that still stands today. He briefly took charge at Reading and returned to Saints as manager in 1925. After six years at in the dugout at The Dell, he retired and returned to Exeter when he died in 1936 whilst watching his old side in action.

Chadwick, David

Winger
Born: *1943 Ootacamund, India*
Playing career: *Southampton, Middlesbrough, Halifax town, AfC Bournemouth, Gillimgham Town, Dallas Tornado, Ft. Lauderdale Strikers (NASL)*

Chadwick, a winger born in India, started his career at Saints but made only 25 appearances in his six year stay, scoring once. This was mainly due to the fact that he was competing for a first team place with Terry Paine and John Sydenham. He then moved onto greater success with Middlesborough and Halifax where he went on to play a further 278 games, before eventually moving onto finish his playing career in the USA. Worked for 30 years as a coach in the NFL combining this role with a job as a hotel wall-cladding salesman. Retired in 2007 after 16 years with AFC Lightning, a prestigious coaching academy in Atlanta.

Chadwick, Edgar

Inside-left
Born: *1869 Blackburn* **Died:** *1942*
Playing career: *Little Dots F.C, Blackburn Olympic, Blackburn Rovers, Everton, Burnley, Southampton, Liverpool, Blackpool (1884-1908)*

Chadwick,was already a title-wining international of some acclaim when he signed for Southampton. Nicknamed "Hooky" because of his party trick of cutting parallel to the byline, cutting in, drawing the goalkeeper out and hooking the ball past him. An ever present in Everton's First Division title of 1890-91. Signing for Saints in 1900, he rekindled his left-wing pairing with Alf Milward, a partnership that had enjoyed much success on Merseyside. He plundered 14 goals in his debut season to fire Saints to the Southern League championship, reaching the FA Cup final the following year. Later turned out for Liverpool, Blackpool, Glossop and Darwen before retiring and moving into management. Became the first boss of the Netherlands national side - winning two Olympic bronze medals in 1908 (London) and 1912 (Stockholm). He also later took charge of HVV, HFC and Sparta Rotterdam (winning the league) in the country. Died in 1942 aged 72.

Chala, Cleber

Midfielder

Born: *1971 Imbabura, Ecuador*
Playing career: *El Nacional, Southampton, Deportivo Quito (1990-2008)*

At club level he played mostly for Nacional Quito in Ecuador, appering over 450 times and winning four league titles. He had also tried his hand in Peru before joining Saints along with compatriot Augustin Delgado. Chala failed to make an impact in England and never played for the first team. This clearly was not due to a lack of talent, as Chala earned 86 caps for Ecuador (scoring six goals). Currently works as a coach for former club El Nacional.

Chalk, Norman

Half-back

Born: *1916 Bitterne, Southampton* **Died:** *2005*
Playing career: *Southampton (1937-1939)*

Strong and rugged, centre-back Chalk signed pro in 1937, but spent most of this stay in the reserves. After a handful of chances, Chalk joined the Borough Police which offered job security, where he stayed until 1969. Having retired from the police, Chalk worked for a solicitor's firm and continued to live in Southampton.

Channon, Mick

Forward

Born: *1948 Orcheston, Wiltshire*
Playing career: *Southampton Manchester City Newcastle United, Bristol Rovers, Norwich City, Portsmouth, (1965 -1987)*

Saints' all time record goalscorer and second only to Terry Paine in the list of top appearance makers, Mick Channon was rewarded with forty six England caps.

One of the "Boys of 76" Channon plundered 229 in 607 games for Saints across two spells, and is widely regarded as one of the club's greatest ever players. Channon has remained a prominent name in sport, as a highly successful stable owner and racehorse trainer. Channon has over 200 horses, at his West Ilsley stables, formerly owned by HM the Queen. He has produced over 300 winners, with horses owned by several of his old colleagues and illustrious football names such as Kevin Keegan, Alan Ball and Sir Alex Ferguson. You can see the extent of the influence Channon has on the racing world here: *https://www.mickchannon.tv*. Channon has had several books released, covering his double life as prolific net buster turned serial horse race winner. "How's Your Dad" (2015) is an interesting account written by his son Mick Channon Jnr which documents his relationship with his racehorse trainer father, and his authorised biography "Mick Channon", an updated version of his earlier book "Man on the Run" are still available today from Amazon.

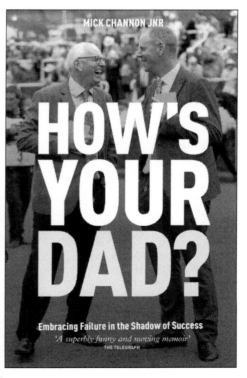

Charles, Alfred

Inside-forward
Born: *1909 Trinidad and Tobago* **Died:** *1977*
Playing career: *Everton, Burnley, Nelson, Darwen, Stalybridge Celtic, Southampton (1933-1938)*

The infamous exploits of the notorious Ali Dia aside, Alfred Charles is perhaps the most well known of all Southampton's "one match wonders." The reason? He was the Saints first black player. Trinidadian born, Charles arrived in England with the touring West Indies cricket team - but not as a player, rather as a valet to esteemed all rounder Learie Constantine. Or so the story goes. His first club, Everton (Trinidad, not the English one) were serial winners with Charles a key part of the side. Having become embroiled in a mass brawl, Charles and his brother Frank were sent off and banned for three years. He then made for England where he signed for Burnley before a spell at Lancashire neighbours Nelson. Recommended by a scout, he moved south to sign for Southampton and made his first, and only, appearance at inside left against Bradford City the following day. A "powerful presence", he wouldn't get another chance with the senior side and after a few outings in the Reserves he was forced to retire through injury. Turned out for a West Indies cricket XI at Lord's in 1944 and then played for Lowerhouse CC in the Lancashire league. He died in 1977 in Burnley, his brief if unique place in Southampton FC history already assured.

Charles, Bob

Goalkeeper
Born: *1941 Bursledon* **Died:** *2014*
Playing career: *Southampton, (1959-1960)*

Having become Southampton's then youngest ever player, aged 17, Charles kept his place throughout his debut 1959-60 season. Having suffered a dip in form, Saints manager Ted Bates moved to sign Ron Reynolds for the remainder of the campaign, but Charles played 24 matches and more than played his own personal part in Southampton's league-winning season. He kept goal for the Saints side that won the English Schools Trophy in 1957 and could call Nobby Stiles and

Geoff Hurst team-mates at youth level for England, although he never earned a senior cap. Twelve months on, a career that had seemed so glittering had crashed to an abrupt halt. A combination of injury, a lack of discipline and a loss of fitness saw him retire from the game. Charles has since remained in Southampton and ran a car sales business in the area.

Charlton, Bill

Centre-forward
Born: *1912 South Stoneham* **Died:** *1998*
Playing career: *Southampton, Hull, Wimbledon, QPR, Barnet, Leyton, Fulham (1931-1939)*

Bill Charlton won a soccer' blue' at Oxford and had turned out for the most famous of all amateur clubs - Corinthian - before signing for Southampton. After three appearances at Reserve team level and two for the senior side, Charlton - holder of four amateur England caps (scoring a hat-trick against Ireland) - went on to play for Hull City, Wimbledon, QPR, Barnet, Leyton and Fulham. After the War, he became a headmaster in London.

Charlton, Simon

Fullback
Born: *1971 Huddersfield*
Playing career: *Huddersfield Town, Southampton, Birmingham City, Bolton Wanderers, Norwich City, Oldham Athletic, Mildenhall Town (1989-2009)*

A versatile left sided defender/midfielder who joined Southampton from hometown club Huddersfield in 1993 who played over 100 games for Saints in a four year spell before moving onto Birmingham in 1998. Retiring from playing in 2007 he rejoined Norwich as Youth team coach, before becoming manager of Mildenhall Town in 2009. He holds a UEFA 'A' Licence. He survived four managers at Saints before a fifth - Dave Jones - restored Francis Benali to the team and signed Lee Todd. Moved to Birmingham and also played for Bolton, Norwich and Oldham. As well as his post as manager of Eastern Counties League team Mildenhall, he also worked to establish Global Soccer Network, a Norfolk based talent spotting development course, where he's a director.

Chatterley, Lew

Midfielder
Born: *1945 Birmingham*
Playing career: *Aston Villa, Doncaster Rovers, Northampton Town, Grimsby Town, Southampton, Torquay United (1962-1978)*

Chatterley retired in 1978 having had a lengthy career. He then moved to the United States, where he coached Chicago Sting. He made the move to Southampton in 1979 to become Assistant Manager before taking up a similar role at Sunderland. Played a handful of games for Saints in the mid 70s as a midfielder. Then came a spell as Poole Town manager, and the Assistant's job at Reading where he briefly was handed the role of caretaker manager. He returned to Southampton in 1990 as a youth development officer but was later promoted to coach and then caretaker manager when Dave Merrington was sacked. He is now working as a teacher and a football coach at Winchester College and also briefly scouted for Newcastle United. Described his time at The Dell as "the biggest mistake I ever made." Also ran a guest house.

Martin Chivers

Cherednyk, Oleksiy

Defender/Midfielder
Born: *1960 Stalinabad, Tajik SSR*
Playing career: *Pamir Dushanbe, FC Dnipro Dnipropetrovsk, Southampton, FC Chornomorets Odessa, FC Metalurh Zaporizhya, FC Kryvbas Kryvyi Rih (1974-1996)*

A gold medallist at the 1988 Seoul Olympics, Cherednyk caught the eye of Southampton manager Chris Nicholl when playing against them in a pre-season friendly for FC Dnipro. He became the first Soviet player to appear in the First Division. Despite his Ukranian roots, he was capped twice by the "USSR" (Russia as we know them today). Having started out in Saints Reserve team, he eventually dislodged Jason Dodd and went on to play 23 times for the club. Cherednyk eventually lost his place to Barry Horne, and with Nicholl replaced by Ian Branfoot and Jeff Kenna as Dodd's backup, there was no way back. Returning to his native homeland, he briefly turned out for three different clubs, then worked for Dnipro as a scout. Managed in Russia before another scouting role this time at Ukranian powerhouses and perennial European participants Shakhtar Donetsk.

Chivers, Martin

Forward
Born: *1945 Southampton*
Playing career: *Southampton,Tottenham Hotspur,Norwich City & Brighton & Hove Albion.*

Best known for his net busting exploits at White Hart Lane - he is Spurs' third all time leading scorer - his career at Saints was just as impressive. Chivers, a 24-cap England international, scored 106 times in 189 games at The Dell, including 30 goals in 29 games during the club's promotion season of 1965-66 (four of those in a 9-3 thumping of Wolves). Formed a potent pairing with Ron Davies and his prolific form continued when he joined Tottenham for what was, at the time, a British record of £125,000 plus Frank Saul in part exchange. Plundered 200 goals in 415 games for the north London side and then moved overseas to try his hand at player-management. Became the first ever substitute to score for the Saints in April 1967.

Since retiring, Chivers owned and ran a hotel and restaurant in Hertfordshire as has worked as a radio commentator. A match day host at Spurs, he has been inducted into their Hall of Fame. As a local boy who scored over 100 goals for Saints, Chivers has the credentials to be remembered as one of the club's all time greats.

Christie, Alexander

Half-back
Born: *1896 Glasgow, Scotland* **Died:** *1981*
Playing career: *Royal Navy Barracks, Hamilton Academical, Reading, Walsall, Southampton, Rochdale, Exeter City, Aldershot (1919-1929)*

After serving in the Royal Navy, Glasgow-born Christie moved to England early in his career, playing for Reading and Walsall before joining Second Division Southampton in May 1922. His move to the Dell proved a step too far however, even though he was described as "coolness personified" on his debut in place of Alec Campbell at Old Trafford in March 1923. Dropped for the returning Ted Hough, and second choice to Albert Shelley, there was little future for Christie on the south coast so he moved to Rochdale where he spent the rest of his career, bar a brief stint at Fourth Division Exeter. Later worked in a brewery.

Christie, John

Goalkeeper
Born: *1929 Fraserburgh, Scotland* **Died:** *2014*
Playing career: *Ayr United, Southampton, Walsall, Burton Albion, Rugby Town (1947-1964)*

John Christie came to the attentions of Southampton manager Sid Cann whilst undergoing his obligatory National Service at Farnborough. Snapped up from Ayr in his native Scotland, Christie was "agile and brave" but spent most of his time at the Dell in competition for the no.1 jersey with Fred Kiernan. Having finally established himself as Cann's first choice, Christie went on to play over 200 times for the Saints as one of their finest post War goalies. After a record run in which he played 50 consecutive games, only injury finally saw him usurped in goal by 19-year-old Tony Godfrey. 217 appearances in eight years, he moved to Walsall and

also played for Burton Albion and non league Rugby Town before retirement. He later worked as a sales representative for Dixon industrial cleaners and then as a site supervisor for a school in Winchester.

Christmas, Edwin

Centre-forward
Born: *1886 Southampton*
Died: *1916*
Playing career: *Southampton (1912-1912)*

The wonderfully named Cecil Christmas joined Southampton as an amateur on Hampshire League forms during the 1908-09 season. His business career - running a chain of hotels with his family - meant that football played second fiddle. But Saints Reserve team manager George Carter refused to give up on him, and persuaded Christmas to return in 1912. WIth first choice forward Henry Hamilton discarded for a club breach, Christmas played twice but, despite his pace and trickery, an injury did not help his cause and he sank back to the Reserves, never to be seen again. He died in action on the Western Front in 1916, aged 30.

Clark, Joseph

Outside-left
Born: *1890 Willington Quay*
Died: *1960*
Playing career: *Wallsend Park Villa, Hebburn Argyle, Cardiff City, Aberaman Athletic, Southampton, Rochdale (1913-1924)*

The Saints board signed Clark having been impressed by him during an FA Cup tie with Cardiff. The Welsh side went on to reach the semi finals and Clark had been playing in the Welsh section of the Southern League for Aberaman when Southampton came calling. Went on to play for Rochdale, Norwich, Exeter City and Aldershot. Later worked as a plasterer. Died in 1960.

"DID YOU KNOW?"

"The club that we now know was formed on 21st November 1885 and was originally called St Mary's Y.M.A."

Colin Clarke

Clarke, Colin

Forward

Born: *1962 Newry, Northern Ireland*
Playing career: *Ipswich Town, Peterborough United, Gillingham, Tranmere Rovers, Bournemouth, Southampton, QPR, Portsmouth (1980-1993)*

Colin Clarke had already racked up a reputable career in the lower leagues by the time he arrived at Southampton. Signed by Chris Nicholl from south coast rivals Bournemouth - managed by a certain Harry Redknapp - for £200,000, he became the first Saint to score a hat-trick on his debut. Fresh from scoring for Northern Ireland against Spain in the World Cup, Clarke plundered his treble in a 5-1 win over QPR at The Dell on the opening day of 1986/87. His ratio would remain at a league goal every two games and would go on to hit 39 goals in 86 outings in all competitions during a three year stay at the club. But an acrimonious six months saw him fall out with Nicholl over money, so he was banished to the Reserves, re-joined Redknapp on loan and then moved to QPR - the club he had enjoyed that spectacular Saints bow against. Also turned out for our "nearest and dearest" down the road before suffering a career ending knee injury.

Having been forced to retire, Clarke ran a pub in Lambourn, Wiltshire, before starting a coaching career in the USA. He also managed the Puerto Rico national team and the Carolina Railhawks. Played 38 times for Northern Ireland.

Clarke, Graham

Full-back

Born: *1935 Nottingham* **Died:** *2010*
Playing career: *Southampton, (1953-1966)*

A part-time motor mechanic, Clarke arrived at Southampton having already been capped by England at youth level. He would have to bide his time at the Dell but eventually made the no2 shirt his own at Reserve team level, playing second fiddle to Bill Ellerington, The form of Len Wilkins and Ron Davies restricted him to only three first team games before he left to play at non league level for the next few years. After which he returned home to his native east Midlands working for *Raleigh*. He latterly moved back to Southampton where he was employed by the Post Office.

Clarke, William

Full-back

Born: *1880 Kettering* **Died:** *1952*
Playing career: *Sheffield United, Northampton Town, Southampton (1902-1908)*

William Clarke was plucked from works league obscurity to join FA Cup winners Sheffield United in 1902. He had an unhappy time at Bramall Lane and moved into the Southern League - first with Northampton and then with the Saints (runners up in that Cup final of 1902). A "promising, pacy full-back", Clarke went on to become a Southampton regular, playing in most of their league and cup ties over the next two seasons before succumbing to a plethora of health issues. He never rediscovered the initial form that had marked his rise to prominence and then missed a year with a knee injury. Joined the Coldstream Guards in 1916 and served in France during World War One, before having to withdraw from duty - again because of his ever problematic knee. Saw out the War as a Lance Corporal in Windsor before returning to run a pub in his hometown of Kettering.

Clarke, William

Outside-left
Born: *1916 Leicester* **Died:** *1986*
Playing career: *Leicester City, Exeter City, Southampton, Cheltenham Town (1936-1939)*

A prolific, net-busting winger-turned-forward, Clarke boasted hugely impressive numbers in front of goal for Leicester Nomads and City's Reserve sides. He was never able to get a first team breakthrough, however, and moved on to Third Division Exeter. But having only played 12 times for the Devon club, he was allowed to head along the coast and joined Southampton on a free transfer. Again, though, he found his path to first team football frustratingly blocked by Harry Osman, who had just broken the goals record for a winger at The Dell. Clarke briefly got his moment after Osman's move to Millwall in April 1939, given a debut alongside fellow debutant Eric Webber at Blackburn. Clarke played again in the season's denouement before being released. Returned to his native Leicestershire with non league Hinckley before the war intervened. He later worked in the medical profession. No relation to Saints 'other' William Clarke (above).

George Clawley (middle row right)

Clawley, George

Goalkeeper
Born: *1875 Scholar Green* **Died:** *1920*
Playing career: *Crewe Alexandra, Stoke, Southampton, Stoke, Tottenham Hotspur, Southampton (1893-1907)*

A goalkeeper renowned for his height, reach and "stunning" reflexes, Clawley assured himself in the pantheon of Southampton greats during the most successful era in the club's history. He won three Southern League titles at The Dell in two spells, and was also an FA Cup winner with Spurs in 1901. In his first, two season spell at the club, Clawley became ever present and captained the side to the title and two impressive, eye-catching Cup runs. For a man of such ability and acclaim, it seems almost criminal he was never capped by England - indeed, Clawley was described as "Surely the finest uncapped goalkeeper ever to grace the football field of England" and he possessed "all the ingredients" that made him one of the greats around the turn of the century. Clawley played 267 times for Southampton and - after his retirement - ran a pub as landlord of the *Wareham Arms.*

Clements, Stanley

Centre-back
Born: *1923 Portsmouth* **Died:** *2018*
Playing career: *Southampton (1944-1955)*

Portsmouth born Clements was working as a mechanical engineer on the docks in his home city when, on the recommendation of ex-Saint Stan Cribb, he came to Southampton during the War. His time at The Dell proved a slow burner, with a smattering of games, only 16 in total, during his first four and a half seasons with the club. Had a Hampshire league stint at Basingstoke Town as player/coach before moving to Asia and Africa where he combined his engineering expertise with coaching commitments. Clements managed the Kenya national team - becoming the first Brit to do so - and was later appointed an OBE. Returning to the UK, he settled in Gosport and, outliving Charlie Purves in 2013, Clements became the oldest surviving former Saint just a week before his 90th birthday. He died five years later.

Clifton, Brian

Inside-forward/Half-back

Born: *1934 Whitchurch, Hampshire*
Playing career: *Andover, Whitchurch, Portals Athletic, Southampton, Grimsby Town, Boston United, Gainsborough Trinity, Boston (1953-1973)*

Clifton was serving his apprenticeship at the paper mill in Test Valley when he was scouted and signed by former Saint Stan Woodhouse. Combining his early days at the club with National Service at Boscombe Down, he made sporadic appearances over the next four years before he scored twice on his senior team bow against south coast rivals Brighton. In and out of the side over the next three seasons, Clifton - despite his diminutive size - had an exquisite blend of "height and power". An ever present in 1961-62, he played the entire season at right-half before falling out of favour following the arrival of Ian White. Moved on to Grimsby before finishing in non league with Boston United (twice) and Gainsborough Trinity. Worked as a draughtsman for a frozen food company in Lincolnshire upon retirement.

Coak, Tim

Full-back

Born: *1958 Southampton*
Playing career: *Hampton Park School, Southampton Schools, Southampton, Salisbury City, Waterlooville, Gosport Borough, Bashley, Gosport Borough, Eastleigh, Aerostructures, Romsey Town, Fareham Town Veterans (1974-1995)*

Rising through the ranks at Southampton, Coak - a "two footed, attack full back" made his debut at 19 with regular right-back David Peach away on international duty. Made a handful of appearances in the 1977-78 promotion winning season, staying on the fringes for the rest of his days at The Dell, playing six games in all. Having left his hometown team, Coak embarked on a nomadic non league journey, playing for nine different clubs in the area including Salisbury City, Eastleigh, Romsey and Gosport. Later worked at Saints Centre of Excellence in a coaching role, also doing work for the Hampshire FA, Southampton University and as a shipping manager for a Chandler's Ford engineering firm.

Coates, Arthur

Full-back
Born: *1882 Feetham, North Yorkshire*
Died: *1955*
Playing career: *Salford United, Heywood United, Exeter City, Southampton (1910-1913)*

Heard the one about the Yorkshireman who was plucked from Lancastrian obscurity to become a footballer in the south-west? That tells the story of Arthur Coates who played in the Lancashire Combination league for Heywood United before former Saint Arthur Chadwick - manager of Exeter at the time - brought him to St James Park. After only a season there, Coates moved south to The Dell and slotted straight into the side for the rest of the 1912-13 season - 34 appearances in total. Returning to Heywood, he played alongside Anthony Donnelly at full-back - Donnelly would himself enjoy a brief Saints career after the War. Died in 1955.

Coates, Herbert

Inside-left
Born: *1901 West Ham*
Died: *1965*
Playing career: *Royal Navy, Southampton, Leyton (1928-1934)*

Regarded by colleagues, contemporaries and coaches alike as one of the greatest amateur-only players of all time, Coates devoted his life to the Royal Navy. He served as both sailor and footballer but despite these commitments he still somehow managed to wrack up over a century of games for Southampton. He remained an amateur during his six seasons at The Dell but made the inside-left position his own, scoring 27 goals and earning a reputation as a swashbuckling showman. Coates was known for his "brilliant dribbling, clever anticipation and terrific shooting ability" as one of the finest exponents of his left half craft. Capped eight times by England at amateur level, he multi-tasked for the Navy - serving on the Royal Yacht *Victoria* and *Albert* even turning out for an HMS Victory "Select XI" in the FA Amateur Cup during the 1930-31 season. Played a record 163 times for the Royal Navy and toured South Africa with the combined forces side.

Cockerill, Glenn

Midfielder
Born: *1959 Grimsby*
Playing career: *Lincoln City, Swindon Town, Sheffield United, Southampton, Leyton Orient, Fulham, Brentford.*

Cockerill was known for his shooting ability and power, and later managed Woking and Winchester, also working under Micky Adams as a scout for Brighton. A creative and eye-catching midfielder, Cockerill played 340 times for Saints as the string pulling fulcrum in a side containing Matt Le Tissier, Alan Shearer and Rod Wallace, doing a lot of the pressing and closing down to free up the more prolific forwards. Since retirement, Cockerill has managed Woking and Winchester and worked under ex-Saint Micky Adams at Brighton as a scout. He later coached at Carlisle and reprised his scouting duties with Lincoln, also running coaching courses in Europe and Africa. A "night on the tiles" may have been strictly off limits for Cockerill whilst a player, but today he brings a whole new meaning to the phrase. A father of five, a chance conversation with former team-mate John Buchanan pointed Cockerill in the direction of the building trade and becoming a qualified kitchen and bathroom fitter. On Twitter at https://twitter.com/glennfootball01

Coham, John

Outside-forward
Born: *1891 Southampton* **Died:** *1969*
Playing career: *Southampton, Partick Thistle (1910-1914)*

A "fleet footed" left winger, Southampton born ham played a handful of games for his hometown team in the 1910-11 season as cover foe the stricken Joe Blake. His Saints career, albeit one in struggling side, spanned six matches before he was tempted to try his luck in Scotland's lower divisions with Partick Thistle. That didn't work out and he went on non league Barrow before returning to Southampton. He would get no further chances at The Dell and worked on the Docks during the Great War before serving in the Merchant Navy.

Cole, Norman

Centre-forward

Born: *1913 Woolston, Southampton* **Died:** *1976*
Playing career: *Itchen Sports, Thornycrofts, Newport, Southampton, Norwich City (1932-1936)*

Signed by Second Division Saints as a replacement for the Arsenal bound Ted Bates. Scoring six goals in his first five games including a hat-trick against West Ham, it seemed like the locally born striker would be a like for like replacement for Bates. Despite not playing since February, Cole top scored the next season - an indication of where the struggling Saints problems lay. Cole would hit 13 goals in his 34 games but, having the Saints avoid relegation, he moved to Norwich to link up with former Southampton manager Tom Parker. Lost to the game aged only 23, Cole went on to work for the railway on the Docks and then helped to develop the famous *Gnat* aircraft trough his employment with Hamble-based Folland.

Colleter, Patrick

Full-back

Born: *1965 Brest, France*
Playing career: *Montpellier, Paris Saint-Germain, Bordeaux, Olympique de Marseille, Southampton, Cannes, Saint-Medard-en-Jalles (1986-2003)*

A French "B" international, Colleter had five years at PSG during which time he won the French league, both cups and the UEFA Cup Winners Cup. A series of hugely impressive performances for the Parisian giants persuaded Southampton manager Dave Jones to swoop and bring Colleter across the Channel for what would be his only season outside his homeland. He was a left-back who mixed Gallic flair with British grit. Had a spell at first and Reserve teams level before a controversial parting of the ways with manager Jones embroiled in ugly legal wranglings. His successor, Glenn Hoddle, never warmed to Colleter and he returned to France having made 26 appearances for the club. Since retiring, he has become a respected if outspoken pundit on French TV and taken up a number of coaching jobs - most recently at third tier side *Racing Red Star 93* as assistant manager.

Collins, Eamonn

Midfielder

Born: *1965 Inchicore, Dublin, Ireland*
Playing career: *Blackpool, Southampton, Portsmouth, Gillingham, Colchester United, Exeter City (1980-1996)*

Small in size but mighty in stature, Eamonn Collins became the youngest player to ever appear in a professional English match. He turned out at 14 years 323 days old for Blackpool. Alan Ball was the seaside club's player-manager at the time, but it didn't work out and Ball returned to Southampton. Collins, not yet 16, followed him after only that solitary appearance for the Tangerines. After three years switching between Youth and Reserve level, Collins earned a first team debut and played for Ireland in the World Youth Championship. He only played one further game for Saints before he moved along the coast to Portsmouth - again under Ball. He would go on to play for the World Cup winner at two other clubs in Colchester and Exeter City before retiring. Collins went on to become a manager at lower and non league level, namely with Elmore, Bohemian in his native Ireland, St Patrick's Athletic and Shelbourne. His mentor Ball described Collins as "diminutive", he never grew but had a shrewd football brain and never let me down."

Conner, Richard

Wing-half

Born: *1931 Jarrow* **Died:** *1999*
Playing career: *Newcastle United, Grimsby Town, Southampton, Tranmere, Aldershot (1950-1963)*

Tyneside born Conner got his Football League chance with Grimsby. A string of impressive showings for the Mariners attracted the attentions of Ted Bates who swooped to bring him to Third Division Saints in 1959. Conner would miss only one game as Southampton won the league. Struggled with injury and eventually dropped into the basement tier with Aldershot and Tranmere. After serving as assistant manager with the former, he took charge at Rochdale and Darlington. In 1980 he ran a pub in the North West before returning to Tyneside where he worked as an electrical engineer. Died in 1999.

Connolly, David

Striker
Born: *1977 Willesden*
Playing career: *Watford, Feyenoord, Wolverhampton Wanderers (loan), Excelsior (loan), Wimbledon, Leicester City, Wigan Athletic, Sunderland, Southampton, Portsmouth, Oxford United (loan), AFC Wimbledon, West Ham United (1994-2015)*

A 41-cap ROI international, Connolly - a much travelled veteran - scored four goals in the final six games of the 2010-11 season as Saints returned to the second tier after a two year exile in League One. Game time limited by the dual signings of Tadanari Lee and Billy Sharp, Connolly moved down the Solent to Pompey before finishing his career with a loan spell at Oxford and then AFC Wimbledon, his last club. Conolly played for Ireland in the 2002 World Cup as his nation reached the knockout stages before a penalty shootout defeat to Spain. Briefly coached at Portsmouth having retired before working as a player agent. Connolly netted 18 times in 66 games for the St Mary's side.

Andy Cook

Cook, Andy

Left-back
Born: *1969 Romsey*
Playing career: *Southampton, Exeter City, Swansea City, Portsmouth, Millwall, Salisbury City, Woking*

Neat, tidy and known for his pace, Cook struggled to make the grade at Saints due to a combination of crippling injuries and the presence of the established left sided pairing of Micky Adams and Francis Benali. Having only played 22 games in four seasons at Saints, Cook signed for Exeter and former Southampton manager Alan Ball. A nomadic career also saw him turn out for Swansea, his former side's fierce rivals Portsmouth, Millwall, Salisbury and Woking. After retirement, Cook managed Salisbury's reserves and became their physiotherapist, a role he currently holds at National League Eastleigh. He also briefly served as Woking's caretaker player-boss.

Cook, Lee

Winger
Born: *1982 Hammersmith*
Playing career: *Southampton, Watford, York City (loan), Charlton Athletic (loan), QPR (loan), Leyton Orient (loan), Charlton Athletic (loan), Apollon Smyrni, Barnet, Eastleigh (1998-2015)*

Cook began his career at Southampton but never played for the club at any level before moving on to non league football with Aylesbury United. Played for a plethora of clubs mainly in his native London including Watford, his boyhood side QPR, Fulham, Charlton and Leyton Orient. Later dropped into non league with Barnet and Eastleigh. Cook played over 400 games during his career and since retiring he has worked as an insurance salesman. He is a second cousin of Olympic medal winning boxer James DeGale.

Cooper, John

Centre-forward
Born: *1897 Wednesbury* **Died:** *1975*
Playing career: *Darlaston, Southampton, Notts County (1921-1924)*

Cooper was "the best inside-right in the Birmingham League" - according to The Echo - when he moved south to join Southampton along with fellow Darlaston team-mate Henry Johnson.

Several clubs had chased Cooper, including Chelsea, Cardiff City and Manchester United, but Southampton beat them all to his signature in time for the Saints first ever Division Three (South) season. Whilst his team-mate Johnston became a regular, Cooper found it almost impossible to dislodge the Saints veterans Arthur Dominy and Bill Rawlings in attack - playing only five times in his two seasons at The Dell. Played for Northampton and later returned to Darlaston before becoming a factory worker.

Costello, Frank

Forward
Born: *1884 Birmingham* **Died:** *1914*
Playing career: *West Bromwich Albion, Southampton, Bolton Wanderers, Nelson, Merthyr Town, Salisbury City, West Ham United (1904-1910)*

Failing to make the grade at West Brom, Birmingham-born Costello moved south to link up with Southern League Southampton ahead of the 1907 season. Costello hit double figures in his debut campaign and was an ever present in the Southampton side that reached the FA Cup semi finals - a run that notably included the last eight win over Everton in which Costello was "the best player on the pitch." Having switched to centre-forward, the move proved unsuccessful and Costello was transferred to divisional rivals West Ham before moving to Bolton, ending his career in the non league game. Enlisted in the 2nd Battalion Royal Warwickshire Regiment during the War, Costello fell in 1914 on the Western Front.

Coundon, Cuthbert

Outside-right
Born: *1905 Sunderland* **Died:** *1978*
Playing career: *Southampton, Wolverhampton Wanderers, Southend United (1923-1935)*

Cuthbert Coundon, a sturdily built and youthful looking chap, was an apprentice joiner when he joined the Saints and quickly earned the moniker "The Kid". Brimming with enthusiasm and deceptively sturdy, Coundon scored on his Southampton bow but played the majority of his games as cover for the injured Bill "Tishy" Henderson.

Despite a run of 14 successive games at outside-right, Coundon was never first choice and - when Henderson returned from a broken arm - Coundon's days at The Dell were over. Moved to Wolves for £150. Later joined Southend and Guildford City before becoming a coach at Sutton. Died in 1978. Coundon played 27 games for Southampton.

Cowper, Peter

Outside-forward
Born: *1902 Tyldesley* **Died:** *1962*
Playing career: *New Brighton, Southampton, Southport, Carlisle United, Wigan Athletic, Altrincham, Prescot Cables, Wigan Borough, West Ham United (1923-1936)*

Cowper never transferred his prolific plundering for the second string into first team success (33 goals in 50 games at that level). Indeed, the power mill runner was at the peak of his career during his Southampton days but only played five games for the senior side. Later scouted for Blackpool. Cowper was working as a caretaker at Clifton Hall when he died.

Cox, Walter

Goalkeeper
Born: *1872 Southampton* **Died:** *1930*
Playing career: *Southampton St. Mary's, Bristol St George, Bedminster, Millwall Athletic, Manchester City, Bury, Preston North End, Dundee (1892-1907)*

Southampton born Cox started playing for the newly founded Southampton St Mary's FC in 1892 as an outfield player. Having decided to convert from a defender to a goalkeeper, he made his debut as a replacement for Jack Barrett in the FA Cup two years later. Saints reached the First Round proper of the FA Cup with Cox praised for his 'heroic" performance against eventual winners The Wednesday. Cox lost his place following the arrival of George Clawley, and moved to Bristol where he turned out for Bristol St George and then non league Bedminster. Played for Millwall before a stint with Manchester City. Only played once and was on the books of Lancashire neighbours Bury and Preston but never played. Cox returned to local football in Southampton and later worked on the railway at Eastleigh.

Crabbe, Bill
Right-back
Born: 1878 Southampton **Died:** 1931
Playing career: *Southampton*
Bill Crabbe was plucked from local league obscurity to start the 1899-1900 season as Southampton Reserves' starting right-back. When first team regular Peter Meehan picked up a mid-season injury, Crabbe got his chance in the Southern League. Despite a "plucky" performance, he played but two further senior games. He was never seen again and drifted into obscurity although its thought, like so many of his contemporaries of the day, that he served in World War One. Died 1931. Not much is known about his career.

Crabbe, Stephen
Midfielder
Born: *1954 Weymouth*
Playing career: *Southampton, Hellenic, Gillingham, Carlisle United, Hereford United, Crewe Alexandra, KePS, Torquay United (1970-1997)*
Crabbe racked up well over 300 league games for six different clubs, graduating through Southampton's youth ranks from schoolboy side to senior team. Made his debut in a 1975 FA Cup tie but found further chances limited. 'Buster' was loaned out two years after his Saints bow with Steve Williams now breaking through. Crabbe played for Gillingham, Hereford and Crewe before playing in Finland and winding up at Torquay. Turned for a several non league sides in Kent and Sussex, Crabbe returned to Weymouth to coach under Neil Webb before succeeding him as manager. Coached in Kent and became involved in Saints-in-the-Community and played for the Ex-Saints. Later worked as a carpenter.

Crainey, Stephen
Left-back
Born: *1981 Glasgow*
Playing career: *Lenzie Youth Club, Celtic, Southampton, Leeds United, Blackpool, Wigan Athletic, Fleetwood Town, AFC Fylde (1997-2016)*
Joined Celtic at 16 and would stay with the Glasgow giants for the next seven years, playing in two domestic cup finals and the UEFA Cup.

Capped five times by Scotland by the time he was signed by the Saints, Crainey became the second current Scotland international to join Southampton - Neil McCann was the first. Crainey had played five times for his country by the time he made his debut under Gordon Strachan. Tasked with solving a problem position at St Mary's, Crainey was described as "the right age and a good one for the future" by chairman Rupert Lowe. When Strachan departed, his successor Paul Sturrock loaned Crainey out to Leeds and his days as a Saint were over. Crainey would sign permanently with Leeds, but spent six seasons at Blackpool including their fairytale flirtation with the bright lights of the Premier League. Became academy coach at Fleetwood Town.

Stephen Crainey

Cramb, Colin
Striker
Born: *1974 Lanark, Scotland*
Playing career: *Doncaster Rovers, Bristol City, Walsall, Crewe Alexandra, Notts County, Bury, Fortuna Sittard, Bury, Shrewsbury Town, Grimsby Town, Hamilton Acc, Stenhousemuir (1991-2015)*
Cramb is the true definition of the journeyman player, as the only man to play in all four divisions both in England and north of the border. Cramb joined Southampton from Hamilton Academical for £60,000 making but one appearance in the Premier League (against Everton as a substitute). He went back to Scotland a season later, never regretting his brief stint on stand by at a "great club with lovely people." Helped Bristol City into the second tier as part of his extensive journey through the the football pyramid. Also played in the Netherlands with Fortuna Sittard. After retirement, Cramb continued to play in charity matches and local amateur sides before moving to Bristol where he completed his coaching qualifications.

Cribb, Stan
Outside-left
Born: *1905 Gosport* **Died:** *1989*
Playing career: *Gosport Athletic, Southampton, QPR , Cardiff City, West Ham United (1923-1933)*
Cribb had already gained Hampshire Rep honours through his exploits with non league Gosport Athletic when he arrived at The Dell. Earmarked by the Echo as a "likely" youngster, he demonstrated potential as a pacy outside left He would eventually make the no.11 shirt his own, going on to play 78 times (22 goals) for Southampton during their Second Division days. Making the step up to division higher West Ham, Cribb failed to make the grade before moving across the capital to link up with QPR. Turned out for Cardiff as a "useful" player, Cribb retired and latterly helped to form Gosport Borough. Managing the club on both the football and financial side of things, he remained in the role until 1967 and later scouted for Saints, rarely missing watching his beloved Gosport Borough game in the process.

Crick, George
Half-back
Born: *1891 Newmarket* **Died:** *1982*
Playing career: *Market Harborough Town, Southampton (1914-1915)*
Crick had played solely at non league level in his native Northamptonshire before he was plucked from obscurity and joined Southampton along with Market Harborough team mate Harry Hall. Adaptable and versatile, his nine appearances all came in different defensive positions. He undoubtedly would have played more if not for the suspension of competitive professional football due to the outbreak of WW1. Crick enlisted in the army later that year, serving with the Northamptonshire Regiment and later the Machine Gun Corps. Earned a military medal for gallantry before resuming his career at Kettering FC after the conflict. After retiring from football, he worked as a storeman at the Corby steelworks.

Crowell, Matthew
Midfielder
Born: *1984 Bridgend, Wales*
Playing career: *Swansea City, Southampton, Wrexham, Northwich Victoria, Altrincham, Central Coast Mariners, Central Coast Mariners Academy, Maitland FC (2000-Still playing)*
Capped for Wales at U17, U19 and U21 level, full senior Welsh honours have eluded Crowell, who is still playing in Australia. As a teenager he was part of the youth system at Swansea in his native Wales, before being scouted and signed by Southampton. His move was contentious as Swans believed the move was illegal, with Saints ordered to pay £100,000 plus a further sum of the same based on games played. However, Crowell never made the grade and was released before joining Wrexham after a trial at Bristol Rovers. Crowell went on to a lengthy career at non league level, interjected by a brief spell in Australia with the Central Coast Mariners. In latter years, he's played in Spain and in Wales for Port Talbot Town. Crowell currently plays for NSW Premier team Central Coast United, where he also works in the five-a-side industry as well as coaching at their Centre of Excellence.

Peter Crouch

Striker
Born: *1981 Macclesfield*
Playing career: *Tottenham H, QPR, Portsmouth, Aston Villa, Southampton, Liverpool, Portsmouth, Tottenham Hotspur, Stoke City, Burnley (1998-2019)*
a man synonymous with the modern adage: "A good touch for a big man" and the stereotypical target man. Followed Harry Redknapp up the coast from Pompey to Southampton (always a bold move) and top scored for Saints in his only season at St Mary's, but despite his 16 goals in 33 games he was unable to prevent the side's relegation and moved to Liverpool that summer. Won the FA Cup at Anfield and played in a Champions League final before moving on again for second spells with Spurs and Portsmouth, playing over 200 games for Stoke and then a brief stint at Burnley. Played for eleven different clubs during his career and boasted an impressive net-busting record for England with 22 goals in 42 caps, featuring in two World Cups. A fan favourite at his many clubs for his 6ft 7 frame, affable personality, robot dancing and acrobatic goals, Crouch remains a prominent figure in the game through his media appearances on BT, Sky Sports and a podcast on FiveLive. Crouch has released several books including: "How Not to be a Footballer", and "I Robot". Twitter: https://twitter.com/petercrouch

Cumming, Laurence

Inside-forward
Born: *1905 Derry, Ireland* **Died:** *1980*
Playing career: *Alloa Athletic, Huddersfield Town, Oldham Athletic, Southampton, Alloa Athletic, Queen of the South, St Mirren (1927-1938)*
Cumming - capped three times by Ireland - arrived at The Dell for £500 in June 1930 from Oldham Athletic. He made an explosive start to his Southampton career as he scored four goals in his first eight games, but he would never find the net again during his time at the club. As the pitches dried up, Cumming seemed to lose both his touch and his temperament and was dropped in favour of Peter Dougall. He returned to Scotland with Alloa after just one season and the Laurence Cumming story was over - or so it seemed. Southampton still held his registration and he was transfer listed for £500, the sum they had paid for him. Chester and Bury both came in for him but he refused to leave Scotland and the asking price was eventually dropped to £100. He joined Queen of the South and later St Mirren before retiring and going into the newspaper industry. He wrote for the Scottish version of the *Daily Express* and was a founding member of the Scottish Football Writers Association (SFWA). He died in 1980.

Cummins, Joseph

Inside right
Born: *1910 Plymouth* **Died:** *1992*
Playing career: *Jersey Wanderers, Southampton, US Tourcoing, Newport (IOW) (1933-1935)*
Devon born but Jersey raised, Cummins was signed by Second Division Southampton as full back cover. He spent most his days at The Dell in the Reserves, but made his one nano only first team appearance shortly after turning 24, in place of John Brewis for a game at Millwall. Injured early in the match and before the era of the substitute, he was largely a "passenger" and that proved to be the beginning of the end for Cummins at Southampton. Later played in France and on the IoW for Newport, before he spent the rest of his working life at the Ordnance Survey.

Curran, Terry
Winger
Born: *1955 Kinsley, near Hemsworth*
Playing career: *Doncaster Rovers, Nottingham Forest, Bury, Derby County, Southampton, Sheffield Wednesday, Sheffield Wednesday, Everton, Huddersfield Town, Hull City, Sunderland, Grimsby Town, Chesterfield (1973-1987).*

Memorable, short but not particularly sweet - those six words seem apt when it comes to describing Terry Curran's Southampton career. In little more than seven months as a Saint, Curran only scored once - but it was against the then mighty Leeds United and took Saints to Wembley for the League Cup final. Spotted in local league football by Doncaster manager Maurice Setters, he was plucked from an apprenticeship as a paint sprayer into the world of professional football. Four years on, Lawrie McMenemy - in search of a winger - shelled out £60,000 for Curran's services but Curran soon left. Forced to retire at 30, Curran started a successful pallet business, then dabbled in property development before taking up a job coaching youngsters at Barnsley, Rotherham and first club Doncaster Rovers.

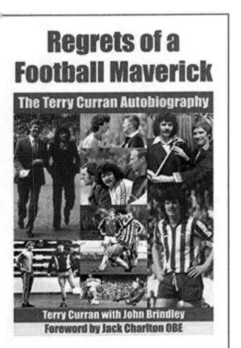

Regrets of a Football Maverick
The Terry Curran Autobiography
Terry Curran with John Brindley
Foreword by Jack Charlton OBE

Curry, Joe
Half-back
Born: *1887 Newcastle upon Tyne* **Died:** *1936*
Playing career: *Scotswood, Manchester United, Southampton, West Stanley (1908-1913)*

Curry started his career at Manchester United but was never going to get past United's famous Roberts/Duckworth/Bell forward line. He did manage to get 14 games in the first team at United, but joined Southern League Southampton in 1911. Reckoned to be energetic and an expert on a heavy pitch, Curry would again chances hard to come by at The Dell - a combination of serious injuries denying him the opportunity to show those attributes. After playing the first league games at left-half, Curry would go on to play another four games for the Saints before retiring from the professional game. The disillusioned Curry later turned out for non league West Stanley before he became a welder.

Curtin, Charles
Outside-forward
Born: *1980 Gateshead* **Died:** *1967*
Playing career: *Ryhope Villa, Norwich City, Southampton, West Stanley, Workington, Caernarvon Athletic (1911-1927)*

Sturdily built but deceptively quick both in mind and in body, Curtin moved to Southampton from divisional rivals Norwich in 1914. Despite the outbreak of war, football - temporarily at least - continued in 1914/15 and new signing Curtin struck up an impressive right-wing partnership with Arthur Dominy. The Curtin - Dominy duo played for two thirds of the league season and in a brief FA Cup run. When league football was curtailed a year later, he returned to his native north east and played some non league football before serving in the army with the Northumberland Fusiliers. After the war, he had a spell with Newcastle United before winding down in the non league game. Curtin was briefly involved in professional sprinting and then found work in a Sunderland paint factory and also as a maintenance worker in Silksworth Colliery.

Curtis, Alan

Forward
Born: *1954 Pentre, Rhondda, Wales*
Playing career: *Swansea City, Leeds United, Swansea City, Southampton, Stoke City, Cardiff City, Swansea City. (1971-1989).*

Played 35 times for Wales at full international level during a career synonymous with the white of Swansea City. Such is his association with the Welsh club, his time at other teams - Southampton included - is often forgotten. He began and ended his playing days with The Swans, and was part of the team to rise from the Fourth Division to the First during seven years at the club. His spell at Southampton came between 1983 and 1986, scoring seven goals in 67 appearances having joined after a fire sale at his beloved Swans. Lawrie McMenemy had first tried to sign Curtis several years earlier but finally got his man for £80,000. In competition with Ivan Golac for the number 4 shirt, Curtis nailed down a place in central midfield but - after McMenemy had departed to Sunderland, his successor Chris Nicholl signed Glenn Cockerill and Curtis' days at The Dell were numbered. Played for Stoke and then Cardiff, booed by both sets of fans during a south Wales derby with Swansea. Returned to The Vetch for a third spell as a player, then dropped into non league with Barry Town at the age of 40. He went back to Swansea, yet again, this time in a coaching capacity. Managed the Wales Under 21 side and served Swansea as both assistant and caretaker boss on three occasions. Curtis currently works as an after dinner speaker and Honorary President at the Liberty Stadium.

Curtis, George

Inside-forward
Born: *1919 Basildon, Essex* **Died:** *2004*
Playing career: *Anglo (Purfleet), Arsenal, Margate (loan), Southampton, Valenciennes (1936-1954)*

Having played in the same Essex schoolboy side as a certain Alf Ramsey, George Curtis joined Arsenal at 17, but war quickly intervened. A dozen games for Arsenal in the 1946-47 season proved a false dawn, but Gunners boss Tom Whittaker was so determined to pluck Don Roper from

Saints that the two clubs agreed to a swap deal with Curtis and Tom Rudkin moving the other way plus an added £12,000. Curtis, the makeweight, was made good. Ruskin barely played but Curtis became a regular. He made the position his own as Saints narrowly missed out on promotion in each of the three seasons between 1947 and 1950. He coached the Indian team at the 1948 Summer Olympics in London, moving on to Valenciennes, in France before finishing his playing days with non league Chelmsford. Managed Brighton, San Diego Toros and the Norway national team either side of two spells in charge of Rosenborg. Suffered from Alzheimer's in later life and died in 2004 aged 84. Curtis was also a founding member of the London Football Coaches Association.

Cutting, Stanley

Right-half
Born: *1914 Norwich* **Died:** *2004*
Playing career: *Norwich City, Southampton, Exeter City (1936-1948)*

Cutting flew into The Dell from the Canaries of Norwich as part of a hat-trick of new arrivals from the Norfolk side. Along with manager Tom Parker and a certain Ted Bates, Cutting signed for Southampton in 1937. He spent most of his time at Saints in the Reserves, before making a first team bow in the Second Division at the end of the final pre-War season of 1938-39, going to have a trio of games at right-half in place of the injured Ray Parkin. Moved to Exeter but War intervened, during which he served in the RAF and posted to Egypt. Later saw service in India, before returning to St James' Park after the conflict where he played until 1948. He then became assistant manager and remained on the coaching staff until 1953 before becoming a hotelier in the Devon town.

"DID YOU KNOW?"

"Albert Brown holds the record for most goals scored in a match for the club - 7 against Northampton Town in December 1901."

Dailly, Christian

Centre-back
Born: *1973 Dundee, Scotland*
Playing career: *Dundee United, Derby County, Blackburn Rovers, West Ham United, Southampton, Southampton, Charlton Athletic, Portsmouth, Southend United (1990-2008)*

With defenders Claus Lundekvam, Chris Makin and Darren Powell all stuck down by injury, Saints manager George Burley swooped to bring a 34 year old Dailly to St Mary's on an emergency two month loan. By the time he arrived at Southampton, Dailly had played almost 300 league games, more than half of them for West Ham and had collected 63 Scotland caps (he would finish his career with 67 in total). Andrew Davies arrived from Middlesbrough and so Dailly's time on the south coast was over after eleven games. He moved on to Rangers and then had two seasons back in London with Charlton. Had brief stints at Portsmouth and Southend United before retiring. He is now qualified with a Sports Science degree and has taken his UEFA 'A' and 'B' coaching badges. A versatile player, Dailly played in eight different positions during his career.

Dainty, Herbert

Centre-half
Born: *1879 Geddington* **Died:** *1961*
Playing career: *Northampton Town, Notts County, Southampton, Dundee, Bradford Park Avenue, Ayr United, Dundee Hibernian (1899-1932)*

A kindred, free-wandering spirit, Dainty never stayed at en of his eleven clubs for more than a year, a trend that continued at The Dell. A "worthy successor" to centre half predecessors Tommy Bowman and Arthur Chadwick, and proved "coolness personified" both when diligently defending and when moving the ball higher up to his forwards. Having left for Dundee, he broke his tangent lifestyle by remaining north of the border for six months before returning to his restless ways, flitting between the English and Scottish leagues. Post war, he served as chairman of Dundee Hibernian and then coached in Canada and Ecuador. Also worked at Ipswich as a trainer before becoming an insurance agent.

Dale, John

Half-back
Born: *1870 Audley, Staffordshire* **Died:** *1948*
Playing career: *Sunderland, Stoke, Southampton St Mary's , Audley Town (1893-1895)*

Having joined the throng of players to move from Football League Stoke to Southern League Southampton St Mary's, John Dale proved less successful than some of his contemporaries. Dale followed Jack Farrell, Willie Naughton and Sam Meston in making the move from Staffordshire to the south coast. He played five games at right-half - winning four of them - in league and Cup in the 1895/96 season. Suffered a 7-3 "thrashing" against Clapton on his debut, in place of Ernie Taylor, and after another handful of games Dale returned to his native Staffordshire to play for Audley. Dale would later work in the coal mines.

Davenport, Calum

Centre-back
Born: *1983 Bedford*
Playing career: *Coventry City, Tottenham Hotspur, West Ham United, Southampton, Norwich City, West Ham United, Watford, Sunderland, Wootton Blue Cross, Elstow Abbey (2000-2005)*

Despite Spurs splashing £3m to bring Davenport to White Hart Lane, the England youth international would play more games on loan from them that he would for them. He had nine games at Saints after Harry Redknapp signed him to partner Claus Lundekvam in central defence. But being in the midst of a gruelling relegation battle, it was no place for a player with no Premier League experience. Andreas Jakobsson displaced Davenport in the team, he moved on again and had a series of loan spells at Norwich, West Ham, Watford and Sunderland. His career ended in off-field ignominy when he assaulted his sister and was then attacked by her boyfriend for stabbing him in the leg - resulting in a serious loss of blood and emergency surgery. Found not guilty with the boyfriend jailed. West Ham ended his contract and he ended up at ninth tier Wootton Blue Cross later becoming their player coach.

Davidson, Andrew

Half-back
Born: *1878 Auchinleck, Scotland* **Died:** *1949*
Playing career: *Ayr United, Middlesbrough, Bury, Grimsby Town, Southampton (1900-1910)*
Spent the majority of his 15 year career with Middlesbrough and was an ageing 31 year old veteran by the time he arrived at The Dell. Despite being known for his pace, Davidson struggled to recapture the form that had made such a success with Boro and a favourite at Blundell Park, where he had captained Grimsby. His neat distribution proved no compensation and after only five games at centre half he returned to Lincolnshire. Eventually dropped into non league football and later worked in the travel industry.

Davie, Alexander

Goalkeeper
Born: *1945 Dundee, Scotland*
Playing career: *Butterburn YC, Dundee United, Dallas Tornado, Luton Town, Southampton, North Shore United, Mount Wellington, Napier City Rovers (1960-1981)*
In 1967, Ted Bates had attempted to sign "Sandy" Davie for £15,000 from his hometown club of Dundee United but ended up with Eric Martin instead. He eventually joined Southampton three years later as cover for Martin, but only played once for the club (a 5-1 defeat at Old Trafford against Man Utd in February 1970). In a second spell at Tannadice, he earned a Scottish FA Cup runners up medal but then emigrated to New Zealand. Residency rules enabled him to play for his adopted country, which he did on eleven occasions. He ten undertook a variety of coaching jobs, in Australia and the US. Returning to New Zealand, Davie became goalkeeping coach for the men's national team and head coach of the wtomen's. Davie also had a spell as manager of North Shore United in the island nation.

Davies, Andrew

Defender
Born: *1984 Stockton-on-Tees*
Playing career: *Middlesbrough, QPR, Derby County, Southampton , Stoke City, Preston North End, Sheffield United, Walsall, Crystal Palace , Bradford City, Ross County (1998-2015)*

Despite breaking a leg, Davies rose to prominence with his hometown team, Middlesbrough, becoming a key man for Gareth Southgate's Teessiders as they reached the UEFA Cup final in 2006. The following season, he was loaned out to Championship Southampton as cover during a crippling defensive injury crisis. Davies impressed with a series of commanding performances at centre-back, asking questions over why Southgate deemed his surplus to requirements. He suffered a broken jaw and then a fractured cheekbone, but despite the fact he was only at the club for a little more than four months, Davies was voted Player of the Year for the 2007-08 season by the fans. Despite this, Davies was not retained by the club and went on to play for Stoke, Preston North End, Sheffield United, Walsall, Crystal Palace, Bradford and in Scotland with Ross County. Capped once by England at Under 21 level, he became a free agent having left Dundee in 2019.

Davies, Arron

Midfielder
Born: *1984 Cardiff, Wales*
Playing career: *Cardiff City, Southampton, Barnsley, Yeovil Town, Nottingham Forest, Brighton & Hove Albion, Peterborough United, Northampton Town, Exeter City, Accrington Stanley (1993-2006)*
Davies joined Southampton's Centre of Excellence at Bath before rising through the ranks to the cusp of the first team. Became a regular at Reserve team level and came to the attentions of first team manager Gordon Strachan, travelling with the seniors to a UEFA Cup tie in Bucharest. He was also named in the initial 20 man squad for Saints 2003 FA Cup Final, but never made the bench. Although seemingly on the edge of a breakthrough, Davies never played a senior game for Southampton and was loaned out to Barnsley. He went on to play for Yeovil, Nottingham Forest, Brighton on loan, Peterborough, Northampton and Exeter City. Capped once at senior level by Wales in 2006 before finishing his playing days with a brief stint at Accrington Stanley. Davies has since worked as a player agent.

Davies, Kevin

Striker
Born: *1977 Sheffield*
Playing career: *Sheffield United, Chesterfield, Southampton, Blackburn Rovers, Millwall, Bolton Wanderers, Preston North End (1993-2015)*

Sheffield born striker who enjoyed two spells with Saints either side of a season with Blackburn. He enjoyed a reputation of being very combative and regularly picked up more bookings than goals. He joined Blackburn in a deal involving James Beattie joining Saints. A wily and battle hardened centre-forward during his playing days, Davies has put his experience to good use in retirement. The well-travelled, one-cap England man has completed his UEFA A coaching licence and has attained a Masters Degree in Sporting Directorship. Managed non league Southport and has since launched his own business, KCD Management - a personal, added value service for professional players both past and present. The company helps out of contract players to find new clubs, and to set them on a future path that helps them to get by after football. Davies often promotes the work of his business on Twitter, https://twitter.com/Kevin__Davies

Davies, Reg

Inside-forward
Born: *1929 Cymmer, Wales* **Died:** *2009*
Playing career: *Southampton, Southend United, Newcastle United, Swansea Town, Carlisle United, Merthyr Tydfil F.C. (1949-1964)*

Davies began his career at Southend after serving in the British Army, having been on the books at Southampton as an amateur. He never made the first team at The Dell, but impressed at Roots Hall and earned a mega £10,000 move to Newcastle United in 1951. Whilst with the Toon Army, he earned the first of six full senior caps for Wales. After he hung up his boots, Davies was player/manager of King's Lynn in 1970 before emigrating to Australia. There, he coached several local sides and remained in Perth until his death in 2009.

Davies, Ron

Forward
Born: *1942 Holywell, Flintshire* **Died:** *2013*
Playing career: *Chester-City, Luton Town, Norwich City, Southampton, Portsmouth, Manchester United, Millwall (1959-1975).*

Rated by Terry Paine and Ted Bates as the "best I've ever seen in the air", even John Sydenham - whose crossing was less accurate - praised the incredible ability and agility of this one of a kind striker. Davies could turn bad crosses into good ones and is still fondly remembered as the greatest header of the ball The Dell has ever seen. Bates had been seeking a striker but, having baulked at Chelsea's valuation of Bobby Tambling, he instead signed five-capped Welsh international Davies for £55,000 from Norwich. He scored 43 times in his debut season, and topped the First Division goalscoring charts again - jointly with a certain George Best - and by the end of his third Southampton season, he had plundered 85 goals in 199 games. Perhaps his most famous feat came at Old Trafford in the fledging days of the 1969-70 season when he was credited with all four of the goals in a 4-1 win against an admittedly far-from-vintage Man Utd side. He eventually lost his touch in front of goal and went on to join Portsmouth, also playing for Manchester United and Millwall.

COMPLIMENTS OF **Typhoo Tea** L[TD] BIRMINGHAM 5

RON DAVIES
(Southampton and Wales)

Freely acknowledged as one of the best strikers in the world and without doubt the most famous son of the tiny Welsh village of Holywell. Chester snapped him up straight from school, passed him on to Luton, who quickly cashed in when Norwich made an offer, and subsequently cost Southampton £55,000 in August, 1966. And it's been goals and caps all the way—more than 250 goals and more than 25 caps. He has twice been the Football League's top scorer, with 37 goals in 1966-67 and 28 the following season.

Had a spell Stateside and played 29 times for Wales. His Saints record read 153 goals in 277 games. Worked in the construction industry in Albuquerque, New Mexico, upon retirement. An appeal was organised by Southampton fans to raise money for Davies hip replacement. A Saints legend, Davies died in the USA aged 71 in 2013.

Davies, Ronald

Full-back
Born: *1932 Merthyr Tydfil, Wales* **Died:** *2007*
Playing career: *Merthyr Tydfil, Cardiff City, Southampton , Aldershot, Andover (1952-1967)*
The 'other' Ron Davies was a full-back for Saints a few years earlier than the legendary striker. Less heralded, but just as important, Davies was an ever present in the Saints Third Division title win of 1960. Deemed unlucky not to gain recognition with his native Wales, it was another Welshman - compatriot Stuart Williams - whom eventually usurped him from the side. Spent much of the rest of his time at The Dell in the Reserves before - after 185 games for Southampton - he moved to Aldershot. Eventually wound up at non league Andover before being overcome by Alzheimer's.

Davies, Thomas

Outside-right
Born: *1882 Swindon* **Died:** *1967*
Playing career: *Swindon Town, Nottingham Forest, Reading, Salisbury City, Southampton (1900-1910)*
Described as a "dapper" little forward, Davies soon became a fans favourite, scoring in his second game. but only played ten games for the first team in total before ending up in the Reserves where he suffered a leg break that prematurely ended his career. Became a coach fitter at the railway depot at Eastleigh, and served as a corporal in the Army Service Corps during WW1. His younger brother, Bert, also played professionally at Swindon.

Davis, Kelvin

Goalkeeper
Born: *1976 Bedford*
Playing career: *Luton Town, Torquay United (loan), Hartlepool United (loan), Wimbledon, Ipswich Town, Sunderland, Southampton (1991-2006)*
In an attempt to rebuild his career after a harrowing spell at Sunderland, Davis moved south to join another club synonymous with the iconic red and white. It was a tough time for a new time for a new keeper to come to Saints, with huge gloves to fill in the absence of the brilliant fans favourite Antti Niemi. Despite collective poor form in 2008/09 Davis was impressive and he comfortably scooped a clean sweep of individual awards, despite his status as captain of the relegated Saints. He then went on to post a record that still stands to this day of 20 clean sheets in a single season during the promotion campaign of 2010/11. He then captained the side that won promotion into the Premier League and was again voted into the Championship Team of the Year. During the 2011/12 season he overtook the club's appearance record. Davis began life in the third tier but went on to play - and win - at Wembley and captain Saints in the Premier League. He earned three caps for England at U21 level and had one game in caretaker charge at St Mary's following the sacking of Mark Hughes as manager in 2018. Davis has stayed with the Saints and is currently first team assistant to Ralph Hassenhuttl. Played 284 games in total.

Davis, Richard

Full-back
Born: *1943 Plymouth*
Playing career: *Plymouth Argyle, Southampton, Bristol City, Barrow, Falmouth Town (1960-1976)*

Left-back Richard Davis spent a solitary season at The Dell, becoming a one game wonder for the Saints in a match against his hometown team Plymouth in 1965. It's fair to say his debut did not to go plan with The Echo describing his performance as "a nightmare." He moved to divisional rivals Bristol City where he had to wait two years for his senior bow. He eventually left, after only six games, for Third Division Barrow. Barrow were relegated but Davis and his young family could not settle in Cumberland and so he was on the move again after 50 games for the Cumbria club. Had a brief dalliance at non league level in Devon and trained as a PE teacher - a career that would fill the rest of his post playing days. He retired in 2003 and continues to live in the area.

Davis, Stephen

Centre-back
Born: *1968 Hexham*
Playing career: *Southampton, Burnley, Notts Co, Burnley, Luton T, Blackpool, York City (1986-2006)*

Rising through the ranks at Southampton, he failed to ever nail down a regular spot in the first team with manager Chris Nicholl having a preference for more uncompromising defenders rather than Davis' cultured style. Despite his reserve team ever presence, Davis only played six games for the senior side before returning to Burnley - the Clarets had cleared marked his card - on a permanent basis. Went on to play for Luton, Burnley again, Blackpool and York City before retiring. Having hung up his boots, Davis just couldn't stay away from Turf Moor and returned again, initially in a scouting role before taking up the reigns of first team coach and reserve team manager. He was soon installed as caretaker boss following Steve Cotterill's sacking. Three years later he filled in again prior to Brian Laws arrival. Latterly worked at Lancashire rivals Bolton as first team coach under former Burnley colleague Owen Coyle.

Dawe, Leonard

Centre-forward
Born: *1889 Brentford* **Died:** *1963*
Playing career: *Southampton (1912-1915)*

Dawe certainly led an eventful life, one that hit two early stumbling blocks - his classes and his glasses. Combining his football career with that of a teacher, he was known for wearing spectacles whilst playing. Despite only sporadic appearances, he did earn amateur recognition with England, capped once in 1912 - appearing for Great Britain in the Stockholm Olympics. After eleven games for Saints in his only season, Dawe left football to take up a job as a master at the Forest School in Walthamstow. Served in the Hampshire Regiment during WW1, before returning to teaching. Dawe later became famous for compiling the cryptic crosswords for the *Daily Telegraph* newspaper.

Dawtry, Kevin

Midfielder
Born: *1958 Hythe, Hampshire*
Playing career: *Southampton, Crystal Palace, Bournemouth, Reading (1978-1984)*

Having served two years as an apprentice, Dawtry turned pro for Saints in the summer of 1976. A cultured midfielder, Dawtry went on to play over 200 games at Reserve level in the next three years, without ever getting a first team opening. Dawtry made his his one and only senior appearance when he replaced the injured Oshor Williams as a substitute in a match against Nottingham Forest. A skilful dribbler "willing to take on opponents", he returned to the Reserves and eventually moved on to Crystal Palace. He never played for them either, and left in time to sign for Fourth Division Bournemouth. He helped the Cherries to promotion and went on to feature 64 times in a three year stint with the south coast club. Had a brief stint at Reading, and them embarked on a nomadic non-league career. Dawtry moved into coaching and management, which he combined with working at a chemicals company at the Fawley Oil Refinery. Managed Totton & Eling in the Wessex League for five years, but stepped down claiming he was "all footballed out."

Day, Alfred
Wing-half
Born: *1907 Ebbw Vale, Wales* **Died:** *1997*
Playing career: *Tottenham Hotspur, Millwall, Southampton, Tranmere R, Swindon T (1928-1940)*
Solid but often guilty of dwelling on the ball, he slipped to third choice behind King and Frank Hill, and left for Third Division Tranmere after only one season. After another solitary campaign on Merseyside, he moved on again to Swindon but War was declared and his football career was over. Day operated telephones for the RAF during the conflict, guesting for numerous clubs and later held a job at a power station in Enfield.

Day, Eric
Winger
Born: *1921 Dartford* **Died:** *2012*
Playing career: *Southampton (1946-1956).*
Heard the one about the promising rugby star turned accidental footballer? Enter, Eric Day - the first man to top 400 post war games for the Saints.

During his eleven-year career with the club, in which he made the number seven shirts his own and plundered 158 goals in 422 games to sit seventh on the club's all time list of net busters - despite not starting out until he was 25. Yet the one club man almost never had a football career at all. Educated at the rugby union mad Watford Grammar, Day seemed set for stardom in the oval-ball sport until he broke his hand and played football whilst in recovery. Ex-Saint Bill Luckett, his PT instructor, recommended Day to another ex-Saint, Arthur Dominy, and the rest is history. Topped the Third South scoring charts for four years in succession, a remarkable feat for a winger and with manager Bill Dodgin struggling to replace the injured Charlie Wayman. The Echo piled on the plaudits for the Southampton hit man, eulogising that "No one had ever seen anything more perfect in pace and precision than the way Day scored his goals." Having helped the club into the second tier, Day left Southampton for a stint at Kent non league side Gravesend & Northfleet - a sad, anti-climatic end to a brilliantly prolific career. Worked at Hartham Park Estate in Corsham in later life, initially as a chauffeur and then as caretaker.

Dean, Norman
Forward
Born: *1944 Corby*
Playing career: *Corby Town, Southampton, Cardiff City, Barnsley, Bedford Town (1961-1974)*
Dean joined the club's CPC nursery side as a part time amateur whilst working as a welder. Singed by Ted Bates, Dean struck up a potent strike pairing with Martin Chivers as the friends and team-mates shared a lot of goals for the Reserves before reprising their partnership in the first team, with Dean breaking through after Chivers had already become established. Formed part of the influential Dean - Paine - Sydenham - Chivers quartet as Southampton earned Second Division promotion in 1965-66, hitting double figures including a hat-trick against fierce south coast rivals Portsmouth, instantly endearing himself to The Dell faithful. Ron Davies would replace him for Saints

Division One debut, moving on to Cardiff where he would play - and score - in the quarter final and both legs of the semi final in the Welsh side's European Cup Winners Cup campaign. Broke a leg at Barnsley which ended his career, returning to Corby to work for British Steel and later Oxford University Press. He also held a job as head of security at the Saints training ground.

Delamotte, Freeman

Forward
Born: *1870 Birkenhead* **Died:** *1933*
Career: *Southampton St. Mary's (1888-1893)*
The wonderfully named Freeman Delamotte is but a footnote is Southampton history, playing as he did before the days of Southern League football and The Dell. The club played at the Antelope Ground, The Dell's precursor, during Delamotte's time at the club. In his day, winning the various regional cups was the priority, although Delamotte did play, and score, in the Saints first two FA Cup ties in the 1981.92 season. A centre-forward who played with an edge and an aggression, his trademark was to close in on the goalkeeper as he went to catch the ball. He scored six goals in 22 appearances for the Saints and, after a brief spell on trial at Derby County, he returned to gain county Rep. honours in 1892 against the Corinthians and Surrey. Moving to Wales, he played for Conwy and Wrexham before becoming the Borough Surveyor in Conwy.

Delap, Rory

Midfielder
Born: *1976 Sutton Coldfield*
Playing career: *Carlisle United, Derby County, Southampton, Sunderland, Stoke City, Barnsley, Burton Albion (1992-2013)*
Capped eleven times by the Republic of Ireland, Delap was known for two things - his penchant for the spectacular and for rapier like throw ins. The latter would become synonymous with Stoke's robust approach during their time in the Premier league with Delap responsible for their major weapon. Also fond of giving away penalties due to his zealous commitment, Despite his niche talents, Delap was forced to compete with Matt Oakley, Chris

Rory Delap

Marsden and Anders Svensson but played regularly in their FA Cup run of 2003, missing out on a place in the final through injury. Having hardly missed a game in 2004/05, relegation meant a cull and Delap moved north to Sunderland. Fell out of favour under Roy Keane and was loaned to Stoke - his third successive club to play in red and white. Became a key ever-present in midfield for Tony Pulis workmanlike Potters and Delap - a javelin champion at school - became renowned for that throw in raison d'etre. Played for Barnsley and Burton Albion in the twilight of his career and has now returned to Stoke where he works as first team coach to Michael O'Neill - no doubt helping the current crop of Potters to refine their throw-in prowess.

"DID YOU KNOW?"

"The Dell was 'home' for over 100 years before the move to St Mary's Stadium in 2001."

Delgado, Agustin

Forward
Born: *1974 Ambuqui, Ecuador*
Playing career: *ESPOLI, Barcelona SC, El Nacional, Independiente Medellin, Cruz Azul, Necaxa, Southampton, Aucas, UNAM, LDU Quito, Emelec, Valle de Chota (1991-2010)*

Arrived at Saints with a modest price tag but a mighty reputation as the poster boy of Ecuadorian football. Dogged by injury during his time at the Saints, Delgado would start only twice in the league during his three year stint at the club - although he did score against Arsenal and Liverpool, Gordon Strachan became alienated by his new striker's refusal to learn English and when asked about the player's future, once famously replied: "I've got more important things to consider, I've got a yoghurt to finish by today - the expiry date is today." Things may have worked out differently if Delgado had missed the 2002 World Cup instead of playing through injury. Having plundered nine goals in qualifying, Ecuador pinned their hopes on the fitness of the striker and although he did score at the tournament, he was never fully fit. Scored 31 goals in 71 games for his country and later played for a string of sides in his homeland. Currently works as a politician, serving as a member of the National Assembly in his native Ecuadorian province.

Denby, John

Half-back
Born: 1892 *Sutton-in-Ashfield* **Died:** 1977
Playing career: *Southampton (1911-1915)*

In summer 1911, Saints manager George Swift signed an entire team's worth of new players including John "James" Denby for £820 from former side Chesterfield. Alongside Bert Lee and Jim McAlpine, Denby became an integral part of the Saints defence until competitive football was halted due to the outbreak of War. According to the local press, he was "a strong, reliable player who could play anywhere across the defence with equal merit." He demonstrated this versatility by frequently switching from centre-half to right-back and back again - filling in at left-back and inside right when required to do so. He must have done something right as he became an ever present to steady the Southampton ship all the way through to the aforementioned halt in the professional game. Later returned to Southampton to work on the docks.

Dennis, Mark

Left-back
Born: 1961 *Streatham, Greater London*
Playing career: *Birmingham City, Southampton, QPR, Crystal Palace, (1978-1990).*

A stormy career was wrecked by brushes with authority, he was cautioned 60 times, sent off on twelve occasions and appeared before the FA on disrepute charges more than once. Dennis moved to Spain to work as a sign writer. He spent time as assistant manager at Eastleigh F.C. and as at February 2009 was a presenter on 107.8 Radio Hampshire. Dennis was twice accused of beating up his wife with the police called to several domestic disputes with the marriage eventually and inevitably breaking up after a drunken fight. Dennis would later end up before the courts in Southampton, charged with aggravated assault and the threat of burning down a house. The former full-back was acquitted of all charges and now works as a roofer. The original "Pyscho", despite his fiery and colourful history, Dennis remains a popular figure at The Dell.

Dewar, George

Centre-half
Born: *1867 Dumbarton, Scotland* **Died:** *1915*
Playing career: *Blackburn Rovers, New Brighton Tower, Southampton (1887-1899)*

Capped twice by Scotland, he was a two time FA Cup winner at Blackburn before moving to Southampton - via a brief stint at non league New Brighton Tower. Despite that club's acceptance to join the Football League, Dewar had already decided to move south and organised his own transfer to Southampton. In hindsight, it wasn't the best move for Dewar. Aged 31 and in the twilight of a nomadic career, he had to wait for his chance at the Saints settled into their new home at The Dell. He had but four games at half-back in the league - 14 in total - and duly moved to near neighbours Eastleigh. He worked as an upholsterer - a trade he had originally taken an apprenticeship in on ships - at the railway factory and played for the works side, Eastleigh Athletic. Later in life, he worked as a trimmer at a motor works in Kings Norton.

Dia, Ali

Striker
Born: *1965 Dakar, Senegal*
Playing career: *Beauvais, Dijon, La Rochelle, Saint-Quentin, Chateaubriant, FinnPa, PK-35, VfB L ubeck, Blyth Spartans, Southampton, Gateshead, Spennymoor United (1988-1997)*

The Southampton story simply would not be complete without paying homage to probably the most famous - or should that be infamous - foreign signing in the club's history. Dia somehow managed to dupe the Saints hierarchy that he was the cousin of the great George Weah in a phone call that later transpired to have come from a friend of his, and so signed a one month contract with the club. Many of the team's stars - Matt Le Tissier among them - thought that Dia was a competition winner when he was first seen in training. Dia only played one match in his very short spell at Southampton - but wrote himself into club folklore for all the wrong reasons. In the match against Leeds in 1996, Dia stepped off the bench to replace the injured Le Tissier after 32 minutes and simply "ran around wherever the ball wasn't." With five minutes remaining, manager Graeme Souness substituted the substitute and so the most talked about 53 minute cameo in Premier League history was over. Played a handful of games for Gateshead before he again faded into obscurity having failed a trial at Bournemouth.

Digby, Derek

Outside-forward
Born: *1931 Teignmouth*
Died: *2005*
Playing career: *Dawlish Town, Exeter City, Southampton, Ledbury Town, Welwyn Garden City (1949-1955)*

A lightning quick winger, he was described as "quick off the mark" and "lively and persistent" by his Southampton boss George Roughton. Roughton had signed Digby when manager of Exeter and linked up with him again at The Dell. But despite his pace - he ran a lap of the pitch in 53 seconds - but despite creating the winner on his debut, he was always second fiddle behind the two Johns, Flood and Hoskins. He was released by Saints and moved into non league football with Ledbury and Welwyn Garden City. He gained a PhD in Economics from London University and then qualified as a teacher in Cambridgeshire and Essex, teaching Maths for two decades retiring in 1981.

Dixon, Kerry

Striker
Born: *1961 Luton*
Playing career: *Reading, Chelsea, Southampton, Luton, Millwall, Watford, Doncaster R. (1980-1996)*
Chelsea's third highest net buster of all time, he was capped eight times for England and played at the 1986 World Cup. Failed to hit the heights at Southampton, before moving on to Luton, Millwall, Watford and Doncaster. Since retirement, Dixon has kept himself busy, working for Chelsea TV and BT Sport as a commentator, presenter and match summariser. He is also involved in match day hospitality at Stamford Bridge and managed Doncaster Rovers, Hitchin and Dunstable Town as joint boss. A known gambling addict, Dixon has released two books "Up Front" in 2017 and the earlier "Kerry" in 2003. Dixon had a drugs charge against him dropped in 2014 but was jailed for nine months a year later having been found guilty of attacking a man in a pub after a night out. As of 2019, Dixon, now out of prison and continuing with his life, works as a pipe fitter for central hearing company Oakray. https://twitter.com/real_kerrydixon?

"DID YOU KNOW?"

"Rank Xerox became the club's first official shirt sponsors in 1980."

Dodd, Jason

Full-back
Born: *1970 Bath*
Playing career: *Southampton, Plymouth Argyle, Brighton & Hove Albion, Eastleigh (1989-2006)*
Dodd developed into a mainstay of Southampton's backline for the best part of two decades. During 16 years at the club, the Bath-born defender played 453 times for Saints and was was capped by England at U21 level on eight occasions. His consistency, longevity and loyalty made him a £15,000 steal from Bath City. Went on to captain the side as first choice right-back under Dave Jones. Theo occasional deployment in midfield and the odd game at centre back or midfield sweeper apart, Dodd stayed in the no.2 shirt during the rest of his playing days at Southampton. Injury denied him the chance to lead Southampton out in the 2003 FA Cup final. Known for his dead ball prowess, Dodd became the seventh post War Saint to pass 400 games. Following a brief spell at Brighton and Eastleigh, he returned to Southampton as first team coach under George Burley. When Burley failed to resist the lure of the Scotland national team job, Dodd held the reigns at St Mary's, jointly with John Gorman. Managed Eastleigh and Aldershot Town on a caretaker basis and then rejoined Saints as director of football and head of Academy (Under 18s coach). Credited with developing the likes of Luke Shaw, Calum Chambers and James Ward - Prowse, Dodd then became head of football at Winchester College.

Dodgin, Bill

Centre-half
Born: *1931 Gateshead* **Died:** *2000*
Playing career: *Southampton , Fulham, Arsenal, Fulham, (1948-1964)*

Dodgin arrived at The Dell in the summer of 1939. He signed in time to make two league appearances before the outbreak of War and the subsequent abandonment of competitive football. Dodgin played four more official games in the FA Cup but stayed with the club and continued to turn out in wartime cup games and unofficial fixtures. He also played for the Folland Aircraft works side, combining this role with coaching duties at Saints. In 1946 Dodgin was appointed as first team manager and inherited a strong core of players, signing Bill Rochford, Charlie Wayman and Ian Black to put together a team that would finish third in the Second Division in Dodgin's first two seasons in charge. Went on to manage Fulham, Brentford, Sampdoria in Italyand Bristol Rovers. He lived until the ripe old age of 90 when he died in 1999. Dodgin also ran a sweet and tobacco shop during his days as boss of Yiewsley.

Dodgin, William

Wing-half
Born: *1909 Gateshead*
Playing career: *Huddersfield Town, Lincoln City, Charlton Athletic, Bristol Rovers, Clapton Orient, Southampton (1928-1946)*

The son of Bill Dodgin Sr, he began as an amateur at non league level before signing for Southampton, where his dad was manager. He never played a league game for the Saints and followed in his father's footsteps to play under him at Fulham. Faced accusations of nepotism during his time at the club, but went on to become first choice centre-back at London rivals Arsenal after the departure of Ray Daniel. A tall if somewhat cumbersome defender, Dodgin lost but then regained his regular place and featured over 200 times for the Gunners. Returned to Fulham where a broken leg ended his playing career. He had clearly caught the football bug from his old man, and decided to follow the same path into management.

Went on to manage a string of clubs but resided over QPR's worst ever start to a league season, a run of 12 games without a win during his first managerial job. Despite this inauspicious start to life in the dugout, he returned to Fulham as their boss and went on to take charge of Northampton Town (across two spells), Brentford and Woking. He died in 2000 aged 68 after a long struggle with Alzheimer's.

Dollin, Albert

Outside-forward
Born: *1866 Southampton* **Died:** *1955*
Playing career: *Freemantle, Southampton St. Mary's , Eastleigh Athletic (1892-1893)*

Albert "Jack" Dollin is believed to have created a slice of club history as their first ever full-time, paid, professional player, a fact kept secret for many a year to avoid being ostracised by Southampton's rivals. Versatile and unpredictable, he played for the Saints in the era before organised league football, meaning that he only ever played in FA Cup, Hampshire Senior Cup and friendly games. By the end of that first season, however, he was carrying an injury in both knees and returned to his previous club, Freemantle. Later joined Eastleigh Athletic where he became a club stalwart, managing them and serving as secretary whilst working on the railways.

Dominy, Arthur

Inside-forward
Born: *1893 Southampton* **Died:** *1974*
Playing career: *Weston Grove, Peartree Athletic, Bitterne Guild, Woolston, Southampton, Everton, Gillingham, Clapton Orient (1911-1931)*

A boiler maker by trade, Southampton unearthed a gem when they plucked Dominy from the backwaters of a Woolston works team. He made an immediate impact in his first full season, scoring 13 goals in a front line consisting of Len Andrews, Percy Prince and Sid Kimpton. His second season was even better as he plundered 30 goals in 36 games, making him the top scorer in the Southern League. Dominy was described as a "special talent, ball control was second to none and he had that priceless ability, for a forward, of being able to beat an opponent at close quarters."

Presented with "Boys' Magazine"

A. DOMINY, Southampton

in the Royal Garrison Artillery despite Britain's peace time status. Spotted by Manchester United, he went on to star in the club's second league title win of 1910-11 but, deemed surplus to requirements at Old Trafford he crossed the Irish Sea to play for Glentoran. Brimming with "zeal and abundant energy" he returned to local football before war broke out. Amongst the first of the many men to arrive on the Western Front in 1914, Sgt Donnelly was injured at Flanders and transferred to RAMC. Joined Southampton in time for the first post-War football season, but by then was in the twilight of his career and aged 33. A one match wonder for Saints, he soon opted to wind down down his career in his native Lancashire, later serving as a police constable.

War disrupted the next phase of his career, but went on to strike up a formidable partnership with Bill Rawlings and captain Southampton during their promotion to Division II in 1922. After 392 games and 155 goals, Dominy moved on to Everton and wound down his career with Gillingham and then Newport on the Isle of Wight. In retirement, Dominy became the licensee of *Mason's Arms* in St Mary's Street and combined this role with scouting for the Saints. He also helped to run a leisure centre in Bournemouth. When Tom Parker resigned as Southampton manager. Dominy stepped in to take charge, although it was a part time role until his successor Bill Dodgin (above) arrived. A local, dyed-in-the-wool Saint, Dominy would later become president of the Saints Supporters Club.

Donnelly, Anthony

Full-back
Born: *1886 Middleton, Lancashire* **Died:** *1947*
Playing career: *Heywood United, Manchester United, Glentoran, Chester, Southampton (trial), Middleton Borough (1908-1919)*
A talented, busy and multi purpose teenager, Donnelly was working as a Lancashire coal merchant whilst active

Dorkin, Jack

Forward
Born: *1866 Aboard the SS Tamar, at sea*
Playing career: *Ipswich Rangers, St Bernard's, Royal Engineers, Southampton St. Mary's, Basingstoke (1883-1902)*
Born at sea to an English father and Greek mother, Dorkin took up a career as a draughtsman, connected to the Ordnance Survey offices. He moved to Aldershot and caught the eye of Southampton St Mary's when playing for The Engineers as they faced the former in the Hampshire Senior Cup. Offered terms by Southampton, he became one of the club's first professionals and was a prolific goalscorer during the pre Southern League era. He stayed long enough to play League football and scored in each of his three outings but retired in 1895 (four goals in six games for the club). He coached Southampton's Reserves side and ran a sports shop with ex-Saint and Hampshire cricketer Victor Barton. Worked as a pub landlord in Ryde, Isle of Wight, and had a brief comeback as a player at non league Basingstoke. Later the coach/manager at Hampshire League club Romsey Town. He moved to London in 1910 becoming a company secretary for a radiator manufacturer before migrating to Canada.

Dougall, Peter

Inside-left

Born: *1909 Denny, Falkirk, Scotland* **Died:** *1974*
Playing career: *Burnley, Clyde, Southampton, Arsenal, Everton, Bury, Manchester U (1926-1940)*

Billed as one of the most promising players of his time, Dougall's spell at Saints was ultimately disappointing. Having made the step up from Clyde, he only played 29 times across three seasons at The Dell. True, he combined skill with the ability to beat his man on the proverbial sixpence, but this was outweighed by his over elaborate style. The club made a £100 profit on Dougall when he made the hop across the Channel to France. He returned to England with Arsenal where he was to appear in the same team as Alex James and former Saint Ted Drake. Later played for Everton and Bury before guesting for Man United during the war.

Dowie, Iain

Striker

Born: *1965 Hatfield, Hertfordshire*
Playing career: *Cheshunt, St Albans City, Hendon, Luton Town, Fulham, West Ham United, Southampton, Crystal Palace, QPR (1983-2001)*

Dowie had earned seven of 59 eventual Northern Ireland caps by the time Ian Branfoot signed him for Saints.

The design is screen printed onto a white t-shirt, made in limited numbers. See: http://inbedwithmaradona.com

Playing as a striker in an Alan Shearer-spearheaded side made things hard for Dowie, but - a rugged, committed player - he still weighed in with his fair share of goal as well as holding the ball up to allow Shearer to run the channels. Later linked up with David Speedie and Kerry Dixon but Alan Ball - Branfoot's successor - signed Neil Shipperley and Dowie moved on to divisional rivals Palace. Also turned out for London sides West Ham and QPR before retirement. His post playing days saw Dowie work in the media and as manager of QPR, Oldham, Palace, Charlton, Coventry City and Hull City. Dowie still appears on Sky Sports Soccer Saturday.

Dowsett, Dickie

Inside-forward
Born: *1931 Chelmsford*
Playing career: *Tottenham Hotspur, Southend United, Southampton, Bournemouth & Boscombe, Crystal Palace (1952-1965)*

James "Dickie" Dowsett played once for Spurs before being spotted and signed by Frank Dudley, who recommended him to former colleague and then then Saints manager, Ted Bates. Dowsett played three times for Saints, twice in the league and in the FA Cup against Dowsett's future club Weymouth. He was unable to break the symbolic wing pairing of Terry Paine and John Sydenham, and moved further along the coast to Bournemouth for £100. He flourished there - finishing as top scorer in three of his five seasons. Determined, agile and useful in the air, Dowsett's value sky rocketed when he joined Palace for a record £3,500. Finished his playing career at Weymouth, then returned to Dean Court as Bournemouth's head of operations. He remained in the town as a production manager of a toy firm, while his wife Cynthia worked as PA to the Saints secretary at The Dell.

"DID YOU KNOW?"

"The club's 'Saints' nickname is due to its history as a church football team - St Mary's Church of England Y.M.A."

Drake, Ted

Centre-forward
Born: *1912 Southampton* **Died:** *1995*
Playing career: *Southampton, Arsenal, Reading. (1931-1945)*
Southampton born, Drake rose through the ranks to become one of his home town team's most prolific post war goal grabbers. Described as the archetypal number nine, he was "strong, powerful, brave and unstinting" in his approach to the game. Drake plundered 50 goals in 78 games for Southampton having initially joined the club on a part time basis whilst combining playing with a job as a gas meter inspector. Remarkably, his record at Saints was rendered relatively mundane by his extraordinary exploits at Arsenal, netting 124 goals in 167 games to become their fifth highest goalscorer of all time. He set the record for most goals in a single game - seven - against Aston Villa and scored 42 goals in 41 games in his debut season. Won two FA Cups and a league title with the Gunners, but despite his prolific goal ratio, he only played five times for England. Went on to manage Hendon, Reading and

Chelsea where he steered the west London club to the First Division championship - the first man to win it both as a player and a manager. Drake also turned out at both amateur and professional level for Hampshire county cricket club.

Draper, Mark

Midfielder
Born: *1970 Long Eaton*
Playing career: *Notts County, Leicester City, Aston Villa, Southampton, Dunkirk (1988-2009)*
A talented and tenacious midfield maestro, Draper became recognised by Notts County supporters as one of the greatest young players ever developed by the club. He spent most of his playing days in the Premier League with Leicester City, Midlands rivals Aston Villa and retired in 2003 after a spell with Saints. He played 21 times for Saints under Glenn Hoddle. Draper made a brief comeback in 2009 when he signed for non league Dunkirk. Won the League Cup with Villa in 1996 and earned two call ups for the senior England side (although he never played for his country). Having hung up his boots, Draper made the move into coaching and joined his former side Notts County in a dual role as first team coach and kitman. He later spent two years at Stoke City working for the Potters Academy. Obtained his UEFA 'A' and 'B' licences and coached at non league sides Radford and Nottinghamshire-based club Arnold Town FC. He has since set up his own football academy with former team-mate David Norton where they coach 16-18 year olds.

Dryden, Richard

Defender
Born: *1969 Stroud*
Playing career: *Bristol Rovers, Exeter City, Manchester City, Notts County, Plymouth Argyle, Birmingham City, Bristol City, Southampton, Stoke City, Northampton Town, Swindon Town, Scarborough, Worksop Town, Tamworth, Shepshed Dynamo (1987-2007)*
Dryden was signed for Saints in 1996 by Graeme Souness and made his debut opposite Gianluca Vialli and Frank Lebouef against Ruud Gullitt's Chelsea - a somewhat elaborate baptism of fire.

Richard Dryden

Known for his heading ability and power, Dudley plundered 120 goals in 195 games and played 73 times for Saints (33 goals) and was equally adept playing anywhere across the front line - inside forward, centre forward or on either flank. Appendicitis disrupted his latter days at Southampton, and, after a brief spell at non-league Folkestone, Dudley went on to work as a local government officer and coached at hometown team Southend United.

Dryden's mentor Terry Cooper had arrived at The Dell at the same time as Souness's new assistant. Dryden dispelled his doubters to form a solid and at times spectacular if unlikely partnership with fellow newbie Claus Lundekvam. Loaned out three times, Dryden played over 50 games for Southampton but fell out of favour after the arrival of Dave Jones who preferred Ken Monkou. Played and won the Auto Windscreens Shield at Wembley and then moved to Stoke. Dryden wound down his playing days at Luton then played for Tamworth under Terry Cooper's son Mark, whom he also worked under as assistant manager at Darlington. Managed Tamworth, Worcester and had a brief spell as caretaker boss of Notts County. Dryden later worked in the transport industry as a partner in haulage firm BWD Logistics.

Dudley, Frank
Centre-forward
Born: *1925 Southend-on-Sea* **Died:** *2012*
Playing career: *Southend United, Leeds United, Southampton, Cardiff City, Brentford (1945-1956)*
The archetypal free-scoring forward, Frank Dudley set a record in the first three games of the 1953-54 season. By scoring his first three goals of the campaign for as many clubs - Southampton, Cardiff and Brentford - he achieved a feat that is impossible in today's modern era where players can't flit freely between sides. He scored in the First Division when on loan at Cardiff, in the Second for Brentford and the Third for Saints. Unusually, he signed for Southampton when on a London bound train from Leeds and slotted into a forward line consisting of speed demons Eric Day and Eddy Brown.

Dunmore, Alfred
Outside-right
Born: *1911 South Shields*
Died: *1991*
Playing career: *Stanhope Road School, Simonside, Newcastle United, Derby County, Southampton, Mansfield Town (1928-1934)*
Having never made the first team at top level Derby, Dunmore would barely fare better upon joining Southampton. Although he would top score for the Reserves, his only Second Division chance came against West Ham in 1932 when he deputised for the injured and otherwise ever present Dick Neal. A one game wonder at The Dell, Dunmore was released in the 1932-33 season and returned to the north east where he worked in the coalmines and played for Mansfield.

Dunn, William
Centre-forward
Born: *1910 Lambhill, Scotland*
Died: *1980*
Playing career: *Ashfield, Celtic, Newton Villa, Brentford, Southampton, Raith Rovers, Bo'ness, Dumbarton, Leeds United (1933-1942)*
On his arrival at The Dell, the local press praised his "skill and marksmanship" as Dunn scored on his Saints bow after a couple of unfulfilling years in Glasgow. Taking over from departed namesake Jimmy Dunne, he played in the first nine matches of his debut season - but manager Tom Parker realised Dunn wasn't his answer. He spent most of the rest of the season in the reserves and would reject terms, going to return to his native Scotland where Raith snapped him up for £750. Also played for Bo'ness and guested for several Scottish sides during the War.

Dunne, Jimmy

Forward
Born: *1905 Dublin, Ireland* **Died:** *1949*
Playing career: *Sheffield United, Arsenal,
Southampton, Shamrock Rovers (1923-1942)*

Capped for two separate Ireland sides -
the Northern Ireland based IFA XI and
later the Republic when he arrived at
Southampton. Dunne holds the all-time
record of consecutive goals scored at the
elite level of English football as he scored
in 12 successive games during the 1931-32
season. He won the First Division with
Herbert Chapman's all conquering Arsenal
in the 1930s. Nicknamed Snowy because
of his fair hair, Dunne was the Saints' top
scorer in 1936-37 as he scored 14 goals in
26 goals to help secure Second Division
survival. He made the centre forward
position his own but, with a new manager
appointed at The Dell, he returned to his
native Ireland after one season. Eighteen
months after leaving the club, Dunne
was given a standing ovation by the
Southampton dockers as he passed through
the port on the way to an Ireland game. He
later served Shamrock Rovers as player-
manager and went on to coach Bohemians.

Dunne, Martin

Forward
Born: *1886 Padiham* **Died:** *1955*
Playing career: *East Lancashire Regiment,
Oswaldtwistle Rovers, Accrington Stanley,
Southampton, Stalybridge Celtic (1910-1911)*

Having cut a swathe through the
downtrodden backwaters of the lowly
Lancashire leagues, Duane moved
south in time for the 1910-11 season. A
regional champion sprinter, Dunne was
"exceptionally quick off the mark" and
he used his greatest asset to good effect -
top scoring in a struggling, goal shy side,
including a goal on his debut. He scored
nine times and might have had more if not
for a foot injury in the final weeks of the
season. After which he was gone, linking
up with former Southampton team-mate
John Johnston at Stalybridge Celtic. He
served in the east Lancashire regiment in
1914 before being discharged on medical
grounds. He recovered to re-enlist and later
became a factory engineer.

Durber, Peter

Full-back
Born: *1873 Stoke-upon-Trent*
Died: *1963*
Playing career: *Wood Lane, Audley Town, Stoke,
Southampton, Glossop North End, Northampton
Town (1896-1908)*

Plucked from coal to the Potteries, Durber
struggled to establish himself at Stoke
but became a regular at The Dell having
signed for Saints after two seasons. Durber
became first choice left-back, winning a
Southern League championship medal in
1899 and playing for the club in their first
ever FA Cup final a year later (Saints lost
4-0 to Bury at Crystal Palace). Strong in
the tackle with a good range of passing,
Durber earned an England trial but never
- much to his disappointment - earned a
call up for the national side. After almost
100 games for Saints, he returned to Stoke
- via Second Division Glossop - and then
to Saints divisional Southern League rivals
Northampton Town. Briefly coached the
Cobblers, and returned to coal mining
before he took over a pub in his beloved
Stoke-on-Trent. His league and cup medals
later sold for over £2,000 at an auction.

Dyer, Albert

Inside-forward
Born: *1886 Portsmouth*
Died: 1918
Playing career: *Southampton, Gainsborough
Trinity, Eastleigh Athletic, Southampton Cambridge ,
Woolston, Bitterne Guild, Romsey Town (1906-1915)*

Dyer spent much of his career on the south
coast marooned in second string, but
would get his one - and as it turned out,
only - appearance in the 1907-08 away at
Northampton when Sam Jepp was taken ill
shortly before kick off. Dyer remained with
the Saints for another year, but as a fixture
in the reserves until he joined division
Gainsborough Trinity. Within a month he
had returned to Hampshire with Eastleigh
Athletic, winning the Hampshire Senior
Cup before retirement. Played briefly at
non league level before the outbreak of
War. Dyer died in 1918 at the painfully
young age of 31 after a long illness.

Earles, Pat

Forward

Born: *1955 Titchfield, Hampshire*
Playing career: *Southampton, Reading (1974-1982).*
A local lad and schoolboy international, Bobby Stokes-esque striker Earls had to bid his time for a Southampton opening. Made his debut in the South Coast derby and featured only sporadically in his second campaign as a squad player for Lawrie McMenemy's Cup winners. Although he did not play in the final, he had a key role in getting the side to Wembley as he set up Hugh Fisher's last-gasp equaliser in the Third Round tie with Villa. That was as good as it got and, after only six games at The Dell, he moved on to Third Division Reading. The Royals were relegated but he was top scorer in 1979-80 as they went straight back up. Forced to retire from League football with a plethora of injury problems aged only 28, Earls briefly played for Road Sea. He combined this role with working with young offenders and qualifying at University of Southampton. Later went on to employment at Winchester Prison where his eleven minutes of FA Cup fame proved to be a big hit with in-mates and officers alike!

Earls, Mick

Defender

Born: *1955 Limerick Ireland*
Playing career: *Southampton, Aldershot (1973-1978).*
Nicknamed "Irish" to distinguish him from unrelated namesake Pat Earls, Mick signed for Saints as a 16-year-old and was renowned for his ability to play out from the back. Second choice to Paul Bennett in a relegated side, Earls made his debut at Anfield but played only three more games before dropping into the Reserves. Played eight games for Southampton in total before moving to Third Division Aldershot - suffering another relegation in the process. Combining playing with a coaching role for the Shots, Earls 81 professional league games were spread across all four divisions. Having turned out for non league Woking, serious injury put paid to his playing days and he worked part time in residential child care. Social work would become his main job, as he eventually gained employment as Children Services Manager for Hampshire. Played for ex Saints sides into his 50s and continues to live in the city.

Ex-Saints traise money for charity

Eastham, John
Full-back
Born: *1883 Blackburn* **Died:** *1932*
Playing career: *St Peter's School, Blackburn Rovers, Glossop, Southampton (1900-1912)*

Eastham featured only sporadically for Blackburn and - in their Football League heyday - Glossop before earning his move to Southampton. There, he would develop into one of the club's finest Southern League era full-backs. Robust, wholehearted and fearless, he racked up over 200 games at The Dell having dislodged previous right-back incumbent Bill Clarke. He went on to become Saints captain and was known for his mentoring of the younger players. Southampton reached the FA Cup semi-finals and finished second and then third during Eastham's stint as skipper in the club's early rise to Southern League prominence. An ever present in 1910-11, his unstinting service earned him a benefit match against Portsmouth. Dan Gordon and Frank Grayer slowly started to phase Eastham out the side so he left for Blackburn before becoming a publican. When he died in 1932, he was the owner and manager of the Boars Head Hotel in Stalybridge.

Edmonds, Thomas
Centre-half
Born: *1878 Edinburgh, Scotland*
Died: *1940*
Playing career: *Dundee, Preston North End, Southport, Southampton (1903-1906)*

Having never featured in the Preston side that won the Second Division in 1904, Edmonds was plucked from Southport and non league obscurity to move to the south coast and The Dell. Hit by a succession of injuries during his time at the club, Edmonds was never able to hold down a regular starting place as the "slim and wiry" centre-back often served as cover to regular no.5 incumbent Bert Lee. Played nine games - all of them across the defence - before he left Southampton and returned to Lancashire. Became a mining contractor at the Preston Links Colliery and was also a competent golfer, winning several amateur titles and serving as chairman of his local club in his native East Lothian.

Edwards, John
Inside-forward
Born: *1924 Salford* **Died:** *1978*
Playing career: *Nottingham Forest, Southampton, Kidderminster Harriers, Notts County, King's Lynn (1944-1954)*

By 1947, the prolific form of the Salford-born inside forward was turning heads with both Arsenal and Liverpool willing to pay up to £14,000 (an astronomical fee at the time) for his services. But the two First Division powerhouses ultimately missed out and Edwards instead joined Southampton for £10,000. Described as a "clever box of tricks", Edwards was a true crowd pleaser but manager Sid Cann never settled on a stable, consistent combination between his fast and tricky forwards. Edwards - otherwise known as Jack - was capable of playing anywhere across the front and finished the 1951/52 season as Saints regular number 11 at outside half. He was eventually loaned to non league Kidderminster and then returned to the League with Second Division Notts County as part exchange for Alec Simpson (who moved the other way). Having retired to Nottingham, Edwards met a sticky end with a violent death after a street mugging. He was 54.

Ekelund, Ronnie
Midfielder/Striker
Born: *1972 Glostrup, Denmark*
Playing career: *Brondby, Barcelona, Southampton, Manchester City, Coventry City, Lyngby, Odense BK, Toulouse, Walsall, San Jose (1988-2006)*

Heard the one about the Danish international residing in the Sunshine state and running a baby business? That brings us neatly to the story of Ronnie Ekelund, a former midfielder, capped by Denmark at U17, U19 and U21 level. Ekelund played seventeen games for Southampton before embarking on a nomadic, ground hopping and two decade journey in England, Denmark, Sweden, France and across the pond in the USA. It was during his sojourn Stateside, in which Ekelund played for and then managed San Jose Earthquakes, that he, wife Claire and their six month old daughter, settled and eventually emigrated to California.

Having initially designed infant products for their own children, the two began to experiment with nursing covers and a business was born. Today, Ekelund - former pro turned small business entrepreneur - and his wife run two companies, *Bebe au Lait* and *Puj,* offering the full range of baby products from covers to bibs, beakers and blankets. The business are on Twitter at: *https://twitter.com/bebeaulait*

Elkes, Jack
Inside-left/Centre-half
Born: *1894 Oakengates, Shropshire* **Died:** *1972*
Playing career: *Birmingham, Southampton, Tottenham Hotspur, Middlesbrough, Watford, Stafford Rangers, Oakengates Town (1911-1937)*
Moved to division lower Saints having already won the second tier title with Birmingham City. Manager Jimmy McIntyre sprung a surprise on his promotion chasing charges when Elkes arrived at The Dell as part of a complex, protracted four-way deal. Elkes and Blues team-mate George Getgood moved south with Fred Foxall and Joe Barratt going the other way. The gamble paid off, though, as Saints pipped Plymouth to the Third South title on the final day of the pair's debut season. Elkes suffered a broken collarbone that meant he mainly had to watch from the sidelines as the team took the championship but he became a regular the following season but when Tottenham offered the eye watering fee of £1,000 for his service, the Southampton board were unable to resist. Played 200 times for the north London side and racked up another century of games for Middlesbrough. He played in four international trials without ever earning 'proper' England recognition. After his playing career came to an end he coached the Ford Motor Works team at Dagenham. He played on into his 60s, representing Rainham Old Boys.

"DID YOU KNOW?"

"The first match at the Dell was in September1898 - a 4-1 victory over Brighton."

Ellerington, William
Full-back
Born: *1923 Southampton* **Died:** *2015*
Playing career: *Southampton (1938-1956)*
A one club man, William Ellerington - "Mr Southampton" spent more than four decades at the south coast club. Born in the city, he had moved to Sunderland before returning south when his father (also a professional footballer) got a job with the Harland & Wolff shipping firm. Guesting for the Saints during the War, he signed full time in 1945 having served in the RAF. Ellerington became Saints first choice, unstinting right-back for the best part of 12 years, notching up 237 games in the famous red and white. With ambitious adversary Alf Ramsey for competition, Ellerington was struck down with pleurisy and had to watch on as Ramsey rose to England recognition until he suffered a knee injury in 1949. Back came Ellerington, and so good was his form that he, too, was capped twice by England - against Norway and France. He became a key man as Second Division promotion wasnarrowly missed in 1949 and 1953 before joining joining manager Bates coaching staff. He went on to serve the club as coach, scout and secretary and created the tactical blueprint to beat division higher Man Utd in the 76' Cup Final. Widely credited with unearthing the raw talent of Mick Channon, and continued to assist the club's historians until his death in 2015, aged 92.

Elliott, Bernard

Half-back
Born: *1925 Beeston*
Playing career: *Nottingham Forest, Boston United, Southampton, Poole Town (1942-1960)*

The teenaged Elliott had been plucked from the obscurity of non league Boston United by Southampton manager Sid Cann, having played for hometown club Forest and served for two years in India in wartime. He soon became an established member of the Southampton side and went on to play over 200 times during a decade long stint at The Dell. Leaving the club in 1959 he embarked on a short voyage along the coast to Poole where he would play for two seasons along with former Saints teammates Barry Hillier and Pat Parker. He ran an off licence in Freemantle, a stone's throw away from the Dell, with his wife and played tennis, squash, badminton and possessing a "4" handicap as a gofler.

Ellison, James

Full-back
Born: *1901 St Helens, Lancashire* **Died:** *1958*
Playing career: *Tranmere Rovers, Rotherham County, Rhyl United, Southampton, Rochdale, Connah's Quay & Shotton (1921-1930)*

James Ellison was plucked from the Welsh League to join Second Division Southampton. Initially signed as an amateur, Ellison turned professional in the 1927-28 season and played 56 games for the reserves but only one game for the first team, against Port Vale in 1928. Picked up a serious injury after bursting a thigh muscle and was never the same. Later coached at Connah's Quay before drifting out the game to take up a job at Forster's Glass Company in St Helen's, where he also played for their works teams.

"DID YOU KNOW?"

"Theo Walcott still holds the record as the youngest player to appear for Saints. He was only 16 years and 143 days when he played against Wolves in August 2005."

Emanuel, Thomas

Full-back
Born: *1915 Treboeth, Wales* **Died:** *1997*
Playing career: *Swansea Town, Southampton, Swindon Town, Wrexham (1935-1948)*

Born in the heart of the rugby-mad Welsh valleys, Tom Emmanuel played for Swansea Rugby Club as an amateur but went to work for ICI where he played for their works football team and was duly scouted and signed by Swansea Town. Meanwhile, Southampton manager Tom Parker deployed four different left-backs in the first six games of the 1938-39 season after the retirement of Tom Sillett. Parker parted with - at the time - an eye watering £2,200 to bring Emanuel south to The Dell. He would play in all but three games in his debut season and the first three games of the next campaign until the declaration of war saw the professional game shudder to a halt. Emanuel, as was common at the time, joined many of his football contemporaries in joining the war efforts - serving with his battalion in North Africa, India, Burma and Madagascar. When League football eventually resumed, Emanuel was no long first choice. He returned to his native Wales with Llanelli and retired after a couple of years to become a bus inspector in Swansea.

Englefield, Frank

Outside-left
Born: *1878 Southampton* **Died:** *1945*
Playing career: *Southampton (1898-1902)*

Locally born and playing for Freemantle, he moved across town to join back-to-back Southern League champions Saints but his handful of games came largely in the Western United league and hence were not officially recognised. He represented Hampshire against neighbouring Dorset but Englefield became a one game wonder. He later wnt back to play for Freemantle before returning to the Southern League with Fulham. A boot maker by trade, Englefield became the brother in law of the legendary Hampshire and Ashes cricketer Phil Mead when he married Englefield's sister Beatrice. Mead played one game for Southampton as an emergency goalkeeper in 1907.

Ephgrave, George

Goalkeeper
Born: *1918 Reading* **Died:** *2004*
Playing career: *Guernsey Rangers, Northfleet, Aston Villa, Swindon Town, Southampton, Norwich City, Watford, Deal Town, March Town (1935-1955)*

Until the arrival of Paulo Gazzaniga in 2012, George Ephgrave held a unique 127-year old distinction of being the club's tallest ever goalkeeper. Towering over his team-mates at 6' 4", Ephgrave had 10-inch hands and could reach the crossbar without lifting the heels of his enormous size 12 feet. Boasting a "wing span" of 6' 8", he was known for his ability to pick up the old leather balls one handed but, despite his imposing size, he was impressively agile for such a tall man. Having started out in non league football on Guernsey, he was on the books at Villa but never played for the first team. Turned out once for Swindon and then served in the War where he was captured and made a POW in Odessa, Ukraine. On his return to England after four years, he was signed by Southampton and became first choice throughout the 1946-47 campaign. Sharing goalkeeping duties with Len Stansbridge the following year, he played another season-and-a half of Second Division football having been dislodged between the sticks by Ian Black. Ephgrave moved to Norwich for £500 but played only five games in three season in East Anglia. Featured briefly for Watford before ending his career in non-league with Deal Town and also March Town United. After running a pub, he returned to Guernsey where he became a market-gardener.

Evans, Harry

Forward
Born: *1919 London* **Died:** *1962*
Playing career: *Fulham, Romford, Aldershot, Southampton, Exeter City, Aldershot (1943-1950)*

Evans spent his early working life as a clerk in the wine and spirits trade while playing as a part time amateur for Sutton FC. Served in the RAF during the War, as a PT instructor in Farnborough, Hampshire. The town's football club had links with Southampton at the time and it was they whom Evans signed for in 1943.

He went on to play 53 times in unofficial wartime competition, mainly as a forward but would find 'official' appearances hard to come by. His solitary league outing - after four FA Cup games - came in 1946-47 as a centre-forward. After leaving Saints, Evans played for Third Division (South) Aldershot having briefly turned out for Exeter City. Forced to retire with a stomach infection, he took up coaching and having also gained physiotherapy and secretarial qualifications, he served "The Shots" as manager, trainer, coach and physio. When sacked in 1959 after four years in charge, he joined up with the legendary Bill Nicholson, working in tandem as Nicholson's assistant, a position he would hold throughout Spurs iconic Glory Years. He died suddenly in 1962 aged 43.

Evans, Michael

Forward
Born: *1973 Plymouth*
Playing career: *Plymouth Argyle, Plymouth Argyle, Blackburn Rovers, Southampton, West Bromwich Albion, Bristol Rovers, Plymouth Argyle, Torquay United (1987-2006)*

Welcomed to The Dell by manager Graeme Souness as an "explosive and barnstorming striker", Michael Evans was signed to add muscle and presence to Southampton's relegation-battling forward line in March 1997. He went on to plunder four goals in three games, all of them crucial, that earned Southampton seven points to finish a place and a point clear of the dreaded Premier League drop. Known for his brave approach to the game, Evans earned the April Player of the Month away but fell out of favour after the arrival of Kevin Davies - then David Hirst - and his stint at The Dell lasted a mere six months. A brief, but impactful, spell. A one cap wonder for the Republic of Ireland, he went on to give service to West Brom, Bristol Rovers, Plymouth Argyle and Torquay United. After retirement, Evans set up his own property development and construction business, MJ Evans. The company shut down in 2013 having gone into administration. Evans donated 75% of the money from his 2008 testimonial to five local Hampshire charities.

Evans, Richard

Outside-right
Born: *1874 Smallthorne* **Died:** *1942*
Playing career: *Newcastle White Star, Burslem Port Vale, Reading, Southampton, Burslem Port Vale (1894-1904)*

After five seasons with Midland League Port Vale and non league cohorts Reading, Richard Evans signed for Southampton to fill the void left by the departed Arthur Turner. With his pace, indomitable spirit and a potent shot, Evans had all the ingredients to become both a regular and fans favourite at The Dell. But having played a part in Saints Southern League title win in 1903, he look set fair for a long career at the club until injury struck. He returned to the team for the final throes of another championship success, before a strange quirk saw Arthur Turner go back to Saints and, as a result, Evans returned to former side Port Vale. Ill health and injuries forced him to hang up his boots - in his two year at The Dell he made 41 appearances (16 goals) and will be most remembered for those successive championship trophies. In later life, he returned to the area and, in retirement, ran the *London Arms* pub on The Docks.

Everist, Frank

Outside-forward
Born: *1885 Orpington* **Died:** *1945*
Playing career: *Grasmere United, Cray Wanderers, Orpington, Southampton, Croydon Common, Dartford, Orpington (1906-1919)*

An accomplished sprint runner, Everist had accumulated over 40 honours on the athletics track when he was recommended to the Saints by a local supporter. As a former sprinter, Everist's pure fleet of foot enabled him to distinguish himself from his peers, initially in the reserves and eventually earning him a first team call up. During his one year stint at The Dell, Everist's contract included work as Saints groundsman, before linking up with a number of former Saints at divisional rivals Croydon Common during their Southern League heyday. Played nine times for Saints, scoring twice, before a spell in the Kent League and a job working in the local gasworks. Everist died in 1945 aged 60.

Eyene, Pedro

Winger
Born: *1982 Equatorial Guinea*
Playing career: *Sector Sant Feliu, Hospitalet, Espanyol, Southampton, Hercules, Alaves B, Dundee, Gramenet, Levante Las Planas (1992-2010)*

Eyene, also known as Jacinta Ela, from the small central African nation of Equatorial Guinea, signed for Southampton in the 2001 off-season having turned down Coventry City. During his three years at the Premier League side, Eyene never officially appeared in a senior first team game, having to make do with several fleeting reserve team outings. He suffered a bad knee injury which spelt the end of his career in England. Bar a very brief two game stint with Dundee in Scotland, Eyene played the rest of his career in Spain at amateur level except for eight games with third-tier Gramenet in 2007. After retiring, Eyene moved to Barcelona where he started his own clothing range called Malabona, working alongside his wife in the production of T-shirts and a variety of fashion items.

Fairgrieve, Walter

Outside-right
Born: *1874 Edinburgh, Scotland*
Died: *1915*
Playing career: *Dalry Primrose, Glasgow Perthshire, Southampton, Luton Town, Hibernian, Partick Thistle, Heart of Midlothian, Dunfermline Athletic (1898-1900)*

Any hopes Walter Fairgrieve may have had of helping steer Southampton's ship to a third successive Southern League title were quickly scuppered. Hit hard by his drinking habits and general misconduct, Fairgrieve only played four games for the first team before he was allowed to go to Luton. His stay at Dunstable Road was even shorter, however, and he returned to his roots with a whistle stop tour of Scotland to play for the two Edinburgh clubs, Partick Thistle and Dunfermline Athletic. A wood turner for many years, on the outbreak of war he enlisted in the 15th Battalion Royal Scots. However, Fairgrieve would die of angina before he saw any action on the Front. A case of what might have been.

Fairman, Bob

Full-back/Wing-half
Born: *1885 Southampton* **Died:** *1916*
Playing career: *Southampton, Birmingham City, West Ham United , Birmingham City (1907-1917)*
Southampton born Fairman began his career with his hometown team but never played a first team match. Fairman finished his career at Birmingham before retiring from the game in 1917. Served in the RAF and later became a railway signalman.

Farrell, Jack

Forward
Born: *1873 Tunstall* **Died:** *1947*
Playing career: *Southampton St. Mary's, Stoke, Southampton, Northampton , West Ham (1894-1903)*
At the time of his arrival on the south coast, the local press dubbed John "Jack" Farrell as "fast, tricky and reliable" and he soon justified his burgeoning reputation with a series of impressive showings at centre-forward in his debut season. He top scored in each of his first two campaigns at the Dell, and was an ever present in 1896-97 as he captained Southampton to their first Southern League title. The team reached the FA Cup semi finals the following year in a cup run noted for the controversial blizzard in a replay with Nottingham Forest.

Jack Farrell

At the end of that season, Farrell returned to Stoke but later returned to Saints for a second stint on the south coast - going to make 116 appearances across his two spells at the club. Having fallen out of favour amid rows with Saints, Farrell moved on to New Brighton Tower, taking in Northampton and West Ham before becoming a publican in Tunstall.

Farwell, Arthur

Forward
Born: *1940 Forward*
Died: *1940*
Career: *Southampton St. Mary's (1888-1893)*
Farwell served Southampton St Mary's for five seasons during which time he helped to establish them as the county's top dogs. Quick, pacy and full of skill, he led the line in the days before organised League football but had a knack of plundering goals in important games. He scored goals regularly and played in two FA Cup matches, remaining with the club until 1893 and the arrival of professionalism. He was employed in the drapery department of Edwin Jones department store, and remained in the St Mary's area of Southampton and assisted the choir at the church that founded the football club.

Fashanu, Justin

Forward
Born: *1961 Hackney, London* **Died:** *1998*
Playing career: *Norwich City, Nottingham Forest, Southampton (loan), Notts County , Brighton & Hove Albion, Manchester City, West Ham, Leyton Orient, Newcastle United (1978-1997)*
A former A.B.A. heavyweight boxer and elder brother of John, he started his professional career with Norwich City and after shooting to fame with some spectacular goals, Brian Clough took him to Nottingham Forest in a one million pound deal. However his stay was brief and despite repeated comebacks from injury with a variety of clubs both here and abroad, he never recaptured the form that brought him to prominence. The first loan player to score for the Saints, his manager Lawrie McMenemy wanted to make the move permanent but was unable to do so due to lack of funds.

Justin Fashanu

The first openly homosexual footballer, Fashanu was dogged by allegations of sexual assault against young teenage men. He was playing in America at the time where homosexual acts were illegal at the time, Fashanu fled to England and was found hanged in his garage a month later. A flamboyant personality with a tortured life off the field, Fashanu played eleven times for England at Under 21 level but never played for the senior England team.

Fenwick, Herbert

Half-back
Born: *1900 Wallsend*
Died: *1961*
Playing career: *Harland & Wolff, Southampton (1919-1920)*
Harrison 'Herbert' Fenwick - a product of the footballing hotbed of Wallsend - moved south to work at Harland&Wolff and became one of the better players in their rapidly expanding work force team. He helped their shipyards team to victory in the South Hampshire War League in 1919 and signed for Southampton having guested for them during the conflict. Whilst continuing to work as an engineer for the shipping firm, he became a Southern League regular for the opening months of the first post-War season, 1919-20. A reliable right-half, Fenwick was hit by a succession of injuries and had his contract terminated at his own request. Returning north, he later re-emerged in professional football at QPR in Third Division South. Retired in 1924 and, back in his native Tyneside, took up a job as a coal miner.

Ferguson, Eric

Forward
Born: *1965 Fife, Scotland*
Playing career: *Rangers, Southampton, Dunfermline, Clydebank, Raith Rovers (1983-1989)*
Not much seems to have been written about this Scottish forward, apart from the fact he played his football almost exclusively in his native homeland. Turning out for a handful of clubs north of the border, Ferguson played for Rangers, Clydebank (twice), Dunfermline, Raith Rovers and Cowdenbeath. Went on loan to Southampton in 1986 but only featured thrice for the reserves and never made the first team squad. Returning to Scotland, he coached at Rangers, worked for Dunfermline in several different roles and continues to live in Scotland to this day.

Fernandes, Fabrice

Winger
Born: *1979 Aubervilliers, France*
Playing career: *Rennes, Southampton, Bolton W, Beitar Jerusalem, Dinamo Bucharest (1998-2008)*
French winger Fernandes got his Premiership break when Gordon Strachan brought him to the the south coast in 2001. Wide man, Fernandes excited the St Mary's faithful with feints, shimmies and dummying runs. Primarily a left winger, Fernandes would become an early demonstration of an increasingly modern trend, where he would be stationed on the "opposite" flank and whip crosses and dangerous, in-swinging free-kicks to either a lone striker, or sometimes two, with his "wrong" foot. Cutting in to score or create with his stronger foot, Fernandes was unpredictable, eye-catching and a fans' favourite. He struggled with injury but earned an FA Cup runners up medal in 2003, featuring in every round and playing in Saints final as a late substitute. Fernandes remained a key man but, with Harry Redknapp brought in to try and stave off relegation, Saints needed to reduce their payroll for life in the Championship and Fernandes became a casualty and joined Bolton. Later played in Israel and Romania before returning to France with Le Havre. Played almost 100 games for Saints in a four year stint.

Fisher, Hugh
Midfielder
Born: *1944 Pollok, Glasgow, Scotland*
Career: *Blackpool, Southampton (1962-1980)*
Southampton manager Ted Bates had been eyeing Preston's Howard Kendall (later of Everton managerial renown), but was priced out a move so turned his attentions elsewhere. Fisher - then employed by Preston - became the new apple of his eye and this time Bates was successful. In his near decade at The Dell, Fisher was an ever present in 1970-71 only to break his leg the following year in a collision with Arsenal goalkeeper Bob Wilson. Fisher featured heavily in 1976 and all that, but injury kept him out of the semi final and Fisher was the unused substitute for the Cup final itself. He left Southampton in 1977 to become player-manager of Fourth Division Southport. Narrowly missing out on a much-deserved Saints testimonial for ten years service, he described the position at Southport as one that was "too good to turn down." The Merseyside club would drop out of the Football League, Fisher left to return to Hampshire and conrtinued to play, but at semi-professional level. He retired from the game in 1980 and went on to work as a brewery rep for many years. Still living in the Southampton area, he is a regular spectator at St Mary's and also an after-dinner speaker for the club.

Fishlock, Laurie
Defender
Born: *1907 Battersea, London*   **Died:** *1986*
Playing career: *Crystal Palace, Southampton, Millwall (1936-1947)*
A multi-talented sportsman of considerable renown, cricket would ultimately trump football in the life of Laurie Fishlock. Despite two impressive seasons as Southampton's regular outside-left, leather and willow came first and Fishlock would miss the entire 1936-37 season whilst in the heat of battle for England's Ashes campaign Down Under. After a brief spell at Fulham, he joined Gillingham and also played for Millwall. Fishlock played in two amateur international games for England, but cricket continued to dominate and - despite breaking a bone in his hand - he excelled for Surrey. Played in his fourth and final Test on England's 1946-47 tour of Australia before retirement five years later. He coached at all levels of cricket including, for many years, St Dunstan's College in Catford.

Fitchett, Jack
Full-back/Half-back
Born: *1879 Chorlton-cum-Hardy*   **Died:** *1942*
Playing career: *Talbot, Bolton Wanderers, Southampton, Manchester United, Plymouth Argyle, Manchester City, Fulham (1897-1910)*
A colourful and controversial character, John "Jack" Fitchett's time on the south coast was dogged by controversy. Mainly used as cover for Sam Meston, Fitchett's tendency to be over elaborate - even if he was energetic in the tackle and a neat passer - certainly endeared him to the fans but less so to his bosses. Even so, it was his off-field antics that proved his downfall. While drunk, he had insulted and threatened to throw two members of the public into the sea and ordered to leave town or face police action. Having decided upon the former, he returned to Manchester United and briefly turned out for Fulham. After hanging up his boots, he worked for the impresario Fred Karno as a touring actor and then as manager of Karno's vaudeville theatre in Exeter. Briefly served the Devon club as player-manager and later became a pub licensee.

Flahavan, Aaron

Goalkeeper
Born: *1975 Southampton* **Died:** *2001*
Career: *Southampton, Portsmouth (1992-2001)*
Flahavan - young brother of Darryl
(below), also a goalkeeper - played for
Southampton at youth level before turning
professional with south coast rivals
Portsmouth as an 18 year old. Flahavan
twice had blackouts during matches, the
first attributed to a virus and the second
to a drop in his blood pressure. He died
in a car accident outside Bournemouth in
2001, sustaining fatal injuries having been
three times over the legal drink drive limit
when he lost control of his BMW sports
car. Brother Darryl named his son Aaron in
memory of his brother.

Flahavan, Darryl

Goalkeeper
Born: *1978 Southampton*
Playing career: *Southampton, Woking, Southend
United, Crystal Palace, Portsmouth, Bournemouth,
Crawley Town (1996-2015)*
Like elder brother Aaron, locally born
Flahavan began his career at Saints but
never played for the first team (although he
did make the bench in the Premier League
on a few occasions). Went on to have a
successful career in the lower leagues,
playing over 300 times for Southend
and also turning out for Crystal Palace,
Leeds, Oldham (twice), Portsmouth, AFC
Bournemouth and Crawley. Played in goal
during The Shrimpers famous 1-0 League
Cup win over Manchester United - with
Wayne Rooney and Cristiano Ronaldo et al
- in 2006. Having retired in 2016, Flahavan
stayed involved in the game and took up
numerous coaching roles. Linked up with
former Southampton team mate Garry
Monk at Leeds as goalkeeping coach, and
reprised this role at Middlesbrough and
Birmingham - again under the managerial
guidance of Monk.

"DID YOU KNOW?"

*"The most goals scored for Saints
in one league season is 44. Achieved
by Derek Reeves in 1959-60."*

Fleming, James

Centre-forward
Born: *1864 Leith, Scotland* **Died:** *1934*
Playing career: *Vale of Leven, 93rd Argyll and
Sutherland Highlanders, Southampton St. Mary's,
Aston Villa, Lincoln City (1891-1893)*
John Fleming signed for Southampton after
impressing the club's hierarchy during an
exhibition match against 93rd Argyle &
Sutherland Regiment. Along with fellow
soldier John McMillan, both men moved
to The Dell to bolster Saints ranks for
the 1891-92 FA Cup campaign. Both men
duly made their debuts in a 7-0 thumping
of divisional rivals Reading with "Jock"
Fleming netting a hat-trick. But trouble
was brewing - the Saints had failed to sign
both Fleming and McMillan before the
28 day deadline and were removed from
the FA Cup - McMillan would never been
seen again whilst Fleming moved to play
for Aston Villa, Lincoln City and in India,
where he played whilst serving in the
Army.

Flood, John

Winger
Born: *1932 Southampton*
Playing career: *Pennington St. Marks,
Southampton, Bournemouth, Headington United,
Cowes (1949-1959)*
Southampton born and bred, Flood was
a 14-year-old whippersnapper when
Saints manager Bill Dodgin made him a
member of the ground staff in 1946. With
World War Two a receding memory, Flood
signed pro in 1949 and went on to play
129 times for the Saints - scoring on his
debut and another 28 times henceforth.
He also played for England at schoolboy
level before finding his progress hindered
by two obstacles - his obligatory National
Service and new Saints arrival Eric Day.
New manager George Roughton, managed
to shoehorn the two into his team by
moving Day to centre-forward and giving
Flood the number seven shirt. From then
on, he became an ever present until a
17-year-old by the name of Terry Paine
rose through the ranks to become Flood's
new heir apparent. Flood moved on. After
retirement, Flood worked on the Docks as a
fitter's mate.

Flowers, Tim

Goalkeeper
Born: *1967 Kenilworth, Warwickshire*
Playing career: *Wolverhampton Wanderers, Southampton, Swindon Town, Blackburn Rovers, Leicester City, Stockport County, Coventry City, Manchester City (1984-2002)*

Flowers earned eleven caps for England and kept goal for Saints for seven years, playing over 200 games in the process. Sold by Fourth Division Wolves to balance the books, a young and rookie Flowers joined Chris Nicholl's Southampton as understudy to compatriot Peter Shilton. His first two appearances for the first team proved inauspicious - heavy 5-1 and 4-0 defeats against the heavyweight duo of Manchester United at Old Trafford, and Arsenal. An ever present during the inaugural Premier League season, Flowers soon received that England recognition, making his national team debut against Brazil. Third on the list of all time appearances for a keeper at Southampton (behind only Eric Martin and Kelvin Davis). Blackburn bought him for £2m as Jack Walker's millions built the team that would unexpectedly win the Premier League. Flowers also turned out for Manchester City twice, Stockport and Coventry on loan. Since retirement, Flowers has stayed involved in the game as a coach - managing Stafford Rangers, Northampton Town and, most recently, National League club Solihull Moors. He was involved at League Two side Macclesfield until they were relegated and folded amidst the Covid pandemic in 2020.
https://twitter.com/timflowersgk

Tim Flowers

Forrest, Gerald

Full-back
Born: *1957 Stockton-on-Tees*
Playing career: *South Bank, Southampton, Rotherham United, (1977-1992)*

Described by none other than Matt Le Tissier as "excellent and under-rated", Forrest began his career as an out-and-out winger before reverting to full-back. Starting out at Rotherham, where he made the number 2 shirt his own during a decade of service, he attracted the attentions of new Saints manager Chris Nicholl. £100,000 later, the 29-year-old Forrest had made the step from the basement division to the top flight. He admitted he was as "surprised as everyone else" by the move, but he immediately replaced Steve Baker and remained in the team until midway through his third season when he was usurped by Ray Wallace. A knee injury - sustained in a collision with Wimbledon hardman Dennis Wise - ultimately put paid to his ambitions. By the time he was fit again, he was third choice behind Jason Dodd and Aleksey Cherednik and was given a free transfer. Forrest returned to Rotherham for his swansong at The Millers during which time he passed 500 professional appearances, 131 of which came for Saints. Coached at Darlington - taking charge as caretaker manager for a four match stint - and then worked as a kitchen installer and shop fitter in his native Stockton.

Forsyth, Robert Campbell

Goalkeeper
Born: *1934 Plean, Stirlingshire, Scotland*
Playing career: *Falkirk, Shettleston, St Mirren, Kilmarnock, Southampton (1955-1968)*

One of the few men to play in the European Cup for Kilmarnock when 'Killie', in a brief malaise from the Glasgow duopoly, won the League and faced Real Madrid in a 1965 Second Round tie. Ted Bates was a known admirer of the Scottish stopper and thrashed out a deal at Heathrow airport when the team arrived back from a 5-1 defeat at the Bernabeu. Capped four times by Scotland, Forsyth was described by Terry Paine as "my kind of keeper: big, agile, and commanding."

F

Forsyth came straight into a Southampton side sitting seventh in Division Two and became number one during the club's ultimately successful challenge for promotion. Worked for *Watney's* brewery for several years in retirement, combining this role with a scouting job in Scotland for Bates. Three of his recommendations - Jim Steele, Gerry O'Brien and Ally MacLeod - would all play in the first team for Southampton. He later became a corporate host for *Marriott Dalmahay Hotel and Country Club*. Peter Shilton - another ex-Southampton keeper, once scored against Forsyth at the Dell whilst in goal for Leicester in a 5-1 victory for the visitors - Forsyth came to claim his opposite number's long clearance but the ball bounced over him, a moment both men would describe as a "pure fluke." Died in November 2020 at the age of 86.

Foster, John

Centre-forward
Born: *1877 Rawmarsh* **Died:** *1946*
Playing career: *Blackpool, Rotherham Town, Watford, Sunderland, West Ham United, Southampton, Huddersfield Town (1901-1910)*

Arriving at The Dell in 1909, John Foster did not live up to the reputation he had earned for himself at Watford. It was his 33 goals in 55 games that had attracted the attentions of First Division Sunderland, with the Wearside club shelling out £800 to bring Foster to Roker Park. He lost both his form and fitness, however, and things did not improve at West Ham. Foster scored once in his first six games on the south coast, and struggled to have an impact. He eventually lost his place and was on the move again after only one season. He rekindled his old magic as he top scored for new club Huddersfield, albeit in the inauspicious surroundings of the Midland League. He eventually dropped down into non league while working as a chimney sweep, before returning to Huddersfield as assistant coach. He worked as number 2 to Colin Veitch at Bradford City, stepping in for a stint as caretaker boss for the final four months of the 1927-28 season. He also worked as a scout for Portsmouth.

Foster, Robert

Goalkeeper
Born: *1911 Deane* **Died:** *1983*
Playing career: *Accrington Stanley, Southampton, Wrexham, Bury, Oldham Athletic (1931-1940)*

Foster joined Second Division Southampton as cover for Bert Scriven. During his 12 month at the Dell, he only played once in the first team, deputising for the injured Scriven early in 1932-33 season. Moved on to Wrexham, Bury, Oldham and non league Mossley but his career never got going again and he would wind up running a newsagent's.

Foster, Steve

Central defender
Born: *1957 Portsmouth*
Playing career: *Southampton, Portsmouth, Brighton & Hove Albion, Aston Villa, Luton Town, Oxford United, Brighton & Hove Albion (1972-1996)*

Ian St John's decision to try the man affectionately known as "Fozzie" in defence during a reserve game proved to be a key moment in the career of the Portsmouth born player. Although he had regularly scored goals as a youngster, he never played for the Saints first team but immediately looked comfortable in the centre-half position. He went on to earn three England caps and now lives in Brighton where he runs a successful insurance business offering cover to professional footballers.

Foulkes, William

Inside-forward
Born: *1926 Merthyr Tydfil* **Died:** *1979*
Playing career: *Cardiff City, Chester, Newcastle United, Southampton (1945-1961)*

Foulkes scored with his first touch on his Wales debut against England. Foulkes won the FA Cup with Newcastle before Tommy Roughton paid £12,000 to bring the dual signing of Foulkes and his Magpies team-mate Tommy Mulgrew to the Dell. After only 23 games for the side, Foulkes suffered a back injury, one that the club claimed he had been carrying since his arrival. The board sought a reduction in his transfer free and moved Foulkes on to non league Winsford Utd whilst the case was heard. Later ran a milk bar in Chester.

Foxall, Frederick

Outside-left

Born: *1898 Stourbridge* **Died:** *1926*
Playing career: *Aston Villa, Blackheath Town, Southampton, Birmingham, Watford (1914-1924)*

Halesowen-born winger Fred Foxall was spotted by Southampton coach Jimmy McIntyre. Foxall immediately made the outside-left position his own and proved an excellent winger, going on to play more than 100 games at The Dell. Known for his crossing, Foxall was an ever present as Saints finished their debut Football League campaign in second place. At the end of the 1920-21 season, he caused controversy when he signed a contract to join Aston Villa but was still registered with Saints. He was ordered by the FA to rejoin Saints and went on to win the Third Division South title the following year. Went on to play for Birmingham and Watford but broke his leg and never fully recovered. He died two years later aged only 28 from complications caused by the injury.

Foyle, Martin

Striker

Born: *1963 Salisbury*
Playing career: *Southampton, Blackburn Rovers, Aldershot, Oxford United, Port Vale (1980-2000)*

Martin Foyle's debut season at The Dell would co-incide with the swansong of two Saints legends and Foyle's idols - Mick Channon and Kevin Keegan. The Salisbury-born striker would only play seven games for Saints under the tenure of Lawrie McMenemy and scored his only Saints goal in front of the TV cameras at Old Trafford. Competing with Danny Wallace and Steve Moran, opportunities were limited for Foyle and became even more so when Frank Worthington arrived. Moved to Aldershot for £40,000 and also played for Blackburn Rovers, Oxford United and Port Vale. Having notched up his 150th League goal and dogged by a persistent knee injury, he retired to take up coaching full time. Managed Vale, Wrexham as caretaker, York City, Northwich Victoria, Hereford United and Southport. Foyle has since worked as Head of Recruitment at Northampton and as chief scout for Motherwell.

Martin Foyle

Fraser, Bill

Inside-forward

Born: *1907 Cowpen*
Died: 1974
Playing career: *Blyth Spartans, New Delaval Temperance, Cowpen Celtic, Royal Tank Corps, East Stirlingshire, Northampton Town, Aldershot, Southampton, Fulham, Northampton Town, Hartlepools United, Salisbury City (1926-1934)*

A serving soldier, he combined his job in the forces with playing part-time for Aldershot. Joined Southampton in a protracted transfer deal, making the considerable step up from the Southern League to the Second Division in 1929. Despite his tendency to become riddled with nerves, he endeared himself to the Southampton faithful and went on to feature over 50 times in the next two seasons, mainly at centre-forward or inside-right. Later sold to newly promoted Fulham, but found himself surplus to requirements in west London and dropped down in non league via a brief stint at Northampton. Fraser later worked as a landscape surveyor.

Fraser, John

Winger
Born: *1876 Dumbarton, Scotland* **Died:** *1952*
Playing career: *Dumbarton, Motherwell, Notts County, Newcastle United, St Mirren, Southampton, Dundee (1896-1905)*

By the time John Fraser had joined Southampton as Arthur Chadwick's replacement, he had already taken in five different clubs. Although naturally a winger - thereby belying his 'stocky" frame - he started out as centre-forward and scored a hat-trick on his Southern League debut against Brentford. Dovetailing with compatriots and new signings John Robertson and Mark Bell, Fraser top scored with 15 goals as Saints swept to their fifth league title in seven years in his debut campaign - including four goals in an 11-0 win over Watford, still, to this day, Saints joint highest margin of victory. They went on to win the league again the following year with Fraser again at the heart of things, before returning to Scotland for a final flourish, winning the Scottish Cup with Dundee and earning his only Scotland cap. Later worked for Chelsea as a scout.

Freeman, Alfred

Inside-right
Born: *1920 Bethnal Green*
Died: *2006*
Playing career: *Tottenham Hotspur, Southampton, Crystal Palace, Reading (1939-1954)*

Alf Freeman was unquestionably one of those players to be born into the wrong generation. He seemed set to become Spurs next big thing until the outbreak of WW2 scuppered any hopes he may had of making it in north London. Seeing service with the Duke of Cornwall Light Infantry in Normandy, it was there that Freeman met a certain Alf Ramsey and the two men became good friends. Guested for Sunderland in the war before linking up again with Ramsey at Southampton, although the future mastermind of England's World Cup win would have notably more success. Freeman was mainly used as cover for Ted Bates and filled in when the latter was away on military service, going on to make seven "official" appearances at The Dell once

competitive fixtures resumed in 1946. Bill Dodgin would often rebuke Freeman for his languid approach to the game, and moves to Crystal Palace and Reading respectively failed to revive his floundering football fortunes. He ended up working in the cardboard manufacturing business in North London.

French, Joseph

Centre-half
Born: *Portslade, Sussex 1878*
Died: *1948*
Playing career: *Clifton, Southampton Oxford, Southampton, New Brompton, Freemantle (1899-1902)*

French spent most of his time at Southampton in the reserves as a "capable" understudy to Arthur Chadwick. Played a handful of games on the rare occasion his international colleague was absent, six games in total. French made three further appearances in the early days of 1900/01 season but relinquished his number 5 shirt to Bert Lee, a new signing whom would go on to play more than 300 games for Southampton. Played for divisional rivals New Brompton and non league Freemantle closer to home before gong to work on the docks.

Fry, Alfred

Half-back
Born: *1864 Southampton*
Died: *1930*
Playing career: *Southampton Harriers, St. Mary's (1885-1888)*

Little is known about Alfred George Fry, with evidenced research on this player stretching to barely two paragraphs. A more than capable half-back in the club's first three years in existence, he played in the Saints first two Hampshire Junior Cup fixtures and unofficial friendlies, in the days before organised professional league football. He went on to become a prominent builder in Southampton. His brother in law John played in goal for Hampshire and was on the books "down the road" at Portsmouth in the early 1920s. John's son Charlie was the Saints first choice keeper during the unofficial war time season of 1940-41.

Fry, Charles

Midfielder
Born: *1872 Croydon* **Died:** *1956*
Playing career: *Corinthian, Southampton, Portsmouth (1891-1903)*

The story of C.B. Fry sounds almost unbelievable and better suited to a TV drama series than a book about former footballers. He lived in the early 1900's and earns his place on these pages by virtue of three games in a Pompey shirt, the third of which was due to be his last ever match due to injury. Apart from his brief footballing career, he was also a sportsman, politician, diplomat, academic, teacher, writer, editor and publisher, and first class cricketer. He played for both the England international football and cricket sides, played in an FA Cup final for Southampton and equalled the world record for the long jump. If that was not enough, he also stood as an independent candidate in the General Election and was reputedly offered the chance to take over the throne in Albania. He later launched and edited two magazines for boys, C.B. Fry's Magazine and The Captain, and then started a career in broadcasting.

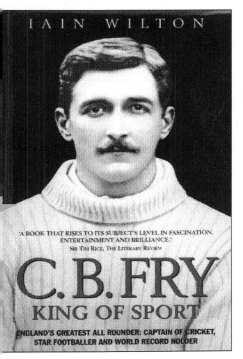

IAIN WILTON

'A BOOK THAT RISES TO ITS SUBJECT'S LEVEL IN FASCINATION, ENTERTAINMENT AND BRILLIANCE.'
SIR TIM RICE, THE LITERARY REVIEW

C.B.FRY
KING OF SPORT
ENGLAND'S GREATEST ALL ROUNDER: CAPTAIN OF CRICKET, STAR FOOTBALLER AND WORLD RECORD HOLDER

In the late 1920s, he had a breakdown and became paranoid. For the rest of his life, he dressed in bizarrely unconventional clothes and was occasionally seen running stark naked down Brighton Beach. This remarkable man died in September 1956 aged 84.

Fry, Roger

Defender
Born: *1948 Southampton*
Playing career: *Southampton, Walsall (1967-1977)*

A boyhood Saints fan, Fry combined schoolboy football with an apprenticeship working on the docks. Spotted and signed by the club's hierarchy, he signed pro as a 19 year old, he developed into a man marking full-back, modelling his game on idol Denis Hollywood. It would be Hollywood whom Fry would come in for to make his first team debut, but - facing stuff competition for his place from Hollywood, Francis Burns and Joe Kirkup - Fry had to make do with the occasional game in defence. Played 26 times in total before a 7-0 defeat at Leeds, when he was in tandem with Bob McCarthy at full-back, proved the nadir. Went on to Walsall where he would played 136 times before retirement. Had a spell at Salisbury and later held employment in plumbing, moving into film production and then the aeronautics industry.

Fuller, Ricardo

Striker
Born: *1979 Kingston, Jamaica*
Playing career: *Crystal Palace, Hearts, Preston North End, Portsmouth, Southampton, Ipswich Town , Stoke City, Charlton Athletic, Blackpool, Millwall, Oldham Athletic (1999-2016)*

Jamaican international striker who joined Pompey on a pay-as-you-play deal in 2004. He struggled to find the net and Alain Perrin was happy to let him re-join Harry Redknapp who had since moved on to Southampton. The fee, of only £90,000, reflected his value at the time and gave no clue to the fact that he would become a feared Premiership striker in future years. Fuller joined Stoke City in 2006 and became a key part of the club's unlikely rise to Europa League football.

Ricardo Fuller

He scored Stoke's first ever Premier League goal, conjuring up a grit and guile strike partnership with Mamady Sidibe. Fuller, capped 77 times by Jamaica, and now in his 40s, dropped down to the Northern Premier Division and signed for Nantwich in 2019 before moving on again in August 2020 to Hanley Town.

Funnell, Anthony

Forward
Born: *1957 Eastbourne*
Playing career: *Newhaven, Eastbourne United, Southampton, Vancouver Whitecaps, Gillingham, Brentford, Bournemouth, Poole Town (1975-1983)*

Plucked from non league, he plundered ten goals in his first 16 consecutive starts for Saints at reserve team level. Unfortunately for him, the first team had a rather prolific pairing of Ted MacDougall and Phil Boyer up top, which meant Funnell's chances were limited. Yet, having scored on his senior debut as a sub, he starred in the promotion run with seven goals in 12 games including a spectacular header at Leyton Orient. He therefore outscored Messrs Boyer and MacDougall. He failed to kick on from nine goals in 20 games and was shipped out to Gillingham. Signed by two ex Saints - Bill Dodgin and David Webb respectively - for Brentford and Bournemouth, before being forced to retire with a bulging disc injury in his lower back aged only 25.

Briefly made a comeback at Poole Town where he became the Dolphins all time top scorer and completed a hat-trick of promotions with three southern clubs - Saints, Bournemouth and Poole. He also worked as the club's commercial manager and ran a community coaching scheme whilst frequently appearing at St Mary's as an analyst for the PFA and the Press Association.

Furby, William

Half-back
Born: *1871 Staffordshire* **Died:** *1969*
Playing career: *Southampton St. Mary's, Freemantle (1894-1895)*

A Staffordshire amateur player of some repute, Bill Furby joined Southampton St Mary's ahead of their first ever Southern League season. However, he rquickly returned to amateur status and joined Freemantle. Furby played eight games for Southampton and remained in the town after retirement where he worked, with delicious irony, as a *tailor.*

Futcher, Ron

Striker
Born: *1956 Chester*
Playing career: *Chester City, Luton Town, Manchester City, Minnesota Kicks, Portland Timbers, Southampton, Tulsa Roughnecks, NAC Breda, Barnsley, Oldham Athletic, Bradford City, Port Vale, Burnley, Crewe Alexandra, Boston United*

Futcher started out at hometown team Chester in the Fourth Division before moving with brother Paul to Luton Town in 1974. He made over 100 appearances for The Hatters and played for Manchester City before crossing 'the pond' for a stint in the NASL. before a brief spell back in England on loan at Saints, although he never played for the first team. Latterly played in Europe with NAC Breda in Holland before winding down his career with a succession of Football League clubs including Barnsley, Bradford City and Burnley. After retirement, the former striker became involved in college soccer in the USA, coaching at Oakland University and he also worked for Bradford City as Community Officer and Head of Youth Development.

Gabriel, Jimmy

Defender
Born: *1940*
Playing career: *Dundee, Everton, Southampton, Bournemouth, Swindon, Brentford. (1957-1973)*

Prominent in Harry Katterick's all-conquering League and FA Cup winners of the 1960s, Jimmy Gabriel had been capped twice by Scotland by the time he came to Ted Bates attentions. He was initially reluctant to leave the increasingly trophy-laden Toffees in favour of The Dell, but - having lost his place to Howard Kendall - and with Alan Ball also waiting in the wings, he signed for £42,500. Told that he "would win nowt down there", Gabriel decided to see for himself. He relished the challenge of keeping Saints in the First Division and formed an imposing three-man defensive unit with John McGrath and Dennis Hollywood. A "tough defender with no little skill", with a steely determination to stand him in good stead, Gabriel also occasionally filled in as a striker. He played 224 games for Saints, scoring 27 goals, and went on to turn out for Bournemouth, Swindon and Brentford. He played Stateside for Seattle Sounders and went on to manage the club. Served as boss of San Jose Earthquakes, returned to Bournemouth as coach and was twice caretaker manager at Everton in the 90s. He has since scouted for the Toffees and also been involved in the management of two youth soccer schools both in the UK and Stateside. https://twitter.com/jgabrieloffical

Gallego, Jose

Outside-forward
Born: *1923 Errenteria, Spain* Died: *2006*
Playing career: *Brentford, Southampton, Cambridge United, Colchester United. (1947-1952).*

An evacuee to England from the Spanish Civil War, Gallego would make his first, and last, appearance for the first team, at outside-left against Barnsley in October 1948. After a stint with Colchester, the Spaniard eventually dropped into the non league game and worked for the gas board as well as becoming a proficient golfer. Died in Cambridge in September 2006 at the age of 83.

Gandy, Alfred

Born: *1864 Southampton* Died: *1914*
Playing career: *Southampton*

Alfred and brother George both played in St Mary's YMA first ever match in 1885, but the latter would never play a competitive game at any level for the club. He would go on to chair its committee until the formation of the Limited Company two years later. Whilst George's business acumen was notable, he soon retired but continued to live locally, working both on the Docks and as a tinsmith.

Gandy, George

Defender
Born: *1861 Southampton* Died: *1905*
Playing career: *Southampton*

The eldest of the two Gandy brothers, George reportedly showed more promise as a player than his sibling Alfred, whom would play six times for Southampton St Mary's. He would later turn out for Freemantle and the works team at Eastleigh railway depot. Gandy would work as a signalman and also took employment on the Docks.

Gaughran, Benny

Forward
Born: *1915 Dublin, Ireland*
Died: *1977*
Playing career: *Bohemians, Celtic, Southampton, Sunderland, Rochdale, Dundalk (1935-1940)*

Previously a salesman, Gaughran's goal grabbing exploits for Bohemians in Ireland turned heads aplenty on the UK football scene. Arsenal, Wolves, Blackburn and Man Utd were all interested in the Irishman but it wasn't until Tom Parker came calling that Gaughran got his chance. The striker had first come to Parker's attention when he was manager at Norwich, but by now the boss of Southampton, he took his chance and snapped up the striker when he released by Celtic after only one season. Gaughran's time at The Dell was brief, but effective, as he plundered four goals in seven games to persuade Sunderland to prise him away for £1,000. Went on to Rochdale and Dundalk before working as a beekeeper later in life.

Gay, Leslie

Goalkeeper
Born: *1872 Brighton, Sussex*
Died: *1949*
Playing career: *Southampton (1892-1900)*

A talented multi-sportsman, Gay is one of an elite group of men to be capped for England in two different sports - in a solitary Test match against Australia in 1894-95 (scoring 33 and took three catches with one stumping) and three times for the England football team. As a first-class cricketer, he played for Cambridge University, Hampshire and Somerset. He also represented Devon at golf, adding yet another string to his considerable sporting bow. He represented Cambridge University as a goalkeeper in a Varsity match and - in 1900 - joined Southampton as back up to England compatriot Jack Robinson. Gay never played at The Dell in the first team, but had drifted out of professional spot by the early 1900s. Died in 1949.

Gennoe, Terry

Goalkeeper
Born: *1953 Shrewsbury*
Playing career: *Bury, Halifax Town, Southampton, Crystal Palace, Blackburn Rovers(1972-1993).*

Rejected by Man United and West Brom, Terry Gennoe had seemingly settled for a career in the classroom, occasionally turning out for amateur club Bricklayer Sports in the Shropshire League. It was here that Gennoe was scouted and signed by Bury, offering him his break as a professional footballer. He began his career with the Shakers, and moved to Halifax where he made 78 appearances. Despite the admiring glances of Graham Taylor at Watford, Halifax manager Alan Ball Sr recommended Gennoe to his son's club. Saints came calling and Lawrie McMenemy had his man for a fee of £35,000. Gennoe soon displaced Peter Wells as number one and played against Nottingham Forest in the 1979 League Cup final. Although he ended on the losing side, McMenemy was pleased with Gennoe's performance and he went on to establish a post-war club record of six consecutive clean sheets. But after an error in an FA Cup replay at Highbury,

Gennoe was dropped and would eventually become third choice behind the returning Wells and new signing Ivan Katalnic. He went on to play more than 300 games for Blackburn, and - after retirement - remained heavily involved in the game as a goalkeeping coach. He held that role for Tim Flowers during Rovers League title win in 1995, and also coached under Kenny Dalglish at Newcastle and Celtic. After briefly living in Spain, Gennoe returned to England with a job at Aston Villa, where - once again - he took up his old role as goalkeeping mentor. Terry's wife Suzie is on Twitter, describing herself as "more than just a WAG" and posting regular photos of her husband in action during his time between the sticks https://twitter.com/susiegennoe

George, Charlie

Forward/attacking midfielder
Born: *1950 Islington*
Playing career: *Arsenal, Derby County, Southampton, Nottingham Forest, Bournemouth, Derby County. (1969-1981)*

A colourful and flamboyant personality both on the field and off it, Charlie George became best known for his exploits in the red and white of north London powerhouses Arsenal. A key man in their Double winning campaign of 1971, he played more than 150 times for the Gunners, but his latter days at the club were marred by a combination of injuries and moments of controversy. Not content with getting sent off for head butting Kevin Keegan, he flicked a "V sign" at Derby County's fans after scoring in a game at The Baseball Ground.

Charlie George

As the Double winning side slowly broke up, George fell out with manager Bertie Bee and moved on to Derby, scoring twice against Real Madrid in a European Cup tie. Also had a short spell at Derby's fierce local rivals Nottingham Forest, winning the UEFA Super Cup in 1979. He went to enjoy a long career playing overseas and 52 times for Lawrie McMenemy's Southampton side, scoring 14 goals. George lost a finger in a lawn-moving accident in 1980 and went on to run a pub in the New Forest. For a man of such talent, it comes as a surprise that he only played for England at senior level, against Republic of Ireland in 1976. Also worked in a garage business and is still a prominent figure at Arsenal, hosting the "Legends" tours and working in match day hospitality at the Emirates.

George, William
Winger
Born: *1878, Southampton* **Died:** *1917*
Playing career: *Southampton (1902-1902)*
A local find, William George made three appearances were spread across as many seasons. He drifted out of the game in 1904 to enlist in the Royal Sussex regiment for half a decade before becoming a bricklayer's labourer in Sussex, but rejoined the Army upon the outbreak of the First World War. He was reported missing - presumed dead - in France in 1917.

Getgood, George
Half-back
Born: *1892 Coylton, Ayrshire, Scotland*
Died: *1970*
Playing career: *Ayr United, Reading, Birmingham, Southampton, Wolverhampton Wanderers, Shrewsbury Town (1912-1931)*
George Getgood played eleven times at The Dell in his debut season as Southampton won the Third Division South. After a further 23 games for the Saints, he was involved in another exchange transfer, moving back to the Midlands with Wolves as Bill McCall went the other way. Went down and then back up again at Molineux, before joining Kidderminster Harriers and ending at a flurry of non league clubs. Later worked as a bus conductor and then hotel porter.

Gibbens, Kevin
Midfielder
Born: *1979 Southampton*
Playing career: *Southampton, Stockport County, Oxford United, Basingstoke Town, Sholing, Blackfield & Langley, Andover Town (1996-2016)*
A locally born midfielder, Gibbens was tipped for stardom having burst onto the scene as an 18 year old, making his Saints debut away to West Ham in 1998. Despite his impressive start to life in red and white, he was released in 1999 having made only three further League starts over the next four seasons. Gibbens will always be remembered as a "Sholing legend" where he played over 1,000 games. He dropped down a division to help Blackfield & Langley enjoy best ever runs in both the FA Cup and the FA Vase. Later went on to manage B & L as player-manager.

Gibbins, Vivian
Forward
Born: *1901 Forest Gate* **Died:** *1979*
Playing career: *West Ham United , Clapton, Brentford, Bristol Rovers, Southampton, Leyton, Catford Wanderers (1923-1939)*
School teacher Viv Gibbins arrived at Southampton with an impressive reputation having been capped by England at both amateur and professional level. He had combined scoring goals for First Division West Ham - becoming their first top scoring amateur - with turning out for part time Isthmian League side Clapton (winning the FA Amateur Cup twice in successive years). At a time when amateur and pros freely intertwined, he had short stints with Brentford and Bristol Rovers before arriving at Saints. By now in the twilight of his playing days, his time at the Dell was over before it really began - only playing twice in the second tier and failing to catch the eye. Returned to teaching after retiring, although he was an occasional spectator at West Ham's Upton Park. Gibbins boasted an impressive scoring ratio as an international, with three goals in his two full international games for England. Capped 12 times at amateur level as well, Gibbins plundered seven goals as one of the last amateur players to feature for his country.

Gibson, Andrew

Inside-forward

Born: *1890 Glasgow, Scotland* **Died:** *1962*
Playing career: *Kelvinhaugh,Strathclyde,*
Southampton, Celtic, Leeds City (1911-1913)

Plucked from under the noses of the two Glasgow giants, Saints manager George Swift described Andrew Gibson as the best he had ever seen and that his new signing would "easily be a thousand pounds man." Gibson failed to live up to such lofty expectations. Playing at inside left, Gibson had featured 19 times for the Saints before an incident in a casino that triggered his premature departure. Fined £5 and suspended, Gibson's contract was terminated and he subsequently returned to Scotland. Joining Celtic on trial, he scored on his debut but soon moved to Leeds United forerunners - Leeds City, where he played a handful of times before retiring. Gibson later became a locksmith. Died in 1962.

Gilchrist, Paul

Forward

Born: *1951 Dartford*
Playing career: *Charlton Athletic, Doncaster Rovers, Southampton, Portsmouth, Swindon Town, Hereford United (1969-1979)*

Moving from the backwaters of Fourth Division Doncaster to top flight prominence with Southampton for £30,000, Paul Gilchrist became part of an impressive Saints forward line. Featuring Ron Davies, Mick Channon, Bobby Stokes and Peter Osgood. His subtlety of touch meant he was well equipped for a deeper role, as he most effectively demonstrated during Saints never-to-be-forgotten Cup run in 76'. Having scored a spectacular goal in a Dell replay against West Brom, he became a midfielder upon the return of Osgood, replacing Nick Holmes in the quarter final and Hugh Fisher for the semi. He played on the right-wing in the final win over Man Utd. Having played 118 times (22 goals) and ensured his place in Southampton folklore, Gilchrist would find himself down the pecking order as the Cup-winning side swiftly broke up. He played on loan in Saudi Arabia - a move that Gilchrist himself described as a "disaster" - before

returning to England and moving the short distance to Third Division Portsmouth. Also turned out for Swindon and Hereford in the lower leagues, before his career ended in ignominy with a snapped cruciate ligament in a behind closed doors friendly. Gilchrist would go on to open and run a fitness centre in Swindon and also worked for BMW in Redhill, Surrey, as a sales/ service adviser.

Gilchrist, Robert

Forward

Born: *1892* **Died:** *1973*
Playing career: *Southampton (1982-1982)*

Striker Robert Gilchrist spent only two months at Southampton St Mary's. In those pre professional league days, only the FA Cup counted towards "official" recognition. Gilchrist featured in two Cup ties in two different positions. He never settled in a struggling Saints side, and a 4-1 win over Newbury was the team's only victory in a run of eight Cup and unofficial friendly games. Shortly after a 4-0 defeat to non league Maidenhead, he departed and played briefly for Basingstoke, before retiring. Gilchrist worked on Southampton Docks after his retirement as a player.

Gilkes, Michael

Left midfield

Born: *1965 Hackney*
Playing career: *Reading, Chelsea, Southampton, Wolverhampton Wanderers, Millwall.(1984-1991)*

An exciting young player brimming with pace, Gilkes was unable to convert his Reading form - he played over 400 games as a Royals legend - into his days at The Dell. A fast, tricky winger, loan spell at Saints saw him link up with former boss Ian Branfoot, but he failed to demonstrate Premiership potential in his four games, despite his status as Reading's best ever left winger. Gilkes latterly became a coach at Basingstoke and briefly served the "Dragons" as their manager in the 2015-16 season. Gilkes currently works at his beloved Reading as first team coach. Played five times for the full Barbados national side. He has also worked as a mortgage consultant for an estate agent.

Gill, Ernest
Full-back
Born: *1877 Mountsorrel*
Died: *1950*
Playing career: *Poole White Star, Bridgwater Town, Bristol City, Grimsby Town, Southampton, Freemantle, Leicester Fosse, Melton Amateurs, Excelsior Thursday (1899-1902)*

Ernest Gill would have been forgiven for choosing a full time cricket career over football, coming as he did from a leather and willow family. His father had played for Leicestershire and elder sibling George would play more than 100 first class games for Somerset. Gill would follow in his dad's footsteps by turning out on five occasions for Leicestershire, scoring 23 runs and taking 12 wickets. When it came to football, Gill would play in one friendly for Southern League champions Southampton, as a trialist at right-back in a 5-0 win over Sheppey United in March 1900 ahead of regular incumbent Peter Meechan. Despite failing to excel, the Saints board offered Gill a contract to sign full time, but he refused. He later turned out for local rivals Freemantle before returning to his native Leicester with the town's football club, Leicester Fosse. He broke his leg, ending his career, but went on to become a trainer and also worked as a groundsman in Hull.

Gill, Mervyn
Goalkeeper
Born: *1931 Exeter*
Died: *2007*
Playing career: *Bideford , Portsmouth, Woking, Southampton, Torquay United (1948-1962)*

Ted Bates first signing as Southampton manager, Gill spent most his career at Torquay under the tutelage of former Saint Eric Webber. He spent six seasons at Plainmoor, playing 174 times for the Devon coastal club. Gill was a one-game wonder for Saints, standing in for Fred Kiernan in the final match of the 1955-56 season a 3-1 win at Walsall. Gill served in the RAF during the War and also played for Portsmouth. He then worked for *English China Clay Quarries* for 28 years , combing his job with playing part time for non league Bath City. Died in Bridport, Dorest, in September 2007 at the age of 76.

Gittens, Jon
Centre-back
Born: *1964 Moseley*
Playing career: *Southampton, Swindon Town, Middlesbrough, Portsmouth, Torquay United, Exeter City (1985-2001)*

Gittens started his coaching journey in 2009 when he worked for the FA delivering coaching courses at both grass roots and professional level. As an affiliate member of staff, he would oversee youth and adult development across the board before becoming a full time coach educator in 2012. A former Saints, Swindon and Pompey player, Gittens brought over 40 years of experience to the dugout - as manager of Fareham and then Blackfield & Langley - and the classroom. Also coached Team Solent and taught on the Football Studies course at Solent University. Two of his most prominent positions at the top of the coaching ladder included leading the FA's position-specific courses and head of the "A" licence badge scheme with the governing body, becoming one of the only BAME coaches to do so. Gittens died in 2019 at the age of 55.

Glen, Alex
Inside-left
Born: *1878 Kilsyth, Scotland* **Died:** *1966*
Playing career: *Clyde, Grimsby Town, Notts County, Notts County, Tottenham Hotspur, Southampton, Portsmouth, Brentford (1902-1909)*

Glen's long term ambition to become a medical professor was put on hold by the Boer War, in which he served as a surgical dresser. Upon his return from service, Glen managed to combine his future aspirations whilst playing for Grimsby and Notts County and Tottenham abefore moving to divisional rivals Saints in 1906. He plundered eight goals in ten games until a breach of club discipline - being drunk along with Bill Gray and Robert McLean - led to misconduct charges and a suspension. A ban ended the Saints career of all three men but Glen would resume his playing days, first with south coast neighbours Portsmouth, and then at Brentford. His ambition to become a doctor came to fruition when he set up and ran his own practice in Glasgow in 1913.

Glover, Horace

Full-back
Born: *1883 Ashford, Kent*
Died: *1967*
Playing career: *Southampton, West Ham United, Boscombe (1906-1914)*

An architect's assistant and amateur player, Glover was playing for Hastings & St Leonards in the Sussex league when Jimmy Yates - a free-spirited player whom often alternated between them and Saints - recommended him to the Southampton board. Glover made his debut at left-back in the opening game of 1906-07 and quickly went on to prove Yates' judgement right. Glover became a virtual ever present and never missing an FA Cup tie in his half decade of service at the Dell. He helped to steer Saints to the last four of the cup in his second season at the club and eventually took over the captaincy. After over 200 games and and six superb years, Glover moved on to divisional rivals West Ham. After World War 1, Glover worked for his father in law R.C Hallett, at a scrap merchant and then as a stevedore in Southampton Docks. Later worked on the railways in his home town of Ashford.

Gobbel, Ulrich van

Defender
Born: *1971 Paramaribo, Suriname*
Playing career: *Willem II, Feyenoord, Galatasaray, Southampton (1988-2002)*

Graeme Souness clearly saw something in the relatively unknown quantity of Ulrich van Gobbel. The Scot signed the Suriname-born Dutch international twice - once for Galatasaray (where he won the Turkish Cup Final) before the Saints manager made him the club's then-record signing at a record £1.3m. Known for his aerial power and strength, his finesse and subtlety were not so much in evidence, but Van Gobbel was good enough to play eight times for Netherlands, featuring at the 1994 World Cup. Having hardly missed a Saints game for Souness, Van Gobbel played twice under successor Dave Jones, playing 32 times in total for the club. Returning to the Netherlands and former club Feyenoord, he played for another five seasons before finally retiring from the game.

Went on to run a sports shop in Rotterdam - unusually specialising in cultural Surinamese objects - before he was jailed for four months after selling rented cars through a third party from hire- purchase. The sentence was reduced to 129 hours of community service and van Gobbel went on to coach at 66' VV Alexandria, an amateur club in Rotterdam.

Godfrey, Tony

Goalkeeper
Born: *1939 Pangbourne*
Playing career: *Norwich City, Southampton, Aldershot, Rochdale, Aldershot (1956-1985)*

An apprentice bricklayer, Godfrey had become Basingstoke's youngest ever player at 16 years and 123 days. After a brief period on the books of Norwich, he was signed by Southampton of the Third Division (South) for £500, having being championed by Basingstoke's former Saint Stan Clements. Godfrey quickly became established as first choice for the Reserves before his first team debut - described as "confident, cool and agile" saw him keep a clean sheet in a 1-0 win over QPR in an FA Cup tie. Godfrey kept his place for the next five games until the return of John Christie but - when the latter departed that summer - Godfrey had. A run of games until injury saw Bob Charles usurp him. His career was then interrupted by his National Service which was spent in the Army, also turning out in the game for the forces sides. Godfrey vied with Ron Reynolds as Southampton gained promotion in 1960, playing in every season from debut to departure - a span of seven years - without every truly becoming undisputed number one. Nevertheless, he still featured 150 times for the club before he was sold to Aldershot with Campell Forsyth and John Hollowbread now staking their claims as no.1. He returned to Basingstoke Town where his career was book-ended by becoming their oldest ever player - aged 45 - three decades after he had the set the record as their youngest. Both still stand today. Godfrey served Basingstoke as player/coach before spells as manager of Andover, Alton Town and Fleet. He later set up his own building business.

Goodchild, Jim

Goalkeeper

Born: *1892 Southampton* **Died:** *1950*
Playing career: *St Pauls Athletic, Southampton, Manchester City, Guildford City (1909-1929)*

Plucked from the backwaters of local parks football, "Jack" Goodchild was barely 18 and still only an amateur when he was drafted in for his Saints debut in place of the injured Tom Burrows. Signed pro that summer, but Arthur Brown returned from Portsmouth which meant - now third choice - Goodchild would only get a handful of games the following season. He drifted out of the game to work on the Docks but was tempted back when First Division Manchester City came calling. He would on to feature over 200 times for City and played in the 1926 FA Cup Final - not bad for a young talent almost lost to the game. He later returned to Southampton to run the *Royal Albert Hotel,* while playing part time for non league Guildford. Took over the running of the *Cricketers Arms* pub in Eastleigh and turned out for Stoneham Nomads at the age of 50. Goodchild died of a heart attack in October 1950.

Gordon, Dan

Full-back

Born: *1881 West Calder, Scotland* **Died:** *1958*
Playing career: *Everton, Southampton, St Mirren, Middlesbrough, Bradford PA, Hull City, (1903-1912)*

Failed to make the grade at Everton and barely made an impact at the Dell either. Gordon played in six Southern League games, as cover for the stricken George Molyneux at left-back. Having captained the Reserves to 1905 Hampshire Senior Cup glory, he left and went on to turn out for a plethora of clubs both in England and north of the border. Played for St Mirren, Falkirk, Middlesbrough, Bradford PA and Hull City Represented Scotland at youth level but never earned a senior cap. He later returned to The Dell to play a further 12 games for a struggling side, one that would eventually be relegated. He dropped into the league's second division to play for Luton before winding down at Pontypridd in Wales, going on to work in a slate quarry after the war.

Golac, Ivan

Fullback

Born: *1950 Koprivnica, FPR Yugoslavia*
Playing career: *Southampton, Bournemouth, Man City, Southampton, Portsmouth. (1978-1984)*

A "silly rule" prevented Golac from playing outside of his native, communist, Yugoslavia until the age of 28 so the first 6 years of his playing career were spent at Partizan Belgrade in his nation's capital. Free, in the summer of 1978, to get his longed-for move overseas, Golac seemed set to sign for Galatasaray in Turkey until Lawrie McMenemy intervened. Pushed on by a love of English music and culture, Golac did not need asking twice and he moved to Saints, making his debut at The Dell, at right-back, in August 1978. Formed a "smashing" triangle with Alan Ball and Mick Channon. He achieved one of his big ambitions, playing in a Wembley cup final as Saints lost 3-2 against Nottingham Forest in the League Cup final. His time at Southampton ended in a dispute with McMenemy over terms although be briefly returned in 1984. Golac went on to play for Portsmouth before turning his hand to management. He took charge of Torquay and Dundee United with whom he won the Scottish Cup, as well as teams in Yugoslavia, Serbia, Iceland and the Ukraine. Ran a chocolate factory in Belgrade for a number of years and worked as a technical director for the Libyan FA. Now 70, Golac has retired to his native Serbia.

Gotsmanov, Sergey

Winger

Born: *1959 Minsk, Belarus, Soviet Union*
Playing career: *Dinamo Brest, Dinamo Minsk, Brighton & Hove Albion, Southampton, Hallescher FC, Dinamo Minsk, Minnesota Thunder.*

Gotsmanov's career spanned both side of the Soviet Union's break up, playing 31 times for the USSR, scoring against England at Wembley. The four-time Belarussian Player of the Year, he came to England in February 1990 to play out the rest of the season on a trial basis at Brighton. Gotsmanov instantly endeared himself to the Seagulls faithful, but Chris Nicholl scuppered any plans they may have had for a longer term or permanent deal. Tempted to tested himself in higher league, it was a case of right place, wrong time for Gotsmanov as he only made eight appearances - six of those as sub - and struggled to displace Rod Wallace, Alan Shearer and Matt Le Tissier. Nicholl was forced to deny suggestions that he'd signed Gotsmanov merely as company for his compatriot, Aleksey Cherednik. Later went on to coach in his home country of Belarus.

Granger, Keith

Goalkeeper

Born: *1968 Southampton*
Playing career: *Southampton, Darlington, Basingstoke Town (1982-1994)*

Keith Granger's two games first team games came about more by luck than judgement. With Peter Shilton hamstrung two games out from the end of 1985-86, his deputy Phil Kite had left on loan and Tim Flowers had returned to Wolverhampton. Granger would deputise for games away to title chasing Everton and mid-table Spurs - Saints would lose 6-1 and 5-3 respectively. Despite conceding eleven goals in those two outings, Chris Nicholl clearly saw something in the young keeper and signed him as a pro. When Shilton left, he was replaced by John Burridge and so Granger headed north, with Darlington in need of an emergency goalkeeper signing. Ever present for the next two seasons, his League career was ended with his left knee shattered in a collision. He returned to Southampton to work on the Docks and played for a succession of non league clubs - including back at Saints for the Reserves during an injury crisis.

Granger has gone on to work for the English FA, and also in Scandinavia and Poland. Worked under Mark Wotte as Scotland's U16 goalkeeping coach. Coached at the Saints Academy and head of goalkeeping at Matt Le Tissier's coaching school.

Grant, Wilfred
Winger/Centre-forward
Born: *1920 Bedlington* **Died:** *1990*
Playing career: *Newcastle United, Manchester City, Southampton, Cardiff City, Ipswich T (1937-1958)*

Having failed to make the grade at local professional side Newcastle, Wilf Grant moved to Manchester City but War was declared and he served in the RAF. Grant guested for Southampton during the conflict and signed for them in the first post-war season of 1945-46. His brother worked on the railways at Eastleigh so the move made sense. With his blistering pace and diminutive size, Grant had all the attributes of the archetypal winger but would soon be made to share wide man duties with another rapid new arrival, Eric Day. Manager Bill Dodgin tried them both in tandem, with Grant on his preferred right wing and Day on the left, but - halfway through his third season at The Dell - Dodgin transfer listed Grant, having signed yet another winger, Bill Heaton, for the run-in. He went on to play for Cardiff and Ipswich and - moved to the role of centre-forward - scored 26 goals from 42 games in south Wales, earning an England 'B' cap in the process. He later managed in non-league and was a Sports teacher at Worcester College. He died in Worcester aged 69 in 1990

Gray, Steven
Centre-back
Born: *1981 Dublin, Ireland*
Playing career: *Leixlip United, Cherry Orchard, Verona, Southampton, Drogheda United, Derry City, Bohemians, Dandenong Thunder SC, Oakleigh Cannons FC, Melbourne Heart FC (2003-date)*

Gray can still be found on the football field, but in Australia these days. He featured at Reserve level for Southampton but never played for the first team despite making it on to the bench on three occasions.

Played for the Republic of Ireland at age group level. Gray has played for a succession of lower league clubs in Austria, Italy, his native Ireland and Australia and briefly held the role of player-manager Dandenong Thunder in Australia. A tough-tackling centre back, he has taken his UEFA coaching badges in preparation for when he finally hangs up his boots.

Gray, Stuart
Midfielder
Born: *1960 Withernsea*
Playing career: *Nottingham Forest, Bolton W, Barnsley, Aston Villa, Southampton. (1980-1994)*

One of an elite group of men to have served Southampton as both player and manager, Stuart Gray's time at Saints will be best remembered for his exploits in the dugout, rather than on the pitch. He played only 20 times at The Dell before injury curtailed a promising playing career He made over 300 appearances for four different clubs his Saints second coming. He began it as community officer, tasked with the general day-to-day running of the club, but then worked his way through the corridors of power to become first team coach under first Dave Jones and the Glenn Hoddle. When the latter left for Spurs, Saints needed a new manager and Gray - on a caretaker basis at least - was their man. Despite two draws and five defeats in his first seven games at the end of the 2000/01 season, chairman Rupert Lowe wanted continuity and minimum upheaval so - despite a young David Moyes interest in the job - Gray and his assistant Dennis Rofe were made permanent. Eight games into the first St Mary's season, however, both men were sacked with Gordon Strachan appointed as replacement. Gray later linked up with Hoddle to work at Wolves, and with former Saints boss Dave Jones at Hillsborough. Also served Portsmouth as caretaker manager in four different stints.

"DID YOU KNOW?"

"It used to be normal for players and fans to travel to home games at the Dell on the bus together."

Gray, William

Left-half
Born: *1882 Inverness, Scotland* **Died:** *1916*
Playing career: *Inverness Thistle, Partick Thistle, Southampton (1900-1909)*

After making his name in his native Scotland, William Gray moved north of the border to bring his accomplished passing game to Southampton. He soon made the left-half position his own, and had missed only three Southern League games in two seasons when catastrophe struck. Suspended *sine die* along with Alex Glen and Rob McLean for drunken misconduct, he was released from his contract and returned to Scotland with Partick Thistle. Moving back to his native Inverness, he combined a job on the railways with playing for the town's football club, Caledonian Thistle. Enlisted in the 4th Battalion Highlanders, he was wounded in action during WW1. Died of his injuries and is buried at Abbeville, France

Grayer, Frank

Full-back
Born: *1890 Brighton, Sussex*
Died: *1961*
Playing career: *St Mary's Athletic (Southampton), Southampton, Liverpool (1908-1915)*

Despite having all the ingredients for a top quality right-back - solid, reliable and a good turn of pace - local lad Grayer spent his early years at The Dell paying in the reserves until, tow day before he turned 21, he got his first team chance. It would be the first of seven games for the senior Saints side across four years, with his path to stardom often blocked by Jack Eastham, Dan Gordon and occasionally the versatile John Robertson. Surplus to requirements, Grayer attracted the attention of many scouts until First Division Liverpool but the bullet and paid £100 to take him to Anfield. There again, he found opportunities hard to come by playing only once in three years on Merseyside. He joined the Royal Garrison Artillery and was so badly wounded at Ypres that his football career was over. He found employment with a furniture company *Shepherd & Hedger* where he continued to work until retiring in 1955.

Green, George

Full-back
Born: *1891 Dartford* **Died:** *1958*
Playing career: *Southampton (1914-1919)*

The outstanding full-back of his day, George Green was plucked from Kent League Northfleet and arrived at Southampton after a three-way battle for his services between Saints, Brighton and Fulham. Neat in style and quick both in body and mind, he would have made more of his career if not for the outbreak of War and his own discretion - with Green banned *sine die* for drunken antics whilst in Swansea for an away game. He only played 19 games for the Saints, a criminally low number for a player whose talent was so well regarded. His ban lifted on request, Green played war-time football for Millwall and guested for the Saints during the conflict. He later rejoined Northfleet and worked as a maintenance manager in later life.

Greenlees, Donald

Half-back
Born: *1875 Glasgow* **Died:** *1955*
Career: *St Mirren, Southampton (1899-1900)*

Considered Scotland's finest exponent of full-back play, Greenlees moved to Southern League Southampton - at the time reigning champions - in May 1899. Greenlees was never able to command a regular place in the Saints defence, playing third fiddle to compatriots Sam Meston, Peter Meechan and Bob Petrie king only eight appearances in total. Played once for the Scottish League Rep. side in 1904 and returned to his native homeland after one season on the south coast. Played for St Mirren for a time before returning to Southampton where he played locally while working on the Docks for the infamous *White Star Line* of Titanic fame. After retirement he moved to Atherton to become a blacksmith.

"DID YOU KNOW?"

"The record fee paid by Saints was £20 million to bring Danny Ings in from Liverpool in 2018."

Gregory, John

Full-back
Born: *1925 Southampton* **Died:** *2008*
Playing career: *Southampton, Leyton Orient, Bournemouth & Boscombe Athletic (1944-1963)*

John "Jack" Gregory captained the 1952 Combination Cup winning second string to victory but soon got his first team chance and went on to play 68 times for Saints, even captaining the senior side on three occasions. Finished in the non league game but continued to live in Southampton. He regularly turned out for the ex-Saints and became a regular at the Woolston & District Bowls Club until Alzheimer's took hold.

Griffit, Leandre

Winger
Born: *1984 Maubeuge, France*
Playing career: *Southampton, Leeds United, Rotherham United, Elfsborg, Norrkoping, Crystal Palace, Centre, Columbus Crew (2002-2016)*

Given his debut under Gordon Strachan, the unknown Frenchman scored a stunning goal against Blackburn on his Southampton bow despite only coming on as a sub. Described as a "great talent with good skill and ability", Griffit would start only twice before Strachan left and Paul Sturrock took over.

Griffit never fully lived up to his blistering potential. In the end, he played only seven times for Southampton and featured for ten other clubs before retirement in 2016. Griffit has since become a qualified UEFA coach having gained his 'A' licence, and is a player consultant for both the MLS and the Premier League. You can follow him on Twitter here: *https://twitter.com/elgdix*

Griggs, Philip

Inside right
Born: *1918 Southampton*
Died: *1980*
Playing career: *Sholing Boys, Spring Albion, Southampton (1937-1939)*

A member of the 1932 Southampton Schools side to reach the national final, Phil Griggs is one of those men to be a "one game wonder" for the Saints. Played for an FA Amateur XI in 1939, and then signed pro before a Saints debut against Plymouth in May the same year - the last game of the final pre-War campaign. Still only 27, like so many of his contemporaries he served on the Western Front in WW2 but lost a leg and ended any chance he had of resuming his playing career.

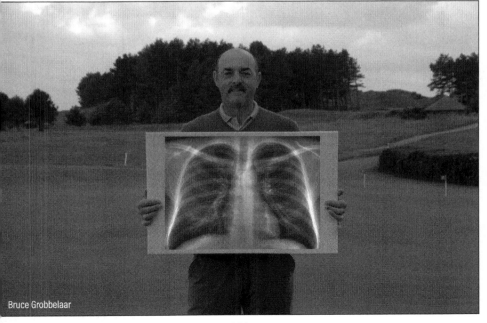

Bruce Grobbelaar

103

Grobbelaar, Bruce

Goalkeeper
Born: *1957 Durban, South Africa*
Playing career: *Crewe Alexandra, Liverpool, Stoke City, Southampton, Plymouth Argyle, Oxford United, Sheffield Wednesday, Oldham Athletic, Chesham United, Bury, Lincoln City, Northwich Victoria, Glasshoughton Welfare (1976-2007)*

A colourful and eccentric custodian, Bruce Grobbelaar was known for his plethora of idiosyncrasies. Having played for three clubs in his native South Africa and capped for Rhodesia, he arrived in England - via Fourth Division Crewe - scoring a penalty in his last game before going across the pond to Vancouver in the NASL. Then came the move which saw him rise to prominence as he signed for First Division Liverpool, initially as deputy to Ray Clemence. He would go on to win everything it was possible to win at Anfield, including six First Division titles, three FA Cups and the European Cup during Liverpool's decade of dominance in the 1980s. Eccentric, confident, agile and flamboyant, he instantly became a cult hero who played with a swagger that bordered on arrogance. Whilst his move Southampton was seen as a step down, he continued to delight and despair in equal measure, vying for the goalkeeping gloves with Dave Beasant. Grobbelar would go on to be declared bankrupt and he was cleared of match fixing after a jury failed to reach a verdict. He sued the Sun but was awarded £1 and was forced to pay £500,000 on the grounds of dishonesty, going on to a whistle stop tour of England's lower leagues. He returned to Africa and coached Supersport - the South African club founded by "Mr Southampton" Terry Paine. Capped 32 times by Zimbabwe and still fondly remembered to this day.

Groves, Perry

Left winger
Born: *1965 Bow, London*
Playing career: *Colchester United, Arsenal, Southampton. (1981-1994).*

Twice won the League at Arsenal after George Graham took him to Highbury from Colchester for £75,000. Groves dazzled with his wing play and movement.

The "ginger wizard" played 155 times for the Gunners and winning the League Cup in addition to the two championship wins. He signed for Southampton as an injury prone 27 year old, with Alan Shearer money to burn and manager Ian Branfoot sceptical. All for a handful of appearances - eight in total but only starting twice - before his ongoing Achilles problem ended his career. Still idolised at Arsenal, Groves has since worked as a TV and radio pundit and has also gained employment in some bizarre, mundane jobs. Having worked for Franny Lee's company designing playground markings for junior schools, he moved into coaching at that level.

Gueran, Sid

Inside-right
Born: *1916 Grays, Essex* **Died:** *1944*
Playing career: *Arsenal, Margate, Southampton (loan) , Exeter City (1935-1938)*

Manager Tom Parker used his connections to sign the "thoughtful and constructive" inside-forward Gueran - from Margate via Arsenal. Gueran spent most of his Saints career in the second string but made his debut as stand in for Wilf Mayer on the final day of the 1936-37 season. Made two further showings before Arthur Holt became established at inside right. He was soon on his way to Third South Exeter, but failed to break through again and had a stint in non league in his native Kent. A sapper in the iconic Royal Engineers, Gueran fell in the Allies ill-fated attempt to take the bridge at Arnhem in September 1944. Buried at Nijmegen, Netherlands.

Gurr, Gerald

Goalkeeper
Born: *1946 Brighton*
Playing career: *Arsenal, QPR, Guilford City, Southampton, Aldershot Town (1962-1972)*

From stopping shots to strumming strings, Gerald Gurr certainly didn't stop taking centre stage even after he finished his football career. Sandwiched between a gym and a hairdressers, Gurr - together with his two Saints team-mate Dave Paton and Mick Judd - strutted their post-match stuff in Shirley's After8 nightclub as four piece band The Sunsets.

Irish musician Tony Cattoire completed the charismatic quartet. Gurr, musically gifted since he was eight, was lead guitarist with Messrs Paton and Judd as drummer and vocalist respectively. He played 49 games for Saints before being forced to retire through injury, but - his footballing days behind him - continued to go from strength to strength with the band. The Sunsets would tour the world, performing in Thailand, Sydney, Los Angeles, Paris, London and Moscow to name but six, with his days as a footballer never getting in the way of his other life passion. In later life, Gurr would marry Liane (or Lee-Anne), a professional singer, and became her musical director and manager.

Gurry, Jack

Half-back/Inside-forward
Born: *1907 Barking* **Died:** *1983*
Playing career: *West Ham United , Barking, Leicester City , Southampton, Chester (1929-1937)*
A jack of all trades, Gurry was a versatile player capable of filling in anywhere when required. His ten games for Southampton demonstrated this and owed much to his adaptability, coming as they did in five different positions. A half-back by trade, he failed to make the grade at West Ham before his job in the hosiery industry took him to the Midlands and a crack at the First Division with Leicester City. He played seven times in five seasons before leaving the relegated club to join new divisional rivals Saints. Played nine league games and one in the Cup before leaving for Third Division Chester after one season at The Dell. He later returned to the Leicester area to continue in his original trade.

Hackett, Reginald

Half-back
Born: *1891 Cradley Heath* **Died:** *1967*
Playing career: *Cradley Heath St. Lukes, Blackheath Town, Southampton (1919-1920)*
Reg Hackett was an engineer in a munitions factory when he came to the attentions of Southampton. Turning out for Blackheath Town of the Birmingham League, Hackett and team-mate Fred Foxall were scouted and signed by Saints Midlands-based trainer Jimmy McIntyre.

Messrs Foxall and Hackett arrived at The Dell in time for the first post-war season of 2019-20 ahead of the club's last ever Southern League campaign. Capped twice by England at junior level, Hackett instantly made the left-half position his own for the remainder of the season but when he picked up an injury Bill Turner replaced him and Hackett's League career was over. He returned to his native Birmingham and drifted around the west Midlands, playing at non league level whilst resuming his former trade as a factory worker.

Haddleton, Arthur

Centre-forward
Born: *1910 Chester-le-Street* **Died:** *1971*
Playing career: *Southampton, Fulham, Swindon Town, Walsall, Pirelli General, West Hartlepool Belle Vue Congs, Horden Athletic, Easington Colliery WelfarHorden Colliery Welfare (1930-1935)*
From the moment this centre-forward plundered 12 goals in 17 games at Reserve level for Saints, Arthur Haddleton was marked out as a first team star in the making. His moment came late in the 1930-31 season when - with Will Haines injured - he deputised at centre forward. Haddleton went on to establish a record that would stand for more than three decades as he scored in seven consecutive matches - a feat later smashed by Ron Davies in 1966. But the goals soon dried up as am emerging Ted Brake began to rise to prominence. Football League new boys Fulham, knowing the full extent of cash-strapped Saints financial issues, made the most of it. Haddleton, along with team-mates Bill Fraser and Arthur Jepson, moved to Craven Cottage and would go on to play for Swindon and Walsall in the Football League. A broken leg during his debut season with the latter saw his career come to an untimely end as a man who promised plenty but delivered little. Haddleton worked for *Pirelli General* cable works in Eastleigh - turning out for their works team - and served in the RAF during the War. This would end in tragedy for Haddleton when his wife and new born son were killed by the *Luftwaffe* when they visited his mother-in-law in Swaythling.

Hadley, George
Half-back
Born: *1889 Darlaston, Staffordshire* **Died:** *1954*
Playing career: *Southampton, Aston Villa, Coventry City (1913-1922)*

A press-tool setter with a lock manufacturer, George Hadley had been playing for Willenhall Swifts where Southampton came calling. Ever looking to better himself. Hadley headed south to stake his claim in a struggling Southampton outfit. A "stocky, versatile half back also capable of playing up front", Hadley was soon a regular in the team and became a fans favourite. He became a virtual ever present, only missing five games in two seasons but - by the end of the campaign - England was at war and "normal" football was suspended. Played once as a guest for Southampton during the conflict, before joining Aston Villa in 1919. He only made four appearances for the Second City side before signing for second tier Coventry. A broken collarbone put an end to his pro career and he died in 1954.

Hadley, Harry
Wing-half
Born: *1877 Barrow-in-Furness* **Died:** *1942*
Playing career: *Colley Gate United, Halesowen, West Bromwich Albion, Aston Villa, Nottingham Forest, Southampton, Croydon Common, Halesowen, Merthyr Town (1895-1919)*

Harry Hadley was an energetic if "methodical" wing-half, capped once by England against Ireland in 1903. He had won the Second Division title with West Brom and played eleven times for Midlands rivals Villa by the time he joined Southern League Southampton for £250 in 1907. He was a steady regular during Saints mid-table Southern League Division One finish during his debut season, tasked with "looking after" the forwards with his link up play. Hadley went on to play at non league level for Croydon Common, Halesowen and Merthyr Town before becoming a manager, primarily in Wales, with Aberdare Athletic, Bangor and his last club - Merthyr Town - on three separate occasions. He also had a brief five month spell in charge of Second Division Chesterfield.

Haines, Wyndham
Centre-forward
Born: *1900 Warminster* **Died:** *1974*
Playing career: *Frome Town, Portsmouth, Southampton, Weymouth (1922-1938)*

It takes some doing to be universally loved by fans of both Portsmouth and Southampton. But that was Willie Haines. He plundered an impressive 119 goals in 164 games at Fratton Park and a further 47 in 70 when he moved to The Dell, firmly securing his place in the hearts of fans of the two fierce south coast rivals - an endearment that still lasts to this day. Despite being plagued by injuries during his time at Southampton, Haines still managed to finish as top scorer in two of his four seasons at the club. Nicknamed the "farmer's boy", fans of both clubs would voice their approval of Haines with a rendition of the popular refrain "To be a Farmer's Boy." He eventually lost his place to a young Ted Drake and left Saints for a brief spell at Weymouth before retiring. Having hung up his boots, he took over a pub in Frome, remaining landlord until 1949. He later ran a paper shop in Havant.

Hajto, Tomasz
Defender
Born: *1972 Poland*
Playing career: *Schalke, FC Nurnberg, Southampton, Derby County, (1990-2011)*

Capped 62 times by his country having captained Poland and played in the World Cup of 2002, Tomasz Hajto came to Saints in search of first team football. Hajto started well for Saints under Harry Redknapp in the Championship. After 20 appearances and with Redknapp replaced by George Burley, Hajto's contract was cancelled and he was allowed to join Derby. He soon return to football in his native homeland however, without having added to his international tally of caps. Retired in 2010. Hajto had a brush with the law in 2008 when he was handed a suspended two-year jail sentence for killing a pedestrian whilst speeding at a crossing in Lodz, Poland. He pleaded guilty to the manslaughter charge but did not serve any time behind bars allowing him to move into management.

1,000 professional UK-based players on matters including negotiating transfers, organising sponsors and corporate events, media training and legal advice. https://basesoccer.com/

Hall, Harry

Inside right
Born: 1889 *Fleckney*
Playing career: *Market Harborough Town, Southampton (1914-1915)*

A former runner in the hosiery trade, Harry Hall was playing for Market Harborough when he and team mate George Crick were whisked away - surprisingly so - to the south coast and the Dell. Crick would fare better than Hall, whom saw only 90 minutes of first team action when he replaced the injured Arthur Dominy at centre-forward in a game against Bristol Rovers in March 1915. Crick played at centre-half. The two men played regular second string football until "official" action ceased upon the outbreak of War. He briefly played for th Santa in wartime, and went to war but it is not known what happened to him after that.

Hall, Marcus

Defender
Born: 1976 *Coventry*
Playing career: *Notts Forest, Southampton, Stoke City, Coventry City, Northampton T (1992-2011)*

Marcus Hall had 17 years as a professional, during which time he played for five different clubs - Coventry, Nottingham Forest, Stoke City, Coventry City and Northampton - and captained England at U21 level (eight caps, two goals). Most associated with his days in the sky blue of Coventry, Hall rose through the ranks of his hometown team, his first two games at Highfield Road coming in the Premier League against Spurs and Man Utd respectively. Played one game for Forest before moving south to St Mary's, where he failed to get a game any any level at the club. He went on to Stoke before returning to Coventry for a second stint where he racked up another 150 games and earned a testimonial. Had a final swansong at Northampton before yet again moving back to Coventry, this time as a coach.

Hall, Fitz

Defender/Striker
Born: 1980 *Leytonstone*
Playing career: *West Ham, Barnet, Oldham Ath, Southampton, Crystal Palace, Wigan Athletic, QPR, Newcastle United, Watford (1997-2014)*

Fitz Hall has stood out from many of his contemporaries for more than just his nickname. "One Size" (obvious enough if you think about it), a tall 6ft 6 centre-back, caught the eye of Oldham's Iain Dowie where he made a breakthrough before his move to the Premier League and Saints in 2003-04. Hall would fail to become a first team regular at St Mary's but still went to enjoy a career of some renown elsewhere in the top flight. He appeared in a Bruce Willis sci-fi film - *The Fifth Element* - a major hit at the box office in the US, aged 16. Hall became a football consultant and director for player development group "Base Soccer Agency" The agency - used by players such as Kyle Walker, Harry Kane and James Ward - Prowse - is a highly reputable and award winning company, providing a service for over

Hall, Richard

Defender
Born: *1972 Ipswich*
Playing career: *Ipswich Town, Scunthorpe United, Southampton, West Ham United (1987-1999)*

Chris Nicholl handed on to Ian Branfoot a teenage centre-back of some repute plundered from Coventry City. Hall had signed for Nicholl's side for a paltry £200,000 and soon proved his worth. Hall would quickly establish himself in a Saints side seemingly forever battling Premiership survival. After five seasons at The Dell, Hall had played over 150 games when yet another manager - this time Dave Merrington - was sacked. Wheeler dealer Harry Redknapp, then manager at West Ham, took Hall to east London for a fee fixed by a tribunal at £1.4m. Seven games latter, Hall was forced to quit at the age of 27 after suffering a foot injury. In his post-playing days. Hall would go on to join former side Ipswich as a coach before joining Colchester as professional development coach and then assistant boss. He was appointed as caretaker manager of the "U's" for one game in 2015 following the dismissal of Tony Humes. Later became Head of Academy at the Essex side.

Hamer, David

Full-back
Born: *1866 Rhayader, Wales* **Died:** *1948*
Playing career: *Royal Engineers Aldershot, Southampton St. Mary's, Cowes (1891-1898)*

David "Taffy" Hamer won the Hampshire Senior Cup with the Royal Engineers side twice in succession before setting sail for Southampton St Mary's. Leaving the Armed Forces, he arrived at Southampton but only played once in a Hampshire Cup tie before crossing the Solent to play for Cowes. He soon returned to Saints in time for the club's inaugural Southern League campaign but never nailed down a regular place in the team, going on to play only 12 times in the next three seasons including in a 14-0 FA Cup thumping of Newport - still to this day, Southampton's biggest ever competitive victory. Later emigrated to the USA where he worked as a tunnel miner. He returned home in 1920 to live on Merseyside and run a fish and chip shop.

Hamill, Rory

Forward
Born: *1976 Coleraine, Northern Ireland*
Playing career: *Southampton, Fulham, Glentoran, Coleraine, Ballymena United (1992-2014)*

Hamill had been capped at youth level for his country Northern Ireland when he arrived at Premier League Southampton in 1993 as a trainee. He never played for the first team and left to make the step down to third tier Fulham less than a year later. Having played over 50 games for the Cottagers, he moved back home to play for clubs in the League of Ireland and to be capped for Northern Ireland - under former Saints manager Lawrie McMenemy - in a 1999 friendly with Canada. Won the League and Cup double with Glentoran in 1998 and scored in the UEFA Cup in 2001. Later banned for a year after traces of a banned substance were found following a routine drug test. Now 43, Hamill works as a coach at his hometown team of Coleraine.

Hamilton, Henry

Centre-forward
Born: *1887 South Shields*
Died: *1938*
Playing career: *Craghead United, Sheffield Wednesday, Huddersfield Town, Southampton, Belfast Celtic, South Shields (1908-1914)*

The boat building apprentice's prolific form at Huddersfield - 13 goals in 19 league and cup games - persuaded the new Southampton manager George Swift to make Hamilton one of his first purchases.

He instantly became a first team fixture, and even top scored during that first season with nine goals - an indication, perhaps, of Southampton's struggles. That would be as good as it got, though, as Hamilton was suspended along with team-mate Andrew Gibson for a drunken and fatal breach of club discipline, putting him on the transfer list as a move away beckoned. A succession of players took over from Hamilton at centre-forward, all with varying degrees of success, and he went on to play for Belfast Celtic and South Shields before becoming a labourer.

Hamilton, Ian
Midfielder
Born: *1967 Stevenage*
Playing career: *Southampton, Cambridge United, Scunthorpe United, West Bromwich Albion, Sheffield United, Grimsby Town, Notts County, Lincoln City, Woking (1982-2003)*

Stevenage born Hamilton never the senior side. He went on to make his name at Scunny and West Brom where he made nearly 300 appearances. After hanging up his boots in 2003, he worked as an IT business development manager.

Hammond, Dean
Midfielder
Born: *1983 Hastings*
Playing career: *Brighton, Aldershot Town, Leyton Orient, Colchester United, Southampton, Leicester City, Sheffield United (1998-2016)*

Sussex born and bred, Dean Hammond played over 100 games at St Mary's but, in truth, his time at Saints was nothing more than the filling is a Seagulls sandwich. Brighton's penchant to be a "selling" club saw Hammond pitch up at newly relegated Saints bemoaning Brighton's "lack of ambition". Under Alan Pardew and his former Albion coach Dean Wilkins, Hammond instantly became a key cog in midfield, with his hassling, harrying style, coupled with his experience, eventually earning him the captain's armband. Led Saints out at Wembley as they won the Johnston's Paint Trophy in 2010 before they were promoted back to the second tier the following season, pipped to the title by no one other than... Brighton.

With Southampton now in the Premier League again, Hammond returned to his old stamping ground and attempted to win over the Falmer faithful he had previously left incensed. Now retired, Hammond remained in football and works at former club Leicester City's academy setup.

Handley, George
Winger
Born: *1886 Totley, Sheffield*
Died: *1952*
Playing career: *Hallam, Chesterfield Town, Bradford City, Southampton, Goole Town, Barrow, Sheffield United (1905-1922)*

George Handley had two stints in the Football League with Chesterfield and Bradford before new Southampton manager George Swift made him one of his first signings. Handley's stay would only be a short one, though, playing 24 times at outside left . He was considered to be one of the manager's better buys but would depart The Dell at the end of Handley's only season on the south coast. The lure of a player/management role - albeit only at non league Goole Town - was too good for him to turn down. In a ground hopping end to a nomadic career, Handley coached in Switzerland and served with the Royal Flying Corps in the war. Died in 1952.

Harding, Dan
Defender
Born: *1983 Gloucester*
Playing career: *Brighton & Hove Albion, Leeds United, Ipswich Town, Southend United (loan), Reading (loan), Southampton, Nottingham Forest, Millwall (loan), Eastleigh (1999-2015)*

Harding's career had notable similarities with that of his team-mate Dean Hammond (above). Both played together at their first club, Brighton, later linking up with Alan Pardew at League One Saints in a bid to return Southampton to the second tier. The pair played at Wembley in that 2010 final, and are similar in style with an energetic and combative approach to the game. Instantly recognisable by his blond, flowing locks, Harding had played for Leeds and Ipswich when he arrived at Saints as a stylish, even swashbuckling, defender.

Dan Harding

As Saints stormed to League One promotion in Harding's second full season, he was one of five members of the Saints side to be named in the PFA Team of the Year - a record for any one club. Played four times for England at Under 21 level and also turned out for Nottingham Forest, Millwall, Eastleigh and Brighton based Whitehawk, whom he also served as caretaker player/manager in 2017.
https://twitter.com/danharding03

Harkus, George
Half-back
Born: *1898 Newcastle upon Tyne*   **Died:** *1950*
Playing career: *Nuns Moor, Aston Villa,Southampton,Olympique Lyonnais ,New Milton Town,Southampton (1921-1934)*
Newcastle born centre half Harkus turned professional in 1922 but, where his opportunities at Villa Park were limited, his time at Southampton proved an outstanding success. He turned out to be worth every penny of his £250 fee, featuring anywhere across the backline over seven seasons and more than 250 games. A captain, a mentor to the younger players and not only a crowd pleaser but a quality footballer too, he was a man of

"dynamic personality" he came close to the international recognition he craved when he toured Canada with an FA Select XI in 1926. He finished his career as player/coach of Southport and was later awarded and MBE for his service in the RAF during the War. Later serving Southampton again as a board member - after a brief two game stint back at the club, he also worked for the RAF (on the ground this time) at Andover before his sudden death at the age of 52.

Harris, George
Inside-left
Born: *1881 Rocester*
Died: *1947*
Playing career: *Uttoxeter Town, Stoke, Reading,Southampton, Tutbury Town (1900-1908)*
In April 1905, Harris was one of massive influx of nine new players to arrive at The Dell as the club bid for their seventh Southern League title in nine years. In and out of the side during that first season, Harris retired out the blue in 1907 aged only 26 having become first choice up front. He later became landlord of the *Leopard Inn* in Burton upon Trent and then turned out for his local non league team almost a decade after officially hanging up his boots.

Harris, Jimmy
Outside-forward
Born: *1907 Tunbridge Wells*
Died: *1974*
Playing career: *Folkestone, West Ham United, Southampton (1929-1933)*
Started out at top flight West Ham where Jimmy Harris played a handful of games before his move to join lower division Saints in time for the 1932-33 season. With regular outside left incumbent Jimmy Arnold away on cricketing duties with Hampshire, Harris filled the position for two games until Arnold was ready to resume his football career. That would be the zenith of his Southampton days, with the rest of his time on the south coast spent in the Reserve team where he would remain a regular over the next few months. Released come May, Harris returned to his native Kent where he worked at the Paper Mills in Aylesford and turned out for their works team. Died aged 67.

Harrison, Bernard

Outside-right
Born: *1934 Worcester* **Died:** *2006*
Playing career: *Portsmouth, Crystal Palace, Southampton, Exeter City (1952-1968)*

Bernard Harrison holds au unique place in the annals of both Hampshire County Cricket Club and Southampton FC - winning the County Championship as a cricketer with the former and helping the latter to promotion into the Second Division in the 1959-60 season. Harrison would only play three games for Saints before he moved down to Devon to try his luck at fourth tier Exeter City. Later returned 'home' to become a maths teacher and sports coach at Farleigh School in Andover.

Harrison, Fred

Centre-forward
Born: *1880 Winchester*
Died: *1969*
Playing career: *Fitzhugh Rovers, Bitterne Guild, Southampton, Fulham, West Ham United, Bristol City (1900-1914)*

Southampton stumbled upon this "fast goal getter with an accurate shot" when Joe Turner recommended him to the club's board after watching him in a local game on Southampton Common. "Buzzy" Harrison spent most of his early days at The Dell in the second string, but once he made the centre-forward berth his own, he could not stop scoring. Harrison plundered 16 goals in nine games - including two five-goal hauls - and then 27 in 32 games as Saints stormed to a second successive Southern League title in 1903-04 to top score for the second campaign in a row. As his goal grabbing exploits rose to prominence, an international trial with England beckoned but nothing came of it. In his seven years at Southampton, he played 249 times (156 goals) and led the scoring charts for four of those seasons. With a struggling Southampton side increasingly strapped for cash, Harrison was sold to Fulham and also later turned out for West Ham and Bristol City. Served in the First World War where he was gassed, later returning to the south coast to set up his own master plasterer business.

Harrison, Mark

Goalkeeper
Born: *1960 Derby*
Playing career: *Baroka, Southampton, Port Vale, Stoke City, Hellenic, Kettering Town, Stafford Rangers, Telford United (1977-1989)*

Harrison was a trainee on the books of Saints but never played for the first team before joining Fourth Division Port Vale where he became an ever present. He would later play for Vale's fierce rivals Stoke in two spells but left England after a succession of long term injury problems. Played in South Africa for Hellenic and also turned out for Kettering Town, Stafford Rangers and Telford. Harrison embarked on an extensive career in management and coaching after retirement as a player. Has coached the youth team at Bristol City, the goalkeepers at Everton, managed Stafford Rangers, coached at Barrow, managed the reserves at Oxford United and coached the Bangladesh national team.

Hartley, Abe

Right-back/Centre-forward
Born: *1872 Dumbarton, Scotland* **Died:** *1909*
Playing career: *Dumbarton, Everton, Liverpool, Southampton, Arsenal, Burnley (1892-1900)*

Five goals in eight games for Dumbarton in their spell as back-to-back Football League champions in Scotland encouraged Everton to tempt him south. He bagged 25 goals in his 50 appearances as a right-back turned centre forward, before crossing the city to sign for Liverpool. After just one season at Anfield, Hartley had the opportunity to earn more money by signing for Southampton. They were members of the Southern League and therefore free to pay more than their Football League counterparts and the investment paid off - with 41 goals from 43 games including one on his debut in the first game at the Dell - to help steer them to the title. He died in 1909, nine years after retiring from the game, at the age of only 37. He had taken up employment with the London and South West Railway but collapsed and died outside their offices. During his playing days, it was claimed that he used to put a rolled-up cigarette behind his ear before kick off and smoke it at half time!

Hartshorne, Albert

Left-back
Born: *1880 Darlaston* **Died:** *1915*
Playing career: *Moxley White Star, Wolverhampton Wanderers, Burslem Port Vale, Stoke, Southampton, Northampton Town (1900-1907)*

Hartshorne arrived at The Dell, quickly becoming both a regular and a favourite due to his combative, all action style. After a season as Southern League runners up and a run to the FA Cup's last eight (1905/06) - with Hartshorne playing 25 times as Saints regular left - back - he upped sticks and left for relegation bound Northampton. Having become a tool maker in his post playing days, Hartshorne linked up with the Staffordshire Regiment at the outbreak of WW1. Died in action during the conflict near Boulogne.

Harwood, Lee

Central Defender
Born: *1960 Perivale*
Playing career: *Southampton, Wimbledon, Leatherhead, Port Vale, Leatherhead (1976-1981)*

Harwood started out at Southampton, turning pro at 18 and playing in the reserves. Having not made the grade at The Dell, he was released by manager Lawrie McMenemy. With his knee battered by injury and after four operations, Harwood was forced to retire in 1984 and went into coaching at local club Hanwell and Greenwich Borough. Later worked in the property industry.

Hassli, Eric

Forward
Born: *1981 Sarreguemines, France*
Playing career: *Sarreguemines FC, Metz, Southampton, Neuchatel Xamax, Servette, FC St. Gallen, Valenciennes, Z urich, Vancouver Whitecaps FC, Toronto FC, FC Dallas (2000-2015)*

A French striker known for his physical strength and technical ability, Eric Hassli had five months on loan at Southampton in which he scored twice in eight games for the reserve side but made no appearances for the first team. The club decided against signing the little known forward and so he returned across the Channel to his native France. Also played in Switzerland, Canada and USA.

Hassli was capped three times at Under 21 level for France. Made his name whilst in Switzerland with St Gallen (26 goals in 47 games) and then Zurich (32 goals in 85 games) but drifted out of the game. Is believed to be living in America and coaching a youth side in Louisiana.

Haxton, Frederick

Left-half
Born: *1879 Southwark* **Died:** *1933*
Playing career: *Southampton (1899-1909)*

Haxton stepped on the first rung of the ladder with Saints feeder side Eastleigh Athletic, before leaving their launchpad to stake a claim at The Dell. Haxton was described as "hard as nails" but despite this endorsement he spent most of his time at Saints in the Reserves, winning the Hampshire Senior Cup in 1905. Over a season and a half at the Dell, he eventually deputised in the first team for the injured Bert Houlker, going to play three times in the Southern League. After which, he had a brief stint at newly relegated Wolves but again failed to make the grade, returning south for another crack with Eastleigh Athletic - his third at that club. Moved to Manchester in 1909 to work as a railway carriage fitter in the area. Died in 1933.

Hayes, Austin

Left winger
Born: *1958 Hammersmith* **Died:** *1986*
Playing career: *Southampton, Millwall, Northampton Town. (1976-1984)*

Austin Hayes never looked back from the moment he scored twice on his Southampton debut in the Cup Winners Cup. Two years later he was capped by Republic of Ireland in a win over Denmark and then played for Saints at Wembley in the League Cup final - a 3-2 defeat to Nottingham Forest. With Keegan, Boyer and Charlie George et al for illustrious company at the Dell, his undoubted talent was never able to command a regular place in the side. Scored five times in 22 games for Saints before moving on to Millwall, Northampton and then Barnet before a brief stint in Sweden. Died at the tragically young age of 28 in 1986, only three weeks after being diagnosed with lung cancer.

Haynes, Harry

Wing-half/Full-back
Born: *1873 Walsall* **Died:** *1902*
Playing career: *Wolverhampton Wanderers, Small Heath, Southampton (1891-1900)*

Stable-fitter Haynes signed his contract with the Saints on Birmingham New Street station with a borrowed pen. Haynes was an ever present as Saints became the dominant force of the early Southern League era. In his four seasons at the club Haynes made more than 100 appearances before retiring having won three consecutive Southern Leagues. He went on to take over as landlord of the *Turks Head* pub and the *Edinburgh Castle Inn,* combing pulling pints with scouting talent for Southampton. Died in 1902 aged 29.

Hayter, Fred

Inside-left
Born: 1876 *Christchurch* **Died:** 1952
Playing career: *Southampton*

Plucked from parks football, page boy Domestic Hayter only played two Southern League games for Southampton but continued to play locally while working in the transport industry as a coach driver, chauffeur and on the railway. Worked on the board at Saints and donated 100 shillings towards a fund set up to help the survival of financially struggling Saints.

Heaney, Neil

Winger
Born: *1971 Middlesbrough*
Playing career: *Arsenal, Hartlepool United, Cambridge United, Southampton, Manchester City, Charlton Athletic, Bristol City, Darlington, Dundee United, Plymouth Argyle (1987-2002)*

After failing to break into the Arsenal first team in seven years in north London, Middlesbrough born Heaney became Alan Ball's third Southampton signing. Saints, as is their wont, were struggling but Heaney described his time on the south coast as the "happiest time of my career." A player with the pace and ability to change a game out of nothing, his tendency "to frustrate by running up blind alleys" meant he represented the archetypal mercurial winger, capable of delight and despair in equal measure. Earned six caps for England at U21 level but never got a senior call up. Played in the famous 6-3 win over Man United and went on to make 61 league appearances in his two and a bit seasons at The Dell. Later turned out for Charlton, Bristol City and Darlington in England also having a stint north of the border with Dundee United and Plymouth. After retiring, Heaney drifted out the game and became CEO of *Judicare* a company of solicitors which deals the legalities of buying and selling properties overseas.

899

Heaton, William

Winger
Born: *1918 Leeds*
Died: *1990*
Playing career: *Leeds United, Southampton, Rochdale, Witton Albion (1946-1951)*

Leeds born Heaton had carved out an impressive reputation with his hometown team, becoming known as the "wizard of the dodge" before the play named Bill Dodgin paid £7,000 to bring him to the south coast. Settling into a number 11 shirt that had been swapped between - remarkably - nine different men, his arrival co-incided with a run of seven wins and a draw as Saints surged to the summit of the second tier. But form fell off a cliff, the club finished mid table and that was that for Heaton at the Dell. Served in India and represented the FA and England at amateur level (seven caps), but never turned out for the full senior England side despite interest from selectors. Heaton was unwilling to move to the south coast and so he returned north to play in the Greater Manchester area. Having retired from the professional game, Heaton became a tradesman for a Leeds based roofing firm. Died in 1990.

Hebberd, Trevor

Midfielder
Born: *1958 Winchester*
Playing career: *Southampton, Bolton Wanderers, Leicester City, Oxford United, Derby County, Portsmouth, Chesterfield, Lincoln City. (1976-1994)*

Signed for Saints straight out of school having been spotted by scout Tom Parker playing in the Hampshire League. Known as "Smiler", Hebberd - nonchalant and "unhurried" - helped Saints into the top flight in his debut season before coming of age in 1978-79. He featured in more than half of their league games and was an ever present in the run to the League Cup final, setting up the winning goal for Terry Curran in the semi final. Hebberd describes missing out on selection for the Wembley showpiece against Nottingham Forest as the "biggest disappointment" of his life. In and out of the team following the arrival of Kevin Keegan, he would move on for Southampton to plough a nomadic furrow through the lower leagues.

Hebberd finally got his hands on some silverware in the unlikeliest of manners, winning the League Cup that eluded him in '79, this time with unfashionable Oxford - scoring in the final on the way to a Man of the Match award. He later worked in a steelworks warehouse in Leicester. Played almost 100 for Saints yet probably should have had more.

Hedley, George

Born: *1876 Middlesbrough* **Died:** *1942*
Career: *Sheffield United, Southampton (1903-1906)*

In an eventful career, Hedley played in four FA Cup finals for two different clubs - winning it with Sheffield United (twice, in 1899 and 1902, with the latter at Saints expense) and with Wolves, winning it again six years later - Hedley scored in both the semi and the final. He was also on the losing side in the Steel City a year before the second of those triumphs with the Blades. Not content with 'only' three FA Cup winners medals, during his time on the south coast with Saints he struck up a potent partnership with Fred Harrison. The pair plundered 42 goals between them in Hedley's debut season to help Saints to a second successive Southern League title. Instantly endeared himself to the Southampton faithful by starting as he would go on with a goal on his bow against the "nearest and dearest" from up the road at Pompey. Moved on to Wolves and went on to manage second tier Bristol City as well as being licensee of the *George and Dragon* pub in Bristol. Guested for Chesterfield during the War and later ran a boarding house in Wolverhampton. Capped once by England against Ireland.

The trophy cabinet

Henderson, Bill

Right-back
Born: *1878 West Lothian* **Died:** *1945*
Playing career: *Broxburn Athletic, Everton, Reading, Southampton, Reading, Clapton Orient, New Brompton (1896-1908)*

Henderson moved to Southampton - a club which had just just won four titles in five seasons - after spells at Everton and divisional rivals Reading. A capable defender he was often let down by his 'over zealousness' and the presence of the iconic amateur right-back CB Fry hardly helped Henderson's cause. Although Henderson only missed four league games in his only season at the club but returned to both former clubs Everton and Reading before playing for Clapton Orient and New Brompton. Later became a labourer.

Henderson, Bill

Outside-right
Born: *1899 Carlisle* **Died:** *1934*
Playing career: *Carlisle United, Arsenal, Luton Town, Southampton, Coventry City (1921-1930)*

The 'other' Bill Henderson was widely regarded as enigmatic puzzle with his play wildly veering between a "queer combination of brilliance and error", capable of a dazzling concoction of pace and trickery but also of a tendency to become careless on the ball and the failure to take the easier option of passing to a team-mate. His unconventional style made "Tishy" a fans favourite at The Dell, becoming an ever present at outside right as the Henderson-Rawlings-Dominy triangle propelled Saints to two FA Cup semi finals in three years. In his five years at the Dell, Henderson made 168 appearances scoring ten goals but creating many more. A broken arm ultimately ended his Southampton career and he moved to Coventry, spending a season there before returning to hometown team Carlisle. He stayed living in his native Carlisle after retirement, initially emptying meters for the council for its gas work, then collecting rents and later in the housing office. "Tishy" was so called after a racehorse of the day, a thoroughbred that had a similar running style to that of Henderson.

Henderson, Douglas

Half-back/Right-back
Born: *1913 Southampton*
Died: *2002*
Playing career: *Southampton, Bristol City, Park Avenue (1934-1940)*

Southampton born and bred, it always seemed to be Doug Henderson's destiny that he would have a crack at stardom for his hometown team. It was not until coach Bert Shelley spotted him playing for Park Avenue on Southampton Common that his destiny became reality. Joining as an amateur, he signed pro shortly afterwards and had to bide his time with Bill Adams ahead of him in the pecking order at full back. He got a run of games towards the end of his debut season but only made a handful of further appearances in League and Cup across the next few campaigns as cover to the ageing Arthur Bradford and Stan Woodhouse. Eventually taking over from Charlie Sillett, he briefly became first choice but always struggled for regular selection and moved on a free transfer to Bristol City. The outbreak of War put paid to that, and Henderson would join the Southampton Police during the conflict. He remained in the force until his retirement.

Hennigan, Michael

Central defender
Born: *1942 Thrybergh*
Playing career: *Sheffield Wednesday, Southampton, Brighton & Hove Albion, Durban United (1961-1965)*

Hennigan was the victim of Tony Knapp's unbroken, 103 game dominance at the heart of the Southampton defence. Finally given his chance through his team mate's injury, Hennigan and his Southampton side made history on the young defender's debut it being the first time Saints had travelled by air to an away game (on this occasion, at Newcastle). After only two further games, Hennigan moved up the coast to link up with Saints geographical - if not divisional - rivals with a stint at Brighton in the basement league. Played in South Africa with urban before retiring from the game to take up management. Served Blackpool as caretaker and had a brief spell in charge of the Malawi national team.

Higginbotham, Danny

Defender
Born: *1978 Manchester*
Playing career: *Manchester United, Royal Antwerp (loan), Derby County, Southampton, Stoke City, Sunderland, Stoke City, Nottingham Forest (loan), Ipswich Town (loan), Sheffield United, Chester, Altrincham (1994-2014)*

Manchester born Higginbotham started with 'United' and moved to Derby for £2 million in July 2000 but joined Saints following the Rams' relegation from the Premier League. Became a tough tackling regular as Saints reached the FA Cup final in 2003. After a succession of managers with Higginbotham outspoken about the running of the club, he joined divisional rivals Stoke and quickly cemented a place in Tony Pulis's Premier League bound Potters. Despite being born and raised in England, Higginbotham played three times for Gibraltar (by virtue of his maternal grandmother), including the tiny nation's first ever match as a full UEFA member. Since retirement, Higginbotham has worked in the media for *TalkSport*, *Five Live* and *Sky Sports*. His autobigraphical memoir "Higginbotham: Rise of the Underdog" (2015), tells the story of his rise to stardom.

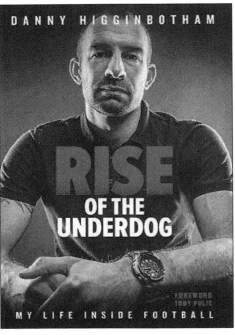

Hiley, Scott

Right-back
Born: *1968 Plymouth*
Playing career: *Exeter City, Birmingham City, Man City, Southampton, Portsmouth (1986-2009)*

Devonian defender, joined Saints initially on loan from Manchester City having played for Saints scout Terry Cooper at Exeter and Birmingham. Stayed eighteen months (32 games) before joining Pompey (three years, 75 games) but was then sold back to his first club by former manager of both south coast clubs Harry Redknapp - got all that? Hiley, dropped into non league football with Crawley and then Tiverton in his native Devon. Now runs a Bed & Breakfast with his wife Tina in the village of Clyst St Mary, just outside Exeter. He still attends Exeter City matches and features for the legends team .

Hill, Frank

Right-half
Born: *1906 Forfar, Scotland* **Died:** *1993*
Playing career: *Aberdeen, Arsenal, Blackpool, Southampton, Crewe Alexandra (1924-1948)*

After four seasons with Aberdeen, Hill joined Herbert Chapman's all-conquering Arsenal they would win three consecutive First Division titles together. He then captained the Seasiders of Blackpool to their first ever campaign in the top division before another coastal club, Southampton, came calling in an attempt to follow suit. Tom Parker recruited Hill as part of his drive to take Southampton into the First Division. Earning the nickname of "Tiger", Hill was made captain of Saints and he hardly missed a game. Injuries eventually took their toll and Hill would fall out with the Southampton board amid tensions over his future ambitions - unbeknownst to his employers, he had covertly applied for several managerial jobs whilst still registered as a player. Served in India during the War, later becoming player/manager of Crewe and also taking charge of Burnley, Preston, Notts County and Charlton in his managerial career, but never fulfilled his ambition of becoming Southampton manager. Played three times for Scotland and later became the owner of a fish and chip shop in California.

Hill, Leonard

Goalkeeper
Born: *1899 Islington* **Died:** *1979*
Playing career: *Cranley Rovers, Southend United, QPR, Southampton, Rochdale, Lincoln (1919-1929)*

After seeing out his military service during the Great War, Hill - despite suffering a double skull fracture during the conflict - still had a successful career as a player, starting out at QPR. In 1925, he joined Second Division Saints as cover for regular keeper Tom Allen. Hill would begin his debut season as the club's first choice, but Allen then agreed terms and reclaimed his place with Hill bumped down the food chain. Played in two FA Cup games when Allen was injured but left for Rochdale at the end of his only season at The Dell, also going on to Lincoln City and non league Grays. Having hung up his gloves, Hill became a cricket coach in Watford and also had a spell as manager of a multi sport club in the Netherlands.

Hinton, John

Inside-forward
Born: 1892 *Southampton* **Died:** *1955*
Playing career: *Southampton, RAF Farnborough, Thornycrofts, Exeter City, (1912-1922)*

Southampton born joiner Hinton was making his name in the backwaters of the Hampshire League when he was spotted by Saints and invited for a trial. Having plundered a hat-trick in a Reserves game, Hinton seemed like the answer to Saints scoring problems but would only play twice at first team level as cover for the injured Fred Jones in the closing months of the 1914-15 season. Despite being registered as a Southampton player for three full seasons, those two games would be as good as it got for Hinton, and he joined the RAF with the professional game halted amid the outbreak of war. Played for the Forces team and moved back to the area having been demobbed in 1919, to play for Thorneycrofts (the club known today as Sholing). Captained them in the FA Cup first round at Fratton Park as they took the relative might of Burnley to a replay. Hinton later played for Barnstaple Town and Exeter City before retiring to work in the building trade.

Hirst, David

Striker
Born: *1967 Barnsley*
Playing career: *Barnsley, Sheffield Wednesday, Southampton (1985-1999)*

Yorkshire born and bred, Hirst was an integral part of Sheffield Wednesday's League Cup winning side in 1991, top scoring to fire Wednesday into the top flight and ultimately, Europe. England recognition swiftly followed, as Hirst would go on to play three times for his country and score in a friendly against New Zealand in tandem with another future Saint, Alan Shearer. Eyebrows were raised when Dave Jones paid £2m for Hirst, now 30 something. But despite his advancing years, Hirst was an ever present in the 1997-98 season, scoring on his debut. Injured during an innocuous training jog, Hirst would only make two further brief substitute appearances before being forced to retire on medical grounds. A strong, agile and pacy striker, he would return to his native Yorkshire, setting up his own business, booking celebrities for corporate events. He continues to work at Wednesday in matchday hospitality and is also involved in local radio.

Hoare, Joe

Full-back
Born: *1881 Southampton* **Died:** *1947*
Playing career: *Southampton, Liverpool, Southampton (1902-1912)*

Combining his town jobs of builder and joiner with a career in the amateur game, Southampton born Hoare was signed by Southern League champions Saints as cover for England's George Molyneux. but would depart for top flight Liverpool having played only four games in the 1902-03 season. His time at Anfield was similarly short lived and he returned south to The Dell for a second crack at the Saints. He went on to make three further league appearances before again falling out of favour. Hoare retired from the professional game at the end of that season to pull on his boots in the lower echelons of the Hampshire League. Played for Bitterne, Salisbury and Woolston, where he became the owner of a tobacco shop in later life.

Hobson, Gordon
Forward
Born: *1957 Sheffield*
Playing career: *Grimsby Town, Southampton, Lincoln City, Exeter City, Walsall. (1977-1992)*
Wary of the professional footballer's short lifespan at the top level of the game, Hobson began planning for his future whilst still playing. He began to invest in yachting, buying a fleet of boats to renovate, refurbish and then sell on. It was after he stopped playing, having turned out for Lincoln, Exeter and Walsall after a spell at Saints, that his ambitions really set sail. Settling in the Southampton area, Hobson set up his own business, Fairview Sailing, in Hamble. The business enables clients to buy or charter yachts and boats, as well as offering sea safety training, yacht handling courses and RYA-accredited workshops. Hobson serves as the company's director and manager, and - as of 2020 - Hobson has also been running another local firm, Fareham-based company Stow Away Storage. This firm allows boats users to keep their belongings and equipment dry whilst out on the water. I've started a yacht building business in my attic - sales are going through the roof! https://twitter.com/fairviewsailing

Hodgkinson, Albert
Outside-left
Born: *1884 Pembroke Dock, Wales*
Died: *1939*
Playing career: *Old Normanton, Hinckley Town, Derby County, Grimsby Town, Plymouth Argyle, Leicester Fosse, Bury, Southampton, Croydon Common, Southend, Ilkeston United (1902-1912)*
Bert Hodgkinson - a one cap wonder for Wales - arrived at Saints from division higher Bury, forming an established partnership with compatriot John Lewis and George Smith. Described as a "mercurial player, who would suddenly produce the sensational only to just as suddenly disappear from prominence", he also left the Southampton expecting the unexpected. Despite his unpredictability, he became a virtual ever present in his debut season for the Southern League Saints as the team reached the FA Cup semi finals.

Having left the Saints after two seasons, he dropped into non league with Croydon Common, Southend and Ilkeston. Hodgkinson played baseball at professional level, twice winning gold at the NBA (National Baseball Association) finals, later going on to become the owner of the Rose & Crown Inn near Derby. Died 1939.

Hodgkinson, John
Half-back
Born: *1871 Tunstall, Staffordshire* **Died:** *1944*
Playing career: *Southampton (1895-1898)*
Scouted and signed by Southern League Southampton, John Hodgkinson (no relation to Albert), aka "Ironside" due to his cropped locks (giving him a rather tough and daunting appearance) quickly staked his claim ahead of George Marshall at left-half. In his first full campaign at the club - Saints in those days played at The Antelope Ground - he captained the side to an unbeaten season as part of a defence that only conceded 18 goals in 20 games. It would be the first of six Southern league titles in the next eight years. He departed to divisional rivals New Brompton following the signing of Bob Petrie and later played at non league level in Lancashire and Derbyshire. Returning to his native Staffordshire, he worked in the pottery industry synonymous with the area, placing the pots and other wares inside the kiln for finishing.

Danny Hoekman

Hoekman, Danny
Midfielder. Left winger
Born: *1964 Nijmegen, Netherlands*
Playing career: *NEC Nijmegen, Roda JC, VVV Venlo, ADO Den Haag, Manchester City, Southampton (1983-1997)*

Talented winger Hoekman had been touted as the next big thing to step off his nation's rich conveyor belt of footballing talent. Seemingly on the verge of international recognition, Hoekman was playing for NC Roda when he was on the receiving end of a 'hefty' challenge from Utrecht goalkeeper Jan - Willem van Ede. His knee was so badly damaged that Hoekman was sidelined for 22 months by the tackle, but recovered sufficiently to play in the lower reaches of the *Eredivisie* and even had a brief stint in England with Man City. Quit playing in 1997 to become a coach in his native homeland, Sweden and France. He took van Ede to court and won damages for a fee of around 10m Euros. Had a trial at Saints in 1992 but never played for the club at any level.

Hogg, Jack
Half-back
Born: *1881 Sunderland*
Died: *1944*
Playing career: *Sunderland, Morpeth Harriers, Sheffield United, Southampton, West Stanley, Hartlepools United (1900-1909)*

A right-half turned centre back, Hogg had a brief Football League career upon joining Southampton where he earned a reputation as a "destructive" player rather than a "constructive" one. A reliable workhorse, he became a regular during his debut season, helping the Saints to finish runners up in the Southern League in a defensive triumvirate alongside England men Bert Lee and Kelly Houlker. A particularly horrid time in the FA Cup at the hands of eventual winners Sheffield Wednesday spelt the end of Hogg's days at the Dell, with John Robertson going on to become first choice. Released by the the club, he returned to his native North East to play at non league level whilst working in the colliery at Ashington. Later became the manager of Parsons Works engineering firm near Newcastle.

Hogg came from a talented football family, with both of his brothers - Bill, who won the title with Sunderland and three Scottish Cups with Rangers (being capped by England in the process), and Rob, who also played for Sunderland and Blackpool.

Hollands, Fred
Outside-left
Born: *1870 Poplar, London* **Died:** *1947*
Career: *Southampton St Mary's (1890-1896)*
Diminutive and quick, Hollands was one of nine new recruits shipped to Southampton ahead of their first ever season in competitive league football. Making his debut in their inaugural game alongside fellow new signings Charles Baker, Lachie Thomson and Alf Littlehaes, Hollands scored on his bow against Chatham and went to become an ever present featuring in every League and cup game in that 1894-95 season. He also scored twice in Southampton's biggest ever competitive win - a 14-0 FA Cup win over Newbury in 1894. But he then returned to former side and Saints divisional rivals Millwall Athletic and also played briefly for Fulham before becoming an electrical engineer.

Hollins, Arthur
Centre-forward
Born: 1888 *Wolverhampton* **Died:** *1960*
Playing career: *Wolverhampton Early Closers, Walsall, Wellington Town, Southampton (1914-1915)*
A tailor by trade, Hollins was snaffled up by Saints from the flirtatious advances of Wolves, and instantly repaid the south coast club's faith - going on to plunder seven goals in his first eleven Southern League games (including five goals in six days in the April of 1914 against Norwich and Millwall). Quick in both body and mind, Hollins was said to be "quick to see, and seize, any opportunity" but the rest of his days at The Dell were shrouded by injury and ill discipline. Hollins would later be suspended and dropped for misconduct - with his family business and personal life also affecting his time at Southampton. After a few more fleeting appearances, Hollins was released and served the Navy during WWI. He was awarded the Meritorious Service Medal.

Hollowbread, John

Goalkeeper
Born: *1934 Ponders End, Middlesex* **Died:** *2007*
Career: *Tottenham H, Southampton (1950-1966)*

Born in the shadow of the then mighty Spurs, John Hollowbread could never have imagined that he would get his chance for the north London giants. But get a chance he did, even if most of the time he played the role of understudy to Ted Ditchburn and Ron Reynolds. Stepping into the first team goal when required, he played once during Spurs double winning season of 1960-61, before Ted Bates signs him for Southampton for £3,000 in 1964. He played 30 consecutive games for "Saints" before sustaining a serious knee injury in a match against Coventry - becoming the first player in Southampton history to be subbed off. More pertinently, the injury ended his career after a total of 40 games on the south coast having become first choice. Hollowbread played for Mullard and was a coach at Hampshire League Netley, later running the *Manor House* Inn at Bursledon and then the *Sun Inn* pub in Romsey. Also worked as the manager of a golf club in the New Forest and moved to Spain where he and his wife were keen golfers. Died 2007.

JOHN HOLLOWBREAD

Testimonial Match

Souvenir

Programme

SOUTHAMPTON
v
PORTSMOUTH

TUESDAY, 10th MAY, 1966
Kick-off 7.30 p.m.

Programme 6d.

Hollywood, Dennis

Left-back
Born: *1944 Govan, Scotland*
Playing career: *Southampton (1962-1971).*

A one club man and Scotland Under 23 international, Hollywood made his debut for Saints at 17 and would make the left-back spot his own for the next decade. Despite interest from London clubs Spurs and West Ham, it was Southampton and their manager Ted Bates whom ultimately reaped the rewards of the addition of Hollywood. He would develop into one of the finest exponents of his craft in the 1960s having wrestled the no 3 shirt off previous incumbent Tommy Traynor to become main man. A classy and tenacious full-back equally as adept at going forward as he was at his defensive duty, his willingness to run through brick walls and back his team mates to the hilt made his a hugely popular figures amongst players and coaches alike. Played in Saints first ever top flight season, scoring four goals before leaving for another coastal club, Blackpool, after 266 games for Saints. Retired at only 27, he returned to Southampton after a spell with Basingstoke and Bath City. He initially worked on the Docks then in the Air traffic control centre at Swanwick. Also had employment at the oil refinery in Fawley and latterly in matchday hospitality at St Mary's.

Holmes, Nick

Full-back/Midfielder
Born: *1954 Southampton*
Playing career: *Southampton (1973-1986).*

A loyal, locally born one club man, Nick Holmes was third on the list of all time appearance makers for Saints by the time he hung up his boots after 15 years of unstinting service. Described as "thoughtful, thrusting and as reliable as he was skilful", Holmes is still fondly remembered as one of Southampton's greatest ever not least because of his exploits as one of the Boys of 76 and all that. Started on the left of midfield against Man United at Wembley in the FA Cup final. Also played, and scored, in the 1979 League Cup final for Saints against Forest, albeit in a losing cause.

In retirement, Holmes had a brief spell as manager of Salisbury and ran an open all hours village shop in Winterslow for a decade. Holmes moved to Florida and worked in property management before returning to the UK where he was employed in the Amesbuey offices of Oakley's sunglasses. As of 2020, Holmes works alongside a friend as stock control manager for an Internet company.

Holt, Arthur
Inside-forward
Born: *1911 Bitterne Park, Southampton*
Died: *1994*
Playing career: *Totton, Southampton (1932-1939)*
Brought in as cover for an emerging Ted Drake, Holt scored twice in his first five games and soon became established in Saints forward line alongside Drake, Dick Neal, Tommy Brewis and Fred Tully. A "punchy and enterprising" player, Holt went on to play over 200 times for Southampton, top scoring in his second season and setting a record, along with Vic Watson, as being the only two men to score a hat-trick in the same game for the club. After a move up the coast to Bournemouth fell through, Holt stayed with the Saints during wartime before coaching the Reserve side after the conflict. Holt was also a cricketer of some repute, as an opening batsman for Hampshire with a first class best of 116. He later coached the county and opened a successful sports shop - Holt & Haskell - which still exists today. A pavilion at Hampshire CCC's Rose Bowl ground is named in Holt's honour.

Hooiveld, Jos
Centre-back
Born: *1983 Zeijen, Netherlands*
Playing career: *Twente, SVZ, Achilles 1894, Emmen, Heerenveen, Zwolle, Kapfenberger SV, Inter Turku, AIK, Celtic, Copenhagen, Southampton, Norwich City, Millwall, AIK, FC Twente, Jong FC Twente (2003-Still playing)*
Having initially joined Saints and Nigel Adkins on a loan deal after his time at Celtic was limited, the deal for the towering Dutchman was soon made permanent.

Adkins was impressed by the big defender's repertoire and he quickly became a virtual ever present in the side as the Hooiveld - Fonte partnership to help Southampton back into the Premier League in his debut season, weighing in with eight goals along the way. Having picked up an injury and being displaced by Maya Yoshida, consistent game time in Southampton's newly-promoted defence proved hard to come by and he eventually moved out on loan, playing for Norwich, in Sweden with AIK, FC Twente in the Netherlands and across the pond for California based Orange County. Played for four times for Nettherlands a U19 but a senior call up has, so far, eluded him. Now aged 37, Hooiveld has not yet officially retired but is a free agent. He coached in the Netherlands at Herenveen in 2019.

Hooper, Harold
Full-back
Born: *1900 Brierley Hill* **Died:** *1963*
Playing career: *Brierley Hill Alliance, Southampton, Leicester City, QPR (1921-1927)*
At the Dell, Hooper nicknamed "Rufus" due to the colour and style of his locks, would have to clear the significant hurdle posed by established full-backs Tom Parker and Fred Titmuss. Not surprisingly, he would only make 19 appearances in the first team in his three years at the club, primarily due to the calibre of his international contemporaries rather than any lack of ability. Hooper eventually moved back to his native Midlands to join Leicester City where he was described as "reliable and resolute" in playing another 30 odd games before moving to London and the hoops of QPR. Hooper was the cousin of one of Manchester United and England's early greats, Charlie Roberts.

"DID YOU KNOW?"

"Matthew Le Tissier was the first Saints player to score 20 premiership goals in one season. Since then James Beattie and Danny Ings have done the same."

Horne, Barry

Midfielder
Born: *1962 St Asaph, Wales*
Playing career: *Wrexham, Portsmouth, Southampton, Everton, Birmingham City, Huddersfield Town, Sheffield Wednesday, Kidderminster Harriers, Walsall (1984-2002)*

After a few years of retirement, Horne - capped 59 times for Wales - returned to his spiritual home of Wrexham, coaching the Welsh side before moving 'upstairs' on to their board. Notably, Horne would follow an educational path, earning a first class Honours degree in Chemistry from Liverpool University, putting that qualification to good use in 2015 where he could be found dishing out detentions as a science teacher at a private school in Chester. He would take charge of the school's sports coaching. Horne has continued to stay involved in the game, combining his teaching and coaching role with writing a football column for the *Liverpool Echo.* He has also appeared on BBC Radio Merseyside, Radio City 96.7FM where he hosts a football phone-in show and he has appeared BT Sport as a pundit. *https://twitter.com/1barryhorne*

Horsfall, George

Half-back
Born: *1924 Perth, Australia* **Died:** *1992*
Career: *Southampton, Southend Utd (1943-1950)*

Australian born Englishman Horsfall served in the Royal Navy and dropped by Southampton for a trial. Yet once peacetime football resumed, he would make only two first team appearances at left-half. Played a full season in the Reserves but never managed to displace Bill Ellerington, Alf Ramsey and Bill Rochford for regular first team duty. However, Horsfall would certainly go on to serve Southampton to good effect as a coach after a brief stint in non league with Southend and Guildford City. He had been at the latter for five years when newly appointed Saints manager Ted Bates brought him back to the south coast to assist in his backroom team. He would spend the next 30 years in a variety of roles from coaching, physio, kit man, ground renovation and taking training. He died whilst on duty at the Dell in 1992.

Horton, James

Forward
Born: *1907 Aldershot*
Died: *1972*
Playing career: *Woking, Aldershot Town, Millwall, Southampton, Aldershot, Royal Engineers, Wellington Works, Aldershot & District Traction (1928-1935)*

An eccentric and unpredictable character, Horton would change into his strip whilst still wearing his trademark bowler hat, which he would only remove at the last possible moment. At The Dell, he was used as cover and made only four first team appearances in three different positions. Returning to recently relegated divisional rivals Aldershot - having started out at Millwall - he quit football prematurely due to a leg injury without making an appearance for The Shots. Played non league for a while before working as an electrician and Aldershot's groundsman after the War.

Horton, John

Centre-forward
Born: *1902 Thurnscoe*
Died: *1970*
Playing career: *Southampton (1921-1922)*

Plucked form the obscurity of the unknown backwaters of the Yorkshire league, a 40 goal season at that level catapulted Horton (no relation to James, above) into the national spotlight. It was hoped he could reprise that form at Third Division Southampton, and things started well as Horton grabbed seven goals in his first eight games at Reserve team level. As a centre forward playing second fiddle to the indomitable Bill Rawlings - one of the best strikers of his era - however, chances to shine were at a premium for Horton. He deputised once for Rawlings in a game at Watford in 1921 but that would be his only first team appearances and Horton soon returned to the second string. On the day that Rawlings earned his second cap for England, Horton was playing in a Reserve team game at Bristol and broke his leg, ending his brief football career. He later worked in the transport industry. Died 1984 aged 69

Hoskins, Albert

Forward
Born: *1885 Southampton* **Died:** *1968*
Playing career: *St. Mary's Guild, Freemantle, Southampton, Wolverhampton Wanderers, Dudley Town, Shrewsbury Town (1904-1929)*

Locally born Hoskins caught the eye of the area's only professional club when he turned in a series of impressive displays, notably at the Dell against Saints reserves. Scored in each of Southampton's FA Cup ties during his debut season as he made 21 league appearances - in three different positions - always being on "the brink" of the first team before moving to Wolves after four seasons on the south coast. After a brief stint at non league level he returned to Molineux as "official" football resumed in 1919, in time for the first post War season. He joined the office staff at Wolves, serving on the board and secretary and director of football having retired from playing. After serving as assistant boss, he became the main man in the dugout, combining the role of manager with his secretarial duties. During his time in charge, Wolves found themselves near the top of the table in both of his seasons at the helm but Hoskins left to take up the manager's job at Gillingham. Later worked as a trainer, coach and scout for a variety of lower and non league clubs before War broke out again in 1939. Hoskins later returned to his native Southampton to work as a solicitor's clerk.

Hoskins, John

Outside-left
Born: *1931 Southampton* **Died:** *2006*
Playing career: *Millbrook Rangers, Winchester City, Southampton, Swindon Town, Cambridge United (1952-1960)*

The great nephew of Edwardian Saint Albert Hoskins (above), John arrived at The Dell as Saints searched for a solution to their problems with the no.11 shirt. He soon became a regular in that position - when not sidelined by a plethora of injuries - making 20 appearances in his debut season, scoring five goals in a struggling Southampton side - a side that would be relegated to the Third South at the end of that 1952-53 campaign.

A goalscoring winger, albeit a "languid and relaxed" player, Hoskins hit 67 in 238 games for Southampton - a six in eleven matches when on an unorthodox tour of the West Indies with a FA select XI. A popular and hard working team player, Hoskins seemed to be "on the threshold" of stardom until injuries - and the emergence of a certain Terry Paine - saw him slip down the pecking order. He moved on to Swindon but only made a handful of appearances for them and briefly played for non league Cambridge before returning to Southampton where he worked in Shirley as a bus driver.

Hough, Edward

Full-back
Born: *1899 Walsall*
Died: *1978*
Playing career: *Talbot Stead Tubeworks, Southampton, Portsmouth, Bristol Rovers (1921-1933)*

Head the one about the young centre half who signed for Southampton with 52 pints of beer as a transfer deal? The story goes that "Ted" Hough was procured from works team Talbot Stead by virtue of his boss agreeing to release Hough if the Southampton director got the drinks in. He duly did, and Hough moved south to sign for Saints. Despite the fact he played almost 200 games at the Dell, Hough would have to bide his time as understudy to not only centre-half Alec Campbell, but also Southampton's incumbent full backs Tom Parker and Fred Titmuss. Vying for the number 3 shirt with the latter, Hough eventually made the left back position his own after the two were sold, falling victim to an unfortunate deflection off him against Arsenal in 1927-28, denying lowly Southampton a place in the FA Cup final. Injuries took their toll and Hough moved up the Solent to "nearest and dearest" Pompey but things did not work out as he only made one appearance before jumping ship again this time to Bristol Rovers. After retiring, he returned to the south coast to work at a power station as a fitter's assistant.

Houlker, Albert

Left-half
Born: *1872 Blackburn*
Died: *1962*
Playing career: *Blackburn Hornets, Oswaldtwistle Rovers, Cob Wall, Park Road, Blackburn Rovers, Portsmouth, Southampton, Colne (1894-1909)*

One of England's finest Victorian-era masters, "Kelly" Houlker had already been capped at international level by the time he arrived at Southampton - via Southern League champions Portsmouth - ahead of the 1903-04. Dovetailing with Tommy Bowman and fellow England man Bert Lee, Houlker formed part of an impressive half back line that helped Southampton to win, and then retain, the league title. Tenacious and strong, Houlker remained at The Dell for three seasons, and went on to earn a further four caps at full international level before falling out of favour with the ever evolving England set up. Intending to retire, he left Southampton - and fond memories amongst an adoring fanbase - intending to retire, but instead returned to hometown team Blackburn for a final swansong. After another First Division season, Houlker - now in the twilight of his career - had a final dalliance with non league Colne before he did finally call it a day - discounting the War time game he played for Rovers as a guest - aged 46! In retirement, Houlker worked in the milling industry and then set up his own coal haulage business.

Howard, Brian

Midfielder
Born: *1983 Winchester*
Playing career: *Southampton, Swindon Town, Barnsley, Sheffield United, Reading, Millwall, Portsmouth, Bristol City, CSKA Sofia, Birmingham City, Oxford United, Eastleigh, Alresford Town, Romsey Town, Whitehawk (1999-2017)*

Despite the fact Howard never made the grade at Southampton, he still went on to enjoy an impressive career, being capped by England at every level from U16 to U21. Howard could have made it big having been offered a contract by Chelsea but he was unlucky as the start of the Russian revolution saw a mass influx of expensive foreign imports. Made his name mainly at Barnsley, starring in that club's unlikely

Cup run in the 2007-08 season as the Tykes reached the semi finals with Howard scoring an injury time winner at Liverpool in the fifth round. Played for Sheffield United, Reading, Millwall, Pompey, Bristol City, a brief stint abroad with CSKA Sofia and mainly in the second and third tiers. He went on to play over 300 games at Football League level and last turned out for Brighton based Whitehawk, then of the National League South. He has since coached at Eastleigh and now works as a player agent.

Howell, Henry

Inside-forward
Born: *1890 Hockley, West Midlands*
Died: *1932*
Playing career: *Burslem Swifts, Wolverhampton Wanderers, Southampton, Northfleet, Accrington Stanley, Mansfield Town (1913-1923)*

Howell - a talented cricketer with five Tests for England under his belt - played for non league Burslem and then Wolves prior to the outbreak of WW1. Guesting for Stoke, Lance Corporal Howell served a fusilier for him 'home' regiment during WW1, before resuming his full time professional career after the conflict. He returned to Wolves in the first post-War season and then moved south to The Dell, joining Southampton of the Third Division (South) but he never played for the club at any level and soon left after five weeks, for Kent League Northfleet. He also played for Accrington Stanley and Mansfield, also playing cricket for Warwickshire as a middle order batsman and fast bowler, returning a career best of six for seven during a Championship game in 1922. Represented England in the 1920-21 Ashes series although he'll want to forget it (the tourists lost 0-5). Died in Birmingham in 1932.

Howells, David

Midfielder
Born: *1967 Guildford*
Playing career: *Tottenham Hotspur, Southampton, Bristol City. (1985-2000).*

Signing for Spurs aged seven, Howells rose through the ranks to burst on to the scene as an 18 year old with the north London powerhouses.

He would go on to play 335 games in 12 years with the capital club, winning the FA Cup in 1991 before moving to Southampton in 1998. He would only play nine times in the red and white, scoring once, but had a dramatic debut as he moonlighted in goal at Charlton after regular stopper Paul Jones was sent off, conceding four goals in the process. After that dramatic beginning, Howells' Southampton's career petered out and was ultimately ended by a knee injury. After a loan spell at Bristol City and some time in non league with Hartley Wintney, Havant & Waterloovile and hometown team Guildford, Howells was forced to call it a day in 2000 after his knee flared up again. He later set up a soccer school in Majorca, served on the board of Guildford as director and chairman before becoming manager of a sports agency in Middlesex. Currently works as a teacher.

David Hughes

Hughes, Arthur
Centre-forward
Born: *1883 Birkenhead* **Died:** *1962*
Playing career: *Tranmere Rovers, Bolton W, Southampton, Manchester City (1907-1909)*
Arthur Hughes' individual struggles were reflected by his club Bolton's collective shortcomings in a season of toil on and off the field at Burnden Park. Meanwhile, in that 1907-08 season, Southampton needed re-inforcements so that position was perhaps up for grabs when Smith and the new arrived Hughes linked up in time for Saints first foray into Europe - albeit a pre-season tour. Tragically, Smith collapsed and died a few months later, leaving Hughes as the main option at centre-forward and he did not disappoint. He grabbed 12 goals in 14 games, going on to hit 18 in 28 before being curtailed by injury. He would later turn out for Manchester City but made no tangible impact with his days at Southampton the zenith of his playing days. In retirement, he worked for a bricklayer in his native Birkenhead.

Hughes, David
Midfielder
Born: *1972 St Albans*
Playing career: *Southampton (1991-2009)*
A case of what might have been, 64 appearances in nine years at Southampton is no blemish on David Hughes' ability. Rather, an incredible catalogue of crippling injuries stopped his promising career in its tracks. Two broken legs, fractured ribs and back problem all required major surgery - indeed, Hughes had 16 operations in ten years. When fit, Hughes was a tenacious, tough tackling ball winner and earned four caps for Wales at U21 level, although he was never called up for the senior squad. His time at Saints was ultimately ended by another injury, this time to his knee, in a pre-season friendly at Aldershot - ending his career prematurely. Later went into the building trade before coaching at Eastleigh, briefly managing the Spitfires as successor to another ex-Saint - Jason Dodd - in 2007, also serving as player/assistant boss. Played for Sutton before winding down and now works as a sports consultant for *Midas Sports Management.*

Hughes, Paul

Midfielder
Born: *1976 Hammersmith, London*
Playing career: *Chelsea, Norwich City (loan), Southampton, Luton Town (1994-2006)*

Scored an impressive solo effort on his debut for Chelsea against Derby County, however, was eventually released on a free transfer. Was then signed by Glenn Hoddle who was by then Southampton boss. Never played for the Saints before moving to Luton where he wound down his career. Hughes helped form a company that provides park teams with websites. Has also coached at Brunel University and been reserve team coach at Hayes and Yeading.

Hughes, Mark

Forward
Born: *1963 Ruabon, Wales*
Playing career: *Manchester United, Barcelona, Bayern Munich, Chelsea, Southampton, Everton, Blackburn Rovers (1980-2002)*

A prolific and decorated striker, Hughes won two league titles, three FA Cups, a League Cup, the Cup Winners Cup and the Super Cup during his successful spell at Old Trafford, also scooping silverware at Chelsea and Blackburn after spells at Barcelona and Bayern Munich. Signed by Dave Jones as a partner for David Hirst to spearhead the Saints attack, he was converted to midfield hence only two goals in over 50 games on the south coast. Also played for Everton and was capped by Wales, going on to manage his country also serving as boss of former club Blackburn, Manchester City, Fulham, QPR and Stoke before returning to Southampton as manager. In the dugout at St Mary's, Hughes, aka "Sparky" signed a short term contract to ensure the club's ultimately successful battle against relegation but he was sacked after a poor start to the 2018-19, being succeeded by current Saints boss Ralph Hassenhuttl. There are two books about Hughes available now - "Sparky - Barcelona, Bayern Munich and back" by the man himself, originally released in 1990 but updated in 2002 and "Hughesie! The Red Dragon, his official biography by David Meek on his time at Old Trafford.

Hunt, Stephen James

Defender
Born: *1984 Southampton*
Playing career: *Southampton, Colchester United, Notts County, Lincoln City (2004-2011)*

Hunt began his career at his hometown club but after eight years at the club without ever playing he left for Colchester United. Hunt did make on to the first team bench but never gave his opportunity and later went on to play over 100 games for Notts County, becoming an integral part of the high flying Magpies as they went up as fourth tier champions in 2010. A towering centre back, Hunt was known for his aerial presence and ability to play out from the back, a rare trait for such a big man. Had interested in several Championship and League One clubs for his services but never took the step up, turning out for Lincoln City on loan before retiring. Having hung up his boots, Hunt coached at the U's and now works as a player agent.

DID YOU KNOW?"

"St Mary's Stadium was only built because a planning application to build a site at Stoneham was rejected by Eastleigh Borough Council. However, this can now seen as a homecoming - back to the area where the club was originally formed!"

Hunter, George
Half-back
Born: *1885 Nowshera, British India*
Died: *1934*
Playing career: *Maidstone United, Croydon Common, Aston Villa, Oldham Athletic, Chelsea, Manchester United, Croydon Common, Southampton Brentford, Birmingham, Portsmouth (1907-1919)*
A fiery wing half nicknamed 'Cocky' who had suffered from discipline problems before his time at Pompey, and it is reported that his manager nor his team mates could control him. Wrote a light hearted football book before going onto serve as a sergeant-major in the army during the World War One seeing action in France and Gallipoli. The Indian born enigma served three months hard labour in August 1930 for deserting his wife and children. Died in February 1934 aged 46.

Hurlock, Terry
Central midfielder
Born: *1958 Hackney*
Playing career: *West Ham United, Enfield, Leytonstone/Ilford, Brentford, Reading, Millwall, Rangers, Southampton, Millwall, Fulham (1974-1995)*
Ian Branfoot already knew all about Terry Hurlock's all action hustle and bustle when he signed him for Southampton having managed him at Reading. Recruiting Hurlock for the newly formed Premier League, he went on to play 59 games in the next three years becoming a favourite among fans and team mates for his whole hearted, uncompromising style - perhaps no surprise given his upbringing in the east end of London. As his former Millwall term mate and fellow "hard man" Neil "Razor" Ruddock once said when asked what is favourite animal was, "Terry Hurlock" he replied in a deadpan manner. With a style akin to a pit bull, Hurlock added bite to Southampton's midfield, earning three caps for England "B" whilst at the Dell. He later returned to Millwall for a second spell and finished his playing days at Fulham having also turned out for Brentford, Reading and Rangers. In retirement, Hurlock owned the *Prince of Wales* pub in Walthamstow and has worked for transport union RMT since 2012. He is on Twitter at: https://twitter.com/terryhurlock

Huxford, Cliff
Wing-half
Born: *1937 Stroud, Gloucestershire*
Career: *Chelsea, Southampton, Exeter (1958-1967).*
Huxford was snapped up by Southampton in part exchange for Charlie Livesey having been spotted in Chelsea's footballing hotbed by assistant manager Bill Ellerington. It quickly became apparent how highly rated Huxford was by the Saints hierarchy having been made captain after only twelve games, going to become an ever present in his debut season as Southampton won the Third Division title. He remained an ever present figurehead in an increasingly settled Saints side, even deputising in goal when Ron Reynolds was injured. He played over 300 games for Saints, helping them into Division One for the first time in 1965-66. Later played for Exeter City and non league Worcester City before coaching widely in Hampshire and working as a painter and decorator. He also served his former side as matchday host and is still a keen Saints supporter.

Idiakez, Inigo
Midfielder
Born: *1973 San Sebastian, Spain*
Playing career: *Real Sociedad B, Real Sociedad, Oviedo, Rayo Vallecano, Derby County, Southampton, QPR (1989-2007)*
Saints second Spaniard a, Idiakez was signed by his former Derby boss George Burley in an attempt to return Saints to the Premier League. An attacking, eye catching midfielder, Idiakez - capped six times by Spain at U21 level - spent more time on the treatment table than he did on its pitch.

Inigo Idiakez

Unfortunately for him, Idiakez is most known for missing the decisive spot-kick in the play off semi finals during his debut season, when his former club Derby beat Saints 4-3 on penalties to consign Burley's men to another season at that level. After 35 appearances in two years, he had a loan spell at QPR before retiring and going into coaching in Spain, Cyprus and latterly, back in England with the Hatters of Luton. Idiakez currently works as youth team manager of the League One side.

Ireland, Sid

Left-back
Born: *1889 Tamworth*
Playing career: *Kingsbury Colliery, Southampton, Merthyr Town (1911-1920)*

Sid Ireland swapped the coal mines of Warwickshire for the red and white of the south coast, joining the Southern League club in 1911 and becoming a permanent fixture. An excellent leader and natal born captain, Ireland skippered the Saints for the next three years, earning an fearsome reputation as one of the best left backs in the land, making the position his own under new manager Jimmy McIntyre.

It was only Southampton's status as a Southern League side that prevented him from getting an England call up but he would be rewarded by representing the division in a trial fixture against the Scottish and Irish counterparts. With an improving Southampton denied progress by the outbreak of WW1, Ireland guested for Saints and Man United before being pressed into service in the Durham Light Infantry where was captured and made a PoW for eight months. He survived to resume his career at Merthyr Town - where he was an "outstanding contributor" before retiring and working on the railways.

Jaidi, Radhi

Centre-back
Born: *1975 Tunisia*
Playing career: *Esperance, Bolton Wanderers, Birmingham City, Southampton (1993-2012)*

The Premier League's first Tunisian, Jaidi brought power and dominance to a Saints defence in need of a commanding, physical presence. Jaidi had played at Premier League level for Bolton and Birmingham so it was a considerable step down when he joined League One Saints in 2009. Jaidi instantly endeared himself to the Saints fans with a series of towering displays and scored a 95th-minute equaliser at Carlisle on his first away start. The Fonte - Jaidi partnership would prove to be the best in the third tier as Southampton surged to promotion into the Championship during 2010-11, but the Tunisian would miss the entirely of Saints return to that level with injury. Jaidi played 105 times for Tunisia, winning the AFCON tournament in 2004 and captaining them four years later. He also played in their 2006 World Cup campaign, scoring against Saudi Arabia - although he credits Saints 2010 Football League Trophy win at Wembley as the proudest moment of his career. In retirement, Jaidi remained at Southampton in an internal development role, eventually taking over as manager of the Under 23 side at St Mary's. He left that role in 2019 to take charge of Connecticut-based Hartford in the USA, getting to know his players virtually with quizzes and video training sessions as the global pandemic derailed his debut season in charge. https://twitter.com/radhijaidioff

Jakobsson, Bo

Defender/Defensive midfielder
Born: *1972 Lund, Sweden*
Playing career: *Teckomatorps SK, Landskrona BoIS, Helsingborgs IF, F.C. Hansa Rostock, Br√®ndby IF, Southampton FC, Helsingborgs IF (1978-2007)*

Signed to fill the void left by the injury plagued Claus Lundekvam, Andreas "Bo" Jakobsson had been an ever present in the 2002 World Cup and Euro 2004 tournaments for Sweden by the time he arrived ahead of the 2004-05 campaign. In a turbulent debut season in which Saints were relegated under the tutelage of three different bosses, Jakobsson would not stay for a crack at the Championship and duly returned to his native Sweden for a second stint with former side Helsingborgs winning the Swedish Cup twice before dropping into the seventh tier and retiring in 2007. Jakobsson returned to his first club BoIS Landskroma as a coach.

Jefferis, Frank

Inside right
Born: *1884 Fordingbridge*
Died: *1938*
Playing career: *Southampton, Everton, Preston North End, Southport, Preston North End, Southport (1905-1926)*

Born and raised in the tiny market town of Fordingbridge on the edge of the New Forest, Jefferis was playing for his local non league team when his elegant, clever style caught the eye of Saints - always on the lookout for the cream of Hampshire's young talent. Scored two hat-tricks whilst on trial at The Dell, making it a no brainer for the Southampton hierarchy to sign him. A model professional, Jefferis demanded the best from himself and his team mates and quickly became a firm favourite. At Saints, he played in every position across the forward line, linking up well with George Smith and the two Johns, Bainbridge and Lewis, on his way to double figures in front of goal in each of his first two seasons - earning international recognition with England in the process (Jefferis was capped twice in 1912). Later won a league title medal with Everton in the final post-War season, but he continued to play for the Toffees after the resumption of the professional game, going on to Preston where he was an FA Cup runner up in 1922. After retiring via a stint another spell at non league Southport, he joined Millwall as a coach but collapsed and died at their training ground aged 53 in 1938. Played over 200 games for Saints (61 goals).

Jeffrey, William

Defender
Born: *1868 Dalderby, Horncastle*
Playing career: *West Manchester, Horncastle, Lincoln City, Grimsby Town, Gainsborough Trinity, Burnley, Woolwich Arsenal, Southampton St. Mary's (1891-1895)*

Joining Southampton in time for their inaugural Southern League season from Arsenal - then in the new Second Division he made nine appearances in goal for the Woolwich club) - Jeffrey formed a strong partnership with George Marshall at Saints and became an ever present for the rest of that 1894-95 season, winning the Hampshire Senior Cup and steering the Antelope Ground side to third in the table. Jeffrey would only play 13 games for Southampton before drifting into relative obscurity, later playing for non league Newark and working as a school caretaker in his native Lincolnshire. He would work in agriculture, becoming a farmer in Kirkby - on - Bain and then in Waddington. Died aged 66 in 1932.

Jenkins, Stephen

Centre-back
Born: *1980 Bristol*
Playing career: *Southampton, Brentford, Forest Green Rovers, Bath City, Weston-super-Mare (1996-2005)*

Rising through the ranks in Saints Centre of Excellence, centre back Jenkins failed to make a first team appearance for the club with fierce competition for places, and was released at the end of the 1998-99 season. Went on to have a reputable career in the lower leagues, turning out for Brentford and Forest Green Rovers before turning out for Bath and Weston - super - Mare at non league level. Bristol born, he moved to to play in Seattle in 1976, and then the indoor leagues, he still lives in Seattle where he now coaches, and his son Steve Jr. is a player.

Jenkins, Thomas

Outside-left
Born: *1947 Bethnal Green*
Playing career: *Leyton Orient, West Ham United, Margate, Reading, Southampton, Swindon Town, Seattle Sounders, Pittsburgh Spirit, Phoenix Inferno (1966-1982)*

Replacing the direct John Sydenham with the man he nicknamed "The Weaver", Ted Bates unearthed a gem when he brought Jenkins to the south coast after unfulfilling days at Leyton Orient and their local rivals West Ham. At his brilliant best, Jenkins was a jink and glide winger with great pace, dazzling trickery and a low centre of gravity. So much so, that Bates described the man himself as "the most outstanding player I have seen in the lower divisions, and has the ability to win matches on his own." Jenkins' most memorable moment came against his former club when he beat five West Ham players, including the late, great Bobby Moore, for a stunning solo goal. However, despite his undoubted ability, Jenkins never truly realised his full potential at Southampton and moved on to Swindon having played 95 times (six goals) in four seasons at The Dell. Southampton would struggle to replace him, with six different players donning the no.11 left wing shirt as bates eventually dispensed with the out an out winger in favour of Mick Channon. Jenkins would go on to coach in the USA where he linked up with former Saints team-mate Jimmy Gabriel.

Jennings, Roy
Centre-half
Born: *1931 Swindon*
Died: *2016*
Playing career: *Swindon Town, Southampton, Brighton & Hove Albion, Crawley Town (1952-1969)*
Played for England at youth and amateur level and it was in that form of the game that he represented Southampton, whilst training as an accountant. He moved along the coast to Brighton after two years at Saints and would go on to play nearly 300 times for the south coast side, scoring 22 goals, a good return for a centre-half. Became a fans favourite at The Goldstone Ground due to his strong aerial prowess and physical, uncompromising style. Having helped steer the high flying Seagulls into the Second Division, he joined Sussex rivals Crawley and became a penalty specialist (all 38 of his goals for the 'other' Red Devils were spot kicks). Having retired from the game, he stayed at Crawley, working as their third ever manager between 1968 - 70, winning promotion into the Southern League before retiring from football. He continued to serve the Sussex town as a magistrate, also working as a partner in a Crawley accountancy firm.

Jepp, Samuel
Centre-half
Born: *1885 Aldershot*
Died: *1968*
Playing career: *Aldershot Athletic, Royal Army Medical Corps, Southampton, South Farnborough Athletic, Swansea Town (1907-1914)*

Said to be "enthusiastic and reliable", Jepp scored on his Southern League debut and played four different positions in his next seven games, showing his versatility and ability to fill the breach wherever needed. Jepp would eventually make the centre-back position his own, becoming known for his ability to play out from the back and an accurate positional sense, allowing him to strike up a grit and guile partnership with Bert Trueman. Jepp would play 94 times for Saints in all competitions, including as an occasional centre-forward, before being released and going non league. He served in the Army during the War with the Irish Fusiliers, before resuming his career - albeit a lower level - after the conflict, playing in Wales and later returning to Aldershot.

Jepson, Bert
Outside-right
Born: *1902 Glasshoughton*
Died: *1981*
Playing career: *Frickley Colliery, Huddersfield Town, Southampton, Fulham, Brighton & Hove Albion, Hove (1927-1948)*
Most known for his time with two of the three major south coast clubs, Jepson - Yorkshire born and bred - worked in the coal mines before starting out in the professional game as a late bloomer, at the age of 25. There was no place for him on Huddersfield's right wing, thanks to the exploits of Alex Jackson, but things would be on the upturn for him upon signing for Arthur Chadwick's new-look Southampton side. He would instantly get into the team, shrugging off an early injury to become first choice until the arrival of another winger, Bobby Weale, as Saints finished fourth in the Second Division in Jepson's debut season at The Dell. When Weale left, Jepson again became first choice and went on to feature almost 100 times for Saints, with manager George Kay eventually selling him to divisional rivals Fulham. Also played for Brighton for two seasons in the Third South before retiring. Later became manager of a dairy in Brighton, guesting for Port Vale and Swansea during the War, before joining Sussex League side Hove as player-coach.

Jewett, Alfred
Centre-half
Born: *1899 Southampton* **Died:** *1980*
Playing career: *Bitterne United, Southampton, Thornycrofts, Arsenal, Lincoln City, Wigan Borough, Bournemouth & Boscombe Athletic (1921-1926)*
Alfred Jewett was on the books of Southampton and Arsenal, playing for both at youth team level but never getting that first team breakthrough.Later served as a Fusilier in the Hampshire Regiment during the War, then worked as a railway engineer and for the local council as a maintenance operator in the city.

Johansen, Stig
Striker
Born: *1972 Kabelveg, Norway*
Playing career: *FK Bode/Glimt, Southampton, Bristol City, Helsingborgs IF, (1995-2014)*
Appropriately for a man born in the foothills of Norway's fjords in the Arctic Circle, Stig Johansen was ice cool in front of goal, even though he never showed it at Southampton. Despite the fact he rarely played for the Saints, as he struggled to make an impact and the arrival of David Hirst, he clearly had the ability, being capped three times by Norway before he arrived at The Dell.

Stern John

His reward at that level came having plundered 38 goals in 22 games to fire Lotoren to title success before Saints - and reportedly Newcastle - came sniffing for his services. Later played for Bristol City on loan, later returning to Scandinavia with Swedish side Helsingborgs. Played for first club Bobo Glint in two spells before retiring - subsequently making a one game comeback for home club Kabelvag. Later coached the club's youth teams.

John, Stern
Forward
Born: *1976 Trinidad and Tobago*
Playing career: *Nottingham Forest, Birmingham City, Coventry City, Derby County, Sunderland, Southampton, Bristol City, Crystal Palace, Ipswich Town. (1995-)*
A much travelled Trinidadian striker, John arrived at St Mary's from Sunderland as compatriot Kenwyne Jones moved the other way. Capped 115 times by his country, John played in the 2006 World Cup and is currently Trinidad & Tobago's all time top scorer with 70 goals. Hit 18 goals in the Championship during his debut campaign for Saints to help stave off relegation at the last gasp. John was a virtual ever present during that 2007-08 season, but as chairman Rupert Lowe increasingly turned to youth, John was loaned out to Bristol City. He returned home to play Sangre Grande before a fleeting flirtation with the English non league game. John currently manages Central FC in Trinidad & Tobago.

Johnson, Henry
Forward
Born: *1897 Birmingham* **Died:** *1962*
Playing career: *Coventry City, Darlaston, Southampton, QPR, Cradley Heath (1919-1926)*
After two games for Coventry and a stint with non league Darlaston in his native Birmingham, Johnson and team-mate John Cooper moved to the south coast to sign for Third South side Southampton. In his second game, he contributed to the club's biggest ever margin of victory in a league game, scoring twice in an 8-0 thumping of Northampton, becoming an ever present from then on.

Saints would go on to pilfer the league title from coastal rivals Plymouth by the narrowest of margins, goal difference on the final day of the 1921-22 campaign. For Southampton's first ever campaign in the second tier, Johnson struggled to hold down a regular first team spot with Jack Elkes preferred at inside right by manager Jimmy McIntyre. After the departure of Elkes, Johnson became third choice behind Len Andrews and Cliff Price, so he returned from whence he had come - the Third South - this time with QPR. After two years in London, Johnson returned to his roots and had a spell at Cradley Heath as player/manager.

Johnston, John
Wing-half
Born: *1876 Lennoxtown, Scotland*
Died: *1955*
Playing career: *Stalybridge Rovers, Bury, Southampton, Stalybridge Celtic (1898-1915)*
Something of a specialist in his native Lancashire, Johnston starteed his pro career with Bury for six seasons - winning the FA Cup with the Lancashire club in 1903 - and playing almost 200 games before swapping the Shakers for the Saints, together with team-mate Bert Hodgkinson. He would on to feature more than 100 times at wing-half, helping Ernest Armfield's team to the FA Cup semi finals whilst catching the eye with his eccentric habit of having a blade of grass - or something similar - sticking out of his mouth. Described as a "natural leader", he would help mentor his fellow forwards, particularly the younger members of the Saints squad, belying his unusual posture with a natural ability as an "intricate and creative" wing-half. After four seasons at The Dell, before moving back "oop north" to the forerunners of his former club - now known as Stalybridge Celtic - where he served as player/manager. He would remain involved with the club for the two decades and was then chairman of the Stalybridge Amateur League, combining this with the running of a tobacco shop and a sports merchandise dealership in the town.

Jones, Dennis
Half-back
Born: *1894 Shirebrook* **Died:** *1961*
Playing career: *Leicester City, Southampton, Mansfield Town (1921-1929)*
Midlander Jones made his name with Leicester City, playing for that club for three years and made 64 appearances at right-half. Jones moved to the south coast to join Southampton with Leicester team mate Fred Price with £200 and Harry Hooper moving the other way. Jones would struggle for game time at The Dell, however, with Bert Shelley, Alec Campbell and George Harkus firmly established as Southampton's half back triumvirate. He would play in seven first team games for the club on the rare occasion that one of the trio were unavailable, but returned Nottinghamshire, to sign for Mansfield, after that solitary season on the south coast. He again spent a single campaign at Field Mill before dropping into non league football with Shirebrook, Sutton Town and Wombwell in the Midland League. Later worked as a scout for two of his former sides, Leicester City and Mansfield, and then as a coach at the latter after the War.

Jones, Ernie
Winger
Born: *1920 Cwmbwrla, Wales*
Died: *2002*
Playing career: *Swansea Town, Bolton Wanderers, Swansea Town, Tottenham Hotspur, Southampton, Bristol City (1937-1954)*
Despite a relatively successful 1948-49 season in which Southampton had finished third in the second tier, a dearth of wingers - nine men had been deployed in the no.11 shirt - had given manager Bill Dodgin a throbbing headache. So it was that Jones, an ertswhile, wordly wise goalscoring winger, arrived from Tottenham as a certain Alf Ramsay and £6,000 went the other way. Jones was used to being the main creative outlet but was morphed into a more defensive minded player, often having to "chase another winger" and track back to assist the ageing Bill Rochford. Capped four times by Wales, Jones featured 44 times for Saints, scoring four goals, and still never truly solved the left-wing issue.

Appearances became increasingly few and far between and Jones was eventually transferred to divisional rivals Bristol City where he became player-coach. Later managed Rhyl in the Welsh League and ad a spell at Southern League Poole before retiring from the game. He briefly combined his two loves - football and engineering - through a job at CPC coaching the embryonic Saints youth team before working for aviation production company Hawker Siddeley in Bolton.

Jones, Frederick

Inside-forward
Born: *1888 Newstead, Nottinghamshire*
Playing career: *Annesley, Sutton Junction, Notts County, Coventry City, Southampton, Coventry City, Wrexham (1907-1921)*

Described as a "busy, burly and bustling" inside left, Jones had joined Saints for £85 from divisional rivals Coventry and immediately dovetailed with the potent pairing of Sid Kimpton and the prolific Arthur Dominy - the latter would be the league's top scorer in the final pre-war campaign. He played 35 times in league and cup for Saints (14 goals) before the outbreak of WW1 ended his time at the club. He guested for Plymouth during the war but returned to Coventry - for £35 less than he had left them for - but only played once for the recently relegated Sky Blues. He would wind down his career in Wales, playing for Wrexham, Pembroke and Ebbw Vale before becoming landlord of the *Fox and Hounds* pub in Hucknall, Nottinghamshire.

Jones, George

Centre-forward
Born: *1889 Bolton, Lancashire* **Died:** *1969*
Playing career: *Elston Rovers, Crewe Alexandra, Bury, Southampton, Goole Town (1914-1920)*

In a career spanning both the pre and post World War One era, Jones was in the twilight of an unremarkable career when he signed for Southampton aged 29. As cover to Bill Rawlings, his chances were always going to be at a premium and so it proved, with Jones playing only seven times as deputy to the legendary Saints net buster.

Despite only playing on those seven occasions, he still managed to score five times - including on his bow against Luton and two in an 8-1 victory over Merthyr Town during the middle of his run in the first team. Despite his respectable goals-to-game ratio, his stay at Southampton would not last beyond a single season, but he earned recognition for a call up to the South Eastern Counties Representative side, scoring in a game with London. But that was that. With the Saints heading for their debut season in the Football League, Jones signed for non league Goole Town. Later worked on the railways.

Jones, Ken

Full-back
Born: *1944 Havercroft*
Died: *2012*
Playing career: *Southampton, Cardiff City*

A previously unknown quantity, Jones rose to prominence for his sterling service with Bradford PA, featuring over 100 times and being described as the "best full-back in the Fourth Division" by his manager Jimmy Scoular. Southampton manager Ted Bates was firmly in agreement and parted with £15,000 to bring him to the Dell. Jones was capable of playing anywhere across the defence but had to compete with Stuart Williams, Tommy Hare and David Webb for a regular place in the side. Jones would play his part with a handful of games as Saints got promoted in 1965-66. Jones was "excellent" on his debut in the top division but - with the arrival of Joe Kirkup and the breakthrough of a young Bob McCarthy - he was always third or even fourth down the pecking order but a highlight of his time at The Dell saw Jones feature in a hat-trick of wins against an admittedly far from vintage Man United side, the double of 1968-69 and the game at Old Trafford made famous by Ron Davies four goal feat. After 92 appearances for Saints, Jones rejoined his former boss Scoular at Cardiff but again struggled because of a host of injury problems. Having retired from the game he worked on Southampton Docks and coached at non league level. Jones also became a well-known and competent regional snooker player and mentor.

Jones, Kenwyne

Striker
Born: *1984 Point Fortin, Trinidad and Tobago*
Playing career: *Joe Public, W Connection, Southampton, Sheffield Wednesday, Sunderland, Stoke City, Cardiff City, Bournemouth, Al Jazira, Atlanta United, Central (2002-2016)*
Trinidadian striker brimming with pace and power, Jones affiliation with red and white saw him turn out for Saints, Sunderland and Stoke City. Played during the golden age of strikers from the Caribbean nation, Jones bagged seven goals in as many games during his brief loan spell at Hillsborough before returning to St Mary's. Jones was backup to fellow new signing Peter Crouch and the veteran Kevin Phillips as the trio were unable to save Saints from relegation to the Championship. A match for even the most accomplished defender on his day, he drew comparisons with Chelsea's Ivorian net buster Didier Drogba. 19 goals in 71 games for Southampton before moving north to another club synonymous with red and white, Sunderland, in exchange for fellow countryman Stern John. With John, Jones played in the 2006 World Cup finals for his country and has scored 23 goals in 82 caps for T & T. Currently a free agent having left Atlanta United in 2017. He has since set up his own youth soccer school in his native Trinidad and Tobago, KJJA, where Jones is the lead coach. He is on Twitter at: https://twitter.com/kenwynejonestt

Jones, Paul

Goalkeeper
Born: *1967 Chirk, Wrexham, Wales*
Career: *Stockport County, Southampton, Liverpool, Wolves, Watford, Millwall, QPR (1986-2008)*
Capped 50 times by Wales, he joined Southampton having starred in knocking out the Premier League Saints during a League Cup tie for giant killing Stockport in 1996-97. Outgoing County boss Dave Jones signed Jones - whom had been an ever present that year - for Southampton and he would later link up with the same manager again at Wolves during that club's ultimately unsuccessful effort to stave off relegation. Jones again played every game during his first season at The Dell, earning the fans Player of the Year award in the process. Having started 2003-04 at Saints and ending it at Wolves, he was loaned to Liverpool during a goalkeeping injury crisis, therefore becoming the Anfield club's oldest post war debutant. Later played for Watford, Millwall and QPR and for Bognor Regis at non league level. In retirement, Jones had run a goalkeeping Academy in Sussex as well as doing charity work for Chestnut Tree House in Arundel, also in Sussex. https://twitter.com/pauljonesgoalie

Jordan, Frank

Inside-forward
Born: *1883 Southampton* **Died:** *1938*
Playing career: *Southampton, Reading, Stoke, Merthyr Town, Abertillery (1905-1912)*
Served Southampton in two spells,and became an established first choice at inside left, endearing himself to the Dell faithful with his fleet-footed, agile and direct style. Having displaced Sam Shearer, Jordan himself would lose his place to new arrivals Sam Brittleton and Bob Carter, so his future lay elsewhere. Jordan turned out for a succession of other League clubs, playing for Reading, Stoke and Merthyr during their Football League days. Jordan hung up his boots after a year in the Welsh league before returning to Southampton after the War. There, he worked for over 20 years on the gas board, also playing for the company's football and cricket works sides and secretary of their whist team.

Jordan, Joe

Forward
Born: *1951 Cleland, Scotland*
Playing career: *Morton, Leeds United, Manchester United, Southampton, Bristol City, (1964-1989).*
The only Scotsman to score in three World Cup finals, Jordan - a no holds barred, rough, up and at em striker - was in the twilight of his considerable career by the time he arrived at the Dell for a south coast swansong. Despite this, he gave everything for the cause, sticking his head in "where in hurt" with his four lost teeth evidence of his whole hearted style. He had an impressive debut season, hitting 15 as he struck up a 34-goal partnership with Steve Moran in League and Cup. Jordan went on to have a memorable career in the dugout, twice taking of charge Bristol City and taking Hearts to second in the SPL. Coached at Celtic as no.2 to Liam Brady and worked under Harry Redknapp at Portsmouth. Had a stint as former Saints boss Lawrie McMenemy's assistant with Northern Ireland and later linked up with Redknapp again at Spurs and QPR. Jordan has done TV and radio punditry for Five Live and BT Sport, and you can read about his career in his book, "Behind the Dream: Story of a Scottish Footballer".

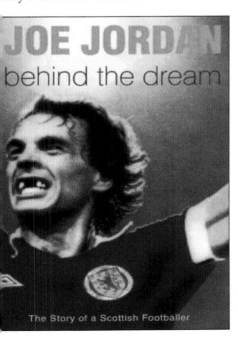

JOE JORDAN
behind the dream

The Story of a Scottish Footballer

Joyce, John

Goalkeeper
Born: *1877 Burton upon Trent* **Died:** *1956*
Playing career: *BSouthampton, Millwall Athletic, Burton United, Blackburn Rovers, Tottenham Hotspur, Millwall, Tottenham Hotspur, Millwall, Gillingham (1895-1920)*
Ironically known as "Tiny" despite standing at 6ft and weighing in at over 14 stone, Joyce joined Southern League champions Southampton as reputable back up to Saints regular 'keeper, England's Jack Robinson. Joyce would have his official debut wiped from the record books as Saints opponents later withdrew from the league. Had a reputaion for long distance goal kicks and ability to reportedly throw the ball from one penalty area to the other! He would go on to play seven times in the league for Saints before turning out for Millwall, Burton United, Blackburn, Tottenham (twice), Millwall again before winding down in Kent with Gillingham and Northfleet United. Joyce once scored a penalty for Spurs and played over 100 games for the north London club before WW1 intervened. Later served Millwall as assistant manager and also briefly took charge as caretaker-manager at The Den. Also worked for the Football Association as liaison officer.

Judd, Mike

Winger
Born: *1948*
Playing career: *Southampton (1967-1969).*
A case of what have been, Judd was touted as Southampton's next big thing when he rose through the ranks to break into the first team at The Dell. Noted for his speed, skill and an eye for goal, Judd played in every outfield position during his first season in the Reserves but despite his talent, game time was at a premium with Judd competing with Mick Channon, Terry Paine and John Sydenham for a place in the team. Judd only played 14 games in in 1968-69 before a nasty injury ended his career - he snapped a cruciate ligament in his ankle after a collision during a Reserve match. Still only 21, he would embark on a new career as a businessman - organising and running ex Saints events, and becoming a successful toastmaster.

Judd, Walter

Centre-forward
Born: *1926 Salisbury, Wiltshire* **Died:** *1964*
Playing career: *Downton, Nomansland,
Southampton (1947-1957)*

Judd was plucked from the New Forest to
the professional game. Having plundered
27 goals in 34 games at Reserve team
level, Judd - an "out and out" striker, he
displaced Eddy Brown and scored nine
goals in his first 19 games at first team
level (a respectable ratio for a player in a
mid table Second Division side) to earn
recognition for England's "B" team. Also
played for Great Britain in the Helsinki
Olympics of 1952 but eventually lost his
place in the Saints side to the emerging
Frank Dudley, dropping back to the second
string before, like the 'other' Judd above, he
suffered a serious leg injury and was forced
into early retirement. He later worked for
the Forestry Commission.

Juryeff, Ian

Forward
Born: *1962 Gosport*
Playing career: *Southampton, IFK Munkfors,
Mansfield Town, Reading, Orient, Ipswich Town,
Hereford United, Halifax Town, Darlington,
Scunthorpe United (1977-1999)*

Juryeff is perhaps better known for his
exploits in Southampton's Reserves,
playing a key role in the side's run to the
FA Youth Cup semi finals, and scoring
24 goals in 41 games at Reserve Team
level. But - hindered by the likes of
Kevin Keegan, Mick Channon and David
Armstrong in the pecking order - he never
played a full senior game for the club.
Indeed, his first team career amounted
to all of 13 minutes with two brief
appearances off the bench. After leaving
the Dell, Juryeff would go on to score over
100 league goals with a plethora of clubs
in the lower leagues. Later played for
Farnborough, Fareham, Havant, Weston
super Mare, on the island with Newport
and Hampshire league Bashley where he
ended his career. Perhaps a case of what
might have been, he later became Football
Development Officer at the Dell, briefly
working the same role at Chelsea before
working in the wine industry in France.

Kachloul, Hassan

Midfielder
Born: *1973 Agadir, Morocco*
Playing career: *Nimes Olympique, Metz,
Dunkerque (loan), Saint-etienne (loan),
Southampton, Aston Villa, Wolverhampton
Wanderers (loan) , Livingston (1988-2005)*

Once Premier League hot property as a
string-pulling enforcer, former Moroccan
international is now a creator of a different
kind as he dabbles in development.
Inspired by frequently moving house as
he would change clubs, Kachloul began
investing in his future whilst playing in
France, buying properties for himself,
renovating them and renting out to
holidaymakers. Son of an architect, an
interest in interior design had always been
in the former Saint's family, and Kachloul
described his early move into property as
"setting himself for when football finishes,
as something on the side." Now, Kachloul
- based in France - buys properties to
rent out, redevelop and then sell on, a
love of "beautiful architecture" inspiring
him. Kachloul has not forgotten football
entirely having completed his UEFA "A"
qualification although he is still awaiting
his first opportunity to move into coaching.

Kanchelskis, Andrei
Winger
Born: *1969 Kirovohrad, Ukrainian SSR*
Playing career: *Dynamo Kiev, Shakhtar Donetsk, Manchester United, Everton, Fiorentina, Rangers, Manchester City, Southampton, Al-Hilal, Saturn Moscow Oblast, Krylia Sovetov (1988-2006)*

Andrei Kanchelskis may have been of Ukranian descent but everyone understood the language of his feet. He had the power to turn a game with deft control and incredible speed. He was signed by United for £650,000 in March 1991 and he soon became a regular. He was part of United's first ever League Cup winning side before helping them lift the first of their Premier League crowns. He then helped do the double in 1994 but a falling out with Sir Alex Ferguson led to his £5.5 million departure to Everton. Continued to play in England for Everton Man City, and Saints. In 2007, Kanchelskis returned to Russia and was appointed sporting director of FC Nosta Novotroitsk. However in December 2009, he became manager of Torpedo Moscow. Played only once for Southampton in a League Cup tie in 2002. His book "Kanchelskis" was released in 2009. The Russian is the answer to the quiz question: "Who is the only player to both feature in and score in the Glasgow, Manchester and Merseyside derbies."

Andrei Kanchelskis

Katalinic, Ivan
Goalkeeper
Born: *1951 Trogir, FPR Yugoslavia*
Playing career: *Slaven Trogir, Southampton, Hajduk Split (1964-1984)*

Becoming the English top division's first Croatia international, Katalinic arrived on the south coast with compatriot Ivan Golac having. A member of Hajduk Split's golden generation, the gloveman had plundered four league titles and five consecutive Yugoslavian cups. Nicknamed "Banks" in homage to the legendary English keeper, Katalinic made 54 appearances for Southampton in his three years at the club, competing with Peter Wells and then having to contend with the arrival of Peter Shilton. Equally capable of brilliance and the customary hiccup, or "Katastrophes" as the media called them. He played 13 times for Yugoslavia and kept goal as the side finished third at France '98. Later went on to have a lengthy career as a coach, goalkeeping mentor and a manager. Most recently worked back at Hajduk Split the club where he made his name.

Keay, Walter 'Watty'
Inside-forward
Born: *1871 Whiteinch, Glasgow, Scotland*
Died: *1943*
Playing career: *Brookland, Whitfield, Whiteinch, Partick Thistle, Darlington, Derby County, Southampton (1893-1900)*

The sight of Walter "Watty" Keay and outside left Joe Turner in tandem became a thrilling sight for Saints fans of the early Victorian era. Indeed, the two would combine for arguably the most totemic duopoly of the Southern League era. With Keay the creator and Turner the dead-eye marksman, Southampton won three successive league titles (1896/97, 1897/98 and 1898/99) to establish themselves as the division - and the day's - predominant team. Scored the club's first ever goal at The Dell before retiring a year later to run the *Bell and Crown* pub in Melbourne Street in Southampton. Later held a job as a shipwright on the Docks before returning to the club as reserve team coach. Also scouted for the club in the 1930s.

Keegan, Kevin

Forward
Born: *1951 Armthorpe, Doncaster*
Playing career: *Scunthorpe United, Liverpool, Southampton, Newcastle United. (1968-1983).*
The very definition of a "coup" or a "marquee signing" in modern parlance, Lawrie McMenemy's acquisition of the affable, bona fide European Cup winner was one that no one outside of Southampton saw coming with the manager arranging an impromptu press conference to announce Keegan's arrival. Keegan - two time World Player of the Year - proved a talismanic figurehead in tpne of the greatest sides The Dell had ever seen, a flamboyant presence at the string-pulling centre of a team boasting the talents of Alan Ball, Phil Boyer, Mick Channon and Charlie George et al. Steered Saints to their highest ever League finish, sixth, in his debut season, with the side even briefly topping the table the following campaign before falling away to seventh. Capped 63 times by England, Keegan embarked on a managerial career with Newcastle (twice), Fulham, England and Manchester City. Considered one of the greatest players of his generation, Keegan scored 37 goals in 68 games on the south coast.

Since retirement, Keegan has remained involved in football - not only as a manager as already mentioned, but he has run a soccer school in Scotland, appeared on Football Focus and Match of the Day and is currently a pundit for ESPN. His book: "My Life in Football" (2019) has proved a best-seller, telling the story of one of English football's greatest ever players.

Keeping, Michael

Full-back
Born: *1902 Milford on Sea* **Died:** *1984*
Playing career: *Southampton, Fulham, Milford on Sea (1919-1939)*
Signing for Southampton as a fresh-faced 16-year-old rookie, Keeping would have to wait four and a half years for his debut, but did become a consistent, ever present cog in Arthur Chadwick's well oiled Southampton machine. It seems a travesty that he was never recognised at international level by England, although he did tour north America and Canada with an FA Representative XI in 1926-27, helping Saints to the FA Cup semi finals that same year. Keeping retired in 1941 to work in his family's motorcar business, later managed in Spain and Holland. Son of Olympic medal winning cyclist Fred Keeping.

Kevin Keegan

Kelly, Gerry

Winger
Born: *1908 Sunderland* **Died:** *1983*
Playing career: *Sunderland, Nelson, Huddersfield Town, Charlton Athletic, Chester-City, Port Vale, Southampton (1927-1939)*

Blessed with blistering pace and power, Kelly had already amassed over 200 games in the upper echelons of the English game when he arrived at The Dell. Although he brought a wealth of experience with him, Kelly would spend more time in the club's reserves than he would in the senior side, playing only 19 games in two years at The Dell. He remained registered with Southampton when war broke out, guesting for Shrewsbury during the conflict but retiring from the game a few months later to become a mechanic. Died in 1983.

Kelly, Hugh

Goalkeeper
Born: *1919 Lurgan, Ireland* **Died:** *1977*
Playing career: *Glenavon, Belfast Celtic, Fulham, Southampton, Exeter City, Weymouth (1936-1956)*

Kelly combined a part time career in Gaelic football in his native Ireland with working in his family's drapery business. After catching the eye with his impressive ball handling skills, he was invited for a trial by Glenavon FC and so his association football days began. He once conceded thirteen goals in a record defeat to Belfast Celtic, but this did not stop him being selected to play for an Ireland Select XI and, ironically, being signed by the very same Belfast Celtic side that he had endured his nightmare against! Having crossed the Irish Sea to England, London and Fulham in particular, Kelly earned four caps for Ireland. Joining Southampton in a straight swap with Ian Black, he became first choice before his time on the south coast ended in ignominy. Breaking a curfew in an unsavoury incident with two women in a Leicester hotel, a scuffle ensued and Kelly gave Southampton coach Jimmy Easson a bloodied nose and a black eye. Falling to fifth choice, Kelly was "rescued" by the Devonians of Exeter City, later spending a brief spell at Weymouth . He later returned to Northern Ireland where he worked as a shop keeper.

Keller, Kasey

Goalkeeper
Born: *1969 Olympia, Washington, United States*
Playing career: *Portland Pilots, Portland Timbers, Millwall, Leicester City, Rayo Vallecano, Tottenham Hotspur, Southampton, Borussia Monchengladbach, Fulham, Seattle Sounders FC (1988-2011)*

His four games for relegation-bound Southampton proved but a whistlestop during Keller's extensive 16 year career both in Europe and his native homeland. Totalled over 500 appearances and capped over 100 times by the USA, playing in two World Cups 16 years apart. Out of favour at Spurs, Keller was signed by Saints on an emergency month long loan deal with Antti Niemi injured. His debut would coincide with the Saints second win of an ultimately torrid season, coming in a south coast derby against Portsmouth under Steve Wigley, but the side would collect only one point from Keller's three further appearances as Harry Redknapp replaced the sacked Wigley, Keller has since served as the USA national side's assistant manager, worked as a commentator and summariser for BT Sport and ESPN.

Kemp, Fred

Half-back
Born: *1946 Salerno, Italy*
Playing career: *Wolverhampton Wanderers, Southampton, Blackpool, Halifax Town, Hereford United. (1964-1974)*

Italian born Kemp brought a classic continental swagger to the Dell, with his "crowd pleasing surges up the pitch", scoring on his debut with a 5-2 win over Preston in 1965. Nicknamed "Fiery Fred", Kemp helped steer the Saints to promotion but then found himself as back up to the increasingly prolific Ron Davies. Following the signing of Brian O'Neil, Kemp was deemed surplus to requirements and moved north to another coastal club, Blackpool. Kemp also turned out for Halifax Town, Hereford United, Durban in South Africa and wound up his career with Weymouth and Telford at non league level. In retirement, Kemp moved to Wolverhampton where he worked in his family's business, supplying furniture to supply offices and schools.

Kenna, Jeff

Right-back
Born: *1970 Dublin, Ireland*
Playing career: *Southampton, Blackburn Rovers, Tranmere Rovers, Wigan Athletic, Birmingham City, Derby County, Kidderminster Harriers (1989-2005)*

Capable of operating on either flank, Kenna became a regular as the inaugural Premier League season kicked off, sharing the no.2 shirt with Jason Dodd as new Saints manager Ian Branfoot shuffled his pack. Kenna would survive a plethora of managerial coming and goings during but would eventually find the lure of Kenny Dalglish's big spending Blackburn Rovers too good to turn down. Moving to Ewood Park for a £1.5 million, Kenna played his part in Rovers' run in to a shock Premier League title, playing the Champions League the following season. A one cap wonder for the Republic of Ireland, Kenna later played for Derby and Birmingham before trying his hand at management in his native homeland with Galway United and St Patrick's Athletic. He's also worked as a coach "across the pond" and currently works as a player agent in Solihull.

Kennedy, Paddy

Left-back
Born: *1934 Dublin, Irish Republic*
Died: *2007*
Playing career: *Manchester United, Blackburn Rovers, Southampton, Oldham Athletic (1950-1960)*

A less well known member of Manchester United's all conquering "Busby Babes", Kennedy only played once at senior level for Busby's well stocked side in 1954 before moving to Blackburn helping Rovers to top division promotion. After which, he moved from the cotton mills of Lancashire to the south coast to join Ted Bates at Saints, along with eight more newly signed men. He moved on to pastures new at the end of a solitary campaign with the Third Division champions. Moved to Oldham but never played a minute for them before moving to Urmston, in the shadows of Old Trafford, where he managed an amateur side and worked for *Massey Ferguson. Died in 2007*

Kennedy, William

Half-back
Born: *1912 Saltcoats, North Ayrshire, Scotland*
Died: *1989*
Playing career: *Portsmouth, Carlisle United, Crewe Alexandra, Southampton, Hamilton Academical (1932-1938)*

Played one game for Portsmouth before a handful of appearances with Carlisle and Crewe paved the way for joining Saints - undergoing an overhaul of players under manager George Goss. Kennedy - described as a "reliable centre half" would form an impressive defensive triumvirate - unfortunately but inevitably known as "KKK" - Kennedy, Cyril King and Billy Kingdon. Kennedy became a virtual ever present until being displaced by Dave Affleck midway through his second season at the club. As new manager Tom Parker shuffled his pack, Kennedy found himself demoted to the Reserves before moving back to his native Scotland with Hamilton Academical. However, the Scotsman did return south after the War, and would serve on the *Queen Mary* cruise liner until 1962. Settling back in Southampton and taking a job with working *Mullard*, a Millbrook based electronic firm. Died in 1989, aged 77.

Kenton, Darren

Defender
Born: *1978 Wandsworth*
Playing career: *Norwich City, Southampton, Leicester City, Leeds United (1996-2010)*

London born Kenton - championed by Saints chairman Rupert Lowe as a "quality English player" - signed on a free transfer in 2003. Kenton was unfortunate that his time at St Mary's dovetailed with a transitional season under Gordon Strachan, and with Saints lurching towards relegation under four different managers, Kenton suffered a string of injuries and never played more than three games in a row. Offered a chance of regular football - albeit in the second tier - with Leicester, Kenton signed permanently for the east Midlands side before playing for Leeds and Cheltenham in England. He would later try his hand across the pond, turning out for the Rochester Rhinos before setting up his own personal trainer business.

Khalej, Tahar El

Defender/Midfielder
Born: *1968 Marrakech, Morocco*
Playing career: *Kawkab Marrakech, UD Leiria, Benfica, Southampton, Charlton Athletic (1990-2003)*

Glenn Hoddle's first signing, the 58-cap Moroccan international endured a baptism of fire. Saints crashed to a 7-2 defeat at Spurs although the centre-back gave his new side the lead before everything went wrong. Faced with stiff competition at centre-half from Claus Lundekvam and Dean Richards, Hoddle shoehorned him into the team in an unfamiliar midfield role. Despite his 6ft 3 frame, El Khalej was as a neat and tidy passer. Was threatened with legal action after injuring Kieron Dyer in a tackle that saw him sent off and put the England international's World Cup in jeopardy. He moved to Charlton after 65 games on the south coast but retired from the game after three appearances for the Addicks, returning to his native Morocco. Played in two World Cup finals for the African nation, in 1994 and again four years later in France. El Khalej later bought his first club as a player, Kawkab Marrakech and oversaw two title wins, first as club president and then as chairman.

Kiddle, Robert

Forward
Born: *1869 Southampton* **Died:** *1918*
Playing career: *Southampton Harriers, Southampton St. Mary's (1889-1895)*

A track sprinter of considerable repute in his heyday, locally-born Kiddle put his prized asset to good use when he joined the newly formed Southampton St Mary's as one of the club's first ever players in 1889. Won the Hampshire Cup at both junior and senior level, but Kiddle was restricted to cup games only as his time at the Antelope Ground largely preceded the club's Southern League era. Kiddle would make one appearance in that competition, in a ignominious 7-3 defeat at Clapton, and the pacy forward was never seen again in Southampton colours. He became a brewery owner but got mixed up in fraud, serving a two year jail sentence. Later worked as a clerk and then as a fish merchant in Southampton.

Kiernan, Frederick

Goalkeeper
Born: *1919 Dublin, Ireland* **Died:** *1981*
Playing career: *Shamrock Rovers, Southampton, Yeovil Town (1942-1958)*

Small in size but mighty in both stature and ability, Fred Kiernan was plucked from Ireland's non league for a then record £4,500. Known for his "tremendous agility", he quickly saw off competition from understudy John Christie to become first choice between the sticks at The Dell. Ireland soon recognised his talent, earning three more caps for the Republic during his time on the south coast to add to the two already won during his time in his native homeland. Over the next five seasons, Kiernan would go to play 136 times in League and Cup for Southampton, playing his last game for the club at the age of 38. After which, he would join division lower Yeovil of the Southern League, applying - ultimately without success - for the vacant managerial job at Peterborough. He later returned to Southampton where he became the secretary of the sport and social club at AC Delco. Won two Irish League titles with Shelbourne and Shamrock.

Killean, Edward

Half-back
Born: *1874 Blackburn*
Playing career: *3rd Coldstream Guards, Blackburn Rovers, Glossop North End, Southampton, New Brompton, Blackpool (1894-1904)*

A "sturdy and diligent" player, Killean - a former Goldstream Guard - arrived at a very strong and well stocked Southampton side having made his name with hometown team Blackburn in the top division. Saints would go on to win a fourth Southern League title in five years, but inside-forward turned wing-half Killean only made two appearances, deputising for the injured Arthur Chadwick at the turn of the year. Killean did little wrong in his two matches, "distributing the ball with precision" but ultimately he failed to do enough. Killean signed for divisional rivals New Brompton, becoming a regular before returning to the Football League with another coastal club, Blackpool. Killean once appeared in court charged with breach of the peace, receiving a fine but nothing more.

Sid Kimpton

Kimpton, Gabriel "Sid"

Striker
Born: *1887 Leavesden* **Died:** *1968*
Playing career: *Leavesden, Southampton*

Unusually for the era he played in when many of his peers flitted freely between clubs, "Sid" Kimpton spent his entire, decade-long career at Southampton. A Watford reject, the Hertfordshire-born striker scored a hat-trick on his Reserve team debut and was instantly promoted to the main man at centre-forward in the first team. He became a regular in Saints Southern League side, staying with the club throughout the First World War while also guesting for Pompey and Thorneycrofts. Re-signed after the conflict, Kimpton - by now a 30 something - only featured twice in the first post-War season, earning a benefit match before retiring having played 149 times for the club, scoring 30 goals. Kimpton went on to have an extensive career as a manager in Europe, including two stints in charge of the France national side - managing the team at the second FIFA World Cup in 1934. Won the French League and Cup as boss of Paris-based Racing Club. Retired back in his native Leavesden. Died in 1968.

King, Cyril

Half-back
Born: *1915 Plymouth* **Died:** *1981*
Career: *Southampton, Darlington (1933-1939)*

A half-back signed as a younger alternative to the ageing and served the club well across a five year stint at The Dell. King would form an imposing "KKK" triumvirate with Bill Kennedy and Billy Kingdon but Saints were perennial strugglers, finishing 18th and then 19th in the Second Division in King's first two years on the south coast. Although officially retained by Saints in the last pre-War season of 1938-39, King moved back to his native Plymouth where he worked on the Docks. Briefly turned out for Darlington before being posted to North Africa where he served in the RAF. After the War, he played part-time for Yeovil and non league Winchester before becoming a prison security guard. Played 100 games for Saints.

King, Ernest

Half-back

Born: *1903 Southampton* **Died:** *1993*

Playing career: *Bournemouth & Boscombe Athletic, Southampton, Guildford City (1923-1927)*

Southampton born, King began life as a journalist working for the *Southern Daily Echo*, combining this role with playing part time for Bournemouth & Boscombe Athletic. Staying local, he joined Southern League Saints to make the step up to the second tier. He never gave up his day job, playing on Saturdays whilst continuing to work in the Echo offices. He went on to play over 100 times for the reserves, but only played twice at senior level. Later joined Southern League Guildford City in the Southern League and had a stint on the island with Cowes before retiring with liver problems. He worked for the paper for almost half a century, finally putting down his typewriter in 1968 after 48 years.

Kingdon, Billy

Half-back

Born: *1907 Worcester* **Died:** *1977*

Playing career: *Kepex (Worcester), Kidderminster Harriers, Aston Villa, Southampton (1924-1946)*

Right-half Kingdon played junior football in the Birmingham & District League for Kidderminster before joining Aston Villa - initially on amateur terms - before signing pro in 1926. In his time at Villa Park, he and the club were moderately successful, finishing First Division runners up in 1930/31 and again in 1932/33, with a third placed finish in 1928-29. The claret and blue reached the FA Cup semi finals in both 1929 and 1934, losing to eventual winners Manchester City. After relegation, Kingdon left Villa in the summer of 1936 to join Saints. At the Dell he proved to have a "nice line of distribution and looked to be a good asset." He briefly skippered the Saints before joining lowly Yeovil & Petters United (known today as Yeovil Town) as player manager after a solitary goal in 49 games for the Saints. He remained with the club through WWII, but left to take charge of Southern League Weymouth. Later worked as a carpenter and ran the Fountain Hotel in the town.

Kirby, George

Centre-forward

Born: *1933 Liverpool* **Died:** *2000*

Playing career: *Everton, Sheffield Wednesday, Plymouth Argyle, Southampton, Coventry City, Swansea Town, Walsall, New York Generals, Brentford, Worcester City (1952-1969)*

With his side rooted to the foot of the second tier, Ted Bates brought in Kirby to add steel and physicality to a Saints side in need of both. An infamous hard-man, Kirby's reputation preceded him as he set about kicking anything that moved. Despite this, he was well liked off the field and there was more to his game - as his ratio of 31 goals in 74 games at Saints shows. They would eventually finish in the top half of the Division Two table during Kirby's debut season, with the new arrival having clearly had an impact. Finishing fifth the following season, Saints were evolving and Kirby was no longer in Bates's plans. In his post-playing days, Kirby had a lengthy managerial and coaching CV, taking charge of Halifax (twice) and Watford on these shores before a spell in Kuwait and back in Europe with IA, one of Iceland's leading clubs.

Kirkman, Norman

Full-back

Born: *1920 Bolton* **Died:** *1995*

Career: *Burnley, Rochdale, Chesterfield, Leicester City, Southampton, Exeter City (1939-1953)*

Kirkman's breakthrough as a professional would unfortunately coincide with the outbreak of World War Two, meaning he was 26 by the time he made a senior bow. Arrived at the Dell in 1950, Kirkman would feature only 20 times for Saints, being hampered by injury. He would then make the step down to Third Division Exeter, lured by the prospect of a player-manager role, with George Roughton moving the other way to take over at Saints as successor to the sacked Sid Cann. He later took over at Bradford PA and Northwich Victoria, dropping out of football to become a baker. He became a scout for various clubs across the country, including Saints, Newcastle, Leeds, Wolves, Stoke and Carlisle. Died back in his hometown Bolton in 1995.

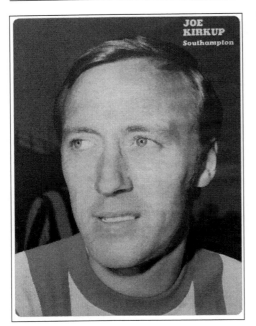

JOE KIRKUP
Southampton

Kitchen, George
Goalkeeper
Born: *1876 Fairfield, Derbyshire* **Died:** *1969*
Playing career: *Buxton, Stockport County, Everton, West Ham United, Southampton(1897-1914)*

Upon arriving at The Dell in 1912, the experienced Kitchen - part of the Everton side to finish First Division runners up in 1901-02 - immediately instilled a sense of confidence and calm composure into a defence that had been struggling. Despite being in the twilight of his playing days, he would retain his place until midway through the next season when, by now 37, Kitchen was displaced in goal by younger upgrade Ernie Steventon. Moving to Boscombe, he went part time to play in the South Eastern League for the club known today as AFC Bournemouth. Kitchen also secured a position as a professional at Queen's Park Golf Club, a job which saw him continue to earn a living in his post-football days. Glance at his stats and you'll see that Kitchen - remarkably for a goalkeeper - scored five goals for West Ham, unusually becoming the Hammers first choice penalty taker including one on his debut - the first ever such instance of a keeper' scoring in his first game!

Kirkup, Joe
Full-back
Born: *1939 Hexham*
Playing career: *West Ham United, Chelsea, Southampton. (1958-1973).*

Kirkup's sporting future looked set to lie with the oval-shaped ball, as a rugby playing teenager in both league and union before he was persuaded to take up football - what a decision that turned out to be! An integral part of one of West Ham's greatest ever sides, he rose through the ranks in east London, winning the FA Youth Cup (with John Lyall and Smith for company) before making his first team debut at 17. Kirkup won the Cup Winners Cup with the Hammers and also earned an FA Cup runners up medal having moved across the capital to Chelsea. He went on to serve Southampton well, running up almost 200 appearances four goals under Ted Bates, until successor Lawrie McMenemy released him in 1974 after Kirkup had played nearly 400 games for his three clubs at League level. Kirkup managed Durban in South Africa before returning to England to run a pub in Alton, a sports shop in Guildford and then a newsagents in Ewell. Retired to France where he still lives to this day.

Kite, Phil
Goalkeeper
Born: *1962 Bristol*
Playing career: *Bristol Rovers, Tottenham Hotspur, Southampton, Middlesbrough, Gillingham, Bournemouth, Sheffield United, Mansfield Town, Plymouth Argyle, Rotherham United, Crewe Alex, Stockport C, Cardiff City, Bristol City. (1980-1996).*

Capped by England at youth and schoolboy level, Kite's career was neatly bookended by turning out for both of his home town clubs, starting at Rovers and ending with City. In between, he played for twelve different sides but, despite three years with the Saints, he was limited to only four Division I appearances. This was mainly due to the presence of England behemoths Peter Shilton and Tim Flowers, with Keith Granger effectively relegating Kite to fourth choice. After p a whistle stop tour of England's lower leagues. Returned to Bristol Rovers to work as physio before serving as player/coach with Bristol City.

Knapp, Tony

Defender
Born: *1936 Newstead*
Playing career: *Nottingham Forest, Leicester City, Southampton, Coventry City, Los Angeles Wolves, Tranmere Rovers, Poole Town (1955-1972)*

Ted Bates paid a then record feee of £27,500 to bring Knapp to the Dell, and the manager's faith in the "commanding" defender soon repeated dividends - even if Knapp's team mates were not so sure. Quickly becoming an ever present, he would make 103 consecutive appearances, until injury kept him out, and developing into Southampton's leader. A man ahead of his time and confident in his own ability, Knapp would ultimately become the first man to captain Saints in the First Division following promotion in the 1965-66 season. Later played for Coventry, Tranmere and non league Poole Town and for LA Wolves in the USA. Knapp would embark on an extensive coaching career, initially in England but then in Iceland where he had two spells in charge of the national side. Managed eleven Norwegian clubs, and continues to reside in the country's fourth largest city, Stavanger, to this day.

Tony Knapp

Knill, Alan

Defender
Born: *1964 Slough*
Playing career: *Sheffield United, Southampton, Halifax Town, Swansea City, Bury, Cardiff City, Scunthorpe United, Rotherham United (1978-2001)*

Started his career as a trainee at the Dell in 1978, signing as a professional four years later but he failed to break into the first team, no surprise given the relative embarrassment of riches Saints boasted at the time with the likes of Nick Holmes, Mick Channon, Phil Boyer and Kevin Keegan at their disposal. Played over 100 games for Halifax and also turned out for Swansea, Bury, Cardiff, Scunthorpe and Rotherham in a lower league career. Capped once by Wales against the Dutch. Mirroring his nomadic existence as a player, Knill went on to have an extensive career in the lower league dugouts, managing Rotherham twice, Torquay United twice (once as a caretaker), Scunthorpe and Bury. He is currently assistant manager to Chris Wilder at Sheffield United.

Kosowski, Kamil

Midfielder
Born: *1977 Poland*
Playing career: *Gornnik Zabrze, Wisla Krakow, FC Kaiserslautern, Southampton, Chievo, CAdiz, APOEL, Apollon Limassol, (1984-2013)*

A skillful, mercurial winger, Kosowski had played for Gornick Zabrze and Wisla Krakow in his native homeland before arriving at St Mary's via a brief spell in Germany with FC Kaiserslauten. With compatriot Tomasz Hajto already in situ, newly relegated Southampton were in the middle of their first post-Premier League season under Harry Redknapp. Considered a "fine dead ball expert who can deliver well to the forwards", Kosowski showed only glimpses of his undoubted skill and hopes of a permanent deal to the south coast were sunk when Redknapp abandoned ship and set sail - for a second time - to Portsmouth. Played in the Champions League for the Cypriots APOEL and also featured in the World Cup of 2006 for Poland. Kosowski has been capped 52 times for his country.

Lambert, Rickie

Striker
Born: *1982 Kirkby*
Playing career: *Blackpool, Macclesfield Town, Stockport County, Rochdale, Bristol Rovers, Southampton, Liverpool, WBA (1992-2015)*

It takes some doing to be compared to arguably Southampton's "God" himself, but that's what happened with Rickie Lambert. Not only did he emulate his idol by donning Saints iconic number 7, but he drew comparisons with Le Tissier because of his extraordinary penalty record - boasting a 100% record from the spot (even Le Tiss missed one) and ability to create something from nothing. Lambert had had an unremarkable career with five different clubs across three different leagues when Saints signed him for a measly £1m. What a bargain that proved to be! Boasting an impressive ratio of 108 goals in 206 games, he plundered 30 goals in his debut season.

Rickie Lambert

Still the goals continued to flow, with 21 the next season as Southampton won promotion back to the Championship. He would top scorer again for the third season in succession, hitting 31 for the 2011-12 to help secure a second successive promotion as Saints returned to the Premier League. But how would Lambert do in his first foray to England's elite league? 15 goals - the joint highest by an English player that year - answered those doubts in style. As a consquence, Lambert made his international debut - the first of eleven national caps - against Scotland in a 2013 friendly. He would score with his first touch, going to play for his country throughout England's brief and ill-fated 2014 World Cup campaign. He scored 34 penalties from 34 at Saints. He later played for Liverpool, West Brom and Cardiff. Retired in 2017. Lambert played and managed to score in each of English football's top four divisions.
https://twitter.com/rickielambert09

Lawrence, George

Midfielder
Born: *1962 Kensington*
Playing career: *Southampton, Oxford United, Millwall, Bournemouth, Mikkelin Palloilijat, Weymouth, Portsmouth, Hibernians , Hednesford Town, Rushden & Diamonds (1979-1997)*

The very definition of the word unpredictable, George Lawrence - London born with West Indian roots - was a selection box of pace, trickery and "heroic" derring do. Full of strong, surging runs, Lawrence at his best would completely perplex defenders and cause havoc for the likes of Mick Channon, Steve Morgan, Kevin Keegan and David Armstrong to exploit. Having played only a handful of games first time round, he moved to Oxford and his days at The Dell seemed numbered. But Saints newly appointed manager Chris Nicholl had other ideas and - its fair to say - he was far more productive second time round. As the old adage often says, you should never go back but - true to form - the opposite was true for Lawrence. Evading tackle after tackle, he would trip over the corner flag and cause delight and despair in equal measure.

A much cherished and popular part of Saints folklore, Lawrence played 83 times over his two stints at The Dell, scoring 15 goals in the process. Following his second departure from Saints, Lawrence would remain in the game for another decade, coaching at non league level and working as a player liaison officer and as an agent. He returned to Saints as an ambassador for their anti-racism arm, *Racism Just A'int Saintly*, a local initiative working alongside national organisations on the issue. Since 2013, Lawrence has been employed as a London bus driver and combined this role with working in the TfL (Transport for London) offices.

Le Saux, Graeme

Left-back
Born: *1968 St. Helier, Jersey*
Playing career: *Chelsea, Blackburn Rovers, Chelsea, Southampton. (1987-2005)*
Jersey born left back, he featured mainly at full back with two spells at Chelsea and Blackburn sandwiched in between. Capped 36 times by England, scoring one goal and an ever present at the France 98' World Cup. A Premier League winner with Rovers in 1995, he also earned a League Cup and European Cup Winners Cup medal at Stamford Bridge.

Le Saux - once the country's most expensive defender - joined Saints in 2003 as part of the deal that took Wayne Bridge to Le Saux's former side Chelsea. Since his retirement from the game in 2005 Le Saux has published an autobiography, worked for the BBC, appeared as a contestant in Dancing on Ice and enjoyed punditry and co-commentary roles for Match of the Day 2 and BBC Radio 5 Live. In a non sporting capacity he's presented on programmes such as Working Lunch. His business acumen earned him an Ambassadorial role in a private banking team for the Sports Desk of financial firm ABN AMRO. He currently runs his own football schools and works as a motivational speaker. He has also released two books since retirement: "Left Field: A Footballer Apart" (2010) and Le Saux: my Life and Football (2007).

Le Tissier, Matthew

Attacking Midfielder
Born: *1968 Guernsey*
Playing career: *Southampton (1986-2002)*
The man known simply as "Le God" by the adoring Southampton faithful continues to hold a special place in the heart of any Saint. A maverick genius, you can be sure that Matt Le Tissier will sit near the top when it comes to any discussion of the greatest ever to don the iconic red and white stripes. Having previously had a trial with Oxford, he joined Saints in 1985 and turned pro the following year. This was to start a remarkable career which saw him play 443 times and score a record breaking 161 goals. Even in retirement, his legacy and legend has not diminished. "Le Tiss" -

capped eight times by England - continues to be heavily involved with the club today. Le Tissier was a regular on Sky Sports flagship results show *Soccer Saturday* until he was axed by the channel in 2020 after 12 years as part of a shake up. He continues to keep busy, though, representing Southampton as a club ambassador, and working for their charity arm Saints Foundation - supporting projects to improve the lives of children and youth people through football in and around the city. This included working both with the Foundation and food charity FareShare in delivering meals and running the food banks to provide for the vulnerable people in the city during the Covid-19 pandemic. Le Tissier has set up two local coaching academies - MLT in the Community and MLTNC (Matt Le Tissier Natural Coaching Academy) - aimed at enabling children and gifted youngsters to improve and develop key parts of their game under the tutelage of Le Tissier and former AFC Bournemouth player Jody Rivers. Since retirement, he regularly participates in Legends matches with the ex-Saints as well as working in hospitality for the Saints as a much anticipated after-dinner speaker and Q & A host.

You can read Matt's musings in his autobiography: "Taking Le Tiss" and follow him on Twitter at: *https://twitter.com/ mattletiss7*

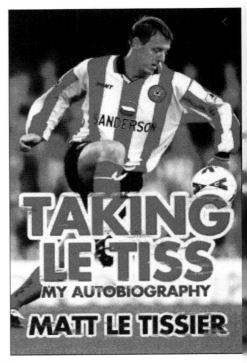

Lee, David

Midfielder

Born: *1967 Whitefield*
Playing career: *Bolton Wanderers, Bury, Southampton, Wigan Athletic, Blackpool, Carlisle United, Morecambe (1986-2001)*

Made over 500 appearances during his career as a professional with the vast majority of these coming for clubs in and around his native north West. Signing for Southampton for £350,000, Lee's foray to the the south coast proved a short lived one. A fast, direct winger "who could motor", Lee arrived as Ian Branfoot's first Saints signing to replace the departed Rod Wallace. He started six successive games in 1991-92 and played once in the inaugural Premiership season but that proved the zenith of his time at The Dell and having played only 20 times for the club, Lee returned north, linking up with Bolton, helping them to back-to-back promotions to get his Premiership chance. Later played for Wigan, before loan spells at Blackpool, Lancashire rivals Morecambe and finally Carlisle. In his his post-retirement days he coached at two of his former clubs, the Trotters and the Latics as Head of Academy.

DID YOU KNOW?"

"Terry Paine holds the record for most appearances He played 815 times between 1956 and 1974."

Lee, Ernest Albert "Bert"

Right-half

Born: *1879 Bridport* **Died:** *1958*
Playing career: *Brewery Rovers, Hamworthy St. Michaels, Poole, Southampton, Dundee, Southampton (1894-1915)*

A figurehead in Southampton's early Victorian era dominance of the Southern League, Lee - a defender of "inexhaustible" energy, would go on to play more games at that level that anyone else. His initial six year spell with Southampton brought storied success - Southern League championship medals in 1901, 1903 and 1904, an FA Cup runners up medal in 1902 and England recognition two years later (against Wales). But Lee was not done there. Not content with an impressive haul of silverware in these parts, Lee moved north of the border to sign for Dundee, playing for them in every position during the next five seasons. Lee became the first man to captain a Scottish club side, winning the Scottish Cup in the process. He would return to the Dell for a further four years before the outbreak of War ultimately ended his playing career. Lee served as a sergeant in the Third Hampshire Regiment and the 17th Royal Fusiliers before taking up a coaching position with the club's Reserves in time for the first post-War campaign. He later helped to coach the first team, getting a benefit match before retiring to become a radio and technology salesman. Lee played 369 times for Saints.

CHURCHMAN'S CIGARETTES.

A. LEE.

Lee, Sammy

Midfielder
Born: *1959 Liverpool*
Playing career: *Liverpool, QPR, Osasuna, Southampton (loan), Bolton Wanderers (1975-1991)*

Sammy Lee proved the epitome of the old adage: never judge a book by its cover. Diminutive and portly, "Little" Sam belied his shortcomings to earn 14 caps for England and prove an integral part of Bob Paisley and Joe Fagan's all conquering Liverpool dynasty in the 70s and 80s. At the peak of his considerable powers, Lee would become known for his strong distribution, relentless running and powerful shot. Lee would live the dream with his hometown club, rising through the ranks to win three First Division championships, four league Cups, and two European Cups. Ageing and past 30 by the time he arrived on the south coast - via QPR and Osasuna - Lee would only play twice as a substitute under Chris Nicholl before a brief spell at Bolton and then retirement. Lee would remain intrinsically involved in the game having hung up his boots, coaching at Liverpool under Graeme Souness before a stint with England in Sven Goran Eriksson's coaching set up. He later went to Bolton as assistant to Sam Allardyce, earning the nickname of "Little Sam" in contrast to his boss who is widely known as "Big" Sam. He also worked under Ronald Koeman at St Mary's.

Sammy Lee

Lewis, George

Striker
Born 1913, Troed-y-rhiw, Wales **Died:** *1981*
Career: *Dartford Watford Brighton Southampton*

A stocky, "well built" centre forward with a never say die attitude, Lewis signed for Second Division Southampton from lower league Watford for a four figure fee. Having served in the war as a PT instructor, the Welshman also guested for Chester and Watford during the conflict before moving south to join Saints. Taking over from the stricken Doug McGibbon, Lewis would make the number nine shirt his own, scoring 14 times in a run of 25 consecutive games up top, including a hat-trick in an FA Cup tie at Bury. Ending his debut campaign as joint top scorer, Lewis was unable to replicate his form in front of goal during his second season - 1947/48. Charlie Wayman took up the mantle, eventually forcing Lewis to go elsewhere, returning to the Third Division South with Brighton. Had a spell at non league level in Kent with Dartford and later became their groundsman. Died in 1981

Lewis, John

Inside-forward
Born: *1881 Aberystwyth, Wales* **Died:** *1954*
Playing career: *Portsmouth, Burton United, Bristol Rovers, Brighton & Hove Albion, Southampton, Croydon Common, Burton United (1899-1910)*

Despite his age, 25-year-old Lewis was a relative veteran when he arrived at Southampton having already turned out for four different clubs, including Saints fierce local rivals Pompey. A diminutive and skilful centre-forward, he won the Southern League title with Bristol Rovers and had been capped by Wales (the first Rovers player to do so), he top scored during his solitary season at Saints. Lewis's ten goals from 24 games was a reputable return, despite regular chop and changing up front to fill the void left by the departed Harrison. A drifting, kindred spirit, Lewis was soon on the move again, having a spell back in the Southern League's Second Division with Croydon Common before a final swansong with the soon-to-be-defunct Burton Albion. Died 1954 aged 73.

Licka, Mario

Midfielder

Born: *1982 Ostrava, Czechoslovakia*
Playing career: *Banik Ostrava, Livorno, FC SlovAcko, Southampton, Banik Ostrava, Brest, SK Slavia Prague, FC Istres, Nieciecza (1986-date)*

Having failed to make the grade at West Ham, George Burley took a punt on the globe trotting Czech international and signed him on a two year deal. It was not until Burley's successor Nigel Pearson's tenure, though, that Licka - named after World Cup winning Argentinian superstar Mario Kempes - made his mark at St Mary's. A string of consistently impressive showings helped stave off relegation to England's third tier but when Rupert Lowe returned and Pearson was out, it spelt the end of an enigmatic two year spell at the club. Licka returned to the Czech Republic, playing for his hometown team of Ostrava and Slavia Prague before a spell in France. Capped three times by Czech Republic, Licka - now 38 - continues to play in the third tier of Czech football for SK Benesov. His father and brother were also both professional players and earned international recognition.

Liddell, Edward

Wing-half

Born: *1878 Sunderland* **Died:** *1968*
Playing career: *Sunderland, Southampton, Clapton Orient, Southend United, Arsenal (1901-1920)*

Liddell would never get a chance on at first club Sunderland, eventually being offered a move to the south coast with second tier Southampton. Adept at reading the game and with an ideal height for a centre-back, his lack of pace ultimately counted against him and Liddell would only play once for the first team - and what an extraordinary outing it would be, Saints memorably beating Northampton 9-1. He left at the end of that season, seeking regular first team football, eventually signing for Clapton Orient and going on to make over 200 appearances in the Second Division. Had a brief stint with Arsenal before going into management with Southend United, QPR, Fulham and Luton. Later worked as a scout for a number of clubs.

Light, William

Goalkeeper

Born: *1913 Woolston, Southampton* **Died:** *1979*
Playing career: *Southampton, West Bromwich Albion, Colchester United (1931-1946)*

A Southampton born and bred goalkeeper, Light would combine an amateur career in the game with working for the iconic Harland & Wolff shipyards of *Titanic* fame before his beloved Saints offered him a contract. He suffered a dislocated kneecap in only his fourth appearance for the side, though, sidelining him for several months. He would get his place back upon his return, but with cash strapped Saints in need of an overhaul, First Division West Brom swooped for a man by now considered one of the country's finest goalkeepers. Light would spend two years in the West Midlands but was between the sticks in Albion's record League loss - a 10-3 defeat at Stoke in February 1937. He would later join Colchester United, winning the Southern League as player-coach before retiring. He returned to the Essex club as a trainer before moving back to Southampton. Died in 1979.

Lindsay, Hugh

Inside-forward

Born: *1938 Ickenham*
Playing career: *London University, Wealdstone, Kingstonian, Southampton, Hampton (1962-1973)*

A fully qualified teacher, Lindsay represented England at amateur level and played for the Great Britain side in the 1960 Rome Olympics. Signing for Southampton manager Ted Bates on amateur terms, Saints last such player, featuring in two games at inside left in the 1960-61 season. Despite being on Saints books until 1965, Lindsay never fully committed and preferred to focus on his teaching career. Teaching Maths and Statistics at Richmond-upon-Thames, Lindsay continued to play football for Kingstonian, Wealdstone and Hampton, gaining 30-odd caps for England and playing in two more Olympics. In Lindsay's post-playing days, he returned to two of those clubs as coach and then assistant manager, before retiring to a quieter life playing golf and bridge.

Liptak, Zoltan
Centre Midfield
Born: *1984 Salgatarjan, Hungary*
Playing career: *Szolnok, PApa, Southend United, Stevenage Borough, Vñjpest, Southampton, Videoton, (2004-)*

Having already played in England for Southend and Stevenage, the central midfielder joined Southampton at a time when the club were cash strapped and on the verge of relegation to the third tier. He would never start a game in Saints ultimately unsuccessful bid to avoid relegation, making seven cameo appearances off the bench. Liptak would soon return to his native Hungary, where he embarked on a ground hopping career in his homeland. Won the first of his 18 Hungary caps at Wembley against England in 2010 and went on win a league title medal with Videoton. Had a trial with Swansea but to no avail. At the age of 35, Liptak was still playing for Gyirmot FC Gyor.

Littlehales, Alfred
Centre-half
Born: *1867 Wellington, Shropshire*
Died: *1942*
Playing career: *Wolverhampton Wanderers, Stoke, Southampton (1892-1898)*

Caught the eye of Southampton after impressing in a friendly game for Stoke, despite being on in a side that lost 8-0. Recruited by Saints ahead of their first ever season in a professional league, Alfred Littlehales joined the club along with team-mates Lachie Thomson and Charlie Baker. "Clever on the ball and with a hard shot" - perhaps unusual assets for a centre-half - Littlehales quickly became a key man for Southampton, winning two league titles and missing only four matches in three seasons. He played 68 times for the club, impressively scoring 12 goals from the back. He would eventually lose his place to new signing Arthur Chadwick with Harry Haynes also in competition. Had a benefit game against Eastleigh before retiring, going on to become a school caretaker in Bevois Valley. Died aged 75 in 1942.

Littler, Oswald
Inside-forward
Born: *1907 Billinge* **Died:** *1970*
Playing career: *Rochdale, Southampton, Southport, Barrow, Winsford United (1928-1933)*

Combined playing part time for Third Division (North) Rochdale with a job as a payroll clerk in the Lancashire pits when Southampton offered him a step up. Then in the Second Division, Saints signed him as a full time player and went on to play 12 times for the club at inside right (three goals). But that proved the zenith of his career and Little would play in the lower leagues for Southport and Barrow being a non league stint at Winsford United. Littler eventually lost his place to Bill Fraser after a poor run of form. After hanging up his boots, Littler worked on the buses in Lancashire and Yorkshire for 25 years before getting a job with the council in St Helen's.

Livesey, Charlie
Centre-forward
Born: *1938 West Ham* **Died:** *2005*
Playing career: *West Ham United, Custom House, Southampton, Chelsea, Gillingham, Watford, Northampton Town, Brighton & Hove Albion, Crawley Town (1956-1970)*

Rejected by Chelsea and their famous, revered scout Jimmy Thompson, Livesey - whom had failed to make the grade at Wolves - was signed by Southampton on the race course at Epsom. Played in all four divisions of English football and instantly made himself at home down south in his debut season - going on to notch 15 goals in 29 games at the Dell despite a brush with the law. Broke a toe and was tried in several different positions, but fell out of favour and was sold, ironically, to Chelsea, now under the tutelage of former Saints man Ted Drake. Joined the Blues in May 1959 from Southampton for £20,000 plus Cliff Huxford. Scored eight goals in his first 14 games but despite his decent scoring record, he was replaced by Ron Tindall and sold to Gillingham for just £2,000 in 1961. Returned to his native east London where he became a painter and decorator. Died in St Bart's Hospital after a short illness in February 2005.

Lock, Herbert

Goalkeeper
Born: *1887 Southampton*
Died: *1957*
Playing career: *QPR, Southampton, Bournemouth and Boscombe (1907-1924)*

Known for his reckless style of play but with an impressive penalty-saving record, Lock was a "daring and acrobatic goalkeeper". He would pace "up and down like a lion" before positioning himself off centre to make the penalty taker aim towards the larger target and develop an uncanny ability to anticipate thee direction of the ball. In his second season at the club, Lock saved eight of the twelve penalties he faced for Southampton. Won three successive league titles with Rangers but was dogged by a succession of injuries. Guested for a number of Scottish clubs whilst working on the docks at Glasgow during the war. Played for QPR before returning to Southampton as cover for the injured Tom Allen. Played another eleven times before moving along the coast to Division Three debutants Bournemouth & Boscombe. After retiring, Lock worked as a carpenter and joiner for Southern Railway but died of a heart attack aged 70 whilst cycling in Bitterne.

Long, Henry

Left-half/Outside-left
Born: *1914 Southampton*
Died: *1989*
Playing career: *Harland and Wolff, Ryde Sports, Southampton, Newport (1933-1939)*

As was common at the time, Long worked on the Harland & Wolff shipyards whilst playing for Ryde Sports FC on the Isle of Wight. Signed for Second Division Saints on amateur forms, but found himself third choice on the left-wing - with Laurie Fishlock, Fred Smallwood and Harry Osman all ahead of him in the pecking order. Played a handful of games when one of the three were injured including the game that saw the debut of a certain Ted Bates. Stayed local and returned to the Hampshire League, going back to the Isle of Wight to play for Newport, where he would later become coach, chairman and manager.

Lovett, Graham

Midfielder
Born: *1947 Sheldon, Warwickshire*
Playing career: *West Bromwich Albion, Southampton (1964-1971)*

Strong and commanding but elegant on the ball, there were comparisons with west Midlands football's most famous son, Duncan Edwards, when Graham Lovett was rising through the ranks at West Bromwich Albion. He was fortunate not to meet the same fate as his illustrious predecessor after a nasty car crash two years after signing with the Baggies. A blow out on the M1 left Lovett with a dislocated vertebrae and partial paralysis. Incredibly, his recovery was so good that not only did he walk again, but resumed his football career - going on to win the FA Cup with Albion in 1968 (having beaten Southampton en route) to add to the League Cup triumph two years earlier. Lovett suffered another near-fatal traffic collision in 1969 when a bus hit his car in Birmingham on the wrong side of the road, later being awarded £14,000. Lovett played three games for Saints in a bid to regain match fitness but retired aged 26. Later worked in the advertising department of the *Express&Star* paper in Wolverhampton, later moving to Spain.

Lowder, Thomas

Outside-forward
Born: *1924 Worksop*
Died: *1999*
Playing career: *Crystal Palace, Rotherham United, Boston United, Southampton, Southend United, Boston United, ,Skegness Town (1946-1962)*

Lowder - who worked as a part-time electrician - caught the eye of Saints manager Sid Cann. Cann duly snaffled him but he struggled at Saints. In his four years at The Dell, Lowder made 39 appearances, scoring twice. Dropped down a level to play for Southern van a second stint at Boston, before a final swansong at non league Skegness where he played alongside the comedian Charlie Williams. Having finished his playing career, he ran an off licence and also worked in a grocery store. Died aged 74 in 1999

Luckett, William

Half-back
Born: *1903 St Helens, Lancashire* **Died:** *1985*
Playing career: *Skelmersdale United, Southampton, Cowes Sports (1927-1939)*

An integral figure in the Southampton sides of the 1920s and 30s, Luckett went on to play over 200 times for Saints despite having to wait three and half seasons to become established. Described as "not particularly skilful but very hard working", Luckett would "chase the ball and opponents around the pitch like a terrier" and eventually made the left-half position his own despite competition from the likes of Stan Woodhouse and Mike Keeping. A one club man, Luckett stayed on the south coast for ten years between 1927 and 1937, before retiring after injury struggles having made 219 appearances. Having hung up his boots, Luckett joined Cowes Sports as player/coach, served in the RAF during WWII and returned to Saints as scout and reserve team trainer. Became landlord of the *Salisbury Arms* in Christchurch and also worked for Ordnance Survey. Died in 1985.

Lucketti, Christopher

Central defender
Born: *1971 Littleborough*
Playing career: *Rochdale, Stockport County, Halifax Town, Bury, Huddersfield T, Preston NE, Sheffield U, Southampton, Huddersfield Town (1989-2010)*

Played four games for Southampton on loan from Sheffield United as the two sides met in an end of season clash in 2008. With Saints facing relegation and the Blades pushing for promotion, Lucketti was allowed to play against his parent club but opted not to in order to avoid a conflict of interests. His career spanned nine clubs and two decades. The bulk of his career came in Lancashire and neighbouring Yorkshire with Bury, Huddersfield, Sheffield United, Halifax and Preston. Also managed Bury and served as caretaker boss of Fleetwood on two occasions. A tall and uncompromising centre-back, Lucketti turned out for Saints at the end of that 2007-08 campaign and continues to stay in the game as assistant manager Graham Alexander at League Two Salford City of Class of 92 fame.

Lundekvam, Claus

Defender
Born: *1973 Austevoll, Norway*
Playing career: *Brann, Southampton (1993-2008)*

A Saints cult hero and a Scandinavian rock at the heart of the defence for more than a decade, Lundekvam's lion hearted displays in the Southampton shirt belief an off-the-field alter ego. Serenaded superbly with "Our Claus" in the middle of defence, those fans knew little of the inner demons that caused the player to twice try and kill himself, leading and an alcohol addiction that took hold upon his 2008 retirement. Struggling with the absence of professional football, Lundekvam turned to drink and drugs - becoming a cocaine addict and, by his own admission, "almost drinking himself to death." Now four years clean, the former centre-back has turned his life around, moving back to his native Norway with his young family and helping to give something back by taking a job with the Psychiatric Alliance in his homeland, helping others with mental health issues, alcohol problems and drug addictions through football, sport and other outdoor activities. Alongside that role, he writes for a Norwegian newspaper and is a pundit for television station, TV2. The ex-Southampton skipper is on Twitter here:https://twitter.com/saintskipper5

Luscombe, Lee

Forward
Born: *1971 Guernsey*
Playing career: *Southampton, Brentford, Millwall, Sittingbourne, Doncaster Rovers (1986-1994)*

Following in the footsteps of Southampton's most famous son, Luscombe - like Matt Le Tissier - was born on Guernsey. Unlike "Le Tiss", though, Luscombe failed to make the grade at Saints and never played for their first team. He left the club after two years and briefly returned to the Channel Islands before going back to the UK to sign for Brentford. Played 42 games in the third tier before spells at Millwall, non league Sittingbourne and later Doncaster. Continued to play at non league level for a while before working as a coach at Warrington Town and Runcorn Linnets.

MacDonald, Elias

Outside-left
Born: *1898 Beswick, Manchester* **Died:** *1978*
Playing career: *Derby County, Burton All Saints, Southampton, Southend United, Southport, Doncaster Rovers, Barrow, Ulverston Town, Chorley, Morecambe, Rolls Royce Welfare (1920-1930)*

Manchester-born MacDonald had played at non league level before he was scouted and signed by Derby County. He represented the Rams across two spells but never played at senior level for the club. But despite a lack of top class pedigree, he was described as a "fine winger" according to The Echo. Something of a surprise swoop for the south coast club, he "did his job without frills and thrills", but MacDonald would have only one season at The Dell before moving to another coastal club, in Southend United. A regular for the Shrimpers, he would move again, staying in the third tier but moving to the North section of the division with Southport where he was a virtual ever present), Doncaster and Barrow. Had a few stints in non league but later returned to work for Rolls Royce, turning out for their works team back in Derby. Died in 1978

Macdougall, Ted

Forward
Born: *1947 Inverness, Scotland*
Playing career: *Liverpool, York City, Bournemouth, Manchester United, West Ham, Norwich City, Southampton, Bournemouth, Blackpool (1966-1980).*

A fantastic goalscorer worked his way down from Scotland to become a hero at Bournemough before a £200,00 move took him to Manchester United. His time at Saints saw him notch up 42 goals in 86 games and forge a deadly partnership with Phil Boyer which helped the club win promotion back to the 1st Division. Went on to become the owner of sports shops in Bournemouth and a licensee of a public house near Romsey. Emigrated to Vancouver, Canada, with his French Canadian wife, where he has become a wealthy property developer. Returned to England for a spell as Portsmouth's reserve team coach, then moved to the USA where he worked with San Jose Earthquakes and the United States Air Force Academy. Now lives in Atlanta, USA, and was Director of Youth with the Atlanta Silverbacks before setting up his own club, Atlanta Spurs, with former Notts County pro, Paul Smith.

1901-02

Mackie, Jerry

Inside right
Born: *1895 Motherwell, Scotland*
Died: *1960*
Playing career: *Motherwell, Blantyre Celtic, Portsmouth, Southampton, Bo'ness (1920-1931)*

Scotsman Jerry "James" Mackie spent the majority of his 13-year career for the south coast. He fell out of favour at Portsmouth and so would move up the Solent to join Saints as a replacement for the Manchester-United bound William Rawlings. Mackie scored a hat-trick on his home debut, going to score six goals in seven games by the time his debut season - albeit one disrupted by injury - was out. Reunited with Pompey strike partner Willie Haines, the pair scored 33 between them to fire Southampton to fourth place in Division Two. Scored his 100th league goal in 1931 shortly before retirement. Took up bowls and became licensee of the *Regents Park* Hotel, a position he held for a quarter of a century. Moved to Bognor Regis in Sussex and continued to play bowls until his mid 50s.

MacLaren, David

Goalkeeper
Born: *1934 Auchterarder, Scotland* **Died:** *2016*
Playing career: *Dundee, Leicester City, Plymouth Argyle, Wolves, Southampton (1956-1967)*

Already the wrong side of 30 when signed, MacLearn had played in goal for the opposition when Saints beat Wolves 9-3 the previous year. Yet when Campbell Forsyth broke his leg eight games into the season, leaving the 18-year-old Gerry Gurr as their old recognised keeper, Saints needed a stand in stopper. Despite conceding nine on that afternoon at the Dell, the Scot had been hailed as "magnificent" and so Bates signed him as his new first choice. The Scotsman would keep four clean sheets in his first six games, but as a relegation battle intensified, so MacLaren fell out of favour. Compatriot Eric Martin was signed by Bates to become the side's third goalkeeper of the season, spelling the end of MacLaren's career in the Football League. He turned out for non league Worcester City and went on to manage the Malaysian national team and Australian club sides Sydney and South Melbourne.

MacLeod, Duncan

Midfielder
Born: *1949 Tobermory, Scotland*
Playing career: *Southampton, Dundee, Dundee United, St Johnstone, Brechin City (1968-1981)*

Born on the Isle of Mull, MacLeod's time at Southampton would be his only experience south of the border. He would never play for the first team but got a handful of games in the reserves before returning to Scotland. Later played for the two Dundee clubs, St Johnstone and Brechin City, making over 150 appearances for the latter before retiring. MacLeod coached at Tannadice and then became a player agent.

Madden, David

Midfielder
Born: *1963 Stepney*
Playing career: *Southampton, Bournemouth, Arsenal, Charlton Athletic, Los Angeles Lazers, Reading, Crystal Palace, Birmingham City, Maidstone United (1981-1991)*

Madden began as an apprentice at Southampton but never made the grade, moving down the Solent to the Jurassic coast for a loan spell at AFC Bournemouth. He played twice for Arsenal and also turned out for Charlton before trying his hand across the pond in Los Angeles. Madden would later help Palace to promotion and played in both games of the 1990 FA Cup - coming off the bench in both the first game and the replay. Having served Maidstone as player/manager, he retired after a decade long career but stayed involved with the Kent club, becoming assistant manager and then a club director.

Maddison, Neil

Central midfielder
Born: *1969 Darlington*
Playing career: *Southampton, Middlesbrough, Barnsley, Bristol City, Darlington (1988-2007)*

Hailing from the iconic north-east hotbed of football, Neil Maddison was moulded into shape at Saints by Dave Merrington, along with perhaps more celebrated cohorts Alan Shearer and Matt Le Tissier et al. He scored on his full debut having risen through the ranks to break into the first team. After more than a decade on the south coast, in which he played 167 times and scored 19 times, Maddison returned to his native north-east, joining Bryan Robson's promotion chasing Middlesbrough. In retirement, Maddison worked as head of Darlington's Centre of Excellence before setting up a coaching school - Premier Player Academy. Maddison later returned to Boro' where he worked as Head of Welfare, tasked with the monitoring of players out of loan or serving their country. He has appeared on BBC Radio Tees as a commentator, remaining a popular figure among the North East football natives.

Madsen, Peter

Striker/left winger
Born: *1978 Roskilde, Denmark*
Playing career: *VfL Wolfsburg, VfL Bochum, FC Koln, Southampton, Brondby, Lyngby (1997-2012)*

Madsen played in his homeland for Brondby in two spells - winning three Superliga titles and the Danish cup. Also played for Lyngby and in Germany. Capped 13 times by his country, Madsen featured at Euro 2004. Unhappy with life in Germany, Madsen jumped at the chance to join George Burley's Championship Saints - albeit on loan - for the second half of the 2005-06 season. Madsen would link up with Grzegorz Raziak in attack, playing nine times and scoring twice as Saints finished in mid table. The pair offered a good balance, with Raziak's aerial ability complementing Madsen's quick and skilful feet. Madsen admitted that he would've like a permanent move to St Mary's, but he instead moved back to Europe with Cologne before returning to Brondby.

Magilton, Jim

Midfielder
Born: *1969 Belfast, Northern Ireland*
Playing career: *Liverpool, Oxford United, Southampton, Sheffield Wednesday, Ipswich Town (1988-2006)*

A gifted Northern Ireland midfielder with 52 caps and five goals, Magilton was Alan Ball's second signing as manager, joining from Oxford for £600,000. He claimed two assists for Matt Le Tissier's hat-trick on the former's debut. Despite the Saints high turnover of bosses, from Ball to Graeme Souness via Dave Merrington, Magilton would be an ever present over the next three years. Dave Jones was not so keen, though, and moved him on to Sheffield Wednesday after 156 games in red and white (18 goals). Went on to continue his fine career with Wednesday and Ipswich, before going into coaching and management after retirement. Magilton took charge of Ipswich, QPR, Melbourne Victory and Northern Ireland's U21 side, also working for the IFA and at Shamrock Rovers as assistant boss and scout.

Makin, Chris

Defender
Born: *1973 St Helens, Lancashire*
Playing career: *Oldham Athletic, Wigan Athletic, Marseille, Sunderland, Ipswich Town, Leicester City, Derby County, Reading, Southampton, Radcliffe Borough (1991-2008)*

Makin was "one of those players" that seemed a perfect fit for a certain type of manager. Having twice played under Joe Royle at Oldham and then Ipswich, he served George Burley three times - at Portman Road, Derby and then at Southampton, by then aged 33. A centre-back adept with either foot, he rose through the ranks at Boundary Park, going on to play over 100 games for the Latics before joining the 'other' Latics of Wigan, Marseille, Sunderland, Leicester and Reading. Played five times for England at Under 21 level, before turning up at Saints for whom he would play 27 times. Makin was forced to retire through injury in 2008 after hip surgery. Since then he has managed his own portfolio of properties and popped up on Qatar TV as an analyst.

Mallett, Joseph

Wing-half

Born: *1916 Gateshead* **Died:** *2004*
Playing career: *Dunston Colliery, Charlton Athletic, QPR, Southampton, Leyton Orient (1935-1955)*

Although born on the banks of the Tyne, Mallett hadn't played outside London until his move to the south coast. Played twice for Charlton and then for QPR before Bill Dodgin, looking to strengthen his squad, swooped to bring him to the Dell. Signing for Southampton for £5,000 after the war (where Mallett had served in the RAF), he proved to be a bargain despite his advancing years. Scored and set up the other on his debut, soon rising to Saints captain and letting others exactly how he felt regarding how the game should be played. Mallett went on to make over 200 appearances at the Dell. before moving into coaching back in the capital but on this occasion it was with Leyton Orient as player/coach. He would later manage Birmingham City (also serving as no.2 to Stan Cullis), and then in Greece as boss of Panionios and Apollon Athens. Also had a spell as manager of San Jose Earthquakes across the pond. He also scouted for Saints and worked as a reserve team coach at Nottingham Forest.

Marsden, Chris

Midfielder

Born: *1969 Sheffield*
Playing career: *Sheffield United, Huddersfield Town, Coventry City, Wolverhampton Wanderers, Notts County, Stockport County, Birmingham City, Southampton, Sheffield Wednesday (1987-2005)*

Eyebrows were raised and questions asked when Dave Jones paid £800,000 to prise this left sided player from Birmingham City. Yet Marsden defied the doubters by immediately impressing in the Premier League as a hard-working, unrelenting fans' favourite. When Gordon Strachan moved Marsden to the left wing form the central midfield, a wonderful partnership was born. Linking with the overlapping Wayne Bridge the duo became one of the best left-sided pairings in the league. He would earn an FA Cup runners up medal in 2003, captaining Saints in the final in the absence of the stricken Jason Dodd. After 137 games and six years, Marsden left Saints to play in Korea under his first manager, Ian Porterfield. He only played two games before returning to boyhood club Sheffield Wednesday for a final swansong. After retirement, Marsden moved into property letting.

Marshall, George

Defender

Born: *1869 Southampton* **Died:** *1938*
Career: *Southampton St. Mary's (1888-1896)*

George Marshall may have only played twice for Southampton but yet still made history. He is the only man to play in the club's first ever match in both the FA Cup and league football. He could also be regarded as their first ever substitute, albeit unofficially, when he replaced "Lachie" Thomson in the early stages of a Southern league tie with Clapton in 1895. Having previously played rugby, Marshall had won the Hampshire Senior Cup twice and county representative honours before St Mary's embarked on their maiden Southern League voyage. He remained strictly amateur, and employed in a variety of defensive positions. After he hung up his boots, Marshall worked for Ordnance Survey but returned to The Dell to work for George Carter in running the second string.

Marshall, Scott

Full-back

Born: *1973 Edinburgh, Scotland*

Playing career: *Reading, Arsenal, Rotherham U, Oxford United, Sheffield United, Southampton, Celtic, Brentford, Wycombe W(1989-2004)*

Having played for Arsenal and been capped for Scotland's U21 side by at age of 19, it seemed Southampton had got themselves a good find when Marshall joined them for only £1m in 1997. But despite the fact he signed a four year deal, he would only play twice for Saints - both games would come in the space of a week and both came away from The Dell. In each of those games, 3-0 and 4-0 defeats to Leeds and Newcastle respectively, Marshall scored an own goal. He never played for the club again, moving to his native Scotland where he played for Celtic - but again would feature once in a 0-3 loss to Glasgow rivals Rangers. Three games, three defeats, no goals scored and 0-10 on aggregate! Went on to play for Brentford and Wycombe, where he would become Wanderers first signing under their new boss and Marshall's old team mate Tony Adams. After retirement as a player, Marshall went into coaching and management, taking charge of Norwich's U21 side and managing Aston Villa and Reading on a caretaker basis.

Martin, Eric

Goalkeeper

Born: *1947 Perth, Scotland*

Playing career: *Blairhall Colliery, Cowdenbeath, Dunfermline Athletic, Southampton, Washington Diplomats (1963-1979)*

Known as Harpo due to his wild hairstyle, Martin was one of three Scottish keeper signed by Ted Bates in 1966. Campbell Forsyth's broken leg and a lack of faith in Dave Maclaren paved the way for Martin to make his mark. Agile and quick, the 5ft 11 Martin quickly became a cult hero and Southampton's number one. A crowd pleaser, his most notable trick would occur just before kick off when he would ping a flurry of training balls in the direction of the man on the touchline, whom would subsequently allow them to fall directly into his bag.

That aside, Martin would only miss one game between December 1969 and the culmination of the 1972-73 season, when Saints finally signed their sought after target Sandy Davie. New manager Lawrie McMenemy also brought in Ian Turner and Martin would move to the USA after 289 games on the south coast. In retirement, he continued to live Stateside and had several different roles and jobs. He was employed as a bar tender, worked as a warden in a San Jose prison, had a job at a zoo, a stint with an American TV network and then as a mail worker in Maryland. Despite being in his 70s, Martin is known admirer of the North American countryside and still looks very much in good nick!

Maskell, Craig

Centre-forward

Born: 1968 Aldershot

Playing career: *Huddersfield Town, Reading, Swindon Town, Southampton, Bristol City, Brighton & Hove Albion, Happy Valley, Leyton Orient, Hampton & Richmond Borough, Aylesbury United, Staines Town (1986-2012)*

A stylish, composed and pacy forward, Maskell (middle name, appropriately Del), rose through the ranks at Saints but found his way barred by the likes of Colin Clarke, Gordon Hobson and Danny Wallace. He scored in his second Saints game but only played a handful of times before moving to Huddersfield, via a loan spell at Swindon. Played for Reading then under Glenn Hoddle back at Swindon, helping them to promotion to the Premier League, only to drop straight back down the following season, By then, Maskell was on the move again as Alan Ball brought him back to The Dell, scoring with a header on his 'second debut' against Liverpool. He again struggled for regular game time and went on to turn out for Bristol City, Brighton, Derby and Leyton Orient. He then played and coached in non league, serving as assistant boss with Staines, teaching at Southgate College before returning to Hampshire, where he taught sports at Eastleigh College.

Matson, Francis

Outside-right
Born: *1905 Cardiff, Wales* **Died:** *1985*
Playing career: *Reading, Cardiff City, Newport County, Southampton (1925-1932)*

An FA Cup winner with Cardiff in 1927, Matson made his name with the Welsh club despite their relegation to the second tier. Had a brief stint with Welsh rivals Newport but made only one appearance before signing for Southampton. In his two years at The Dell, Matson would feature regularly for the Reserves but only played twice for the first team, deputising for the injured Bert Jepson. Manager George Kay would try a succession of players to fill the void until he signed Dick Neal, bringing Matson's hopes of regular football to an end. He retired at the end of the season and went on to work on the railways.

Matthews, Frank

Inside-forward
Born: *1902 Wallsend* **Died:** *1981*
Playing career: *Washington Blue Star, Washington Colliery, Blackpool, Barnsley, Southampton, Chesterfield, Carlisle United (1922-1930)*

Another born in the Wallsend area of the north east, Matthews played for various colliery teams in the area before his big break saw him move to Blackpool. He was unable to nail down a regular place and so switched to divisional rivals Barnsley before Saints manager Arthur Chadwick persuaded him to move to south. Scored on his home debut and would go on to make the left wing position his own, in tandem with Jimmy Carr. Matthews played 19 times for Second Division Saints but Chadwick was looking to rebuild and he would be one of the unlucky ones. Dick Rowley, Alf Bishop and Sammy Taylor were all signed for Saints, all of whom played in the same position as the now out of favour Matthews. He would drop down a division to Chesterfield to play under former Saints team-mate and recently installed Spireites manager Alec Campbell. Matthews only played twice for the club and latterly dropped into the non league game via a brief spell at Carlisle. After he hung up his boots, Matthews returned to his old job as a miner.

Maughan, Wesley

Inside-forward
Born: *1939 Sholing*
Playing career: *Southampton, Reading, Chelmsford City, Cambridge United (1955-1975)*

Southampton born and raised on the Isle of Wight, he started life as a trainee accountant whilst playing part-time for Cowes. He plundered four goals against a Southampton youth side aged 16, persuading manager Ted Bates to take a punt on the pacy, mobile centre-forward. Ironically described as the side's "overseas" player by the local press and his boss, Maughan hit 11 goals in nine games during the young Saints debut campaign in the FA Youth Cup. Despite his impressive form, Maughan was never given a fair crack of the whip at first team level, featuring only six times and scoring once. A £400,000 move to Reading would follow, before a successful stint in non-League football. Later wnt on to work as an IT consultant, play the Salvation Army's brass band and serve as secretary for the Kenya Trust - a Salvation Army charity to help disabled and deprived children and young people in the African nation.

Mayer, Wilfred

Inside-right
Born: *1912 Stoke-on-Trent* **Died:** *1979*
Playing career: *Stoke City, Southampton, Wellington Town (1932-1938)*

Having cut his teeth at reserve level for Stoke, Mayer was one of the first signings made by Southampton's new manager Tom Parker within a month of his arrival at The Dell. Mayer would go straight into the side for Second Division Saints in place of the injured Dick Neal, mostly at inside-right, and went on to play 14 times for the club. A nippy forward, Mayer was capable of playing anywhere across the front or on either wing. He would soon fall down the pecking order though following the arrivals of Ray Parkin and Ted Bates, but he failed to attract any interest for a new club, even when the asking price was halved. He eventually moved to non league Warrington, winning the Welsh Cup and the Birmingham League during the conflict.

McAlpine, James

Left-half
Born: *1887 Lanarkshire, Scotland* **Died:** *1948*
Playing career: *Southampton, Kilmarnock, Wishaw Thistle, Millwall, Gillingham (1907-1923)*

New Southampton manager George Swift embarked on an overhaul having been appointed in the summer of 1911, signing eleven players in six weeks. Inevitably, some of them turned out to be failure, indeed rather like the new boss himself, but he found a gem in James McAlpine. The left half may have lacked stature but he made up for that in tenacity and tirelessness. He would become an ever present over the next four seasons at left half until the outbreak of WW1 saw official football suspended. A fan favourite but an irritating nuisance to his opponents, he returned to his native Scotland after the conflict, working in the Glasgow shipyards and guesting for a variety of clubs north of the border. But love saw him return to the south coast, having married a Southampton girl and got a job at Harland & Wolff, enabling him to continue playing for Saints during wartime. Moved to Millwall for their debut campaign in the Football League, turned out for Gillingham and then retired, moving back to Southampton where he became a pub landlord.

McCall, Willie

Outside-forward
Born: *1898 Maxwelltown, Scotland* **Died:** *1966*
Playing career: *Maxwelltown Juniors, Blackburn Rovers, Wolverhampton Wanderers, Southampton, Queen of the South, Carlisle United (1918-1925)*

Scotsman McCall captained his country at schoolboy level but, as with all players at that time, WW1 temporarily put paid to his career. He served with the 5th Battalion King's Own during the conflict, returning to football with Queen of the South in 1919. After brief spells with Blackburn and Wolves, he moved to the Second Division new boys Southampton. Scored on his debut and played in half of their remaining fixtures, sharing duties with Len Andrews. An archetypal pacy winger, McCall lost his way and returned to Scotland with his first club. Retired after a final stint with Carlisle, later working on the buses for *Caledonian*.

McCalliog, Jim

Midfielder
Born: *1946 Glasgow, Scotland*
Playing career: *Leeds United, Chelsea, Sheffield Wednesday, Wolverhampton Wanderers, Manchester United, Southampton, Lincoln City (1963-1979)*

McCalliog was a lready a well travelled Scottish international midfielder by the time he arrived at Saints in 1975. The following year he set up the goal for Bobby Stokes to score and win the FA Cup against former employers Manchester United at Wembley. Despite this, he was to lose his place to Alan Ball less than 12 months lateranfd moved over to the united States to play for Chicago Sting. These days, however, McCalliog is looking after silver and chasing a clean sheet of a very different kind as he runs an award-winning Ayrshire B&B of national television fame. Having worked as a journalist and a publican in York after his playing days had finished, the Scottish international - five caps for his country - put his expertise in the catering and hospitality industry to good use by opening and running The Langside Bed and Breakfast in Ayrshire. In 2018, the hotel appeared on Channel 4's "Four in a Bed" The Langside, described as a "quirky" venue, emerged victorious on the show and was named best in the region by the Scottish tourist board in 2019.

McCann, Neil

Winger
Born: *1974 Greenock, Scotland*
Playing career: *Greenock Morton, Hearts, Rangers, Southampton, Hearts, Falkirk, Dundee (1992-2011)*

Well travelled Scottish international, capped 26 times for his countr. Played the entirety of his career in his native homeland apart from a three year stint at Southampton, but his time on the south coast was heavily disrupted by injury. He only played 25 times, short change in three years, at a cost of £60,000 each. His contract terminated by mutual consent, he returned north of the border to sign for Hearts and later played in the 2009 Scottish Cup final for Falkirk. Retired and went into punditry work, but later pulled on his boots one last time to help cash strapped Dundee avoid relegation - a club he would later manage during the 2017-18 campaign.

McCarthy, Bob

Right-back
Born: *1948 Lyndhurst*
Playing career: *Southampton (1967-1974).*

Strong in the tackle and with good positional sense, New Forest born right-back Bob McCarthy lived the dream as he rose through the ranks of his local professional club. He would be forced to bide his time due to the presence of the ultra consistent, ever present Joe Kirkup and had a century of reserve team games under his belt by the time his senior debut finally arrived. An ignominious 7-0 loss at Leeds, with young full-backs McCarthy and Roger Fry made scapegoats. However, this did not prevent him from becoming an ever present the following season (1972-73). Saints would be relegated, but a combination of injury and a loss of form saw him leave the game at the age of 26. He played in local football for a bit, before becoming a salesman and toastmaster. Played 137 games for his only club.

"DID YOU KNOW?"

"Staplewood, the club's training ground was opened in 2014 and cost £40million to build."

McCartney, Mike

Full-back
Born: *1954 Musselburgh, Scotland* **Died:** *2018*
Playing career: *West Bromwich Albion, Carlisle, Southampton, Plymouth, Carlisle. (1971-1986).*

Spent most of his career with Carlisle United, making over 300 appearances for the club in two spells, with time at Southampton and Plymouth sandwiched in between. Signing for Alan Ashman's WBA, he failed to make the grade there and so followed the manager to Brunton Park and Second Division United. The Cumbrians would rise into the top flight during McCartney's stay but eventually dropped all the way back to the third tier, by which point he'd already left. Joining Lawrie McMenemy's Southampton, his arrival at the club was overshadowed by the signing of Kevin Keegan on the same day. He would get few chances with Nick Holmes first choice at left-back, playing 24 times in his solitary season on the south coast. Moved on to Argyle and then returned to Carlise before having to retire through injury. Later worked at Gretna as coach, player manager and groundsman.

McDonald, Alex

Inside-forward
Born: *1878 Greenock, Scotland* **Died:** *1949*
Playing career: *Everton, Southampton, West Ham United, Portsmouth, Luton Town (1899-1911)*

Born in Scotland but only ever played in England, McDonald turned out for Everton, scoring against Southampton in an FA Cup tie and duly joining the club. Scored five goals in his three games but the presence of Arthur Chadwick and Harry Wood meant his stay at the Dell was short and sweet. He left for West Ham in December for another four games and by the end of the 1901-02, McDonald had an interesting record - three clubs, 16 games, 14 goals. After leaving the capital, He hit seven in seven for Pompey, a remarkable feat that ensured he will forever be etched in the record books. He had longer stints with Wellingborough, Luton and Croydon Common then returned to his native Scotland. Served in Royal Fleet Auxiliary until his 70s, McDonald would tragically drown at the base in 1949.

McDonald, John

Outside-right

Born: *1921 Maltby, Yorkshire* **Died:** *2007*
Playing career: *Wolves, Bournemouth & Boscombe Athletic, Fulham, Southampton, Southend United, Weymouth, Poole Town (1937-1957)*

Rose through the ranks at Wolves, never became a regular but played twice in the top division before dropping to the third tier with Bournemouth & Boscombe Athletic. McDonald guested widely for many clubs during the suspension of competitive football, including Bristol City, Cardiff, West Brom, York and Southampton. Won the Second Division with Fulham but returned to the second tier when George Roughton signed him for Saints. He lived up to his reputation as a goalscoring winger with four goals in eight games but only played another eight games before moving on to Southend in a season that saw Saints relegated. Dropped into Southern League football with Weymouth before retiring and becoming a PE teacher. Lived on the Isle of Wight in later life.

McDonald, Paul

Winger

Born: *1968 Motherwell, Scotland*
Playing career: *Kilmarnock, Hamilton Academical, Southampton, Burnley, Brighton & Hove Albion, Dunfermline Athletic, Partick Thistle, Greenock Morton, Hamilton Academical (1985-2003)*

After seven years with the "Accies" in his native Scotland, McDonald was signed for £150,000 (a combined fee with team-mate Colin Cramb) by Ian Branfoot in 1993. McDonald would only make four appearances - all of them off the bench - at The Dell - hindered by injury. After his short and sweet stint at Saints, McDonald moved along the coast to join Jimmy Case's newly relegated Brighton, in the basement division. He and ex Saint Craig Maskell played in the match that kept the Seagulls in the Football League the following season. After 52 games for Brighton, McDonald moved back to north of the border where later coached at the Accies, including a brief stint as caretaker manager, working at Kilmarnock as a community coach and then as head of Academy.

McDonald, Robert

Forward

Born: *1857 Inverness*
Died: *1931*
Playing career: *Southampton (1887-1888)*

The first Scot to play for the south coast club, 'Bob' McDonald scored four goals in as many games as part of Southampton St Mary's first ever trophy-winning side. The club won the Hampshire Senior Cup - their first foray into professional competitive football - in 1887-88, with McDonald finding the net twice on his debut and again in his last appearance, the first player ever to achieve that rare feat. He played in the last four games of their run to eventual victory including the replayed final over the amateurs of Southampton Harriers. He worked at the Ordnance Survey as a draughtsman before moving to London, later returning to continue his work with the OS. Retired to his native Inverness until his death in 1931 at the age of 74.

McDonald, Scott

Striker/Attacking midfielder

Born: *1983 Melbourne, Australia*
Playing career: *Gippsland Falcons, Cranbourne Comets, Southampton, Huddersfield Town, Bournemouth, Wimbledon, Celtic, Middlesbrough, Millwall, Motherwell, Dundee United (1998-date)*

The Australian with the Scottish sounding name never made a league start for Southampton and will be remembered as the one to get away. Played three times for Saints, with one League Cup start and two sub appearances in the Premier League. Played for Celtic under Gordon Strachan (ironically the manager who allowed him to leave St Mary's), and then Middlesbrough via Millwall. His unfulfilled potential at Saints did not hold him back though as he went on to enjoy a prolific career in Scotland, his parents birthplace for Motherwell, Dundee United and Patrick Thistle, and in his native Australia with Western United and Brisbane Roar. A pacy, powerful striker, he has represented his homeland at every age group from U17 to the senior Socceroos (26 caps).

McGarrity, Thomas

Inside-forward
Born: *1922 Scotstoun, Scotland* **Died:** *1999*
Playing career: *Morton, Southampton, Headington United, Banbury Spencer (1946-1954)*

Played over 100 games for Morton until, in 1952, Ted Bates paid £4,500 (an astronomical fee at the time) to bring him to the south coast. Although he was 30 by the time he arrived at The Dell, he added experience and guile to the forward line of a team battling relegation. In borrowed boots, McGarritty scored on his Southampton debut - a header in a 5-1 thrashing of Hull City. Played another four games but became embroiled in a financial dispute with the club and refused to sign on for a further season. The short-tempered McGarrity quit professional football for a second time - having already briefly done so whilst with Morton - and moved to Maidenhead to work as a physiotherapist whilst also playing at amateur level. He also held a job at Oxford United FC as physio and coach, becoming head of the Physiotherapy Geriatrics Department at the Radcliffe Infirmary.

McGhee, George

Forward
Born: *1883 Egmanton, Notts* **Died:** *1944*
Playing career: *Doncaster Rovers, Gainsborough Trinity, Southampton, Bitterne Guild, Southampton Pirates, Southampton Cambridge (1904-1909)*

George McGhee's football career took him wherever his other main line of work - teaching - led him to. As his first job saw him working as a schoolteacher in his native Nottinghamshire, so he turned out for Gainsborough Trinity, playing a handful of games for the then Second Division outfit. When he moved to Ipswich and the Municipal Secondary School, McGhee played for the Suffolk club, then an amateur side, before moving to a school just 'up the road' from a place called The Dell in the city of Southampton. And so it followed that McGhee became a Saint, after a spell with Bitterne Guild where he played both football and cricket. At that time, teachers could mix freely with their pupils when it came to representing school XIs with the King Edward's school enjoying a great number of successes during his time with them.

The Dell 1990

Thr club eventually picked him up, and he would be tried in both the Western League and Southern League, making a total of four appearances in the first team. Scored twice on his debut in the former before injury at Millwall ended his career at The Dell. Played at amateur level for a time, serving in WW1 with the Sherwood Foresters Nottinghamshire and Derbyshire Regiment, before resuming his teaching career after the War.

McGibbon, Charles

Centre-forward
Born: *1880 Portsmouth*
Died: *1954*
Playing career: *Woolwich Arsenal, Eltham, New Brompton, Crystal Palace, Southampton, Woolwich Arsenal, Leyton, Reading, Southampton (1905-1911)*

As a sergeant based in Woolwich, Pompey-born McGibbon signed for local club Woolwich Arsenal but never made their first team. Undeterred, he would fare much better at Southern League level for New Brompton (known today as Gillingham FC), Crystal Palace and Southampton twice. He also became one of select few to play football for Saints and cricket for Hampshire when he made one appearance at county level against Yorkshire in 1919 (he scored one run and bowled a solitary over). A prolific centre-forward, he plundered a hat-trick in the FA Cup for New Brompton to knock top flight Sunderland out of the competition. Another treble, this time for Palace against the Saints, greatly impressed the Southampton hierarchy and led to him becoming a Saint. Described as "physically well suited to the role of a centre forward" and "possessing a powerful shot and influential leadership", McGibbon had plundered 19 goals in 23 games for the club by the time he moved back up the coast to resume military duties - heading the scoring charts for Southampton in the 1909-10 season. Helped Arsenal avoid the drop, served in WW1 as a clerk with the Royal Garrison Artillery before returning to Southampton. This time, though, he never played a game for them and continued to work in the army and for *Supermarine* in Woolston.

McGibbon, Douglas

Centre-forward
Born: *1919 Netley*
Died: *2002*
Career: *Southampton, Fulham, Bournemouth & Boscombe Athletic, Lovells Athletic (1938-1951)*

Born in Netley, McGibbon was the son of former Saints forward Charlie McGibbon (above). Like his father, he was a prolific goalscorer throughout his career which included all of the WWII years and the Southern League prior to the start of post-war football. He broke the record for the fastest Southampton goal, 4.6 seconds from kick off. This goal was one of six he scored in a 7-0 victory over Chelsea. His playing career was ended after a bizarre collision with a crossbar. After football he worked in the aircraft industry in Hamble for a while. He died in Aylesbury aged 83 in 2002.

McGowan, James

Inside-forward
Born: *1924 Cambuslang, Scotland* **Died:** *1984*
Playing career: *Celtic, East Fife, Clyde, Dumbarton, Grimsby Town, Southampton, Salisbury (1942-1958)*

Combining an amateur career in Scotland with a job as coachbuilder, McGowan initially joined Celtic, although his time there co-incided with the outbreak of war. As a result, McGowan would never represent the Glasgow giants in an official competitive game, instead turning out in wartime football. By the time official football resumed in 1946, McGowan was in England with First Division Grimsby. 34 games and one relegation later, he joined Sid Cann's Southampton for £8,000 McGowan would later spend eight seasons at The Dell, making the right-half spot his own until being struck down with a lung infection. McGowan returned to captain Saints reserves to Combination Cup glory in 1955, then going on to Salisbury for a few sporadic games at non league level. After retirement he became a pub landlord including the Drummond Arms in Portswood, a popular haunt for many Saints players at the time. McGowan's life ended tragically when he drowned in the boating lake on Southampton Common shortly after his 60th birthday in 1984.

JOHN McGRATH
SOUTHAMPTON

CENTRE
HALF

McGrath, John
Centre-half
Born: *1938 Manchester* **Died:** *1998*
Playing career: *Bolton W, Bury, Newcastle United, Southampton, Brighton & Hove Albion (1955-1973)*
A tracksuited member of the boys of 76 as a first team coach, McGrath - a cultured and commanding centre-half during his playing days - had "graduated" to senior duty having taken charge of the youth team and then the Reserves at Saints following his retirement as a player. McGrath left Saints in 1980 for Port Vale - taking charge of a side 91st in League. He would go on to engineer a remarkable turnaround, steering Vale to safety and then promotion, a feat he would later replicate when boss of divisional rivals Preston. He later returned to Southampton as a scout before becoming a commentator and pundit for BBC Radio Lancashire, also working as an amusing after-dinner speaker. He helped to write Saints publications *Full time at The Dell* and *Dell Diamond,* interjecting both publications with his wry humour and quick wit, assets that would make him a very popular host of ex Saints-events and perfect for radio work. McGrath died suddenly on Christmas Day 1998.

McGrath, Martin
Midfielder
Born: *1960 Hendon*
Playing career: *Southampton, Bournemouth, Oxford City (1977-1981)*
An England youth international of considerable promise, Martin McGrath's senior Southampton career consisted of a single, 30-minute cameo from the bench. Despite being a reserve team regular, McGrath came on as a sub in a 2-0 defeat at Elland Road in march 1980, never to be seen again in the red and white. Released that summer, he moved across the New Forest to Dorset where he signed for Bournemouth, going on to have more success and play 22 times for them. Played under manager Bobby Moore and assistant Harry Redknapp at Oxford but soon drifted out of the game to become a croupier at the Ritz in London. Later worked for British Airways at Heathrow, firstly as a salesman and then in Customer Service where he looked after the VIPs. Moved to France and set up his own business selling designer toothbrushes.

McGuigan, John
Inside-forward
Born: *1932 Motherwell, Scotland* **Died:** *2004*
Playing career: *St Mirren, Southend United, Newcastle U, Scunthorpe U, Southampton, Swansea Town, Crewe Alexandra, Rochdale (1953-1967)*
As Saints became over-familiar with Scunthorpe during 1962-63 (they would play Scunny five times that season), so Ted Bates admired the string-pulling abilities of the Lincolnshire side's deep lying inside forward John McGuigan. He had scored twice across those five ties, so Bates parted with £10,000 to bring McGuigan to The Dell as replacement for the soon-to-depart David Burnside. Eight goals in 21 games - including two on his debut - was a decent return for this "tricky and versatile inside forward" before eventually losing his place to new signing Jimmy Melia. He would fail to score again and moved to Swansea for £6,500. Later returned to Southampton to become licensee of the appropriately named *Swan Hotel* in Woolston, before moving back to his Scottish roots and working for Rolls Royce in Glasgow.

McIlwaine, John

Centre-half/Centre-forward
Born: *1904 Irvine, Scotland* **Died:** *1980*
Playing career: *Irvine Victoria, Falkirk, Portsmouth, Southampton, Llanelly (1928-1937)*
McIlwaine captained Portsmouth and led them to their first FA Cup Final (a 0-2 defeat to Bolton). He moved up the Solent to Southampton for a fee of £2, 650 in time for the 1930-31 campaign. Later became assistant manager at Southampton, and then Grimsby Town. McIlwaine remained at Blundell Park until 1948, when he opened a masseur practice in Grimsby. He remained in the area for the rest of his life, dying there in April 1980, aged 75.

McIvor, George

Born: 1862 **Died:** *1916*
Playing career: *Southampton*
Played in Southampton St Mary's first ever match, a 5-1 win over Freemantle for the newly formed club. McIvor was also headmaster of Eastern District School and never played a competitive senior match for Saints as the side would become the premier club on the south coast. Like McIvor, many of the team from that first Southampton side worked in the city, a line up including teachers, hoteliers and dockyard workers.

McKay, Donald

Full-back
Born: *1876 Inverness* **Died:** *1926*
Career: *Southampton St. Mary's (1896-1897)*
Having initially worked on the banks of the Clyde in Scotland, Donald McKay's army career took him to Aldershot where he was scouted and signed by Southampton St Mary's FC. Buying his way out of the forces, he turned pro full-time but it would prove hard for him to get regular football, playing second fiddle at right-back to his established compatriot Sam Meston. McKay played eight times for Saints as the club won the Southern League title for the first time, before moving to the Bristol area, where he played for a flurry of lower league sides. After he hung up his boots, he stayed in Bristol and worked as a fitter on the tramways

McKeer, Charles

Inside-left/Left-half
Born: *1883 Farnham*
Died: *1957*
Playing career: *Southampton, Royal Army Medical Corps (1904-1911)*
Failed to get a game first time around at Southampton having signed on amateur forms before joining the Royal Army Medical Corps. Turned out for them in the Hampshire League before leaving the forces in 1910 and re-joining Ernest Armfield's Southampton, this time as a professional. Having become established in the reserves, McKeer would get four run outs at first team level, at left half or inside left, deputising for the injured Bert Trueman. Scuppered by injury and a loss of form, McKeer was released and re-joined the Army, later being discharged on health grounds.

McKenzie, James

Outside-left
Born: *1875 Glasgow, Scotland*
Died: *1945*
Playing career: *Gatmore, Possil Park, East Stirlingshire, Cowlairs, Burton Swifts, Southampton, Clyde (1896-1900)*
Glasgow born and trained as an upholsterer, McKenzie played for several lower league Scottish clubs before moving south of the border to join Burton Swifts in England's Division Two. He became a virtual ever present during his single season in Burton upon Trent, before returning to Scotland with Clyde, suffering relegation. Meanwhile, Alfred McMinn's Saints were about to embark on their first season at The Dell and persuaded McKenzie to join them in the venture. He would score and claim an assist in the club's first ever match at the new ground, a 4-1 win over the now defunct Brighton United, but the diminutive and lightweight winger would lose his place to George Seeley after only five further matches. He remained a regular for the Reserves but picked up a bad leg injury and re-signed for Clyde once he had recovered. A Southern League winner with Southampton in 1898-99.

McKie, James

Full-back
Born: *1873 Ayrshire, Scotland* **Died:** *1948*
Playing career: *Southampton St. Mary's, Chatham, Dartford (1896-1899)*

James McKie, known only as John, was posted to the Royal Artillery in Fareham as a 20 year old, four years after he had been kicked in the head by a horse. He had a turbulent early life, being jailed for drunk and disorderly behaviour that led to his discharge from the army. Won county honours with the RA team - a link that took him to Freemantle, combining playing with the job of head groundsman. Freemantle were St Mary's main rivals in the struggle for Southampton supremacy, and McKee came to the Saints attentions. Signed by the club on a paltry £3 a week, the tough and rugged McKie never became a first team regular playing six FA Cup ties and the same number of league games during his single season with the club. Lining up in an all-Scottish backline, Saints would win their first Southern League title in 1896-97, even if he was only a peripheral part of the success. He went on to play in Kent for Chatham and Dartford before he ended up back at Freemantle. Died in 1948.

McLaughlin, Bobby

Wing-half
Born: *1925 Belfast, Northern Ireland* **Died:** *2003*
Playing career: *Distillery, Wrexham, Cardiff City, Southampton, Headington United (1949-1959)*

Bobby McLaughlin arrived in England's third tier at Saints from the League of Ireland via Wrexham and Cardiff. He described his time at Southampton as "the best move I ever made" and would quickly endear himself to the Saints faithful thanks to his committed, tough tackling style. Most of his work was defensive, although he got forward enough to net five goals in 178 appearances. Formed a strong partnership with Bryn Elliott at wing-half during six seasons at The Dell and the pair once said "you could never wind us up and we both never stopped running." After a few forays at lower league level, McLaughlin worked as an engineer for shipping firm *Union Castle* on the Docks for 31 years until he retired to Shirley.

McLean, Duncan

Outside-forward
Born: *1874 Govan, Scotland* **Died:** *1952*
Playing career: *Summerton, Moor Park, Elderpark Rangers, Partick Thistle, Cowes, Southampton, Derby County (1899-1902)*

A trained shipyard engineer, he played in his native Scotland as an amateur - notably for Queen's Park - until his work took him to the Isle of Wight and Cowes. Played for them in the Southern League but was scouted and signed by Southampton director George Thomas, going on to move to The Dell as a professional. He initially struggled to break into a title-chasing side, but played in the last eight games of the 1899-1900 season across four different position. An extremely versatile player, he linked up with compatriot Roddy McLeod (see below) and grabbed three goals whilst deputising at centre forward. Saints went on to win the title but McLeon moved to Derby after Saints had brought in several new players, hindering his chances of regular game time. Moved back to Glasgow after a year but soon returned to Cowes, winning the Hampshire Senior Cup whilst continuing in his day job as an engineer.

McLean, Robert

Half-back
Born: *1879 Bonhill, West Dunbartonshire, Scotland* **Died:** *1936*
Playing career: *Rutherglen Glencairn , Vale of Leven, Millwall, Newcastle United, Southampton, Dumbarton, (1904-1909)*

Another Scot in the Southern League era, Rob McLean had two stints in that division at Millwall and Southampton sandwiched between three months at top flight Newcastle, although he never played for the Magpies. A busy, bustling and energetic half back, tasked with building the play from deep, he had only played a handful of games at The Dell before finding himself in hot water with the board. Suspended indefinitely for drunken behaviour whilst on a team night out, he was forced out of Southampton and returned to Scotland with Dumbarton. Served in WW1 with the Royal Scots Fusiliers where he won two medals for his service on the frontline.

McLeod, Ally

Forward
Born: 1951 Glasgow
Career: *Southampton, Huddersfield T. (1973-1974)*
McLeod would spend the entirety of his playing days north of the border, apart from three games at Saints and four with Huddersfield both on a loan deal. Signed as back up to Mick Channon, Lawrie McMenemy's arrival as manager and the signing of Peter Osgood meant McLeod barely got a sniff, never starting a game and making only three appearances off the bench. Capped four times by Scotland at U21 level, he also played once for their Representative league side. Later worked in financial services and insurance with the Royal Bank of Scotland and an Australian insurance firm.

McLeod, Roderick

Forward
Born: *1872 Kilsyth, North Lanarkshire, Scotland*
Died: *1931*
Playing career: *Westburn, Partick Thistle, West Bromwich Albion, Leicester Fosse, Brighton United, Southampton, Brentford (1889-1906)*
Scottish forward, played in two FA Cup finals for West Brom, winning it in 1892 before his runners up medal three years later. Scored 50 goals in 149 games for the Baggies and moved on to Second Division Leicester Fosse and the short lived Brighton United. Played and scored in the first ever game at The Dell for the latter against the club which would become his future employers. By the end of that season, he was playing for Saints as they stormed to a third successive Southern League title. Small in stature but a splendid forward with deft footwork, McLeod struck three goals in as many games to fire Southampton to the FA Cup final in 1900, but lost his place to Jack Farrell. They would lose 4-0 to Bury with the performance attributed to dressing room dispute over whether McLeod or Farrell should play in the final. Scored twelve goals in 34 games for Saints before a move to divisional rivals Brentford. After retirement, he later worked in a warehouse, a brewery and then as a boiler mechanic before his death in 1931 at the age of 59.

McLoughlin, Alan

Midfielder
Born: *1967 Manchester*
Playing career: *Manchester United, Swindon Town, Torquay United (loan), Southampton, Aston Villa (loan), Portsmouth, Wigan Athletic, Rochdale, Forest Green Rovers (1985-2003)*
Former Manchester United apprentice, who despite never quite managing to break into the first team at Old Trafford, did later carve out a very successful career at both club and international level. Joined Pompey from Southampton in February 1992 for £400,000. Although he had joined from the team 'up the road', he quickly won over the crowd and went on to make over 300 appearances including the 1992 FA Cup run and become club captain. A McLoughlin goal qualified the Republic of Ireland team for the World Cup in the United States and he became the first Portsmouth player to be included in any World Cup squad since 1958. In December 1999 he was sold to Wigan Athletic for £260,000. Injuries prevented him from making a major impact and a slipped disc brought his playing days to an end. As well as being a familiar voice on local radio, Alan has also scouted for Nottingham Forest and run a soccer clinic and summer soccer schools. Won 42 Republic of Ireland caps.

Alan McLoughlin

McManus, Stuart

Forward
Born: *1965 Falkirk, Scotland*
Playing career: *Tottenham Hotspur, Southampton, Newport County, Sandvikens (1983-2011)*
McManus combined playing for Saints reserves whilst working as a PE teacher in Farnham. Plundered 30 goals in his first season at that level and then made his first team debut after a loan spell at Newport. Scored on his senior bow with a "thumping header" at QPR, but he made only one further appearance before moving abroad to play in Scandinavia. There, he would be dogged by controversy as he got banned for five matches having attacked a ref, then cracking the rib of another official in a collision - albeit he insisted it had been accidental. He retired before judgement could be passed and went into property development, resurfacing aged 45 to play for Swedish lower league side Hagastrom.

McMillan, John

Centre-half
Born: *1869* **Died:** *1892*
Playing career: *Southampton St. Mary's (1891-)*
Sgt John McMillan came to the attention of the powers that be at Southampton St Mary's after playing against them in an exhibition match for Argyle & Sutherland Highlanders. Fellow debutant and soldier, Pte Jock Fleming, scored a hat-trick in a 7-0 demolition of Reading that marked the club's second ever FA Cup tie. Neither man ever played for the club again and would be posted to India, although Fleming later played for Aston Villa and Lincoln. As for McMillan, his story came to and end when he contracted enteric fever and died at the tragically young age of 23.

McMillan, William

Half-back
Born: *1872 Glasgow, Scotland* **Died:** *1929*
Playing career: *Dykehead, Heart of Midlothian, Southampton, Burnley, St Mirren, Kilbarchan, Arthurlie, Morton, Arthurlie (1894-1905)*
Southampton St Mary's trainer Charles Robson had tried five different players at right-half before William McMillan, yet another Scotsman, arrived from Hearts, towards the end of the 1895-96 season.

He quickly became an ever present as Saints won the Southern League for the first time the following campaign and played 47 times in total for the club. The man known as "Punt" would find chances limited thereafter, though. Had a brief stint with Burnley but then returned to Scotland with St Mirren, Morton and numerous lower league clubs. Died in 1929.

Mead, Charles Philip

Goalkeeper
Born: *1887 Battersea, London* **Died:** *1958*
Playing career: *Southampton (1907)*
In the midst of a brilliant career as a batsman for Hampshire and England, it is often forgotten that one of the county's most famous sons, Phil Mead, ever played for Southampton FC. But yet he did, as an emergency goalkeeper for the Southern League side in 1907. He kept a clean in his one and only appearance for the club, a 0-0 draw at The Dell. And that was it, as Mead focused on his career as a cricketer. He played in 17 Tests for England and still holds the record as Hampshire's all time leading run scorer (48,892). He later coached at Framlingham College in Suffolk, representing that county at Minor County level in the final post-war season. Mead would later go totally blind and continued to attend Hampshire's matches right up until his death at the age of 71 in 1958.

Measures, William

Half-back
Born: *1867 Leicester* **Died:** *1923*
Playing career: *Southampton (1891-1891)*
A soldier working at the hospital in Netley, Charles William Measures regularly turned out for their works team and registered with Southampton St Mary's as an amateur. He would be called upon only twice, both in cup games, against Cowes in the Hampshire Senior Cup and then Warmley in the club's first ever FA Cup tie the following season. After another friendly turn out, Measures was posted to Barbados and later served in India. Joined the Mediterranean Expeditionary Force during WW1, later becoming a quarter-master with the Red Cross in Manchester.

Meechan, Peter

Full-back
Born: *1872 West Lothian, Scotland*
Died: *1915*
Playing career: *Hibernian, Sunderland, Celtic, Everton, Southampton, Manchester City, Barrow,Clyde, Broxburn Athletic (1892-1904)*

A league champion with Sunderland and Celtic, where he was released after refusing to play in a match against Hibernian. Earned an FA Cup runner's up medal with Everton, playing 28 times for the blue half of Merseyside before moving south for £200. He joined a Southampton team dominating the Southern League and a side that knocked out three top flight clubs - including Meechan's former club Everton - en route to the 1900 FA Cup final where they lost to Bury. The Anglo-Scottish split in the Saints camp concerning selection for the final led to Meechan's departure from the club. Capped once by Scotland against Ireland in 1896. After retirement, Meechan emigrated to Canada where he worked as a coach and then returned to his original trade as a miner. Died at the young of 43.

Melia, Jimmy

Midfielder
Born: *1937 Liverpool*
Playing career: *Liverpool, Wolverhampton Wanderers, Southampton, Aldershot, Crewe Alexandra (1952-1972)*

A midfielder with great vision, played over 300 games for hometown club Liverpool, joined Saints from Wolves in 1964, and stayed for four years before joining Aldershot as player manager, He is probably best known as the manager who took unfancied Brighton to the FA Cup final in 1983 and has coached professionally in five countries - England, Kuwait, Portugal, United Arab Emirates and USA. He now coaches youth teams for Liverpool FC America in The Colony, Texas where he is now Technical Director. Capped twice by England during his time at Anfield and got promoted with Saints in 1964-65 in a team consisting of Terry Paine and Martin Chivers, among others. Played 152 games in four years at The Dell, scoring twelve goals.

Meston, Sammy

Winger
Born: *1902 Southampton* **Died:** *1953*
Playing career: *Southampton, Gillingham, Everton, Tranmere Rovers (1921-1932)*

Sammy Meston Jr. realised his childhood dream to follow in his famous dad's footsteps, even if it was not quite to the same scale. Signing for he club as a young, raw and ambitious 19 year old, he would play six successive games at the start of the 1923-24 campaign and then another four three years later having recovered from a broken leg. He would break the same leg in his second game back, and never played for Southampton again. Played for Cowes and Gillingham before moving to top flight, title-chasing Everton. Returning to Southampton in 1932, he played sporadically for Isle of Wight-based Newport whilst working for a local bookmaker. Briefly worked in the aircraft factory at Woolston but continued as a bookie until his death in 1953.

Meston, Samuel

Half-back
Born: *1872 Arbroath, Scotland* **Died:** *1948*
Playing career: *Stoke, Southampton, Salisbury City, Croydon Common, Eastleigh Athletic (1894-1913)*

Sam Meston Sr was a totemic presence in the era of Southampton's Southern League dominance. Signed as one of several new arrivals from Stoke, Meston won six championship medals, two FA Cup runner up gongs and played over 400 times during a stellar 11-year career at The Dell. He was the first player to achieve the latter feat, and holds several other club appearance-related records - second highest Southern League appearance maker with 246. Strong, agile and versatile, Meston could play anywhere across the back and in midfield, and would leave for a stint in non league in 1906. He turned out for Croydon Common and Eastleigh as player-coach and also coached at a football school in New York. Played and/or trained for several local clubs before taking up a job on the railways at Eastleigh as a brake fitter. He was still playing for the ex Saints two decades on when his son, Sam Jr, was starting out at The Dell.

Metcalf, Thomas

Left-half
Born: *1878 Burton upon Trent* **Died:** *1938*
Playing career: *Burton United, Southampton, Salisbury City, Wolves (1903-1909)*

Metcalf had turned out for Burton Swifts and later the United of the sane name when Southampton came calling. Having played only in the Midland league, the Southern equivalent may have looked a sideways step but Metcalf wanted to try his hand away from home territory. He would play only once for the club at senior level, as a left half during his second campaign, but otherwise had to be content with second strong football. Won the Hampshire Senior Cup at Reserve team level and represented the Western League team (affiliated to Saints but a separate entity from the Southern League side) before he joined division lower Salisbury. Had a brief stint at Wolves before retiring and retuning to his original trade as a barrel-maker for the brewers. Joined the Middlesex Regiment and was mortally wounded on the battlefields with the 67th Royal Engineers. Suffering gunshot wounds, a broken leg, burns and deafness, he retired to Kent.

Mettomo, Lucien

Defender
Born: *1977 Douala, Cameroon*
Playing career: *Tonnerre Yaounde, Saint-Etienne, Manchester City, FC Kaiserslautern, Kayseri Erciyesspor, FC Luzern, Southampton, Veria F.C. (1995-2009)*

Capped 41 times by African powerhouses Cameroon, Mettomo played at the 2002 World Cup and won the AFCON with his nation twice. He was part of the Manchester City side to win the Division One title and promotion in 2001-02, a busy year for him, also winning the aforementioned continental title the same season. He played 31 times for City but fell out of favour after the signing of Sylvain Distin. Played in Germany and had an unsuccessful trial at Norwich before a similar deal with Southampton. However he never played for the Championship Saints and his contract was cancelled after only two months having failed to make a first team appearance.

Middleton, Steve

Goalkeeper
Born: *1953 Portsmouth*
Playing career: *Southampton, Torquay United, Portsmouth (1967-1977)*

Although signed as cover for first choice stopper, Ian Turner, Middleton played 18 successive times during the opening months of the iconic 75-76 campaign. Turner would be restored for the Wembley final after Middleton suffered a "crisis of confidence" according to manager Lawrie McMenemy. Turner would get injured at the start of the following campaign, but the arrivals of Colin Boulton, loanee Jim Montgomery and then Peter Wells saw him slip down the pecking order. Released by Saints, he moved up the Solent to sign for hometown team Portsmouth but played only one season at Fratton Park before retiring. Later worked as a financial advisor for a Fareham based building society.

Millen, Keith

Defender
Born: *1966 Croydon*
Playing career: *MK Dons, Southampton, Crystal Palace, Brentford, Watford, Bristol City (1980-2003)*

A former apprentice at Southampton, Millen never played for the first team but went on to have a successful career elsewhere. Made over 300 appearances for Brentford but also turned out for Watford and Bristol City. In a career spanning two decades, Millen racked up 530 careers games and went into management having hung up his boots. Managed his former Bristol City in three separate spells, two of those as caretaker, and also took charge of another of his ex clubs, Crystal Palace, again on a temporary basis in three stints. Served as manager of MK Dons and is currently boss of Swedish outfit Orgryte IS. Also worked with the youth development at Spurs and Pompey.

"DID YOU KNOW?"

"The club originally used the same crest as the city but it was re-designed in the 1970s."

Miller, Kevin

Goalkeeper
Born: *1969 Falmouth, Cornwall*
Playing career: *Birmingham City, Watford, Crystal Palace, Barnsley, Exeter City, Bristol Rovers, Derby County, Southampton, Torquay United (1985-2016)*

With Antti Niemi departed and new arrival Bartosz Bialkowski injured, George Burley signed the Cornish born keeper as cover for first choice Paul Smith. Plucked out of retirement from the world of corporate hospitality, Miller finished the 2005-06 season as first choice. He played the last seven games. The arrival of yet another new stopper, Kelvin Davis, meant Miller was third choice and he moved to Torquay United. Also, played for his local side Falmouth and for South West Peninsula League side Bodmin Town. Having finished playing, he stayed involved in the game as a football in the community coach, working in local schools and at the Centre of Excellence for Exeter City, his first club.

Miller, Charles

Forward
Born: *1874 Sao Paulo, Brazil* **Died:** *1953*
Playing career: *Southampton*

Brazilian born Scot widely credited with introducing the beautiful game to the football mad South American country. Disembarking from the *SS Magdalena* from Southampton to Rio, he brought with him a rulebook, a couple of shirts, a pump, three footballs and a pair of boots. Having played both football and rugby in Banister Court public school in ther city, Miller returned home ten years later to create a monster. Aside from the many friendlies he played in for the "Saints", his competitive career consisted of seven games in the Cricket Club Charity Cup. With the era of the newly formed Southern League dawning, Charles Miller jumped on a ship down Southampton Water, sailing into the sunset and into history. Went on to set up Brazil's first football club Sao Paulo Athletic and formed the Brazilian Association of football. Went on to work in his uncle's travel business and as British Vice Consul in Santos. He died on 30 June 1953 in Sao Paulo, and is buried in the city.

Mick Mills

173

Mills, Mick
Full-back
Born: *1949 Godalming, Surrey*
Playing career: *Portsmouth, Ipswich Town, Southampton, Stoke City (1964-1987)*

England international full back and captain with 42 caps, played nearly 750 games for Ipswich before joining Saints in 1982, two months before his 33rd birthday. He went on to play over 100 games in the next three seasons, followed by a final playing season at Stoke City. He then entered management with a four year spell as Potters boss, followed by a few months with Colchester United, a scouting job for Sheff Weds & coach at Birmingham City. He was also rewarded with an MBE for his long service to our national game. Since his last job in football management and coaching, he's worked as chief scout at Sheffield Wednesday. He retuened to live in Suffolk and become technical director of Galaxy Sports Management. He is also Suffolk's patron for the Sir Bobby Robson Charity. Mills still appears on BBC Radio Suffolk as a summariser for Ipswich matches.

Mills, Steve
Full-back
Born: *1953 Portsmouth* **Died:** *1988*
Playing career: *Southampton, Miami Toros, Weymouth (1969-1978)*

Pacy and combative, Portsmouth born Mills had already become an established Saint and an England age group international by the time he was 20. Mills was snapped up by Ted Bates as a 15 year old, turning pro in 1971. Went on to play 77 times for Saints and seemed to be set for an illustrious and decorated career. That would come crashing down though when he was critically injured in a car accident. Driving home after a night out with friends, they struck a kerb and overturned the vehicle. Mills sustained pelvic, back and neck injuries but, incredibly, would play again - in the USA for Miami Toros. Played in the final league match of the 75-76 season having returned to Saints but never fully regained fitness and quit the following season. Worked in a newsagents and for Ladbrokes before tragically succumbing to leukaemia aged just 34.

Millward, Horace
Forward
Born: *1931 Sheffield* **Died:** *2000*
Playing career: *Doncaster Rovers, Southampton, Ipswich Town, Poole Town (1951-1964)*

Sheffield born, Horace 'Doug' Millward signed for Doncaster at 16, but never played for the Yorkshire side before moving to Southampton. He would have no better luck there, either, never playing for the senior side and only being restricted to a handful of run outs for the reserves. Millward would finally make his mark and find a home in Suffolk, turning out over 100 times for Ipswich Town and going on to coach their Academy. He would move into management after retiring, worked in Scotland as boss of St Mirren before going "across the pond" and taking charge of the short lived Baltimore Bays NASL side. When they disbanded, he helped to found phoenix club Baltimore Comets, going on to manage them for their debut 1974-75 season. Died in Baltimore in 2000.

Milward, Alf
Left winger
Born: *1870 Great Marlow, Bucks* **Died:** *1941*
Playing career: *Everton, New Brighton Tower, Southampton (1888-1903)*

To describe Alf Milward as a winner seems something of an understatement. He had already won a First Division title and played in two FA Cup finals for Everton by the time Southampton enticed him to the south coast. Saints were building an impressive looking side, a star-studded squad of ex top flight players and experienced internationals. With Milward pulling the strings as a goalscoring winger, he plundered 23 goals in 28 games to fire Saints to their first FA Cup final during his debut season - only for the club to fall at the final hurdle. Milward was noted for his distribution and accurate shot. Capped four times by England at full international level, Milward's record in a Southampton shirt was 87 games, 44 goals. In tandem with ex-Toffee team mate Edgar Chadwick, he fired Saints to their fourth Southern League title the following season. Later became a landlord of the *Diamond Jubilee* whilst working for the Southampton FA.

Mitton, John

Half-back
Born: *1895 Todmorden*
Died: *1983*
Playing career: *Portsmouth Rovers, Padiham, Brierfield, Burnley, Bury, Exeter City, Sunderland, Wolves, Southampton (1914-1928)*

Although his career scanned both peacetime and the horrors of the Great War, John Milton did not truly get started in the professional game until he was 24, when he signed for Southern League Exeter. Having joined top flight Sunderland after a single season, he would spend the best part of the next decade as a Football League player, also with second tier Wolves. Divisional rivals Southampton paid £150 to bring him to The Dell ahead of the 1927-28 season. It would be Mitton's only season on the south coast, providing cover for the defensive areas albeit only playing eight games. Released the following season, he played briefly at Hampshire League level before retiring in 1930. Later worked in the hospitality industry and also on the railways for a while.

Moffat, Thomas

Right winger
Born: *1948 Lanarkshire, Scotland*
Died: *2015*
Playing career: *Southampton, Motherwell, Detroit Cougars, Falkirk, Dumbarton, Toronto Metros, Detroit Express, Washington Diplomats, Detroit Express (1964-1983)*

A winger with a little slice of history as he became the first substitute to score in Scottish league football, whilst playing for Motherwell. He had joined Southampton as an amateur in 1964 but failed to break into the first team and so tried his luck in his native Scotland. Also played for Falkirk and Dumbarton in his homeland before playing overseas in North America and Canada. Turned out for two clubs in Detroit and also the Washington Diplomats. After retirement he settled in Canada with his family and turned his hand to coaching. Worked with amateur side AC Roma (not to be confused with AS Roma the Italian side) before he was appointed head coach of NSL side Windsor Wheels. Died in 2015.

Moger, Harry

Goalkeeper
Born: *1879 Southampton*
Died: *1927*
Playing career: *Forest Swifts, Freemantle, Southampton, Manchester United (1898-1912)*

Such was Harry Moger's successes at Manchester United that his time at Southampton is relatively forgotten about. Tall, lean and agile, he proved himself to be a willing deputy for whenever first choice keeper Jack Robinson was unavailable. He would only play 14 games in three years at The Dell, such was Robinson's pre-eminence, but having moved to Bank Street and then later Old Trafford as United move house, his talent and promise was realised. After a tentative first season in which he seemed to lack confidence, More became a regular for the next eight seasons as United won promotion to the top flight, winning two Division One titles and an FA Cup. He would stay with United until 1912, playing over 200 games and being remembered as one of the club's finest Edwardian era goalkeepers. After retirement, he settled in Manchester where set up his own business as a commissioned agent. Died aged 47.

Molloy, William

Inside-left
Born: *1929 Coventry*
Playing career: *Coventry City, Southampton, Lockheed, Newport County, Millwall, Rugby Town, Snowdown Colliery Welfare, Canterbury City, Dover, Nuneaton Borough, Bedworth United (1945-1957)*

Posted to Aldershot on Army duty, he attracted the attention of Southampton and signed pro after a trial at The Dell. Became a regular in the Reserves but only played one game for the senior side as manager Sid Cann assessed his options. Showing a lack of pace at inside left, that sparked the start and the end of Molloy's career with Saints. A potential move to Aston Villa fell through, and so - disenchanted b the beautiful game - he worked for Lockheed. Played again briefly for Millwall and Newport County he had several non league flirtations before settling in Coventry where he worked in the building trade.

Monk, Frank

Centre-half
Born: *1886 Salisbury* **Died:** *1962*
Playing career: *Salisbury City, Glossop, Southampton, Fulham (1910-1912)*

An extremely multi-talented sportsman, Monk excelled at swimming, cricket, tennis and athletic - winning honours in all four sports including the Salisbury Marathon of 1909 - as well as professional football. He found the time to play 19 times for Southampton in the 1910-11 season as a centre half-turned-occasional striker. Capped four times by England at amateur level, he went on to turn out for Glossop in that club's Football League heyday, and also played for Fulham before a one game finale at The Dell. Called up to British squad for the football tournament in the Stockholm Olympics of 1912 and became a teacher in retirement, also publishing several books on aircraft and flying.

Monk, Garry

Centre-back
Born: *1979 Bedford*
Playing career: *Torquay United, Southampton, Stockport County, Oxford United, Sheffield Wednesday, Barnsley, Swansea City (1995-2014)*

Caught the eye during his time at Torquay but despite seemingly always being on the verge of a first team breakthrough, this never materialised. He played eleven times in the Premier League under Dave Jones, but with Claus Lundekvam the lynchpin at the heart of the defence, the likes of Ken Monkou, Dean Richards, Paul Williams, Tahar El Khalej and Michael Svensson were all ahead of Monk in the pecking order. Despite being able to deputise at full-back, Monk would only play 13 games for the club in eight years and went on loan five times (to old club Torquay, Oxford, Stockport, Sheffield Wednesday and Barnsley). He eventually signed for Swansea, coming club captain and leading the team to top flight promotion, a League Cup triumph and into Europe. After retiring as a player, Monk has carved out a successful career as a manager, taking charge of Swansea - where he remains a club legend - Leeds, Middlesbrough and Birmingham.

Monk was sacked as manager of Sheffield Wednesday in November 2020 after 14 months in charge. Loud, Proud and Positive" by Garry Monk details the story of his time at Swansea during the greatest era in the Welsh club's history, with the book updated in 2014. He's on Twitter: *https://twitter.com/GarryMonk*

Monkou, Ken

Centre-back
Born: *1964 Nickerie, Suriname*
Playing career: *Feyenoord, Chelsea, Southampton, Huddersfield Town (1985-2000)*

A Chelsea legend, the muscular, cultured and agile centre-back - schooled in the Dutch raison d'être of Total Football - and arguably Ian Branfoot's best buy as Southampton manager. He had played over a century of games for Chelsea, where won the club's Player of the Year award and, such was his impact at the Bridge, he deserved more honours than a single Zenith Data Systems Cup triumph. Joined Saints for £750,000 and went straight into a side perennially battling for their Premier League lives. His goal in the 5-4 win over Norwich helped pull off the "Great Escape" and he went n to play over 200 times for the Saints. Never capped by his country, he also played for Huddersfield before retiring to his native Netherlands, where he ran a pancake house. He has since done media work for Chelsea TV, played for Blues legends teams and reportedly now enjoys a far less stressful pastime - fly fishing!

Ken Monkou

Montgomery, Jim

Goalkeeper

Born: *1943 Hendon, Sunderland*
Playing career: *Sunderland, Vancouver Royals, Southampton (loan), Birmingham City, Nottingham Forest (1960-1980)*

Holds the record for the most Sunderland appearances (627) and was particularly noted for his colossal heroics in the Mackems shock FA Cup win over Leeds in 1972-73. An outstanding double save in the final steered the club to their second and, to date, last triumph in that competition. One of his era's best stoppers, he arrived at Southampton for the 1976-77 season but the move never worked out and he played only five times. Ten goals were conceded, the side failed to win any of those five and Montgomery later admitted that Southampton "wasn't the place for me". Won a European Cup winners medal with Nottingham Forest despite never playing for the first time. Montgomery has suite named after him at the Stadium of Light, where he still works as a corporate host.

Moody, Paul

Forward

Born: *1967 Portsmouth*
Playing career: *Southampton, Reading, Oxford U, Fulham, Millwall, Oxford United. (1991-2002)*

Moody failed to get both games and goals at Southampton, despite seeming to be a perfect fit for manager Ian Branfoot's preferred style. He had plundered plenty for Fareham and Havant & Waterlooville at non league level, earning trials at Portsmouth and Coventry with neither proving successful. Moody's status as a Branfoot favourite was only emphasised when he dropped Matt Le Tissier to give Moody a go. It failed to work out, Branfoot would be sacked and his successor Alan Ball sold Moody to Oxford. He enjoyed much more success there, becoming top scorer and a fans' favourite. His time at the Saints is merely an anomaly when you look at his overall career record of more than 100 goals from 300 games. He retired in 2004 to turn his hand to the property market, buying and renovating houses, before buying and running a health club in Havant, *Moods*, with his wife.

Moore, James

Forward

Born: *1891 Felling, Tyne and Wear* **Died:** *1972*
Playing career: *Barnsley, Southampton, Leeds United, Brighton and Hove Albion, Halifax Town, QPR, Crewe Alexandra (1911-1926)*

A carpenter by trade, Moore was part of the Barnsley team that reached - and won - the FA Cup final in 1912. Worked on the Isle of Wight building aeroplanes during WW1, guesting for Southampton in the process. Scored 22 goals in non-competitive action for the club before signing permanently as a pro in time for the first post-War season. Scored again on his 'official' debut as Saints made the jump from the regional Southern League to the Football League. He missed only one game in two seasons but became the first Saint to be sent off in a Football League fixture. He moved to Leeds for "family reasons". Later managed in the Netherlands before returning to live in Barnsley where he purchased and ran a greengrocer's. Also became a director on the board of his first club at Oakwell.

Moore, Kevin

Defender

Born: *1958 Grimsby* **Died:** *2013*
Playing career: *Grimsby Town, Oldham Athletic, Southampton, Bristol Rovers, Fulham (1976-1996)*

A solid, no nonsense centre-back, Moore began his career at hometown team Grimsby for the best part of twelve years and 400 games alongside brothers Andy and David as well as a certain Chris Nicholl. Nicholl would leave Grimsby to manage Southampton and signed Moore two years later. Finally offered a chance in the top flight at the age of 29 thanks to a clause in his contract. Moore - tough and committed - suddenly found himself playing under the tutelage of his former Mariners team mate. Partnering Kevin Bond and then Russell Osman, Moore continued as a mainstay even after the arrival of Neil Ruddock gave Nicholl five centre back options. Scored in the Zenith Data Systems Cup final in 92 with Ian Branfoot now in charge, and stayed with Saints to play 32 games in the newly formed Premier League before rejoining Branfoot at fourth tier Fulham.

He played 180 games for Southampton before staying at Fulham as ground safety officer, training ground manager and club director. Worked as a scaffold engineer in Fawley but diagnosed with dementia. He died on his 55th birthday. Moore later had a 'pub' built and opened by the White House care home that looked after him, with "Kev's Corner" opened by Francis Benali in 2016 for residents to enjoy.

Moorhead, George
Half-back
Born: *1895 Christchurch, NZ* **Died:** *1975*
Playing career: *Southampton, Brighton & Hove Albion, Glenavon, Linfield, Hearts (1918-1931)*

Although born in New Zealand, Moorhead - raised in Lurgan, County Armagh - was capped three times for Ireland. He played the majority of his club football in his adopted country, except for two spells on the south coast with Saints and then Brighton. Having served in the Royal Ulster Rifles during WW1, he joined Southampton and played nine games in succession - fourteen in total - until the FA spotted an irregularity with his contract and suspended him for a year. He would resume his career along the coast at the Seagulls in the Third South but only played once for them before going back to Northern Ireland. Played for Glenavon and had two spells at Linfield - winning the Irish League and the Irish Cup twice . Later worked as a ticket collector at Lurgan station until he was 70.

Moran, Steve
Striker
Born: *1961 Croydon*
Playing career: *Southampton, Leicester City, Reading, Exeter City, Hull City (1975-1995)*

Since hanging up his boots, Southampton's 1984 derby day hero has had several different jobs. Aside from setting up and running an internet business from his his east Yorkshire home - in which he auctions off sports equipment - Moran cycled to 26 football stadia, covering 1,400 miles in 21 days in 2014, to raise money for four muscular dystrophy charities in honour of his adopted son, whom suffers with the debilitating condition.

Having raised over £2,000 through his ride, Moran organised and ran a charity match between legends of two of his former sides, Reading and Southampton, a year later. Since then, he has worked as a mobile crane operator and as a long distance lorry driver out of Hull for Yorkshire based haulage company David Watson Transport Ltd. He is known to dislike the many nuances of the modern game and is on Twitter at: *https://twitter.com/stevemoran*

Moss, Neil
Goalkeeper
Born: *1975 New Milton*
Playing career: *Southampton, Gillingham, Bournemouth (1992-2008)*

Moss served Saints as able cover for Dave Beasant and Bruce Grobbelaar. Reliable and steady, he was nevertheless unable to displace either those two or the soon to arrive Antti Niemi and Paul Jones. After only 24 starts in eight years, Moss returned to his old stamping ground at AFC Bournemouth, playing over 100 times until a wrist injury forced his retirement in 2008. He set up his own goalkeeping coaching company *Between the Sticks* and now works for the Cherries as their full time goalkeeping coach.

Mouncher, Frederick
Winger
Born: *1883 Southampton* **Died:** *1918*
Playing career: *Fitzhugh Rovers, Southampton Cambridge, Southampton, Fulham (1903-1911)*

As a trophy winning sprinter as a boy, Fred Mouncher had all the attributes of an archetypal winger. Locally born Mouncher started out as a pro with his hometown team in 1903 and played ten matches in his first season and 162 times in total. He stayed at Saints for four seasons but with the club cash strapped and needing to sell, Mouncher was one of the casualties. Second Division Fulham made their move. He had an international trial in 1908 but nothing ever came of it and he retired two years later. Worked as the licensee of the *Railway Arms* in St Denys for a while before he succumbed to tuberculosis aged 34. His brother, Sidney, had a spell with Saints as an amateur and also played for Millwall.

Mulford, Arthur

Forward
Born: *1871 Southampton* **Died:** *1920*
Career: *Southampton St. Mary's (1891-1892)*
Mulford's debut co-incided with Saints first ever FA Cup tie and he would go on to play a handful of games for the club over the next year, five in total. He then moved to Croydon to become a shipping clerk with the *Union Steam* ship company. Worked in South Africa and on the docks having returned to Southampton before he died in Egypt aged 49 having worked out there for an insurance firm.

Mulgrew, Tommy

Forward
Born: *1929 Motherwell, Scotland* **Died:** *2016*
Playing career: *Cleland Juniors, Greenock Morton, Northampton Town, Newcastle United, Southampton, Aldershot, Andover (1948-1965)*
Scored twice on his Saints debut, the opener coming after only 15 seconds - the fastest ever goal seen at The Dell (a 6-4 win for the home side). Not content with that piece of history, he created another, albeit this time a dubious honour. Mulgrew became the first post-war Southampton player to be sent off (in fact, the first since 1933), and went on to become only one of thirteen men to score 100 goals or more for the club in competitive peace time football, having played 330 times.

A typically dour and gritty Scot, he had failed to cut it at Newcastle but found his niche at Saints as a deep-lying forward, just as capable as doing the dirty work for the likes of George O'Brien as he was at finding the net himself. The two helped steer Southampton to promotion and then consolidate at First Division level. He was described as a "real glutton for fetching and carrying, a crowd favourite and popular with his colleagues as well." Later moved to Aldershot and also returned to Northampton, working in a steel factory and later for the council.

Mulholland, John

Centre-forward
Born: *1932 Dumbarton, Scotland*
Died: *2000*
Playing career: *Condorrat Thistle, Southampton, Chester, Halifax Town, Lovells Athletic (1951-1958)*
Scotsman whom began his career on the books at Saints but never played at senior level for the club. Also played for Halifax, represented Chester and briefly at Bolton. A "determined and wily" centre forward, he also turned out for the Scottish League XI but was never capped by his country. He was involved in a car crash in 1958 and, although he survived, the injuries he sustained left him unable to continue playing.

On tour 1904

Murphy, William

Winger
Born: *1895 St Helens* **Died:** *1962*
Playing career: *Liverpool, Alexandra Victoria, Manchester City, Southampton, Oldham Athletic, Tranmere Rovers, Ellesmere Port Town (1918-1932)*

A nifty, speedy cross country runner in his youth, Murphy used his transferrable skills to take up football when his athletics club disbanded upon the outbreak of WW1. Had a spell at Liverpool before turning pro and joining Manchester City in time for the resumption of competitive football in 1919. Murphy went on to play over 200 times for City on the left wing before joining Saints and becoming a virtual ever present. He was part of the team that reached the FA Cup semi finals in 1927 but eventually moved on to Oldham. Died in 1962.

Murray, Paul

Midfielder
Born: *1976 Carlisle, Cumbria*
Playing career: *QPR, Southampton, Oldham Athletic, Beira-Mar, Carlisle United, Gretna, Shrewsbury Town, Hartlepool United, Oldham Athletic (1994-2013)*

Carlisle born midfielder with 4 England U21 caps, joined Southampton from QPR in 2001 at the peak of his career, but the Premier League appeared to be a step too far for him and after just one appearance he moved to Oldham to continue his success in the lower leagues. He played for Hartlepool in the 2010-2011 season before becoming head of Academy at Oldham. Also worked as assistant manager at former club and hometown team Carlisle.

Murty, Graeme

Defender
Born: *1974 Saltburn*
Playing career: *Rangers, Middlesbrough, York City, Reading, Charlton A, Southampton (1991-2010)*

A Royal legend, Murty - capped four times by Scotland - proved an integral part of unfancied Reading's rise from the third tier to the Premier League. Murty played over 300 games for the Berkshire club and was voted Reading's best ever right back in an official fans poll in 2006, winning the BBC South Sports Personality of the Year in the same season.

Skippered Reading to their famous 106-point campaign in 2005-06, a record that still stands today. Having been released by the club, Murty joined Southampton but played only eight times for the Saints after an injury ravaged stint on the south coast. He moved into coaching after retiring from playing, staying on at Southampton as assistant youth development coach, before moving to Norwich to take charge of their under 16 side. Worked as head of youth at Rangers before a stint as caretaker manager of the first team, replacing the sacked Pedro Caixinha, later taking the job on a permanent basis.

Naughton, William

Outside-right
Born: *1870 Garnkirk, Scotland*
Died: *1906*
Playing career: *Carfin Shamrock, Hibernian, Uddingston, Celtic, Carfin Shamrock, Glasgow Hibernian, Wishaw Thistle, Stoke, Southampton, Carfin Rovers (1887-1898)*

Talented yet temperamental, William Naughton aka "Chippy" made his name in Scotland with two of his home nation's biggest clubs, Hibernian of Edinburgh and Celtic of Glasgow. Crossing south of the border, he joined Stoke and went on to play over 100 games for the Potters and was briefly suspended for receiving pay whilst still an amateur. He came to the attentions of Southampton during a friendly match between the two sides, with Stoke winning 8-0. Future Saints Charles Baker, Lachie Thomson and Alf Littlehales were also in the Stoke side that day. Naughton would have two good seasons on the south coast, contributing a fair share of goals as a virtual ever present at inside or outside right (a winger in today's parlance). His "elusive wing play and accurate crossing" made Naughton a key man for Saints, going on to play 47 times and scoring 21 goals. Later returned to Scotland following the signing of Jimmy Yates and played local football, working as a coal pit labourer. He would meet a sad end, admitted to a mental asylum to die at the age of 35.

Neal, Richard

Winger
Born: *1906 Fencehouses* **Died:** *1986*
Playing career: *Blackpool, Derby County, Southampton, Bristol City (1925-1939)*
Southampton Supporters Club stumped up the money to bring him to the south coast. "Dick" Neal was a model of consistency and missed only two games in his five years at The Dell. A combination of injury - namely appendicitis - and the arrival of Tom Parker as manager meant he slipped out of favour. Neal subsequently moved to Bristol City. Later played for Accrington Stanley where he retired to work in the colliery mines during the Second World War. After the conflict, he became a landlord in Dinnington, South Yorkshire, and also worked for the gas board.

Neilson, Alan

Defender
Born: *1972 Wegberg, West Germany*
Playing career: *Newcastle United, Southampton, Fulham, Grimsby Town, Luton Town.*
Despite being born in Germany, Neilson was capped five time by Wales - although he reportedly admitted he'd never set foot in the country before his debut in 1992. He was deployed in both full-back positions and in midfield under three different Saints managers - Dave Merrington, Graeme Souness and Dave Jones, having been signed by Alan Ball in his last act as Southampton boss. Neilson played 55 times for the club. After hanging up his boots, he returned to Luton as youth coach and then served as assistant manager and first team caretaker boss in three spells. Neilson then joined Norwich City as Professional Development Coach with the youth and Academy sides.

Alan Neilson

Neville, Steve

Winger
Born: *1957 Walthamstow*
Playing career: *Southampton*
Steve Neville had trials with London clubs Chelsea and West Ham before being invited to another trial with second tier Southampton. A skillful, darting, pacy winger, he made his debut under Lawrie McMenemy whilst still an apprentice, going on to make half a dozen appearances for Saints in 1977-78, a season that saw Saints promoted to the top flight. McMenemy's penchant to play without out and out wingers hindered him, though, but when the manager finally signed an orthodox wide man - Terry Curran - Neville left for Exeter. He would enjoy two spells with the Devonian Grecians, sandwiched between his time at Sheffield United, and played for Bristol City. Tried his luck overseas with South China AA in Hong Kong before retiring and moving into coaching. Worked in Australia at Perth Glory and Newcastle Jets and assistant manager with Perth-based Sorrento FC.

Nicholl, Chris

Centre-back
Born: *1946 Wilmslow*
Playing career: *Burnley, Halifax Town, Luton, Aston Villa, Southampton, Grimsby. (1965-1984).*
Chris Nicholl stacked up over 200 games for Saints, was capped 51 times by his country and enjoyed a fine career as a cultured and composed defender. Yet it's his exploits at the other of the pitch that he is perhaps best remembered for as Nicholl scored all four goals - two at the right end and two into his own net - during Aston Villa's 2-2 draw with Leicester. He signed for Saints in 1977 and became integral in Lawrie McMenemy's largely successful side, helping them to promotion during his debut season and maintaining his record of going up with every team he'd played for. Captained Villa to League Cup glory, winning the competition twice and scoring a 40 yarder to take the third replay to extra time in 1977. Also played for Grimsby before retiring and going into management. Succeeded McMenemy as Saints boss and took them to three semi finals.

Chris Nicholl

Nicol, Thomas
Centre-forward/Full-back
Born: *1870 West Lothian, Scotland* **Died:** *1915*
Playing career: *Burnley, Blackburn Rovers, Southampton, Southampton Wanderers (1891-1903)*
Goalscoring winger, marked his debut for Burnley with a hat-trick but was converted to full back. Had a stint with rivals Blackburn before joining Saints where he would win two Southern League titles and net their first FA Cup goal at The Dell. He would play 58 times for Southampton (four goals) before having to retire through a persistent knee injury. Nicol worked as a landlord at the *Kingsland Tavern* near the ground, then later the licensee of a pub in Portsmouth - the *Criterion* - and the *London Hotel* in Woolston. Nicol became a keen and competent bowls player winning the annual championship at Southampton Old Bowling Green in 1907.

Nicholl was also involved with bringing on the likes of Matt Le Tissier, Alan Shearer, Rod Wallace and Tim Flowers during his six years in charge. Living in retirement in Walsall - the club he managed between 1994 and 1997 - even the quiet life has been tough for Nicholl as he suffers from dementia, bought about by many years of heading the ball for a living. Nicholl lives in warden assisted housing and reportedly remembers little on his playing days or his background as a prominent name of his era.

Nicholls, Ernest
Centre-forward
Born: *1871 Southampton* **Died:** *1971*
Career: *Southampton St. Mary's (1888-1894)*
Started out as a 16 year old full-back, but Nicholls would convert to a striker and become one of the club's most prolific players of the pre-professional era. He scored 40 goals in six seasons and would be the first Saint to score in the FA Cup. A superb cricketing all-rounder, he played for Deanery, later captaining the side, and in two unofficial matches for Hampshire. In later life he was a season ticket holder at The Dell and died shortly before completion of his own personal century.

Niemi, Antti
Goalkeeper
Born: *1972 Oulu, Finland*
Playing career: *FC Copenhagen, Rangers, Charlton Athletic, Heart of Midlothian, Southampton, Fulham, Portsmouth (1989-2010)*
During his time at Hearts, Niemi was amusingly and famously the subject of a call during a phone-in on radio channel talkSPORT, in which a fan queried Niemi's continued absence from the Scotland squad. When the presenter replied that Niemi was in fact Finnish, the caller responded with the classic: "He's not finished, he's only 28." (Look it up on YouTube). Signed by Gordon Strachan for £2m Niemi initially vied with Paul Jones before taking over the gloves from his 35-year-old rival.

Antti Niemi

Played in the 2003 FA Cup Final and was a popular figure at St Mary's. Left for Fulham after thee relegation in 2005 and later joined Pompey although he never played for the Fratton Park side. Capped 67 times by Finland, he worked as goalkeeping coach with the national side and then in the same role at another south coast club, Brighton, under compatriot Sami Hyypia. Niemi has drifted out of the game and currently lives and works in his native Finland, where he has a job in the sorting office of the postal service.

Nilsson, Mikael

Midfielder/defender
Born: *1978 Ovesholm, Sweden*
Playing career: *Halmstads BK, Southampton, Panathinaikos, Brondby IF (1995-2012)*
Swedish midfielder capped 64 times by his country, spent a single season at Saints during which he played 21 times before moving back to his homeland via stints in Greece and Denmark. Played for Sweden at three major tournaments - UEFA Euro 2004 and 2008 and the FIFA World Cup of 2006. Retired in 2012 and did some coaching work in his home country. Nilsson is currently a pundit on Swedish TV.

Nineham, George

Forward
Born: *1873 Southampton* **Died:** *1950*
Playing career: *Southampton St. Mary's, Freemantle (1892-1895)*
Nineham emerged from local football to win a professional contract with his hometown team for their inaugural Southern League season. Nabbed nine goals in ten FA Cup and Southern League ies and played in three Hampshire Senior Cup finals, winning two. Known as "Dukey", he played in Saints first ever competitive league game and also the game that brought a 14-0 walloping of Newbury in the FA Cup of 1894-95. Nineham scored a hat-trick on a day that saw the club's biggest ever margin of victory in a competitive match - a record that still stands. He left after two seasons to join local rivals Freemantle, going on to work in Southampton Docks before he committed suicide after financial issues, aged 77.

Nixon, Eric

Goalkeeper
Born: *1962 Manchester*
Playing career: *Manchester City, Wolverhampton Wanderers, Bradford City, Southampton, Carlisle United, Tranmere Rovers, Blackpool, Stockport County, Wigan Athletic, Sheffield Wednesday, Kidderminster Harriers, Tranmere Rovers.*
A striker in his youth, Robert David "Eric" Nixon played for over two decades at the top level for thirteen different clubs, stacking up over 500 games in the process. Starting out with City in his native Manchester, he had played for Wolves and Bradford by the time he moved to the south coast on a short term loan deal. With Phil Kite and Peter Shilton out of action, Southampton faced the hectic festive fixtures with no recognised keeper, and so called for Nixon. Nixon had a spell at Tranmere as player/coach, suffering a heart attack from which he recovered. Became a personal fitness instructor and held several posts as goalkeeping coach on the Wirral, in Dubai and then latterly in Chesterfield.

Noble, Alan

Right winger/Right-half
Born: *1900 Southampton* **Died:** *1973*
Playing career: *Southampton, Boscombe, Leeds United, Brentford, Millwall (1920-1928)*
Locally born Alan "Smiler" Noble started out in parks football when he was scouted and signed by Jimmy McIntyre. Noble would have a handful of games for the Reserves but never featured for the first team and left The Dell after only a season. Played for Boscombe and then moved to Leeds, playing 60 games over the next three seasons and helping The Whites to promotion. Had stints at London clubs Brentfordand Millwall Brighton before retiring from football and become a fitter.

"DID YOU KNOW?"

"Chancellor of the Exchequor Rishi Sunak is a Saints fan and confessed to the Guardian newspaper that Matt Le Tissier was one of his childhood heroes."

Norbury, Duncan
Centre-half
Born: *1887 Bartley, Hampshire* **Died:** *1972*
Playing career: *Bartley,Brockenhurst, Southampton, Bartley Cross (1905-1907)*

An all round sportsman of considerable acclaim, "Victor" Norbury played cricket for Hampshire and Lancashire and three games for Saints at full-back in 1905-06. As Norbury flitted between Hants' 1st and 2nd XIs, he played football locally before scouted and signed by Southampton. Replacing Horace Glover in the team, he eventually lost his place in the team when Glover returned from injury. He would break his leg playing village football which put him out of action for a while, but he returned to score 180 runs in the summer of 1907, before moving north to play three levels of cricket - Minor Counties (Northumberland), Lancashire League (East Lancs) and first class for Lancashire, spanning the pre and post War eras.

O' Brien, George
Inside-forward
Born: *1935 Dunfermline* **Died:** *2020*
Playing career: *Leeds United, Southampton, Leyton Orient, Aldershot. (1956-1967).*

A relatively unknown Scotsman, O'Brien began his playing days in his native homeland before signing for Leeds where he failed to impress, scoring only six times in 50 games for the Yorkshire side. Despite this, Ted Bate, having freed up funds in the Charlie Livesey - Cliff Huxford deal, brought O'Brien to the Dell. He would strike up an instant "telepathy" with his more illustrious colleagues, namely Terry Paine, and got off the mark immediately as he fired 23 goals in his debut season - in tandem with Derek Reeves 39 - as Southampton surged to the third tier title. Likened to the legendary Jimmy Greaves by Paine, O'Brien plundered 180 goals in 280 games, going to become top scorer in each of the next two Second Division seasons. Despite his prolific record, O'Brien never played for Scotland and went on to play for Leyton Orient and Aldershot before retiring. He later worked in the pub trade, then as a taxi driver and as a scout for several clubs including Saints.

O' Brien, Gerry
Outside right
Born: *1949 Glasgow*
Playing career: *Clydebank, Southampton, Bristol Rovers, Swindon Town, Clydebank. (1968-1977).*

Working in the brickyards of Glasgow and in the backwaters of Scotland's amateur football scene, Gerry O'Brien - despite his lowly status - attracted plenty of flirtatious glances from the upper echelons of English football. Top flight Southampton among them, Ted Bates and his former keeper, O'Brien's compatriot Campbell Forsyth, scouted him and persuaded their board to part with £22,500 to bring O'Brien south. Linking up with the effervescent Terry Paine, he made the no.10 position his own, and played 77 times for the club, but scoring only three times. A diminutive, elusive player, O'Brien was a "clever, skilful player who at times had the ability to turn a game on his own completely". He played twice during Saints victorious run to Wembley in the 75-76' season, his last appearance for the south coast side coming in the 4-0 replay win over West Brom in the fifth round. Became an ever present for Bristol Rovers and also played for Swindon before returning to his native Scotland with the club where it all began, Clydebank. Coached at the club and then set up building firm with his sons.

O'Grady, Henry
Inside-forward
Born: *1907 Tunstall, Staffordshire* **Died:** *1990*
Playing career: *Nantwich, Witton Albion, Port Vale, Southampton, Leeds United, Burnley, Bury, Millwall, Carlisle United, Accrington Stanley, Tunbridge Wells Rangers (1929-1939)*

A one season wonder at nine of his ten clubs, he moved to Southampton in 1931, scoring against future employers Burnley on his debut, but spending much of his time at The Dell with the reserve team. Occasionally filling in for the injured Bill Fraser or Arthur Wilson, he played seven games for Saints before moving to First Division Leeds. Again played only sporadically, scoring twice in eight games, going on to turn out for Burnley, Bury, Millwall, Carlisle and Accrington. Became a labourer in later life. Died in 1990.

O'Neil, Brian

Midfielder
Born: *1944 Bedlington*
Playing career: *Burnley, Southampton, Huddersfield Town, Bideford A.F.C. (1962-1976)*

Combative and physical, putting his most well known attributes politely, Brian O'Neil was capped at U23 for England and made Alf Ramsey's preliminary 1966 World Cup squad of 40. Ever present in his debut season at The Dell, baggy shirt and and socks around his ankles to boot, he described his time at Southampton as the "best time of his career" after signing from Burnley for a club record fee of £75,000. As hard as nails and as tough as ol' boots, his combative midfield play and shooting prowess from distance earned him cult hero status at The Dell, he was described as a manager's dream by Ted Bates and "possibly the best player there has ever been in mud" by team-mate Ron Davies. Suspended almost as often as he played, O'Neil was banned for nine weeks, a record at the time, during the 1971-72 season. Lawrie McMenemy was not such a fan, though and his four year stay came to an end after almost 150 games. He departed for third tier Huddersfield in 1974 before a few seasons at non league level. Hanging up his (borrowed) boots, he turned his hand to building work, later becoming a civil engineer and also owned a racehorse called Cathy Jane, with former Saint Mick Channon. Spent three weeks in a coma after a street brawl but recovered and still attends St Mary's. Son in law of another ex-Southampton player David Prutton who is married to O'Neil's daughter Jenny.

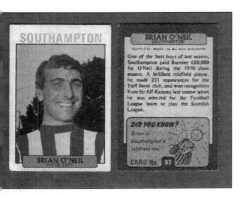

Oakley, Matthew

Midfielder
Born: *1977 Peterborough*
Playing career: *Southampton, Derby County, Leicester City, Exeter City (1993-2017)*

England Under-21 international midfielder who server the Saints well for over a decade. Signing on as a youngster in 1994, he clocked up 311 appearances despite niggling injuries before rejecting a one year deal offered by George Burley in 2006, instead opting to sign for Derby County. The next 10 years saw him give serling service to the Rams, Leicetser City and finally Exeter City. He then followed the well-trodden path of moving into coaching having hung up his boots as a player. He served as assistant manager under Paul Tisdale at MK Dons in 2018-19, but left the club along with his manager at the end of the season and left the day-to-day, pressure cooker world of the professional game. Oakley has not drifted out of sport entirely, though, as he now works for 366 Group. Putting his coaching expertise and contacts from hides as a pro to good use, Oakley has become the figurehead of the agency's work with former professionals, in which he negotiates new contracts, organises image rights, legal issues, tax planning, media training and management, and PR opportunities. The 366 Group's former clients include ex England captains David Beckham, Michael Owen and Gary Neville.
https://twitter.com/366Group

Offer, Harry

Outside-right
Born: *1871 Devizes* **Died:** *1947*
Playing career: *Swindon Town, Royal Arsenal, BurnleySouthampton St Mary's (1887-1895)*

Victorian era forward notable for achieving two "firsts" in his career. Devon born Offer scored Arsenal's first official FA Cup goal and then, upon moving to Southampton, scored the club's first ever goal in league competition. Joined Arsenal from Swindon when neither were affiliated to a league, so played only in cup matches and friendly games. Never made the team at Burnley and so joined Southampton St Mary's, an ambitious club putting together a side to dominate the Southern League. At first a full-back, Offer then reverted to a forward role where he fired the team to Hampshire County Cup success before linking up with Jack Angus, Charles Baker, Fred Hollands and Herbert Ward in the Southern League, finishing third in the inaugural season and reaching the first round proper of the FA Cup. Scored 14 goals in 31 games from Saints before retiring to the Isle of Wight to become a joiner. Died in 1947.

Brett Ormerod

Ormerod, Brett

Forward
Born: *1976 Blackburn*
Playing career: *Blackburn Rovers, Accrington Stanley, Southampton, Leeds United, Wigan Athletic, Preston North End, Nottingham Forest, Oldham Athletic, Blackpool, Rochdale, Wrexham (1995-2016)*

Blackburn born striker and the only player to score in all four divisions of the English game with the same club. Ormerod was a popular figure with team mates and fans alike, procuring the role of forager in chief - mainly for James Beattie - during his time at The Dell. Started the 2003 FA Cup final and earned a runners up medal but became third choice striker behind new signings Kevin Phillips and Peter Crouch. Fell out of favour under Harry Redknapp and returned to Bloomfield Road via loan stints with Leeds, Wigan, Nottingham Forest, Oldham and three seasons at Preston. After retirement, Ormerod moved into coaching and had a stint in charge of non league AFC Fylde as joint caretaker boss with Dave Challinor then first team coach of Preston-based NPL side Bamber Bridge. He has also worked in the media as a co-commentator for BBC Radio Lancashire. Twitter: https://twitter.com/B1orm

Osborne, Frank

Centre-forward
Born: *1896 Wynberg, South Africa* **Died:** *1988*
Playing career: *Netley, Bromley, Fulham, Tottenham Hotspur, Southampton (1911-1933)*

South African born, Osborne joined the Royal Army Medical Corps and moved to England aged 15. A late arrival to the world of professional football, he started at Second Division Fulham. Within a year he had been capped by his adopted nation, becoming the first player from the west London side to do so. Also played for Spurs before a move to divisional rivals Southampton in 1931, where he partnered an emerging Ted Drake as Saints avoided relegation. By now 35 and in the twilight of his career, Osborne played 20 times for the club by failed to find the net. Played briefly for the Reserves before retiring to work as a sales representative. Later returned to Fulham as a director before taking over as manager after the death of Jack Peart. Got Fulham promoted in his first season as boss before moving "upstairs" as former Saints manager Bill Dodgin came in. Osborne had a second stint in charge between 1953-1956 and then served as general secretary/secretary-manager until retirement.

Osgood, Peter

Striker
Born: *1947 Windsor* **Died:** *2006*
Playing career: *Chelsea, Southampton, Norwich City, Philadelphia Fury, Chelsea. (1964-1979).*

A demi god at Chelsea and one the club's greatest ever players became Lawrie McMenemy's first "Galactico" signing at The Dell. Scored both goals on his Blues debut in a 2-0 League Cup win over the minnows of Workington as a 17 year old. A tall and skilful centre-forward, he had forced his way into Tommy Docherty's thinking with an extraordinary record of 30 goals in 20 games at second string level. Broke his leg and missed the club's first ever FA Cup final in 67' (a 1-2 defeat to rivals Spurs) but scored 105 goals in almost 300 games at the Bridge. One of only nine players to score in every round of the aforementioned Cup, finally getting his hands it in 1970, scoring in the replayed final at Old Trafford. Also won the Cup Winners Cup during a golden era for the West London side, scoring in the final, and underlined his reputation as a big game player with another goal in a major showpiece as the Blues lost to Stoke in the League Cup final a year later. Joined Southampton for a club record fee of £275,000 and the "Wizard of Os" would win the FA Cup again as one of the Boys of '76'. Scored 36 goals in 161 games for Saints and later played for Norwich, Philadelphia Fury and Chelsea again. Capped four times for England (a surprisingly low number given his record) and played twice in the 1970 World Cup finals. Later ran a pub in Windsor, married three times and worked in match day hospitality and media at Chelsea. Has a statue at Stamford Bridge and his ashes are scattered under the penalty spot at the Shed End of the ground. "Ossie: Kind of Stamford Bridge," the biography of the man himself, was released in 2002.

Osman, Harry

Outside-left
Born: *1911 Bentworth, Hampshire*
Died: *1998*
Playing career: *Okeford United, Poole Town, Plymouth Argyle, Southampton, Millwall, Bristol City, Dartford, Canterbury City, (1930-1953)*

Despite only playing five times for Plymouth Argyle, Osman caught the eye of then Norwich boss Tom Parker. When Parker took over as Southampton manager three years later, Osman became one of his first buys along with several youngsters from his former side. Scored on his debut against Parker's old side on the way to an impressive tally of 22 goals in 40 games in his debut 1937-38 season, at the time a record for a Southampton winger. This included two hat-tricks. Southampton struggled collectively and Osman failed to replicate the form of his debut campaign as he would score only nine more in the next 30 games before moving to divisional rivals Millwall. Guested for Saints during the unofficial war time season before serving with the Tank Corps in Italy. Played for Third South Bristol City and then in Kent for Dartford and Canterbury (as player manager) and then returned to Hampshire with Winchester whom he later managed. Also ran a pub in the city.

Osman, Russell

Centre-back
Born: *1959 Repton*
Playing career: *Ipswich Town, Leicester City, Southampton, Bristol City, Plymouth Argyle, Brighton, Cardiff City. (1976-1996)*

Won the UEFA Cup with Ipswich in 1981 and capped eleven times by England, but since retirement the former centre-back has been making appearances of a different kind. He has appeared on radio, on stage and even on screen. Osman has done commentary work for BBC Radio Bristol and its Suffolk equivalent and also featured in the 1981 iconic American sports war film *Escape to Victory* as one of a number of famous footballers to appear in the film - Pele, Ossie Ardiles and the two Bobbys, Moore and Charlton, to name but four. Osman's part in the Sylvester Stallone and Michael Caine classic saw him play one of the prisoner of war footballers. Osman has since worked as an after dinner speaker and is now employed by talent agency IEA, a company that secures headline acts and entertainment from the world of music, sport and TV. Osman is booked by the agency to talk about his time at the top at charity dinners, galas, sports awards, Q&A events, fundraisers and after dinner engagements as a brand ambassador and popular sports personality.

Ostenstad, Egil

Forward
Born: *1972 Haugesund, Norway*
Playing career: *Viking FK, Southampton, Blackburn Rovers, Manchester City (loan), Rangers (1990-2005)*

Fondly remembered for his stylish link up with the string pulling Eyal Berkovic, Ostenstad proved worth every penny of the £800,000 that Graeme Souness paid to bring him to the south coast. With Matt Le Tissier and Berkovic creating and scheming behind him, Ostenstad hit nine goals in his debut campaign to help keep Saints up and earn him the fans Player of the Year gong.. Ostenstad was capped on 18 occasions by Norway, scoring six times. Worked at former club Viking FK Stavanger as a scout and director of football having hung up his boots and has since set up his own soccer school in his native homeland.

Egil Ostenstad

He has also worked for a recruitment agency and for the Norwegian FA in a variety of roles including player liaison officer and welfare manager. Ostenstad continues to reside in his native homeland and is currently employed as chief financial advisor for private equity firm DNB. The former Southampton striker is on Twitter at:*https://twitter.com/Egilostenstad/*

Otsemobor, Jon

Right-back
Born: *1983 Liverpool*
Playing career: *Liverpool, Hull City, Bolton Wanderers, Crewe A, Rotherham, Crewe Alexandra, Norwich City, Southampton, Sheffield Wednesday, Milton Keynes Dons, Tranmere Rovers (2002-2014)*

Son of a Nigerian engineer, the right-back joined Liverpool and made his first team debut against Saints in 2002. Only played four times before signing for Southampton via Rotherham. Joining third tier Saints from divisional rivals Norwich, Otsemobor slotted straight in at right-back and made his Saints bow alongside fellow new arrivals Jose Fonte and Danny Seaborne. Missed Saints JPT triumph at Wembley due to being cup tied and played 19 times before being released following Alan Pardew's departure from St Mary's. Otsemobor was once shot in the buttocks by an armed gang member in Liverpool despite being an innocent bystander. Also once scored a goal known as the "Heel of God" to win an FA Cup tie for MK Dons against AFC Wimbledon. He decided not to stay in the game after retirement, instead turning his hand to property management and development.

Paddington, Albert

Half-back
Born: *1881 Bishopstoke* **Died:** *1932*
Playing career: *Southampton, Brighton & Hove Albion (1895-1906)*

A painter on the railway at Eastleigh, "Bert" Paddington joined Southampton as an amateur, captained the reserves and deputised at wing-half for the seniors. At a time when the Saints side was packed with experienced internationals and top class players, Paddington's inclusion was a rare example of a local boy done good. Made his name when he shackled Tottenham's prolific net busting player-manager John Cameron en route to the FA Cup final of 1902 but appearances would remain few and far between for him, and so he moved to south coast rivals Brighton. Paddington played 29 games for Saints and then another 31 during his solitary season at struggling Albion before returning to non league football. Paddington later returned to his original job on the railways.

Page, John

Centre-half/Right-back
Born: *1934 Frimley Green*
Died: *2006*
Playing career: *Mytchett Boys, Surrey Schools, Southampton, Hastings United (1951-1963)*

A goalscoring centre-half, mainly due to his penalty prowess, Page rmade his first team bow having just turned 18. His record of 21 successful spot-kicks was a club record until this was eclipsed by Mick Channon, David Peach, Matt Le Tissier and Rickie Lambert. Page instantly became a virtual ever present, helping Southampton into the second tier and - whilst not a spectacularly flashy player he was greatly appreciated by fans and team-mates alike. Page was never able to shed issues with his weight though, and would leave Saints when Ted Bates signed Leicester's Tony Knapp as Page's successor. A one club man, he played over 200 games for the club before moving to Sussex Southern League side Hastings. Spent only one season there before retiring and later managed Camberley Town. Worked for a plastering company in Farnborough but was affected by dementia in later life.

Pahars, Marians

Forward
Born: *1976 Chornobai, Ukrainian SSR*
Playing career: *Skonto, Southampton, Anorthosis Famagusta, Skonto, Jarmala (1994-2010)*

Dubbed the Latvian Michael Owen, Pahars was a net-busting striker with blistering pace but yet never quite fulfilled his potential due a plethora of injury problems. The story surrounding his move to Saints is one of mystery but after a debut hat-trick for the Reserves on trial, Dave Jones made him a fully fledged Southampton player. The Premier League's first Latvian, he helped to ensure Southampton's survival in that league during his debut season, scoring twice against Everton in the final match to keep them up. Quick, direct and skilful, Pahars exciting style quickly saw him become a fans favourite even when moved out wide by Jones successor Glenn Hoddle. Injuries soon bit, however, starting only 15 games in three years between 2003 and 2006, when he would leave the club. Played 156 times on the south coast, scoring 45 times, and was capped 75 times by his country (scoring 15 goals) including playing in all three of Latvia's matches in Euro 2004. Pahars retired through injury at the age of 35, moving back to his native homeland where he managed former club Skonto, SK Riga and the national team at both U21 and senior level. Pahars has spoken of his desire to return to England and manage Saints at some stage. He was in charge of Jelgava until 2019, and currently works for the club in an advisory role on the board and as chief scout.

Marian Pahars

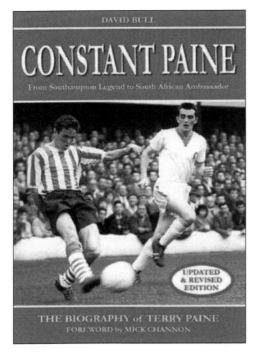

DAVID BULL

CONSTANT PAINE

From Southampton Legend to South African Ambassador

UPDATED & REVISED EDITION

THE BIOGRAPHY of TERRY PAINE
FOREWORD by MICK CHANNON

Paine, Terry

Winger
Born: *1939 Winchester*
Playing career: *Winchester City, Southampton, Hereford United, Cheltenham Town (1954-1980)*

A iconic name synonymous with the famous red and white, men like Terry Paine do not come around very often. Terence Paine MBE may have been something of a late bloomer but he more than made up for that by amassing 800 games for Southampton, becoming one the greats and smashing nearly every record in the book. A goalscoring winger capable of playing anywhere across the front line, Paine served Saints for 18 years, nearly all of them under Ted Bates (Lawrie McMenemy would arrive during Paine's final season). He missed only 22 games in those 18 years and was capped 19 times by England, winning a World Cup winners medal although he didn't play in the actual final. Paine left Saints in 1974 to become player-coach at Hereford United, then managed Cheltenham Town. Now lives in South Africa and works for TV channel Supersport. Became Saints' Honorary President in 2013.

Palmer, Carlton

Midfielder
Born: *1965 Rowley Regis*
Playing career: *Chelsea, WBA, Sheffield Wednesday, Leeds United, Southampton, Nottingham Forest, Coventry City, Stockport County, Dublin City, Mansfield Town, (1984-2013)*

A lanky and combative box to box player who played at Euro 92 and even scored once for his county - albeit against San Marino. Palmer turned out for 12 different clubs including two seasons at Southampton. Signing for Dave Jones, Palmer added grit and bite to the Saints midfield and played 45 times for the club, scoring three goals in the process. An acquired taste, Palmer had smashed Sheffield Wednesday's transfer record - winning the League Cup in 1991 and an FA Cup runner up two years later. He later managed Stockport and had a spell as boss of former club Mansfield. Palmer has since set up his own Football Academy, and now - living in China - has worked as director of football at a Shanghai college. He has done media work for Asian TV and is a Player Representative for any Premier League fan events held in the country. His biography: "It is What It Is - The Carlton Palmer Story' hits back at accusations that fellow ex-Saint Matt Le Tissier had made questioning Palmer's ability and his England selection.

Carlton Palmer

Parker, Patrick

Centre-half
Born: *1929 Bow, Devon*
Died: *2014*
Playing career: *Plymouth Argyle, Newton Abbot, Southampton (1949-1978)*

Pat Parker was deemed not good enough to play professional football - according to himself! Yet, Parker became a Saint and went on to become a loyal, hard working member of the first team. Despite twice suffering a broken leg, Parker recovered to play over 100 at The Dell. Moved to non league Poole Town with Saints team mates Bryn Elliott, Sam Stevens and Barry Hillier and would later go to serve Cowes on the Isle of Wight as player, manager and club secretary. Parker worked as a production controller before becoming an IT salesman. Died in 2014.

Parker, Tom

Right-back
Born: *1897 Woolston, Southampton*
Died: *1987*
Playing career: *Southampton, Arsenal (1919-1933)*

Southampton born right back, Parker went on to play over 250 games for both Southampton and then Arsenal forming a formidable partnership with Fred Titmuss at The Dell . Despite being an FA Cup and League winning captain with the Gunners, he would pick up just the one England cap. Following his successful playing career he moved into management initially with Norwich gaining promotion from the Third Division South. He then returned to Saints as manager in 1937 and would rebuild the side prior to WWII including the capture of his former Norwich charge Ted Bates during a difficult transitional phase. Then WWII broke out and his team dispersed. He left Saints in 1943 to return to Norwich for a second spell after which he retired from football and returned home to Southampton to work for Lloyds registry. A position he held briefly in 1943. When he retired in 1963 he took on a scouting role for Saints under former colleague Bates. He died in Southampton aged 89 in 1987 and will be remembered as one of the finest Saints of the pre-war era.

Parkin, Ray

Inside right/Right-half
Born: *1911 Crook, County Durham* **Died:** *1971*
Playing career: *Esh Winning, Newcastle United, Arsenal, Middlesbrough, Southampton (1926-1939)*

Scored on his league debut for Arsenal as a 17 year old inside right and would repeat the feat for Saints in a 3-3 draw at West Ham. Played for top flight Middlesbrough having left north London before former Gunners team-mate and now Southampton boss Tom Parker signed him as part of a significant overhaul. Signed for £1,500, he became a versatile, dependable and regular member of Southampton's Second Division side. Parkin went on to play 60 times at The Dell, scoring 10 goals before the abandonment of professional organised football during WWII. Guested for a few clubs during the conflict and after the War he worked as an electrician in a coal mine near Leicester. Died in 1971.

Parkinson, Phil

Midfielder
Born: *1967 Chorley, Lancashire*
Playing career: *Bolton Wanderers, Southampton, Bury, Reading (1985-2003)*

Despite never having played for Saints at any level after being on the books as a trainee, Lancashire-born Parkinson still went on to have a creditable playing career. Made his name with Bury in his native Lancashire and also turned out for Reading, playing almost 400 games for the Royals. Since retiring as a player, Parkinson has had a top career as a manager, taking charge of Colchester, Hull, Charlton, Bradford and Bolton and - currently - Sunderland. During his tenure at Valley Parade, Parkinson underlined his potential as one of England's brightest young managers with a historic run to the League Cup final. Although his Bantams team would lose to Swansea at Wembley in 2013, Parkinson remains the only manager to take a fourth tier side to the final of a major cup competition. Most recently was tasked with taking Sunderland back to the Championship but left in November 2020. Voted Reading's greatest ever midfield and remains a legend at the Madjeski Stadium.

Pask, Bernard

Centre-forward
Born: *1936 Winchester* **Died:** *1985*
Playing career: *Southampton (1958-1973)*

Pask was plucked from non league obscurity with works side Pirelli Genera. Signing for Saints, there was little chance of Past becoming a regular as he was second fiddle to ever present incumbent of the no.7 shirt, Terry Paine. He managed to top score in the Reserves side during his debut season, though, and played once for the first team - in a Southern Challenge Floodlit Cup tie against Coventry in the semi finals. That was to be the end of the Bernard Pask story at The Dell as he returned to the non league scene. In later life he worked as a plumber and then as a heating supervisor with *Husband's Shipyard* at Marchwood on the edge of Southampton Water.

Patrick, Roy

Full-back
Born: *1935 Derbyshire* **Died:** *1998*
Playing career: *Southampton*

Roy Patrick became his hometown team Derby's youngest debutant since 1910 in the 1952-53 season, but despite this brilliant promise he would struggle to establish himself with the Rams. So, too, when he moved to their fiercest rivals Nottingham Forest. Forest Reserves coach Joe Mallett recommended the young Patrick to his friend and Saints manager Ted Bates, rebuilding Southampton for a promotion push from the second tier. Patrick's versatility enable him to play 33 games at The Dell but fell out of favour when Stuart Williams arrived as Saints new first choice full back. Moving to Exeter, he helped the Grecians to promotion and played for Burton at non league level whilst working for Rolls Royce. Died in 1998.

"DID YOU KNOW?"

"The club anthem 'When The Saints Go Marching In' was originally an old hymn and jazz tune and sung by fans in different sports all over the world."

Patten, John

Outside-right
Born: *1882 Widnes* **Died:** *1958*
Career: *Shrewsbury, Southampton (1907-1907)*

John Patten arrived from non league Shrewsbury as a triallist at The Dell, and was heading for Ryde, Isle of Wight, with Saints Reserves when fate intervened. Thrown into the first team at the eleventh hour in the midst of an injury crisis, Patten played against Watford at The Dell on the very day he was meant to be crossing the Solent and leaving bemused Saints fans wondering who this slight, agile outside right was. Scored twice in four outings Despite his brief yet eye-catching cameos, Patten did not sign for the club permanently and instead returned to Shropshire, signing pro for Shrewsbury. Later worked as a railway clerk in the Birmingham area.

Peach, David

Full-back
Born: *1951 Bedford*
Playing career: *Gillingham, Southampton, Swindon Town, Leyton Orient.*

His Southampton career may have started amid the ignominy of a 7-0 defeat, but things didn't work out too badly for David Peach, Southampton's Mr Consistent in their star studded side of the 70s and 80s. Peach won the FA Cup in 76', playing at left-back (scoring in the semi final) and also featured in the 1979 League Cup final, again underlining his reputation as the man for the big occasion when he put Saints ahead at Wembley. Peach would score 44 goals for Saints, 24 of those from the spot - a record only since surpassed by Rickie Lambert and Matt Le Tissier. Peach was capped eight times by England's U21 side. One of the best left-backs in Southampton history, Peach amassed 278 games for Saints before he moved on to Swindon and Leyton Orient, becoming the holder of a unique stat as the only man to play at every ground in the Football League. After football became a "bit of a drag" he coached at non league level. Worked as a labourer and at Lymington in the fish trade before taking up a job in the property market as development manager.

Pearce, Ian
Defender
Born: *1974 Bury St. Edmunds*
Playing career: *Chelsea, Blackburn Rovers, West Ham United, Fulham, Southampton (1990-2010)*
Premier League title winning centre-half with Blackburn in 1995, capped by England at U21 level and joined Saints on a 30 day loan in 2008. His first appearance for Nigel Pearson's Championship side would be his last, though, as he picked up a knock and never featured again. Became a mainstay in Fulham's established Premier League side in the mid 00s and also played for Kingstonian and Lincoln. Later worked for the Imps as assistant boss under Chris Sutton, did scouting work for Brighton and took up a post at West Brom as head of recruitment in 2018.

Pearson, Herbert
Centre-forward
Born: *1901 Brierley Hill* **Died:** *1972*
Career: *Southampton, Coventry City, (1923-1925)*
Herbert Pearson, aka "Harold", a quick, determined and versatile centre-forward, made an instant impression at the club, scoring twice on his debut at Sheffield Wednesday. He left the club having played eight games, scoring four times. Played five times for relegation-bound Coventry (again scoring on his debut for them) before dropping into non league football with Nuneaton. Died in 1972.

Peck, William
Forward
Born: *1869 Norfolk* **Died:** *1937*
Playing career: *Southampton (1892-1893)*
Based in Southampton through his work with the Royal Engineers, Peck played for Saints as a triallist in the Victorian, pre-Southern League era. His eight games for the club then known as St Mary's consisted of seven friendlies and one competitive FA Cup tie - a record breaking 14-0 win over Newbury in the preliminary round. Equally as adept on the left as he was as an out and out centre-forward, Peck would be on the move again after that match, moving back to Kent with his army battalion where he played at non league level for a while. Peck later worked as an engineer.

Pele
Defender
Born: 1978 Albufeira, Portugal
Playing career: *Belenenses, Southampton, WBA, Falkirk, MK Dons, (1996- date)*
Unlike his famous four-letter namesake, this Pele was Portuguese and a central defender. Even so, it was a headline writer's dream when he signed for second tier Saints having spurned the advances of several top flight clubs in search of first team shirt. Donning "Pele" on his shirt showed, if nothing else, that he had plenty of confidence and self belief. Moved into an unfamiliar central midfield role by George Burley, he also deputised for injuries to Claus Lundekvam and Darren Powell as Southampton made the play-offs during his debut campaign. Pele played nearly 50 games for Saints before moving to the side beaten in the play-off final, West Brom. Played for several clubs that the 'other' Pele would never have heard of and represented Cape Verde - his parents homeland - eleven times from 2006 to 2009. Later gained coaching badges and was recently working at Matt Le Tissier's academy set up. Full name Pedro Cardoso Miguel Monteiro.

Penk, Harry
Winger
Born: 1934 Wigan
Playing career: *Wigan Athletic, Portsmouth, Plymouth Argyle , Southampton (1953-1964)*
A diminutive, 5ft 4 winger equally adept with both feet, Penk signed for Saints after a successful stint in Devon with Plymouth. He joined Southampton amid ongoing National Service uncertainty for many of Saints locally born players. With John Sydenham one such player unavailable, Penk would replace the flying winger and, although not spectacularly stylish like Sydenham, proved a more than capable deputy. He went on to play 60 times across four seasons at The Dell, giving Bates a versatility and willingness to help out defensively. Penk would move into non league football when only 30, also turning his hand to cricket and playing at Lord's with village club Hursley in 1984, whilst employed at *Husband's Shipyard* in Southampton, as a welder.

Penton, Harry
Centre-forward
Born: *1890 Bournemouth* **Died:** *1967*
Playing career: *Southampton, Boscombe, Southampton, Boscombe (1911-1928)*
A prolific goalscorer at amateur level, which attracted the attention of Saints, in need of a regular centre-forward. Scored on his home debut at The Dell, but would fail to live up to expectations, scoring only three times in his 13 games. Moved back to Boscombe where he became their first ever professional player but rejoined Saints where he played one match under Jim McIntyre before joining Eastleigh. Served in the Royal Artillery during WW1. Played as a keeper in later life, before retiring to work on the railways. Died in 1967.

Pereplotkins, Andrejs
Winger
Born: *1984 Kharkiv, Ukrainian SSR, Soviet Union*
Playing career: *Anderlecht, Southampton, Bohemians, Skonto Riga, Derby County (2001-)*
Latvian international winger, had a trial at Saints but never played for the club. Part of this was due to eligibility issues, with Southampton's struggles to obtain a work permit. Won the League of Ireland with Bohemians and had a two-game loan stint at Derby before a varied career in his homeland Ukraine and his adopted country of Latvia, with whom he played 36 times at international level. Won two league titles and two domestic cups in Latvia during his career and he still plays there, for SK Super Nova.

Perfect, Frank
Full-back
Born: *1915 Gorleston* **Died:** *1977*
Playing career: *Norwich City, Mansfield Town, Wolverhampton Wanderers, Tranmere Rovers, Southampton (1933-1939)*
Full-back Perfect had played under Tom Parker at Norwich, so the manager - by now at Saints - knew exactly what he was getting when he signed Perfect in a recruitment drive after a humiliating FA Cup exit at non league Chelmsford. A "hefty fellow", Perfect had played for Mansfield, Wolves and Tranmere before joining his former boss at The Dell.

Although he would never become first choice, the right-back proved a more than able deputy, but with War imminent and football suspended, Perfect's career would soon be over. Served in the RAF during the conflict and later became a builder.

Pericard, Vincent
Striker
Born: *1982 Efok, Cameroon*
Playing career: *Juventus, Portsmouth, Sheffield U, Plymouth A, Stoke City, Southampton, Millwall, Carlisle United, Swindon Town (1999-2015)*
Cameroon born French international, capped by the latter at U21 level. Most known amongst English fans for two spells with Portsmouth and helping them to a first ever Premier League promotion. He would barely feature during the club's top flight days. Served four months in prison for perverting the course of justice during his time at Stoke. Played five games for Saints under Nigel Pearson, although started only once. After brief spells at Havant & Waterlooville and Moneyfields, he retired to set up his own *Elite Welfare Management*, an agency aimed to help foreign players adapt to life in a new country. Pericard is also involved with *Kick it Out.*

Perrett, Robert
Winger
Born: *1919 Bournemouth* **Died:** *1994*
Playing career: *Bournemouth & Boscombe Athletic, Huddersfield Town, Southampton (1937-1942)*
Perrett was an unlucky victim of circumstance, his career over before it really began due to the impact of WWII. He played in all three games of the curtailed 1939-40 season, and would go on to play another 17 for the club in unofficial wartimes leagues and cup contests. Served in the navy during the conflict, playing a key role in the evacuation of Dunkirk. His commitments at sea - coupled with a serious knee injury sustained in conflict - ended his playing days. He worked on *HMS Illustrious* during the last two seasons of the War and then served in the Fleet Air Arm at Eastleigh as an instructor. With the war over, he was an insurance salesman and then worked for the gas board.

Perry, Chris

Defender
Born: *1973 Carshalton*
Playing career: *Wimbledon, Tottenham Hotspur, Charlton Athletic, West Bromwich Albion, Luton Town, Southampton (1991-2010)*

Wimbledon born and raised, Perry played over 200 games for the Dons. A member of Dave Bassett's "Crazy Gang" he would move to Spurs for £4m and, although small in stature, his pace and positional sense compensated for that. After struggling to break through at Spurs, he played for Charlton and West Brom before arriving at Southampton via Luton. Initially joining Nigel Pearson's Saints on loan in place of the injured Andrew Davies, Perry played six times before making his move to St Mary's permanent, going to play another 50-odd games, winning the JPT in the process, before being released. Despite being widely tipped to play for England by the likes of Sir Alex Ferguson and Harry Redknapp, the coveted call up never came for Perry. He has since became a respected charity worker, raising funds for motor neurone disease and working with the youth teams at Dagenham & Redbridge.

Dan Petrescu

Petrescu, Dan

Full-back/Winger
Born: *1967 Bucharest, Romania*
Playing career: *Steau Bucharest, Foggia, Genoa, Sheffield Wednesday, Chelsea, Bradford City, Southampton, National Bucharest (1985-2003)*

A genuine European superstar whose signing represented quite the coup for Southampton, despite Petrescu's advancing years. Capped 95 times by Romania, Petrescu featured and two European Championships (1996 and 2000) and in the finals of two World Cup tournaments (1994 and 1998) during a golden age for the Romanian national side. Having come to England via his homeland and Italy, Petrescu played for Sheffield Wednesday, Chelsea and Bradford before signing for his former Blues boss Glenn Hoddle at The Dell (Saints final farewell at the iconic ground came during Petrescu's debut season). Played eleven times in red and white, scoring twice before he fell out of favour under Hoddle's immediate successors - Stuart Gray and then Gordon Strachan. He returned to his homeland as player/coach of capital club Nacional before moving into coaching and management. Petrescu has managed 14 different clubs and took charge of Turkish side Kayserispor in 2021.

Petrie, Charlie

Inside-left
Born: *1895 Chorlton-on-Medlock, Manchester*
Playing career: *Manchester City, Sheffield Wednesday, Southampton , York City (1918-1930)*

Manchester born inside left, played 24 games to help Saints avoid relegation to the third tier during his two seasons at the club. Joining for a fee of £150, Petrie provided added competition and depth in the attack. He was in and out of the side during his time at the club, filling in for Charlie Taylor during his best run in the team, seven matches during the run in. He was released on a free transfer after the signing of Herbert Coates and wound down his playing days with non league York City. Having retired, he moved back to his native Manchester, coaching at former side Stalybridge Celtic where he also worked as the club's physio.

Petrie, Robert

Half-back
Born: *1874 Dundee, Scotland*
Died: *1947*
Playing career: *Dundee East End, Gainsborough Trinity, Dundee, Sheffield Wednesday, Southampton, New Brighton Tower, Arbroath, Dundee Wanderers, Brechin City (1888-1908)*

Played in two FA Cup finals for two of his three English clubs, winning it with Sheffield Wednesday (beating his future employers en route to victory over Wolves) and then ending on the losing side with Saints, four years later. Petrie - no relation to the aforementioned Charlie (above), also played for the now defunct New Brighton Tower but spent the rest of his playing career in his native Scotland. Described as a "selfless team player, never showy but always reliable", Petrie made 68 appearances for Saints in three seasons before losing his place to John Robertson after winning two Southern League titles during the club's trophy laden Victorian era. He returned to Scotland to play for Arbroath, hometown team Dundee Wanderers and Brechin City before retirement. After football, he worked in the weaving industry as a jute beamer loading the looms.

Phillips, Gary

Goalkeeper
Born: *1961 St Albans*
Playing career: *Southampton, Chalfont St Peter, Brighton & Hove Albion, West Bromwich Albion, Brentford, Reading, Hereford United, Barnet, Aldershot Town, Aylesbury United (1976-2000)*

Youth player at Saints, he never played for the club at any level but represented England at a semi professional standard. Had a stint with Southampton's south coast rivals Brighton and also turned out for West Brom, Brentford, Reading and Hereford before dropping into non league. Became player-manager at Barnet, taking up the same role with Aylesbury and coached at Aldershot. Later managed at Hemel Hempstead Town in two spells and former club Barnet. Worked as goalkeeping coach at several clubs including Southend, Stevenage, Luton and most recently, youth development goalkeeping coach at Crystal Palace.

Phillips, Kevin

Striker
Born: *1973 Hitchin, Hertfordshire*
Playing career: *Baldock Town, Watford, Sunderland, Southampton, Aston Villa, West Bromwich Albion, Birmingham City, Blackpool, Crystal Palace, Leicester City (1985-2014)*

Upon retirement as a player, Phillips remained with his last club Leicester City as a coach, working with the team's strikers - including Jamie Vardy - on their technique and "close range ability." Moved to Derby under Paul Clement, linking up with his former boss Nigel Pearson when the latter replaced the sacked former. Worked under Steve McLaren and Gary Rowett at Pride Park, also serving as assistant manager at Stoke - again under Rowett - but left that job in 2019. He has played for Sunderland in many ex-Legends events and has occasionally appeared on BBC Radio Wearside. He has also done punditry work for BT Sport. His wife was arrested on suspicion of attempted murder in 2020 after a stabbing incident only to later be released without charge. Phillips book "Second Time Around" was public in 1999 and you can follow Phillips on Twitter here: https://twitter.com/1kevinphillips

Phillipson-Masters, Forbes

Defender
Born: *1955 Bournemouth*
Playing career: *Southampton, Plymouth Argyle, Bristol City, Exeter City, Luton Town, Bournemouth*

Bournemouth born defender, started out at Southampton as a goalkeeper, but was converted to a defender by Saints defensive legend John McGrath. After making just nine league appearances and a couple of loans spells, he joined Plymouth where he started a successful career in the West Country, finishing his playing days at Yeovil. After playing he returned to Dorset to work as a painter and decorator, retaining an interest in local football as a coach and manager, coaching Dorset's representative side and serving as assistant manager at Wessex League Verwood. Phillipson - Masters continues to live in ter area and has his own builders business of the same name, based on the edge of the New Forest and specialising in extensions and conservatories.

Pickering, Mike

Central defender
Born: *1956 Mirfield*
Playing career: *Southampton, Sheffield Wednesday, San Diego Sockers, Norwich City, Bradford City, Barnsley, Rotherham United, York City, Stockport County, Hallam (1974-1989)*

Moved from the Fourth Division with Barnsley to the Second having come south to Saints. Coverted from an all action midfielder to a more refined centre-back, Pickering - under the tutelage of engine room schemer Alan Ball and defensive cohort Chris Nicholl - helped Saints to promotion into the top flight during his debut season. Pickering would go on to play more than 50 times for the stabilising Southampton, but eventually fell out of favour under manager Lawrie McMenemy and dropped down two leagues to third tier Sheffield Wednesday in his native Yorkshire. Pickering went on to captain the Owls and played more than 100 times for them. Pickering went on to work in the brewery trade, staying in Sheffield, also taking work in office facilities and became a match day host at Hillsborough.

Pollard, Walter

Inside-forward
Born: *1906 Burnley*
Died: *1945*
Playing career: *Burnley, West Ham United, Sochaux, Fulham, Southampton, Brighton & Hove Albion, Tunbridge Wells Rangers (1925-1937)*

Broke through with his hometown team Burnley at 16 before swapping claret and blue shirts, moving from east Lancashire to West Ham United. The Hammers would go down into Division Two during his time there but after a brief stint as a coach across the Channel, he landed in Southampton - via Fulham - for another go in the second tier. Industrious and energetic up front, Pollard was not prolific but did the "hard graft" for his team and helped Saints to survival during his debut season of 1934-35. He would play only sporadically the next campaign, combining his playing with coaching some of the younger members of the squad. Spent a season in the third tier with south coast rivals Brighton before retiring. In later life he worked for Ilford Borough Council as an electrician, turning out for their works team.

Ponting, William

Half-back
Born: *Andover, Hampshire*
Playing career: *Ryde, Southampton St. Mary's, Andover (1897-1897)*

A schoolmaster by trade, joined the club then known as St Mary's as a leading amateur player. He had captained Hampshire at both junior and senior level and also turned out for Ryde Sports in the Hampshire League. He would slot straight in to Saints Southern League team In place of the injured John Hodgkinson, initially retaining his amateur status but soon signing pro. Ponting would only play a handful of games, though, and he soon returned to the Hampshire League with Ryde. Played briefly for QPR before retiring from the game and working in insurance brokerage in Hampshire, then Wiltshire and Dorset. Ponting would remain involved with Saints as president of their Supporters Club.

Potter, Darren

Midfielder
Born: *1984 Liverpool*
Playing career: *Everton, Blackburn Rovers, Liverpool, Southampton, Wolverhampton Wanderers, Sheffield Wednesday, Milton Keynes Dons, Rotherham United (2003-date)*

A born and bred, dyed in the wool Toffee, Potter switched allegiances having been released by his boyhood heroes aged 15. He played occasionally for the red half of Merseyside without establishing himself in the side, before joining George Burley's side on loan. Recently relegated Saints were looking for an immediate Premier League return but they would fade into mediocrity despite Potter's impressive debut, assisting a Kenwyne Jones winner at Leicester. He never made the move to the south coast a permanent one - playing twelve games in four months before going to Wolves and Sheffield Wednesday. Latterly played for MK Dons, Rotherham and Tranmere, and has been capped five times at full international level by the Republic of Ireland. Currently a coach at Tranmere.

Potter, Graham

Full-back
Born: *1975 Solihull*
Playing career: *Birmingham City, Wycombe Wanderers, Stoke City, Southampton, West Bromwich Albion, Northampton Town, Reading, York City, Boston United, Shrewsbury Town, Macclesfield Town (1992-2005)*

A steady if unspectacular left-back, Potter had a 13-year career encompassing eleven different clubs. As manager Graeme Souness searched for overseas talent, his no.2 Terry Cooper scouted closer to home and signed Potter for £250,000. Potter would play for England at U21 level, but would struggle to establish himself and left for West Brom having only started three times at The Dell. Having gained coaching qualifications, Potter served as technical director for the Ghana Women national side, going on to earn a reputation as one of Europe's best young managers with FK Ostersunds in Sweden and then, closer to home, at Swansea. Potter is currently back in the Premier League, remodelling Brighton and Hove Albion's existence at that level as the Seagulls head coach.

Powell, Darren

Centre-back
Born: *1976 Hammersmith*
Playing career: *Brentford, Crystal Palace, West Ham United, Southampton, Derby County, Brentford, Milton Keynes Dons (1997-2014)*

Snaffled up by that man with a great eye for a player, Harry Redknapp, on a free transfer, and quickly settled at Saints. Forming a grit-and-guile centre back pairing with Claus Lundekvam, Powell scored twice in his first four games in the red and white for a Saints side treading water in the Championship. Agile and powerful, he would struggle with injury and was released in 2008 having made almost 50 appearances. Later played for Derby, Brentford, MK Dons, and non league Hampton and Richmond Borough. He would manage that club and also worked for Brentford's Academy before taking up a job as Crystal Palace's head of youth development.

Powell, Lee

Forward
Born: *1973 Caerleon, Wales*
Playing career: *Southampton, Hamilton Academical, Yeovil Town (1991-1994)*

Lee Powell's Southampton career was quite literally blink and you miss it. Bursting on to the scene at 18, he was capped by Wales at under 20 level on four occasions and was called up to the senior squad a year later, although never played. He started only twice for Southampton in a three-year stay at the club, playing a handful more times having come on as a sub. He failed to make an impact and would move back to Scotland, playing for Hamilton Academical and Kilmarnock before a stint at Yeovil. After playing for Newport in his native Wales, Powell seems to have retired but there seems to be no record of his current occupation.

"DID YOU KNOW?"

"In 1889-90 Saints wore red and white quartered shirts and were known as "The Cherry and White Squares."

Prado, Guly do

Striker
Born: *1981 Campinas, Brazil*
Playing career: *Cesena, Southampton, Chicago Fire, Ituano, Botafogo FC , Luverdense EC (2002-date)*
Enigmatic striker with dual Brazilian-Italian citizenship. Played the vast majority of his club football in those two countries, save for a spell in the MLS with Chicago Fire and four years with Saints. Despite the fact that Southampton had been relegated into League One and the language barrier with his southern team-mates, Guly do Prado made his debut in a 4-0 win at Bristol Rovers, scoring his first Saints goal in his third appearance. Alan Pardew was already out the door by then, but despite not fitting the typical Brazilian identikit of dazzling skill and impeccable control, he proved to be a hard worker, a goal poacher and a willing foil to strike partner Rickie Lambert. Despite having played under three managers in a matter of months, he chipped in with nine and ten goals respectively over the next two seasons ten-route to the Premier League. Adkins would describe do Prado as a "vital" part of his side's back to back promotions, but he fell out of favour following the arrivals of Jay Rodriguez and Gaston Ramirez. Latterly played in the USA and Brazil where he also coached. Do Prado played 106 games for Saints, scoring 28 goals.

Pratt, Wayne

Midfielder
Born: *1960 Southampton*
Playing career: *Southampton (1978-1981)*
Southampton born, Pratt began his career with his hometown team, becoming a one game wonder for Saints. Whilst a regular for the reserves, his first and last appearance in the senior side came in place of the injured Steve Williams in a draw at Leeds. Dropped for the next match in favour of another debutant, Reuben Agboola, he returned to the second string and would become their captain. He remains involved in grass roots football as director of Eastleigh-based Tyro League side Sarisbury Sharks whilst working in the building trade.

Price, Cliff

Inside-left
Born: *1900 Market Bosworth*
Playing career: *Halifax Town, Southampton, Nottingham Forest (1917-1928)*
Described somewhat formally by the Echo as an "inside left of the rather studious type", Price had worked as a collier whilst also turning out for Leicester as an amateur. After a season and a half as a pro with Halifax he moved to the south coast to join Southampton, greeted by that underwhelming vote of confidence from the local press. He would soon become an established part of the Saints side, as a "good and competent marksman" who looked "here to stay". Despite never being prolific, Price impressed with his link up play and range of passing, combining well with Jimmy Carr, scoring the occasional goal and going on to play 67 times for the club. He went on to Nottingham Forest for two more seasons before returning to his native east Midlands and the non league scene. Price later qualified as a medical officer.

Price, Fred

Outside-left
Born: *1901 Ibstock* **Died:** *1985*
Playing career: *Leicester City, Southampton, Wolves, Chesterfield, (1920-1928)*
Nephew of Cliff (above), Fred Price followed in his uncle's footsteps by playing for Coalville and Leicester before moving south to sign for Saints. Described as a "clever" player during his stint in the east Midlands, Price joined Southampton along with team-mate Dennis Jones with Harry Hooper going the other way. The uncle and nephew partnership briefly overlapped with Saints fans getting two for the Price of one. Six of his nine league games for Saints came in tandem with his uncle, but Jimmy Carr would return to break that up, though, and Fred was unable to establish himself from then on. Moved to Wolves for £250 and also played for Chesterfield. Fred's brother Jack was also a professional footballer. Fred Price later worked as an engineer during the War and also for the council as a warden in his native Leicestershire.

Price, Joseph
Full-back
Born: *1868 Herefordshire* **Died:** *1902*
Playing career: *Geneva Cross, Southampton St. Mary's (1891-1894)*

Amateur player for the Medical Corps at Netley when he joined Saints, then known simply as St Mary's. "A hard-tackling full back with speed and finesse" he had come to the club's attentions with an impressive performance for Geneva Cross in a Hampshire Senior Cup tie despite his side losing 0-5. "Ginger" Price (no relation to Cliff or to Fred, above), he played six times for the Saints mainly in friendlies and cup matches. A serious leg injury ended his career and he returned to the army, later leaving the force to become a carpenter. Price died aged only 33 in 1902.

Prince, Percy
Centre-forward/Half-back
Born: *1887 Liverpool* **Died:** *1973*
Playing career: *Cranbury Avenue, Southampton Oxford, Southampton, Boscombe (1907-1921)*

Born on the red half of Merseyside but raised in Southampton, centre-forward Prince worked in the Merchant Navy whilst playing parks football. Scouted and signed by Southern League Saints, he scored on his home debut but would only make sporadic appearances at either centre forward or inside forward for his first few years at the club. Described as "no one more zealous in the interests of the team" this suggested that Prince was happy to sacrifice his own game for the good of his colleagues. Genial and "a sharp shooting centre forward, keen and enthusiastic" he endeared himself to coaches, fans and players alike, being dubbed "Peewee" by his team mates. Eventually became established having dislodged Andrew Gibson and went on to play over 100 times for the club, scoring 29 goals, top scoring in the 1912-13 season. Released by Saints, he joined non league Boston until the outbreak of WW1 disrupted his career. Had a second stint at Saints and earned county representative honours. After football he worked for the *Cunard Line* and moved to New York in 1930, employed on the trans-Atlantic liners as assistant catering officer.

Prutton, David
Midfielder
Born: *1981 Kingston upon Hull*
Playing career: *Nottingham Forest, Southampton, Nottingham Forest, Leeds United, Colchester United, Swindon Town, Sheffield Wednesday, Scunthorpe United, Coventry City (1995-2014)*

Hull born, cultured and versatile midfielder, capped by England 25 times at U21 level. Played out wide and even at right back for Saints, but his time there was disrupted by two serious injuries (a broken toe and badly damaged ankle ligaments), a fiery streak and seven different managers (five permanent and two caretaker) during his four and a half seasons on the south coast. Sent off for an elbow on Jeff Kenna and then, most notoriously, after a bad tackle and subsequent fight with Robert Pires, refusing to leave the pitch, pushing the referee and swearing at another match official in an ill-fated match with Arsenal in the 2004-05 campaign. Prutton was banned for ten games and fined £6,000. He would return for the final match of the season but was unable to help Saints avoid the drop. He eventually fell out of favour and moved on to Nottingham Forest, also turning out for Leeds, Colchester, Swindon, Sheffield Wednesday, Scunthorpe and Coventry. He currently works for Sky Sports as a presenter, pundit and commentator, often seen on the broadcaster's Football League coverage.

Puckett, David

Forward
Born: *1960 Southampton*
Playing career: *Southampton, Bournemouth, Stoke City, Swansea City, Aldershot, Bournemouth, Woking, Lymington Town (1977-2013)*

Puckett, blessed with "pace, a good touch and no little skill", created two goals on his full home debut against Arsenal as Saints went on to finish seventh and qualify for the UEFA Cup. Capable of playing anywhere across the forward line or in his more natural midfield role, he became the first Saint to make 50 appearances as a sub - useful for the team but frustratingly thwarted for Puckett. Moved to Bournemouth after 111 games (with 52 of those from the bench) in five seasons, going to play for Stoke, Swansea, Aldershot, Bournemouth again and for Woking, Lyminton and Totton at non league standard. He retired in his mid 40s to move into coaching taking his UEFA badges and working at the Saints Centre of Excellence. He played at all levels for Saints and then coached at all levels across their youth and Academy set up, briefly working with the first team until leaving amidst an "overhaul" in 2010. Coached at Lymington and Sholing, before assisting on an FA International Development Programme in Malawi. He has since done some commentary work for BBC Radio Solent and represented the Saints at fundraising events such as golf days and charity galas.

Pulis, Tony

Midfielder
Born: *1984 Bristol*
Playing career: *Portsmouth, Stoke City, Torquay United, Plymouth Argyle, Grimsby Town, Bristol Rovers, Southampton, Lincoln City, Stockport County, Barnet, Aldershot Town (2002-2014)*

Not to be confused with his perhaps more well known father, Tony Sr, of considerable managerial prowess. Tony Pulis Jr. began at Pompey but never played for them before brief spells with Stoke (where his old man would become a popular and revered figure), Torquay, Plymouth, Grimsby and Bristol Rovers. Joined Southampton on a free in 2008 under a two year contract, but was released over three seasons later without having made an appearance for Saints at any level. Pulis would have several more loan spells whilst still officially a Saint, including Lincoln, Stockport and Barnet, before playing for Aldershot and a stint across the pond with Orlando. Having retired as a player, he would - perhaps inevitably - follow in his father's footsteps by moving into coaching and management. Capped four times by his native Wales at U21 level, he took charge of former side Orlando City in 2016, also managing Saint Louis FC and is currently assistant boss to Diego Alonso at David Beckham's MLS franchise Inter Miami.

Purves, Charlie

Inside-forward
Born: *1921 High Spen, County Durham*
Died: *2013*
Playing career: *Newcastle United, Shildon, Walker Celtic, Spennymoor United, Charlton Athletic, Southampton, Sittingbourne, Margate, Chatham Town, Dorchester Town, Ford Sports, Basingstoke Town (1946-1963)*

Born in the shadow of his boyhood club Newcastle, Purves was taken on by the Magpies as a trainee but never made the grade. A "nippy and silky forward", he was subsequently picked up by Charlton but. Although they reached the FA Cup final during his debut season, he had riled his manager Jimmy Seed by turning up for the semi final against Newcastle by wearing the colours of his beloved Magpies. Purves did not play in either the semi or the final (a 1-4 defeat to Derby) but he would go on to play more than 50 games for Charlton. He was signed for Southampton by Sid Cann, described by the Saints boss as "constructive" inside right and going to play every other game or two for the next couple of years. He was an ever present during Southampton's FA Cup run in 1953 with the Saints beaten by eventual winners Blackpool after a fifth round replay at The Dell. Saints would be relegated at the end of the season and Purves would move to Kent's non league scene. Later coached at Vosper Thorneycroft (now Sholing) and at Basingstoke Town as player-manager. Died in 2013 at the age of 92.

Quashie, Nigel

Midfielder
Born: *1978 Southwark, London*
Playing career: *QPR, Nottingham Forest, Portsmouth, Southampton, WBA, West Ham, Birmingham, Wolves, MK Dons (1995-2010)*
A steely, intelligent box to box player, Quashie was a mainstay at Pompey, captained Saints and capped for Scotland on 14 occasions thanks to his Scottish grandfather. Having been influential in Portsmouth's rise to Premier League prominence, London born Quashie followed manager Harry Redknapp up the Solent from Fratton Park to St Mary's. He was given the armband after only a month following the departure of Jason Dodd, but was unable to prevent Saints from sliding into the second tier. Since retirement, Quashie has worked in Iceland, where he briefly took charge of IR Reykjavik and has coached te national Under 16 team. The former Scottish international has now returned to the UK where he has set up his own West-Midlands based coaching school, IPDA, aimed to earn 7 - 16 year olds a chance with a professional Academy in the area. Quashie is currently working towards his UEFA "B" coaching licence . Twitter: *https://twitter.com/nigelquashie1*

Radford, Walter

Inside-left
Born: *1886 Pinxton* **Died:** *1943*
Playing career: *Wolves, Southampton, Wolves, Southport Central (1905-1910)*
FA Cup winner with Wolves in 1908 having played at Molineux in two spells, starting his career with them before moving to Saints. Linking with Fred Harrison before losing his place to Frank Jefferis, Radford's 13 games for Southampton would come in two bursts, playing the first six matches as Southampton looked to defend their Southern League title. They would eventually end up eleventh with Radford returning for the run-in, grabbing his only goal for the club before moving back to Wolves. Scored in the semi final against his former side en route to Cup glory with the "Old Gold." Finished his career with Southport before retiring. He would go on to become a Football League referee.

Ramsey, Sir Alf

Right-back
Born: *1920 Dagenham, Essex* **Died:** *1999*
Career: *Southampton, Tottenham. (1946-1954).*
The old adage is that good players do not always make good managers. That was certainly not the case for Sir Alfred Ernest Ramsey, the man who ensured football finally came home in 1966. Ramsey had a fine career both on the pitch and in the dugout, signing for Southampton having come to the Dell with the Army, playing at centre-half in 10-3 defeat to the Duke of Cornwall Light Infantry. Signed pro in 1944, initially as a centre forward in time for the first post-War campaign, switching to full-back and getting his chance with Bill Ellerington sidelined, becoming an ever present for the next two years. Lacking pace but a "fine reader of the game with superb tactical knowledge and great passing", he fell out with manager Bill Dodgin and moved to Tottenham. Won both the First and Second Divisions with the north London side, playing more than 200 games for them and getting 32 caps for England. Ramsey would later go into management with Ipswich, Birmingham and England, delivering the national game's finest hour and being knighted for doing so in 1967. Sir Alf died in 1999, still the only manager to win a World Cup for England.

Sir Alf Ramsey

Rasiak, Grzegorz
Striker
Born: *1979 Szczecin, Poland*
Playing career: *Dyskobolia Grodzisk, Derby County, Tottenham Hotspur, Southampton, Bolton Wanderers, Watford, Reading, AEL Limassol, Jagiellonia, Lechia Gdansk, Warta Pozna (1996-2014)*

Polish international striker, with 37 caps and eight goals for his country. He had made a name for himself in his homeland when George Burley signed him for Derby County but, having failed to get through the play offs, the cash-strapped Rams were forced to sell. Went to Spurs but he barely featured before joining Southampton, rejoining burley, by now appointed Saints manager. Initially a loan deal but joined permanently, Rasiak was described as "languid and laconic" but also as a "tall, honest targetman" with a good goalscoring record. Rasiak plundered 17 goals in his first 26 appearances for the club but lost his place to compatriot Marek Saganowski and eventually fell out of favour having hit 35 goals in over 100 games across his two spells on the south coast. Later played for Bolton, Watford and Reading before stints in Cyprus.

Rawlings, Bill
Centre-forward
Born: *1896 Andover* **Died:** *1972*
Playing career: *Andover, Southampton, Manchester United, Port Vale (1918-1933)*

As so many 18 year olds had to do, Rawlings enlisted in WW1 as part of the Wessex Field Ambulance, playing for their football team in friendlies and unofficial fixtures. It was one such game that brought him to the attentions of Southampton, when he played against their Reserves in 1916. Signed as an amateur two years later and scored 16 in 15 friendlies and war-time games. Smashed 30 goals in 38 games in Saints inaugural season in the Third South to help them to promotion and gaining England recognition for his prolific efforts. He ended his Saints career with an impressive 198 goals from 377 games, before going on to Manchester United and Port Vale. Two caps for England. Later worked as a civil servant in Wareham before taking ownership of the *Glebe* pub near St Mary's.

Reader, George
Centre-forward
Born: *1896 Nuneaton, Warwickshire* **Died:** *1978*
Playing career: *Exeter City, Southampton, Harland and Wolff, Cowes (1919-1930)*

Signed by Saints from Exeter ahead of the south coast side's inaugural Football League season. His first season at Saints would also be his last, having played three times he retired from the professional game to take up teaching at Central School and to play part-time in the Hampshire League. He would go on to become a highly respected referee, earning a spot at the 1950 World Cup Finals as Britain's representative official. Took charge of three matches at the tournament, including the deciding one between hosts Brazil and Uruguay, the first Englishman to do so, an achievement he described as "the best point of my career". He later became a Southampton director and then chairman, plotting the club's rise to prominence under Ted Bates and then his successor Lawrie McMenemy. As Saints lifted the FA Cup at Wembley in 1976, George Reader was sat beside HM The Queen.

Redknapp, Jamie

Midfielder
Born: *1973 Barton on Sea*
Playing career: *Bournemouth, Liverpool, Tottenham Hotspur, Southampton. (1989-2005)*

Capped by England 17 times (one goal) and blessed with superb technical ability and stylish intelligence in a career blighted by a succession of injuries. Son of former Saints manager Harry Redknapp and cousin to Frank Lampard Jr, the two Redknapps became the first father and son duo to represent the club as boss and player, reprising a partnership that had begun further up the coast at Bournemouth. Won the FA Cup and UEFA Super Cup during his time with Liverpool, spending eleven years on Merseyside and playing over 200 games for the Anfield side, captaining the club. He only played sporadically for Saints and became as famed for his off the field exploits as for his on the field achievements. He was married to pop star Louise Nurding of Eternal until 2017. Redknapp is one of Sky's best known pundits, regularly appearing on their coverage of Premier League football and on Sky One's BAFTA-winning sport panel game show *A League of their Own*.
https://twitter.com/jamiredknappsky

Reeves, Derek

Centre-forward
Born: *1934 Poole* **Died:** *1995*
Career: *Southampton, Bournemouth. (1954-1964).*

Headed Southampton's goalscoring charts for four consecutive seasons, and still holds the reborn for most strikes in a single Saints campaign - 39 in 1959-60. A quick, bustling and busy centre-forward, his lack of height did not hinder his predatory prowess anywhere within 18 yards of goal.

Linking up with Terry Paine and John Sydenham, his historic 39-goal campaign helped Southampton into Division Two, scoring four goals in a single game at Manchester City in an FA Cup tie. He would find the second tier harder, but still ended his days at The Dell with an eye-catching ratio of 173 goals in 311 games. Not bad for a player plucked from the obscurity of the Hampshire League and Bournemouth Gasworks! He left Southampton upon the breakthrough of Martin Chivers and the arrival of George Kirby, returning to Bournemouth & Boscombe and later turning out for Winchester City. After retirement, Reeves found employment as a rep for a building firm in his native Poole and then as an ambulance driver in Hampshire.

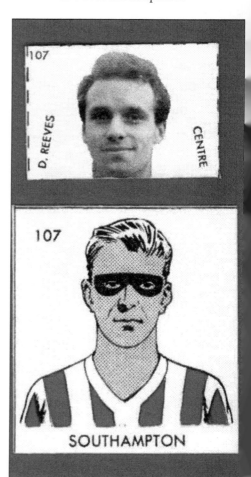

Performing Artistes

Peter Reid

Reid, Peter
Defensive midfielder
Born: 1956 Huyton, Lancashire
Playing career: Bolton Wanderers, Everton, QPR, Manchester City, Bury, Southampton, Bolton Wanderers, Sunderland (1971-1995).

Merseyside born midfielder who arrived at Ian Branfoot's Southampton as an ageing enforcer. With Branfoot beleaguered and under siege, the signing of the England international was a last ditch attempt to spark Saints into life. Even at 37, he inspired Saints to wins over Spurs, Chelsea and Newcastle in three of the eight games he played at The Dell. Once Branfoot was sacked, Reid would follow him out the club. Capped 13 times by England (playing at the 1986 World Cup), Reid played for Bolton, Everton, QPR, Manchester City, Notts County and Bury. Moved into management and coaching after retiring, taking charge of former club Manchester City, Sunderland, Leeds, Coventry, Plymouth (but quit after administration and relegation), Mumbai in India, England's U21 side and the Thailand national team. He has also appeared on Five Live, Sky Sports and ESPN as a pundit. Reid's autobiography: "Cheer up Peter Reid" was released in 2017. *www.performingartistes.co.uk/artistes/peter-reid*

Reilly, Matt
Goalkeeper
Born: 1874 Donnybrook, Dublin **Died:** 1954
Playing career: Benburb, Royal Artillery, Southampton (loan), Freemantle (loan), Portsmouth, Dundee, Notts County, Tottenham Hotspur, Shelbourne (1893-1909)

"Gunner" or "Ginger" Reilly played in an FA Amateur Cup final and won the Hampshire Senior Cup with his Royal Artillery barracks, also winning the second tier of the Southern League with that team. Loaned to Saints, he played twice for the club and kept two clean sheets in a pair of 5-0 wins. Reilly finally earned international recognition in 1900, getting two caps for the Republic of Ireland. He would later become landlord of the *Duke of Devonshire* in Southsea before leaving the south coast for one season stints with Dundee, Notts County and Spurs. Moving back to Ireland, Reilly worked as a labourer.

Reynolds, Jack
Midfielder/Forward
Born: 1869 Blackburn **Died:** 1917
Playing career: Blackburn Rovers, WBA, Aston Villa, Celtic, Southampton, Stockport C (1884-1905)

Due to a dispute over his place of birth that was never fully resolved, Jack "John" Reynolds became one of only two players ever to turn out for both Ireland and England. It was claimed he had been born in Ulster but moved to Blackburn as a boy. There were reports his father was an Irish soldier. Whatever the truth, Reynolds played five times for Ireland (one goal) and eight times for England (two goals), becoming the first man ever to do so (Declan Rice of West Ham has recently trodden the same path). He scored both for and against England setting yet another unique record. Won the FA Cup with West Brom and twice more whilst at Aston Villa, with whom he was also part of three title-winning sides. Had two games for Southampton near the end of his career before playing at non league level and then emigrated to New Zealand briefly working as a player-coach but that didn't work out and he went back to England. Coached at Cardiff and then settled in Sheffield where he worked as a collier.

DAVE BOWLER AND DAVID REYNOLDS

Reynolds, Ron
Goalkeeper
Born: *1928 Haslemere* **Died:** *1999*
Playing career: *Aldershot, Tottenham Hotspur, Southampton (1945-1963)*

A long serving 'keeper and Saints centurion, Reynolds had begun part-time at Aldershot whilst working as a draughtsman helping to design fire engines. He wrote to several clubs, including Saints. He eventually got his move to a bigger club, First Division Tottenham, and played 86 times for them. Reynolds had taken his coaching badges alongside Ted Bates and the latter swooped to give him the chance to play for Saints after all. Reynolds became first choice and would describe his time at The Dell as: "the best club I ever played for." Having played over 100 games for Saints in a career spanning almost 20 years, his playing days would be ended by a dislocated shoulder sustained at Fratton Park. He later moved into financial services to set up his own broker's business with his son David whilst coaching in several schools and also scouted for Crystal Palace and Saints. Died of a heart attack on his 71st birthday.

Richards, Dean
Defender
Born: *1974 Bradford, West Yorkshire* **Died:** *2011*
Playing career: *Bradford City, Wolverhampton W, Southampton, Tottenham Hotspur (1990-2005)*

Genial and unassuming off the pitch, Richards was a lion hearted, committed and strong ball playing centre half centre half described as an "absolute rock" by The Dell's patron Saint, Matt Le Tissier. Despite replacing the departed Ken Monkou, Richards quickly endeared himself to Saints fans with his all action style and was voted Player of the Year by the supporters in his debut campaign. Played 79 times in three seasons (chipping in with the occasional goal) before moving to Spurs. Also played for Bradford and Wolves and earned four caps for England at Under 21 level. Forced to retire prematurely due to illness, after suffering from dizzy spells and nausea, the football world was stunned by Richards premature death in 2011, at the tragically young age of 35, having suffered with a "neurological abnormality"

Richardson, Frazer
Defender
Born: *1982 Rotherham*
Playing career: *Leeds United, Stoke City, Charlton Athletic, Southampton, Middlesbrough, Ipswich Town, Rotherham, Doncaster Rovers (2001-2017)*

Full-back Richardson rose through the ranks at Leeds and stayed with them despite the drop from the Premier League into the third tier. Made over 150 appearances for the Elland Road side before moving to divisional rivals Charlton and then to Southampton, also then of League One, in 2010. Signed by Alan Pardew, a dislocated shoulder would delay Richardson's debut as Pardew was replaced by Nigel Adkins. He would find himself in and out of the team, faced with competition from Danny Butterfield and then Nathaniel Clyne before being released having played 60 times for Saints. He went on to Middlesbrough, Ipswich, Rotherham and Doncaster before retirement. He seems to have kept a low profile since retirement but still works for Leeds as an after dinner speaker and has been involved with a player agent company.

Richardson, Kevin

Midfielder
Born: *1962 Newcastle upon Tyne*
Playing career: *Everton, Watford, Arsenal, Real Sociedad, Aston Villa, Coventry City, Southampton, Barnsley, Blackpool (1980-2000)*

Capped once by England in 1994, the 'Geordie' joined Southampton as a stop gap signing to add further bite in midfield. Richardson kept things simple, and helped Saints to comfortably avoid relegation and finish in mid-table during his solitary season at the club. He had initially been signed by Dave Jones on a two year deal as a replacement for the soon to depart Jim Magilton and Neil Maddison. He would only stay for the 1997-98 campaign though before moving to newly demoted Barnsley and finishing at Blackpool. Richardson also played for Everton, Watford, Arsenal, Villa, Coventry and had a spell in Spain with Real Sociedad. He enjoyed the best time of his playing days with the Toffees, winning the FA Cup, the First Division and the Cup Winners Cup and the Charity Shield twice. Also won the League Cup with Villa and another top flight title during his time with the Gunners. Moved into coaching after retirement as a player, becoming youth team coach at Sunderland and then assistant boss to ex Saint Carlton Palmer with Stockport. He has also worked at Darlington as first team coach and is currently involved with Newcastle's Academy set up.

Richardson, Steve

Left-back
Born: *1962 Slough*
Playing career: *Southampton, Reading. (1980-1992)*

Left-back Richardson started out at Southampton but never played for the club at any level. He moved on to Reading where Richardson would become an ever present, featuring in over 400 games for the Berkshire side. Also had a spell with Newbury at non league level before finishing his playing days with Basingstoke, a club he would later manage as caretaker boss. Richardson also worked at Farnborough FC as assistant manager. Later set up his own youth coaching programme.

Rideout, Paul

Striker
Born: *1964 Bournemouth*
Playing career: *Swindon Town, Aston Villa, Bari, Southampton, Notts County, Rangers, Everton, Qianwei Huangdao, Kansas City Wizards, Shenzhen Jianlibao, Tranmere Rovers (1980-2002)*

Bournemouth born Rideout had to travel to Swindon to start his career at the age of 16 but it would be 8 years before he moved back closer to his birth place. Joined Saints in 1988 for £430,000 having made his name at Aston Villa and then Italian side Bari. Scored 19 goals in 90+ games but was on the move again when Ian Dowie was bought into the fold. Rideout stayed with his last club Tranmere, joining the backroom team, coaching the academy and running the youth sides. Rideout is best known for scoring the winner for Everton against Manchester United in 1995, and he returned briefly to Goodison Park as a scout under David Moyes, also serving in an advisory role. Rideout has remained heavily involved in the beautiful game, working in America with yet another of his ex-clubs, Kansas City Wizards, as Youth Coach, also serving Sporting Blue Valley in a similar role. He continues to live Stateside, residing in Phoenix, Arizona, with his second wife. Rideout now works as head of youth at Sporting Kansas. Twitter: https://twitter.com/paulrideout15

Ridges, George

Inside-forward
Born: *1940 Freemantle*
Died: *1940*
Playing career: *Southampton Harriers, Freemantle, Southampton St. Mary's (1892-)*

Locally born, George Ridges played cricket professionally for Freemantle, Wiltshire and Hampshire County Cricket Club. He played once for the Saints, in an FA Cup tie at Maidenhead during the 1892-93 season. He would turn his attentions to cricket and playing part-time for Freemantle in football, captaining the club to Hampshire Senior Cup glory including a 2-1 win over St Mary's in the semi finals. He later worked in the shipping industry at Hamble, playing for them briefly before becoming an estate carpenter.

Riley, Tom
Full-back
Born: *1882 Blackburn* **Died:** *1939*
Playing career: *St. Mary~ês, Chorley, Blackburn Rovers, Brentford, Aston Villa, Brentford, Southampton (1902-1907)*

Full back Riley started with Chorley in his native Lancashire, going on to sign for hometown team Blackburn in 1902. Although he made 18 appearances during his 1903-04 he found himself often a fringe player during his three years at Ewood Park, playing 23 times in total before taking a step down to Southern League Brentford. He would move to Aston Villa where again he was on the periphery before returning to Griffin Park less than a year later. Continuing the ground hopping nature of his career, Riley signed for Southampton but failed to turned out for the Saints an any level. Having retired from the professional game, Riley returned to his native county in the North West and worked as a bricklayer,

Ripley, Stuart
Winger
Born: *1967 Middlesbrough*
Playing career: *Middlesborough, Blackburn Rovers, Southampton*

Upon retiring from playing, Ripley worked as a physiotherapist in Castleford whilst gaining a Master's qualification in French, criminology and law (not perhaps what you expect from your average ex-pro). Completed his "A' and "B" UEFA coaching badges whilst at non league Allerton United as assistant boss. Also coached at Wigan Cosmos in the Lancashire league, later going on to qualify as a solicitor, setting up his own business. Whilst working for them, Ripley would go into football clubs in the area, both elite and non league, to advise and educate players on the pitfalls of life in the public eye, covering subjects such as agents and social media. Ripley has combined his past life with his new life in later years, working for the FA on their judicial disciplinary panel, hearing cases such as doping, safeguarding, agent legality and discrimination - he was part of the panel to find John Terry guilty on a racism charge in 2012.

Roberts, Albert
Full-back
Born: *1907 Goldthorpe* **Died:** *1957*
Playing career: *Ardsley Athletic, Southampton, Swansea Town , York City (1929-1947)*

Having made the step up from the backwaters of Yorkshire non league, full-back Roberts had the unenviable task of back up to the effervescent and every present Mike Keeping. He would make only 13 appearances over the next four seasons but became first choice when Keeping left for Fulham, making the left-back spot his own and going on to play over 100 times for the Saints. He refused new terms with Saints in the final post-war season of 1938-39 and was sold to Swansea in a swap with Tom Emanuel. He went on to play for York and Doncaster before retiring and become decorator. Died on his 50th birthday in 1957.

Robertson, John Tait
Half-back
Born: *1877 Dumbarton, Scotland* **Died:** *1935*
Playing career: *Morton, Everton, Southampton, Rangers, Chelsea, Glossop (1895-1909)*

Scored Chelsea's first ever League goal and was the first man (player or manager) to ever be paid whilst playing for the club. Capped 16 times for Scotland (three goals) he had played primarily in his native homeland before moving across the border to Merseyside. Spent two years with Everton and made 30 appearances before moving to Southampton. He spent only one season at The Dell but won the Southern League there and picked up another three league titles and the Scottish Cup whilst with Rangers. Worked at newly formed Chelsea as a player, combining this role with a managerial position as well. Moved to Glossop in the same player/manager job and went on to coach the Reserve side at Manchester United.

"DID YOU KNOW?"

"Mick Channon holds the record for most goals scored for the club. He bagged 228 during his two spells, 1966-77 and 1979-82."

Robertson, John Nicol
Half-back
Born: *1884 Ochiltree, Scotland* **Died:** *1937*
Playing career: *Drogan, Rangers, Bolton Wanderers, Southampton, (1902-1913)*

Championed and eulogised by the Echo, John Nicol Robertson was described as a "really classy half-back and an exceedingly capable player" upon his arrival from First Division Bolton. Robertson would prove more than worthy of those accolades as he became a regular, if not quite an ever present. Missed only six games in the 1909-1910 season, being deployed in six different positions and represented the Southern League. Suffered eight different injuries in his six years but played over 200 games before moving back to Scotland with Rangers. Robertson sustained yet another injury, this time a career-ending one on his spinal cord which left him debilitated. Later had a near fatal car accident to underline his reputation as accident prone. Won two Scottish league titles with Rangers and died in 1937 aged 54.

Robertson, Thomas
Full-back
Born: *1875 Lesmahagow, Scotland* **Died:** *1923*
Playing career: *Newton Mearns, St Bernard's, Stoke, Hibernian, Millwall Athletic, Stoke, Liverpool, Southampton, Brighton & Hove Albion (1894-1905)*

An ever present in the Liverpool team that won the top flight in 1901, Thomas Robertson came to Southampton's attentions when he played against them the following season. Southern League Saints stormed to a shock 4-1 win at Anfield on their way to an FA Cup final and Robertson joined them soon after and soon became a key man in an all-conquering Southampton team. A reliable and powerful attacking full-back and strong in the tackle, Robertson hardly missed a game at Saints and helped them to two consecutive Southern League titles. Losing his place to Sam Meston, Robertson fell out of favour and moved up the coast to Brighton having played 76 times for Southampton. Retired to the Sussex coast, becoming a publican at the *Wick Inn* in Hove and, later, the *Fountain* in Worthing, a short distance away.

Robinson, Edward
Full-back
Born: *1903 Hindley* **Died:** *1972*
Playing career: *Southampton, Southport, Wigan Athletic (1916-1947)*

Made a rare foray down south to enjoy - even if it was for only one game. Spent all of his career in the lower echelons of his native Lancashire - for Chorley, Southport, Wigan and a plethora of non league sides. He spent most of his time at The Dell in the Reserves, playing 67 times for the second string before his one and only first team match, at Stoke City on New Year's Eve 1927. Served in the Auxiliary Fire Service during the War and remained with them until the late 1950s. Worked as Wigan's player-coach in the Lancashire League after the conflict before joining the fire service at Hindley. Robinson later became an electrician until retirement in 1970.

Robinson, John 'Jack'
Goalkeeper
Born: *1870 Derby* **Died:** *1931*
Playing career: *Lincoln City, Derby County, New Brighton Tower, Southampton, Plymouth Argyle, Exeter City, Millwall (1886-1912)*

Kept goal 163 times for Derby and instantly became a Southampton hero, battling on through muscle cramps in his hand to help the team to a 4-3 win over Bristol City during the run in to a third successive title. He went on to win two more league medals with the club and two FA Cup runners up gongs. Capped eleven times by England - the first Saint to earn such recognition. This pioneering keeper went on to play more than 200 games for the south coast side, combining his playing days with running a pub, the *Wareham Arms*, before going on to turn out for Pymouth, Exeter, Millwall and Stoke with a brief spell across the pond. His career was punctuated with several unsavoury incidents = from illegally trying to help Saints sign a player from Derby to punching a fan and alleged insubordination when at Stoke. He later became an insurance salesman in his native Derby. Robinson also had a stint as a professional baseball player helping his home town to twice become British champions in the 1890s.

Robinson, Matt
Full-back
Born: 1974 Exeter
Playing career: *Southampton, Portsmouth, Reading, Oxford United, Forest Green Rovers, Salisbury City, Totton, Swindon Supermarine (1993-2012)*

Left winger-turned-full back snapped by Alan Ball upon his return as manager. Went on to play under five different managers in as many years at The Dell before Tony Pulis took him to Pompey in 2000. Played 17 games for Saints but started only four of those. Also played for Reading and Oxford, notching up over 350 career appearances by the time he retired. Played for non league Swindon Supermarine and served them as coach and assistant manager. Became a full time police officer in Andover.

Rochford, William
Full-back
Born: 1913 New House, Co Durham **Died:** 1984
Playing career: *Portsmouth, Southampton, Colchester United (1931-1951)*

It takes some doing to be universally adored and admired by fans of both Southampton and Portsmouth (just ask Harry Redknapp), but yet Bill Rochford managed to achieve that rarest of feats. Worked in the aircraft factory at Hamble during the WW2 before joining Southampton for £550 in time for the first post-War campaign. By now 33, he was seen as a "father figure" to many of the squad, not least a certain Alf Ramsey. He would become an ever present favourite at The Dell despite being overlooked for the manager's position after the departure of Bill Dodgin. Eventually became player-coach under Sid Cann but left for Football League newbies Colchester in 1951 having played 134 times for the club. Only played a handful of times in Essex Later scouted for Saints and served on their board before working as a farmer in the north East.

"DID YOU KNOW?"

"The £75 million paid by Liverpool for Virgil van Dijk is the highest transfer fee received by the club."

Rodrigues, Daniel
Winger
Born: 1980 Madeira, Portugal
Playing career: *Feirense, Bournemouth, Southampton, Bristol City, Walsall, Ionikos, Yeovil Town, Bournemouth, New Zealand Knights ,*

Dani Rodrigues is a Portuguese winger capped at both under 20 and under 21 level. Glenn Hoddle did not show much consideration to his neighbours when he lured th wideman to Saints having made five brief cameo appearances for Bournemouth. Skilfull and quick, he played more than anyone for the Reserves in his debut season, topping the scoring charts and looking set for a bright future. Had a couple of minutes off the bench in two first team games but that would be the end of Dani Rodrigues' Southampton story. Loaned out to Bristol City where he broke an ankle but eventually recovered to play in Greece, New Zealand before ending his playing days in the Cypriot second division.

Rodrigues, Peter
Full-back
Born: 1944 Cardiff, Wales
Playing career: *Cardiff City, Leicester City, Sheffield Wednesday, Southampton. (1963-1976).*

Forced to retire in his 30s, through injury, later moving to California where he worked as a coach. Returned to Hampshire where he was assistant boss with Aldershot, Totton and Christchurch, combining coaching duties with running a pub, the King Rufus, in Eling. Had a second pub in Wales, the Caernarfon-based Whitemill Inn, and he later went on to run a cafe before Rodrigues took over as manager and owner of the Conservative Club in Woolston. Had a brief stint in Spain but never settled. He has since come back to Southampton and most recently worked as a driver for Mercedes Benz. His cup winners medal was purchased at auction by Southampton Football Club in 2004 for more than £10 000 having been under the hammer by his daughter, against Rodrigues' wishes. Unsurprisingly, right-back and Saints captain in 76 at Wembley described lifting the cup to the Saints fans as his finest hour.

Rofe, Dennis

Full-back
Born: *1950 Epping*
Playing career: *Leyton Orient, Leicester City, Chelsea, Southampton. (1967-1983)*

Arriving at The Dell on a free, the full-back would serve Southampton in three stints as player, reserve and first team coach and first team assistant manager. Rofe was already 32 by the time he arrived at Saints, with 500 senior career games under his belt. A tough, no nonsense left-back, he had turned out for Leyton Orient and Leicester under Jimmy Bloomfield, getting capped once by England at U23 level in the process. Used as back up at Saints to Mick Mills, Rofe later captained the Reserves whom he would go on to take charge of. Rofe played 25 times for the club in two seasons, before taking up a coaching role. Joined the staff in 1984 under Chris Nicholl but when both were culled, Rofe moved elsewhere and had a stint in charge at Bristol Rovers and Stoke. Dave Merrington brought him back as youth team coach, but he would leave gain only to return for the third time when Dave Jones came in. He survived five managers - from Glenn Hoddle to Harry Redknapp - before being xed by George Burley and, this time, would never return. Coached at all levels from U14 to first team and later worked for the FA as South East Youth Development Officer. Coached at Bournemouth, taking caretaker charge following the sacking of Paul Groves and before the return of Eddie Howe. Rofe has also done commentary work on Five Live and BBC Radio Solent.

Rogers, Andrew

Midfielder
Born: *1956 Chatteris*
Playing career: *Chatteris Town, Peterborough United , Southampton, Plymouth Argyle, Reading, Southend United (1975-1988)*

Working as a teacher in the capital after being released by Peterborough, First Division Southampton - in Rogers' own words - "lured him back to football). Slotting into a side containing Alan Ball, Mick Channon and Charlie George, his time at the club would prove an anticlimactic one, though, making only five appearances. All of these came from the bench and totalled 30 minutes. Plymouth would borrow him and eventually sign the tricky, pacy winger. Paying £50,000 for his services, Plymouth would get over 200 games out of Rogers. An ever present in Reading's Third Division title win of 1986 he would go on to serve Southend, helping another club to promotion, becoming becoming a probation officer in Devon.

Rogers, Joe

Forward or Full-back
Born: *1874 Macclesfield*
Died: *1955*
Playing career: *Macclesfield, Southampton, Grimsby Town, Newcastle United, Preston North End (1893-1902)*

Started out as an inside forward for hometown team Macclesfield, arriving at Southern League Southampton in 1894 and switching to full-back. He hd barely scored up front but had the "pace, control and kicking ability" required to fill that position. Shortly after signing for Saints, Rogers plundered ten goals in a single game against Wiltshire Regiment in an exhibition match on an Antelope Ground pitch that resembled a ploughed field! He would soon become unsettled on the south coast, though, and moved to Grimsby after only 17 games and less than a year at the club. Spent two seasons at Grimsby and went on to Newcastle and Preston before retirement. Played three times for an FA representative XI, scoring five goals, before coaching in Germany. Later returned to Grimsby where he played part time whilst working in a fish shop.

Roles, Albert

Full-back
Born: *1921 Southampton* **Died:** *2012*
Career: *Southampton, West Ham (1938-1952)*

A local lad, Roles was playing in the
Southampton Junior League when his
hometown team - always on the lookout for
local talent - plucked him from obscurity
and signed him. Joined as an amateur in
1938 but war had broken out by the time he
turned pro. Played more war time games
for Southampton than any other player,
whilst making engines for torpedo boats
on the Docks. These games did not count
towards his official records, though, and
Roles would play only five times for the
club in "official" fixtures. Completed his
mandatory National Service but Saints
had by then signed Bill Rochford whom
would become first choice. Had a stint at
Gloucester City and served Cowes Sports
as player-manager. Hospitalised for two
years along with his wife through TB, Roles
gave up football save a brief scouting role
under Ted Bates. Later worked at *Harland &
Wolff* and as a technician at the institution
today known as Solent University.

Roper, Don

Centre-forward/Winger
Born: *1922 Botley, Hampshire* **Died:** *2001*
Playing career: *Southampton, Arsenal,
Southampton. (1946-1958).*

Worked on Spitfires for Supermarine at
Eastleigh whilst playing wartime football
for Saints. Equally adept with either foot,
versatile and strong, Roper could play
anywhere across the front. Roper clearly
did enough to warrant attention, signing
for Arsenal in 1947 with George Curtis
and Tom Rudkin moving to Saints. Roper
played over 100 games on the south coast
and became a regular for the Gunners, his
only other league club. Won two league
titles with the north London side and
played in an FA Cup final before returning
to Saints, captaining a team containing
talents such as Derek Reeves and a
young Terry Paine. Played for Weymouth
and Dorchester Town and also played
cricket for Hampshire. Later settled in
Southampton and worked as an engineer.

Rosler, Uwe

Centre-forward
Born: *1968 Altenburg, East Germany*
Playing career: *Dynamo Dresden, FC Nurnberg,
Manchester City, FC Kaiserslautern, Tennis Borussia
Berlin, Southampton, WBA, Lillestrom (1981-2003)*

East German centre forward with five
caps, joined Saints on a free transfer
toward the end of his playing career. He
scored the last ever goal at The Dell in a
friendly against Brighton and made 30
league and cup appearances for Saints.
He was forced to retire when he was
diagnosed with cancer in 2003, with an
X-ray discovering that he had a tumour in
his chest. He made a full recovery and was
appointed manager of Lillestrom in 2005
, but left a year later to manage Viking.
He left the club in November 2009. On 31
August 2010, he was hired by Molde FK
on a short-term contract. Has since has
an extensive managerial career, taking
charge of Brentford, Wigan, Leeds and
Fleetwood in England as well as Malmo in
Sweden. Rosler is currently boss of Fortuna
Dusseldorf in Germany's second tier.

Rowe, Douglas
Outside-left
Born: *1909 Nottingham* **Died:** *1978*
Playing career: *Sneinton, Luton Town, Lincoln City, Southampton, US Tourcoing (1932-1935)*

Having failed to establish himself at Luton and Lincoln, Rowe - a forward - signed for Second Division Southampton in search of regular first team game time. He scored on his home debut but lost his place to another new signing Laurie Fishlock and left Saints having only played two games. Played for a time in France and returned to his native Nottinghamshire but he never again returned to top level football. Later became a miner in Ollerton and also turned out for their works team. Doug Rowe was also a wrestler and had already won the England amateur welterweight title before turning his hand to football.

Rowley, Dick
Inside-forward/Centre-forward
Born: *1904 Enniskillen, Ireland* **Died:** *1984*
Playing career: *Swindon Town, Southampton, Tottenham Hotspur, Preston North End (1922-1934)*

Rowley had played rugby at amateur level and represented both Hampshire and Wiltshire in football by the time he signed on amateur forms with second tier Southampton. Played briefly for Swindon in the Third South, and he would slot straight in the team at The Dell following the departure of the prolific Arthur Dominy. He soon rekindled Dominy's former strike partnership in a spot of "R&R" (Rowley and Rawlings) and would finish second top sorer to the latter in his debut season, helping Saints to the FA Cup semi finals. Even after Rawlings had left, Rowley continued to prosper, thumping 26 goals in 23 games including becoming the first Saint to score four goals in a single match away from home. His form inevitably attracted suitors and he signed for divisional rivals Tottenham for £3,750. Served in the Air Force as Squadron leader during the War and received the Distinguished Conduct Medal and was capped six times by Ireland. Scored 62 goals in 117 games for Saints. Rowley later worked as the secretary of Hampshire CCC supporters club.

Ruddock, Neil
Centre-back
Born: *1968 Wandsworth, London*
Playing career: *Millwall, Tottenham Hotspur, Southampton, Liverpool, QPR, West Ham United, Crystal Palace, Swindon Town (1986-2003)*

Known universally as "Razor", one of the beautiful game's most popular hardmen continues to be a larger than life personality to this day. A one cap wonder for England, Ruddock played for Millwall, Spurs and won the League Cup with Liverpool. Despite being anything but a prolific goalscorer, Ruddock slammed home a penalty against fellow strugglers to give Southampton a priceless victory in their battle against the drop. Ruddock helped Southampton to a late "Great Escape" and is still fondly remembered as a combative, uncompromising, kick-anything-that-moved hardman. Went on to QPR, West Ham and Palace before turning out for Swindon including a brief spell as player/coach. Ruddock has become a familiar figure in the media, doing *A Question of Sport, I'm a Celebrity Get me out of Here, Big Brother* and *A League of their Own* as well as working on the after dinner circuit and on TalkSport and Five Live.

Neil Ruddock

Ruddy, Thomas
Inside-forward
Born: *1902 Stockton-on-Tees*
Died: *1979*
Playing career: *Darlington, Derby County, Chesterfield, Southampton (1924-1934)*

The Saints Supporters Club cobbled together the money to bring Ruddy, by now 30 but still a "speedy forward with a hard shot" to The Dell. He had been prolific at Darlington, Derby County and Chesterfield, but failed to replicate at Southampton, scoring only four games in 28 games. Eventually lost his place in the side to Herbert Coates and then Arthur Holt, moving to Spennymoor where he finished his career. Later worked as a miner and then as a joiner on the docks at Gateshead.

Rudkin, Thomas
Winger
Born: *1919 Peterborough* **Died:** *1969*
Playing career: *Creswell, Wolverhampton Wanderers, Lincoln City, Peterborough United, Hartlepool United, Arsenal, Southampton, Bristol City, Hastings United, Weston-super-Mare, Peterborough United (1938-1953)*

Whilst serving as a tank commander in Yorkshire during the War, Rudkin guested widely for clubs up north but also - on a few occasions - for Southampton. A versatile and "unpredictable" wideman, he hd played for Grimsby and Lincoln before signing for First Division Arsenal, scoring twice in five games, before moving on again, this time to Second Division Saints. Rudkin would only make sporadic appearances in two seasons (ten in total), playing on either wing and at inside forward, but never settled and moved on to Ashton Gate after two seasons. Later played for Hastings United and Peterborough and returned to the south west as player-manager of non league Weston-super-Mare. Rudkin found work as a circulation agent for the *Sunday Pictorial* and then worked in security at a nightclub in his native Peterborough. Became licensee of the *Angel Hotel* in Wisbech but suddenly collapsed and died shortly before his 50th birthday.

Ruffell, Daniel
Goalkeeper
Born: *1867 Southampton*
Died: *1940*
Career: *Southampton St. Mary's (1885-1894)*

"Ralph" Ruffell featured in Southampton's first ever official competitive fixture - an FA Cup tie with the Royal Engineers. He also played in the St Mary's side that won three Hampshire Junior Cup finals and two equivalent Senior Cups successes. His arrival preceded the club's days as a Southern League team so his eight games were limited to cup games only, but he was first choice goalkeeper until his departure in 1892. Having left the club, however, Saints were unable to find a regular and reliable replacement keeper, so Ruffell returned to collect another runners up medal before sustaining a dislocated kneecap. He would retire again, this time for good, and went on to work on the Docks as an engineer whilst containing to go to the Dell as a season ticket holder.

Saeijs, Jan-Paul
Centre-back
Born: *1978 The Hague, Netherlands*
Playing career: *Den Haag, Roda JC, Southampton, De Graafschap, (1997-date)*

Had a loan spell with Championship Saints in the 2008-09 season having made his name in his native Netherlands. Southampton's Dutch coach Mark Wotte had been instrumental in bringing Saeijs to St Mary's on loan and was appointed as manager soon after the player's arrival. His compatriot would soon become a regular at the heart of the defence, but despite impressing, Saeijs was unable to help the side avoid relegation to the third tier. Saeijs seemed to adapt well to the physical, robust nature of the English game, with good aerial ability and strength, standing as he did at 6ft 3. Scored twice at Watford in 20 games but, in a turbulent time for the club collectively, he left the club upon the arrival of Alan Pardew as manager and Markus Liebherr as owner. Returned to his native Netherlands to rejoin his first club HBS Craeyenhout whilst working as an accounts manager. Still playing at the age of 42.

Saganowski, Marek

Striker
Born: *1978 Poland*
Playing career: *Feyenoord, Hamburger SV, Legia Warsaw, Vitoria de Guimares, Troyes, Southampton, AaB, Atromitos, Legia Warsaw (1994-2016)*

A case of what might have been, Marek Saganowski never truly fulfilled his blistering potential. Became Poland's second youngest ever full international two months after turning 17 and went on to earn 35 caps for the country (five goals). But his career by a plethora of injuries, including a motorbike accident that put him out of action for almost two years. Played in the Netherlands, Germany, his native Poland, Portugal and France before being brought to England by George Burley. Arriving on loan, Saganowski bagged ten goals in his first eleven starts but, perversely, his form fell away upon signing permanently. He would later return to St Mary's for a second loan stint again scoring plenty early on with six in seven. Saganowski would later say he "loved the area, the city, the football club and its fans", endearing himself to the Southampton faithful by describing them as "the best supporters in the country." A much travelled striker, he played at Euro 2008 for Poland and currently runs a football academy in his homeland.

Salter, John

Inside-left
Born: *1898 Bitterne, Southampton* **Died:** *1982*
Career: *Southampton (1923-1925)*

Called up to the war effort when barely out of short trousers at 16, he served at Swaythling training mules for the gun carriages. Eventually posted to France but was discharged on medical grounds having been mustard gassed. Turned to football and joined Saints as an amateur, turning pro within a month. He would only play once, though, against Fulham in 1923, but he had not fully recovered and was not ready for the regular exertions of pro football. He returned to playing locally and worked for Thorneycrofts as a boiler maker. Later employed by the Post Office as an engineer until retiring. His son, Roland was briefly on the books at Saints.

Salway, Edward

Centre-half
Born: *1891 Nursling*
Died: *1950*
Playing career: *Romsey Town, Nursling United, Southampton (1911-1915)*

A gardener from the outskirts of the Southampton, Ed Salway had humble beginnings but would become a local boy done good. Earned Hampshire Representative honours at both junior and senior level whilst playing for Saints youth team as a "rough, unpolished diamond." Salway would prove something of a late bloomer but eventually got a crack at the first team, utilising his pace and energy in several different positions during his debut season of 1912-1913. Like many of his generational peers, his career at the club would be disrupted - and ultimately ended - by the outbreak of WW1. Served on the Western Front with the Royal Horse Artillery in 1916 and would lose both an eye and arm, being discharged on medical ground to live a life as an invalid. He would recover sufficiently to still work as a flagman on the Docks.

Sarli, Cosimo

Striker
Born: *1979 Corigliano Calabro, Italy*
Playing career: *Schiavonea, Torino, Southampton, Eendracht Aalst, Nice, Crotone, Aglianese, Montichiari, Legnano, Pro Sesto, Cosenza, Scafatese, Catanzaro, Aversa Normanna , Siracusa, Messina, Casertana, Ischia (1997-Still Playing)*

Nicknamed "Cobra", the well travelled Italian striker turned out for 18 sides during his career and was on the books of two others - one of which was Saints - without ever playing at senior level Spent most of his career in his native Italy except for brief spells with Saints, Eendracht Aalst in Belgium and France's Nice. Sarli did make an impact for Saints at Reserve team level, though, scoring 12 goals in 19 games for the second string in the 1998-99 season and featuring in several pre-season tours for the senior side. Dave Jones would never pick him for a senior competitive match, however. Now 41, he is a free agent and still wants to continue playing despite his advancing years.

Sarmiento, Marcelo

Midfielder
Born: *1979 Cardoba, Argentina*
Playing career: *Talleres, Litex Lovech, Olimpo, Argentinos Juniors, Southampton, Larissa, Atromitos, Union (1995-2013)*

Described by the then-Southampton boss as a "George Burley identikit", there was much hype surrounding Saints loan capture of the Argentine with local press describing him as a "top class talent." A midfielder with an eye for an pass and a positive, forward thinking player, he was signed temporarily to give Saints depth, quality and control in the middle but his stint on the south coast proved an ill fated one. He would make only four appearances for the club, failing to play in the Championship with three League Cup appearances and one FA Cup game. Sarmiento returned to his homeland and had a spell in Greece where he later coached and worked for their national Football Association.

Saul, Frank

Forward
Born: *1943 Canvey Island, Essex*
Playing career: *Tottenham, Southampton, QPR, Millwall. (1960-1975)*

Won the FA Cup with Spurs in 1967, scoring a spectacular winner in the final against London rivals Chelsea. Spent the majority of his career with Tottenham, but would move to The Dell as part of the deal that took Martin Chivers the other way. Seen as a replacement for the latter, Saul would never quite live up to the potential that manager Ted Bates and the Saints hierarchy saw in him. His record of 12 goals in 68 goals was far from spectacular, but Saul although he toiled in the league, he would hit some important goals in the cup games, scoring eight in 12 starts with another two as sub. But he would return to London with QPR and Millwall before playing at non league level n his native Essex. Later worked as a builder and decorator in Billericay.

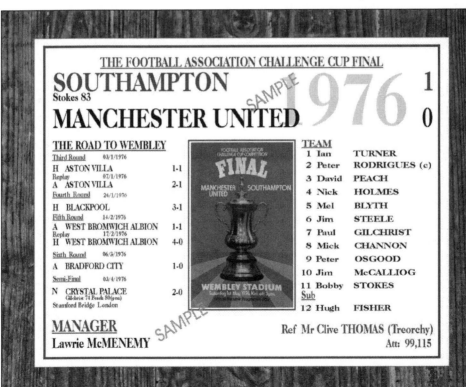

Scott, Augustus

Forward
Born: *1921 Sunderland* **Died:** *1998*
Playing career: *Luton Town, Southampton, Colchester United (1939-1954)*

After the customary stint in pre-war professional football, Scott served in Burma before Bill Dodgin signed him and George Curtis, of Arsenal, for Saints. Whilst the latter would become a regular in the first post-War season, "Augie" only played 47 times fin total. Later became Colchester's then-record signing, before moving to Chelmsford as player-manager. Turned out for Evesham whilst working as a builder before another player-manager role with Cheltenham. Moving back to Southampton, he worked as a labourer whilst also running a timber yard in Hedge End.

Scott, John

Half-back
Born: *1905 Grimethorpe*
Died: *1976*
Playing career: *Pilkington Recreationals, Doncaster Rovers, Norwich City, Southampton (1929-1940)*

Played rugby league with Featherstone Rovers in his native Yorkshire before swapping an oval ball for a spheroid. A part time wrestler - training with British Olympian Harold Angus - Scott initially started out at Doncaster before moving to Norwich after two seasons. Played under Tom Parker at Carrow Road and when the Canaries manager took over at The Dell, he took Scott with him. He would multi-task on the south coast, helping to coach the reserve team, play for that side regularly and be available to fill in with the first team if needed. As it happens, he would only be pressed into service once at senior level, against Swansea in December 1937. Said to be "as strong as an ox and as hard as nails", he deputised at centre forward - with the young debutant Ted Bates alongside him after Ray Parkin, Benny Gaughran and Billy Dunn were all unavailable. He played a couple of games for the club in wartime and later worked for Follands Aircraft at Hamble. After the War had finished he was employed by the council to work at the city library.

Scriven, Herbert

Goalkeeper
Born: *1908 Winsor, Hampshire* **Died:** *2001*
Career: *Southampton, Salisbury City (1929-1939)*

A keeper of both pigs and the Southampton net, Bert Scriven joined Saints on amateur forms before signing pro in 1929. At first deputy to Willie White, Scriven would make the gloves his own and went on to play more than 200 times between the sticks. Firmly established as an ever present for the best part of a decade, Scriven was considered an "alert and agile" keeper and rarely let the team down until Saints manager George Kay brought in 20-year-old William Light to compete with Scriven. The former would eventually usurp Scriven until the cash strapped Saints sold Light to West Brom and Scriven took over once again. A one club man, he retired in 1937 and became the licensee of the *Bear and Ragged Staff* in Romsey whilst turning out occasionally for non league Salisbury.

Sealy, Tony

Forward
Born: *1959 Hackney, London*
Playing career: *Southampton, Crystal Palace, QPR, Port Vale, Fulham, Leicester City, Bournemouth, Brentford, Bristol R, Brentford (1977-1993)*

A product of Tyneside's Wallsend Boys Club - Michael Carrick, Peter Beardsley, Lee Clark and ex Saints Alan Shearer and Fraser Forster amongst their alumnus - Sealy was scouted and signed by Saints North East talent spotter Jack Hixon and brought him south. He came with a reputation as a prolific and net busting striker, but would fail to replicate this form at The Dell. Sealy played only eight times in 18 months at the club. His last ever appearance for Southampton came at Wembley in the 1979 League Cup final loss to Nottingham Forest. Went on to play for several clubs including Palace, QPR, Fulham, Leicester and Brentford twice. Also played in Portugal and Finland before retiring aged 33. Moving overseas, he spent 21 years in charge of Hong Kong whilst also serving in an advisory and administrative role. He is currently Director of Operations for Hong Kong football's governing body.

Seeley, George

Outside-forward
Born: *1879 Torquay* **Died:** *1921*
Playing career: *Southampton, QPR , Southampton Wanderers , Clapton Orient, Leyton (1896-1906)*
Dubbed the "Lion Tamer" upon entering a lion's cage when a circus visited Southampton, Seeley settled for a much safer, more peaceful pastime - as outside half cover to the indomitable Joe Turner at The Dell. Unsurprisingly he spent most of his early days in the Reserves, only playing once for the senior side during his first season at the club. Seeley left in search of regular game time and played for both major Bristol clubs before returning to Saints. Turner had left by then and so Seeley "speedy, versatile and a real trier" filled the void on the left wing, helping the club to win the Southern League again and playing ten games before moving to the capital. Played for Leyton, Clapton, QPR and New Brompton before retiring and becoming a licensee of the *Railway Inn* in Acton. Seeley died whilst on an Isle of Wight holiday at the age of 42.

Selston, Sidney

Outside-forward
Born: *1888 Farnham* **Died:** *1949*
Playing career: *Southampton (1912-1913)*
One of 34 players used in the Southern League season for Southampton during the 1912-13 campaign, Selston - who had played for the Army before joining Saints as an amateur - was one of the players used in the closing months of a season of struggle. It was hardly a time to blood untried youngsters, with Selston know to "part with the ball frequently" in his handful of appearances at outside right. It was nothing more than an experiment, and one that manager Ernest Armfield would not persist with. Selston returned to the Army and served in WW1, becoming a Warrant Officer. He would continue his previous career as a soldier and served in the Royal Garrison Artillery for two decades after the War. Southampton would not use 34 players in a season again for almost a century, during the 2004-05 campaign in a desperate bid to avoid relegation.

Senda, Daniel

Defender
Born: *1981 Harrow*
Playing career: *Southampton, Wycombe Wanderers, Millwall, Torquay United, Bristol Rovers, Barnet (1997-2012)*
Harrow born, centre-back Senda was an apprentice at Saints but would never play for the first team. Having failed to breakthrough, he moved to Wycombe and played as a striker initially until being converted to a defender by Lawrie Sanchez. Senda played over 400 games in his career. Worked as a coach at Brentford before becoming head of youth at former club Barnet in 2017. As of 2020 Senda is employed as assistant manager to Ross Embleton at Leyton Orient.

Shand, Hector

Outside-right
Born: *1879 Inverness, Scotland* **Died:** *1942*
Playing career: *Inverness Thistle , Southampton, Middlesbrough, Millwall (1905-1909)*
Shand - an outside right - made a big step both in terms of quality and geographically to move from Highland League Inverness to Southern League Saints. It would not prove a journey worth making, though, as Shand would only play once and struggled to acclimatise, returning home after only one game in the Southern League. Returned to amateur football in Scotland and later became a taxi driver.

Sharp, Bertram

Full-back
Born: *1876 Hereford* **Died:** *1949*
Playing career: *Aston Villa, Everton, Southampton, Kirkdale, Southport Central (1897-1904)*
A Southern League title winner with Saints in 1900/01, full-back Sharp played 22 times. He later became director of his former club Everton alongside with his brother Jack, also a professional footballer. Sharp was also a competent cricketer and in the summer of 1900 averaged over 40 for Herefordshire. He signed for double winning Villa in 1897 and went on to ma 22 appearances in two seasons with the west Midlands side. Sharp later worked as a landlord of a public house opposite Everton's Goodison Park home.

Sharpe, John

Defender
Born: *1957 Portsmouth*
Playing career: *Southampton, Gillingham, Swansea City (1974-1985)*

Born to a family of Pompey fans, John Sharpe seemed set for stardom with his beloved Blues but when things went wrong at Fratton Park, Southampton swooped. Putting his dream of becoming a professional over any loyal allegiances, Sharpe went behind enemy lines to sign for Saints having been scouted by former player Stan Cribb. He played 22 games but a sending off in a pre-season friendly saw him fall foul of Lawrie McMenemy and he was eventually sold to Gillingham. He played nearly 200 games but injuries curtailed his career and he retired after a brief stint at Swansea. He has remained living and working in Kent, running a kitchen retail business having also managed a sports shop and worked in property maintenance.

Alan Shearer

Shearer, Alan

Striker
Born: *1970 Gosforth, Tyne and Wear*
Playing career: *Southampton, Blackburn Rovers, Newcastle United (1988-2006)*

Shearer's time at Southampton - amidst his heroics for Newcastle and England - is often forgotten. Widely regarded as one of the best strikers of his generation and in Premier League history, he started out at Saints, spearheading an attack scoring 43 goals in 140 games at The Dell. For such a prolific goalscorer, Shearer's time on the south coast was notable for his efforts in "holding off defenders" and doing much of the hard graft for others. Joined Blackburn for a then record fee of £3.6m, winning the title at Ewood Park, before another world record record deal took him to his hometown team of Newcastle where he would become the club's all time top scorer. Since retiring, Shearer had remained in the game as a pundit, regularly appearing on Match of the Day. Shearer had an eight game spell as manager of his beloved Magpies in 2009 in a last-ditch attempt to save the side from relegation - but it would prove futile.

Shearer, Samuel

Inside-forward
Born: *1883 Coylton, Scotland*
Died: *1971*
Playing career: *Southampton, Nithsdale W, Bradford Park Avenue, Trabboch (1908-1913)*

Started out in his native Scotland before impressing on trial at Saint, doing enough to sign for the club in the summer of 1908. In and out of the side, he would often vie with Frank Jordan at inside left, with Shearer described as "naturally skilful." Known for his dribbling and close control, he would often be the target of the opposition's efforts to stop Southampton attacks. Headed back to his native Scotland after 25 games in two fragmented seasons and played anon league level in Dumfries. Briefly played in the English Second Division with Bradford PA, before retiring. Having hung up his boots, Shearer worked as an engineer and later worked in the Canadian Army as a soldier.

Sheerin, Paul

Midfielder
Born: *1974 Edinburgh, Scotland*
Playing career: *Whitehill Welfare, Celtic, Alloa Athletic, Southampton, Ostersunds FK, Alloa Athletic, Inverness Caledonian Thistle , Ayr United, Aberdeen, St Johnstone, Arbroath (1991-2014)*
Scottish box-to-box midfielder, played almost exclusively in his native homeland save for a brief spell at Swedish club Ostersunds, a side known for its championing of British talent. Sheerin was on the books at Southampton, under three different managers - Ian Branfoot, Alan Ball and Graeme Souness - but he failed to make a first team appearance. Capped once by Scotland at U21 level in 1995, Sheerin went on to win the Scottish First Division and the domestic cup during his time at St Johnstone. Later moved into coaching, running St Johnstone's Academy before moving to Arbroath. Helped that club to the third tier title (their first ever national league win) during his first season in charge as player-manager. Had four years as boss at Gayfield Park and has since worked for the Scottish FA as an advisor.

Fred Shelley

Shelley, Frederick

Half-back
Born: *1899 Romsey* **Died:** *1971*
Playing career: *Southampton (1915-1932)*
Southampton's sixth highest appearance maker of all time, Fred "Bert" Shelley served Saints for the best part of two decades as both player and coach. Shelley joined Eastleigh shortly after leaving the Army, before linking up with Southampton and quickly becoming a virtual ever-present. Helped the club to the Third Division title, capable of filling in either at centre-half or in his more accustomed position as a right-half alongside Billy Turner and either Alec Campbell or George Moorhead. Adept at reading the game, Shelley gained a reputation as a consistent and reliable half-back, with "great strength" and had the knack of "smothering opponents" with his ability to anticipate and intercept opposition attacks. He became a key man, going on to play over 400 games during his long career at the club. After eventually hanging up his boots, Shelley worked with the Saints youngsters, scouted for them and worked alongside manager George Kay with the the senior squad. Moved on to Liverpool with the latter and won the league championship before retiring in 1956.

Shields, Robert

Centre-forward
Born: *1931 Derry, Northern Ireland*
Playing career: *Crusaders, Sunderland, Southampton, Larne (1952-1965)*
Centre forward with one cap for Northern Ireland, Shields became Ted Bates first signing as Southampton manager in 1956. Cash strapped Saints borrowed the money from their Supporters Club. Bates spent £1,000 to bring him to third tier Saints and his gamble paid off when Shields scored 18 in his first season including a debut strike against local rivals Bournemouth & Boscombe. Shields plundered 27 goals in 43 games but Derek Reeves arrived and he found himself out of favour. Went on to play at non league level in the North East whilst working as a joiner and, later, as a mechanic.

Shilton, Peter

Goalkeeper
Born: *1949 Leicester*
Playing career: *Leicester City, Stoke City, Nottingham Forest, Southampton, Derby County, Plymouth Argyle, Wimbledon, Bolton W, Coventry City, West Ham United, Leyton Orient (1966-1997)*
One of the greatest goalkeepers to ever grace the field, Peter Shilton was huge in presence, reputation and stature. Nobody has ever played more for England, he is the man with the most number of caps whilst a Saint - in his five seasons on the south coast, he earned 49 of his 125 caps and skippered England on 15 occasions. The records just keep coming. 'Shilts' played 1,390 professional games (no one has played more) and is one of very few goalies to have scored in open play. It came at The Dell but unfortunately against Southampton whilst Shilton was playing for Leicester. Had it not been for Ray Clemence, Shilton probably would have played even more for England. Featured in three World Cups and two European Championships. Considered to be the finest keeper in the world during his playing days, Shilton was revered for his handling, positioning, concentration, agility and consistency. Won the First Division, the League Cup and the European Cup twice during his and Nottingham Forest's Brian Clough inspired heyday. Later managed Plymouth Argyle and is a keen golfer. Shilton makes occasional appearances as a pundit on radio and television.

Shipley, George

Midfielder
Born: *1959 Newcastle*
Playing career: *Southampton, Reading, Lincoln City, Charlton Athletic, Gillingham (1979-1988)*
Brought to the Dell thanks to Southampton's prolific North East scouting system, Newcastle born Shipley - along with Tony Sealey - became Lawrie McMenemy's first academy signings. Shipley played mainly in the Reserves, captaining the club at that level, but would play four times for the senior side. Got an assist in his second game against Liverpool but that would prove the zenith of his time with the club. Played for Reading, Lincoln, Charlton and Gillingham before moving into coaching as the Gills' youth team manager. Took the same job at Middlesbrough before working as no.2 under Lennie Lawrence with Bradford. Most recently, Shipley returned to his boyhood Magpies as their Football in the Community Personnel Manager.

Shipperley, Neil

Centre-forward
Born: *1974 Chatham*
Playing career: *Chelsea, Watford, Southampton, Crystal Palace, Nottingham Forest, Barnsley, Wimbledon, Sheffield United, Brentford (1992-2007)*
London-born striker who had made his name as a young up and coming hitman at Chelsea before joining Saints - via Watford - under Alan Ball. Signed for a record fee of £1.25m, Shipperley immediately displaced a young Iain Dowie and went on to become a virtual ever-present, featuring in 65 of their next 66 Premiership games. By now on his third manager in Graeme Souness, after Dave Merrington came and went, Shipperley earned seven caps for England at U21 level. But Souness signed Egil Ostenstad and promptly sold Shipperley to Crystal Palace, and he went on to fire the Eagles to Premiership promotion. After retiring Shipperley went into management but struggled with financial problems and a gambling addiction in later life. Shipperley was sentenced to a 12-month community order and given a suspended prison sentence for public indecency in 2019.

Sillett, Charles
Full-back
Born: *1906 Plumstead* **Died:** *1945*
Career: *Southampton (1931-1938)*
Father of Peter (below) and of John, whom
also played for Southampton, he had
won several honours with the Army - in
football, shooting and even boxing and
rowing - before joining Southampton as
a pro. He would quickly be thrown into
the first team by manager George Kay
in the midst of an injury crisis. Sillett
would immediately replay his manager's
enforced faith in him with a brace on his
debut and he would instantly become a
regular, playing in five different positions
before converting to left-back. Sillett
missed only two games between the start
of 1934-35 and the end of 1938, captaining
the club in what turned out to be his final
season at The Dell. During his seven years
of loyal, unstinting service in a largely
struggling side - and despite financial
problems - Sillett played almost 200 games
for Saints. Later moved to divisional rivals
Guildford for a swansong before hanging
up his boots. Briefly worked in the New
Forest as landlord of the *The Lamb* before
WWII broke out. Sillett served as a gunner
during the conflict but sadly lost his life
in the sinking of *SS Covus* off the coast of
Cornwall, at the age of 39.

Sillett, Peter
Right-back
Born: *1933 Southampton* **Died:** *1998*
Playing career: *Southampton, Chelsea (1951-1961)*
Southampton born Sillett, a full-back like
his dad, followed in his father's footsteps
and inherited some of his old man's magic
to make the grade. Signing for Saints as
a schoolboy, he was capped by England
at youth level and would go on to earn
three caps for the full national side in
1955. Played 65 times on the south coast
before moving to Chelsea after the cash
strapped Saints were forced to sell several
prize assets in an extensive firesale. Sillett
plundered 34 goals for Chelsea - a record
for a defender and one only since usurped
by John Terry - including the winner that
finally handed the west London side the
top flight title.

Went on to play almost 300 times at
Stamford Bridge, before moving to
Guildford City. Had two stints at Ashford
Town as player-manager (with a certain
Roy Hodgson signed by Sillett) and also
managed Sussex-based Hastings - again
across two spells. Sillett - one of the best
defenders of his era - died aged 65 after a
battle with cancer.

Simpson, Alexander
Half-back
Born: *1924 Glasgow, Scotland* **Died:** *2008*
Playing career: *Wolves , Notts County,*
Southampton, Shrewsbury Town, (1947-1958)
Moving to Southampton as part of the deal
that took Jack Edwards the other way to
Notts County, Simpson was a man with
"an excellent temperament" and he was
made captain after only four games at
The Dell. Simpson would break an ankle,
though, and was unable to save the Saints
from relegation. He would recover but
lost his place to Rob McLaughlin amidst
a catalogue of injuries including a broken
arm, and being knocked unconscious
during a match. Played 75 times in
three seasons for Saints, scoring once.
After retirement, Simpson returned to
Wolverhampton where he worked in his
family's fish and chip business.

Simpson, Terence
Wing-half
Born: *1938 Southampton*
Playing career: *Southampton, Peterborough*
United, WBA, Walsall, Gillingham, (1954-1973)
Rose through the ranks and captained the
Reserves to the FA Youth Cup semi finals.
Terry Paine - one of his team mates in that
side - would quickly go on to first team
stardom, but Simpson would have to wait
a further 18 months for his first team debut.
He would never fully establish himself at
The Dell, playing 27 times without scoring
before losing his place to Ken Birch. He
later played for Peterborough, West Brom
(playing in two League Cup finals), Walsall
and Gillingham. A broken leg ended his
professional career, so Simpson returned to
Southampton to play for Swaythling whilst
employed for the *Ford Transit* works in the
area.

Skacel, Rudi

Attacking Midfielder

Born: *1979 Trutnov, Czechoslovakia*

Playing career: *Hradec KrAlove, Slavia Prague, Marseille, Panathinaikos, Heart of Midlothian, Southampton, Hertha BSC , Slavia Prague, Larissa, Heart of Midlothian, Dundee United, Slavia Prague, MladA Boleslav, Raith Rovers, FK (1985-)*

Described as an "energetic, exciting, all round player," "Rudi" Skacel - capped seven times by the Czech national team - played for George Burley and Hearts and then followed him to Southampton. Won two Scottish Cups north of the border at Tynecastle and would divide much of his career between his homeland, Scotland, Greece - via France and Germany - and his three years at Saints. Although mainly a midfield player, Skacel admitted that Saints fans "never saw the best of him" in part mainly due to him filling in at left-back following the departure of Gareth Bale. Played over eighty games (five goals) and had a brief spell with Hertha Berlin on loan before returning to Saints. Skacel would be released and had a whistle stop European tour before retiring. He most recently coached at former side Slavia Prague in his native Czech Republic.

Slade, Donald

Centre-forward

Born: *1888 Southampton*

Died: *1980*

Playing career: *Southampton Ramblers , Southampton, Lincoln City, Woolwich Arsenal, Fulham, Dumbarton, Ayr United, Dundee United (1908-1923)*

Prolific in schoolboy football, Slade - a bricky by trade - was plucked from local obscurity to Blackpool. He would never cut the mustard in tangerine, and so returned home' to rejoin Southampton and, this time, make a go of things. Despite his impressive form at Reserve team level - 68 goals in two seasons - Slade would only get sporadic chances in the first team. Filled in for the injured Harry Brown for the last matches of the 1910-11 season and then played twice the following season before wrangling a free transfer to Lincoln. Played for them, Arsenal and Fulham in England before playing for three clubs in Scotland after the war. During the conflict,

Slade worked for Harland & Wolff where he maintained the brick linings for the furnaces. Guested for Saints in wartime football before retiring in 1923. Slade ran a succession of pubs - *The Lion* in Reading, the *Green Dragon* in Flackwell Heath, and *The Swan* in Beaconsfield before moving back to Southampton where he worked as a warden for the National Trust.

Slater, Robbie

Midfielder

Born: *1964 Ormskirk*

Playing career: *Anderlecht, RC Lens, Blackburn Rovers, West Ham, Southampton, Wolverhampton Wanderers, Northern Spirit (1982-2001)*

English born Aussie, Slater began his career in his adopted nation but he would return to his homeland, and his native Lancashire, to join Blackburn. Won the league at Ewood Park and then had a season at West Ham before signing for Graeme Souness at Saints. He instantly became a regular and played 30 times s the Saints avoided relegation. Played a further eleven times for Dave Jones but fell out of favour and signed for Wolves. Tried his luck in the NSL in Australia but retired in 2002 to move into coaching. Having established the Robbie Slater Academy, he worked for Fox Sports and regularly featured on Australian radio as a commentator. Slater was capped 44 times by his native Socceroos, scoring one goal. Slater was the subject of an attempt on his life when he was attacked by PSG fans during his days in France, but recovered after a week in hospital.

Robbie Slater

Small, Archibald

Inside-forward
Born: *1889 Droitwich* **Died:** *1955*
Career: *Southampton, (1911-1920)*

A prominent member of the all conquering Royal Engineers side, 'Archie' Small was working for Ordnance Survey when he came to the attentions of Southampton. Scored on his debut for the Southern League Saints against West Ham and went on to earn Hampshire Representative honours, playing nine games in succession to help the Saints avoid the drop. Beset by injury, Small would only feature sporadically until the outbreak of WW1. He served as a sapper (a soldier responsible for jobs such as building and repairing bridges and roads) during the conflict, also becoming a Warrant Officer. He returned to his former side at the Royal Engineers before returning to the OS in the map mounting section. Died in 1955.

Small, Henry

Inside-forward
Born: *1881 Southampton* **Died:** *1946*
Playing career: *Freemantle, Southampton, Manchester United, Salisbury City (1900-1905)*

Henry Small aka "Ranji" scored on his debut for Saints but only made four Southern League appearances in two seasons, many due to his role of understudy to Edgar Chadwick. Having failed to establish himself. Small moved north to an emerging second tier side, a Newton Heath-based club that had just changed moniker to become Manchester United. He failed to make the first team at Bank Street (United's home in their pre Old Trafford days) and so returned south to The Dell. Small eventually turned out for non league Salisbury before becoming a painter and decorator. Died in 1946.

"DID YOU KNOW?"

"Remarkably, Saints won the Southern League championship for three years running between 1897 and 1899 and again in 1901, 1903 and 1904."

Small, John

Half-back
Born: *1889 Middlesbrough* **Died:** *1946*
Playing career: *Sunderland, Southampton, Thornycrofts, Mid Rhondda (1912-1920)*

A "sturdy half-back" John 'Jack' Small spent much of his early career in Sunderland's second string, playing only once for the first team before moving to Southampton. His attitude and influence on team spirit instantly endeared him to colleagues and fans alike. Became a regular at half-back until the arrival of John Denby pushed Small down the pecking order. With his career interrupted by the outbreak of WW1, Small served in the Army Medical Corps but would be invalided home after 16 months in Greece. Once recovered, he worked and played for Harland & Wolff and had a stint with Thorneycrofts before moving to Mid- Rhondda in the Welsh league. He later joined the Merchant Navy as an assistant storeman on the *Empress of Scotland* ocean liner.

Smallwood, Frederick

Outside-forward
Born: *1910 Brynteg, Wales* **Died:** *1965*
Playing career: *Wrexham, Chester, Macclesfield Town, Southampton, Reading, Newcastle United, Sunderland, Hartlepool United (1933-1940)*

Nippy and diminutive yet powerful, Fred Smallwood fitted the mould of the archetypal winger. A superstitious man, he would carry a rabbit's foot amulet in the pocket of his match day shorts, thought to be a symbol of good luck. Whether it worked or not, Smallwood became a virtual ever present, missing only one game in his debut season at The Dell having joined George Goss's side from Macclesfield. Smallwood scored on his debut, but injury in pre-season saw him displaced by new signing Harry Osman and he eventually moved to Reading. Scored ten goal in 50 games for the south coast side. Guested for Wrexham and a string of other sides during the War before settling in Southampton and becoming involved in a band. Later worked as a boiler fitter on the Docks. During his playing days, Smallwood played for his native Wales at amateur level.

Smith, Eugene
Half-back
Born: *1878 Southampton*
Died: *1951*
Playing career: *Bitterne, Southampton St. Mary's (1896-1903)*

Known for his distance kicking, "Victor" Smith would often try to thump the ball the length of the field, although this unusual attribute was rarely utilised during a match. Southampton born and bred, Smith had three stints at Saints but mainly had to be content with long spells at Reserve team level. Captaining the club at that standard, Smith would find regular first team game time harder to come by, featuring only sporadically. Smith played only five Southern League matches, filling in whenever the likes of Al Littlehales or Tommy Bowman were injured or unavailable. Smith retired after a further two Reserve team seasons, going on to work as a full time police officer. He served the force for almost three decades, reaching the rank of Sergeant whilst still watching Saints as a season ticket holder.

Smith, Frederick
Full-back
Born: *1887 Buxton*
Died: *1957*
Playing career: *Buxton, Wigan Town, Stockport County, Derby County, Macclesfield, Southampton, Macclesfield (1904-1923)*

Spent most of his football career in the North West, except for a stint at Southampton in the final post-War season. A relative veteran at 28 by the time he signed for Saints, Smith - a motor mechanic by trade - captained the Reserve side before a run of three straight defeats saw first team manager Ernest Arnfield turn to several fresh faces in a bid to stop the rot. Smith went on to play 16 times in the 1913-4 campaign, where his "determination and speed" proved valuable. He was displaced by Richard Brooks before moving back to Macclesfield to play part time whilst working as a welder during the War.

Smith, George
Half-back/Inside-forward
Born: *1879 Preston* **Died:** *1908*
Playing career: *Preston North End, Aston Villa, New Brompton, Blackburn Rovers, Plymouth Argyle, Southampton (1899-1908)*

Smith (no relation to any of the other "Smiths" mentioned here), started out at his hometown team Preston, going on to Villa and Blackburn. A forward with a "hard shot" but one prone to "over elaboration," he arrived at Southampton in the twilight of his career, covering to an inside forward. Dovetailing in attack with Frank Jefferis, John Bainbridge and John Lewis, his versatility saw him turn out in five different positions during his debut season. Played 21 times for the Southern League Saints and another six in the FA Cup (five goals) as the club reached the semi finals only to fall to eventual winners Wolves. After retirement, Smith played cricket locally but collapsed and died suddenly in 1908 shortly before turning 29.

Smith, George
Full-back/Half-back
Born: *1886 Peartree Green* **Died:** *1978*
Playing career: *Peartree Green, Southampton (1907-1912)*

A brewery bottle maker before turning to football, Smith - locally born - was a one club man but despite his loyalty, he only played 20 times for the first team in five years. He had played locally for Woolston and Netley where he caught the eye of Southampton coach George Carter. Carter was involved in running the Reserve side and Smith had success at second string level, though, becoming captain and winning six honours - two Hampshire Senior Cups, the Hampshire League twice and the Southampton Senior Cup on two occasions. Capable of playing anywhere in defence or in attack, Smith was often used to fill the void and deputise for any of Southampton's more established faces. Despite being far from a regular, he had a benefit match before emigrating to Australia. There, he worked on the ships whilst playing amateur football in Sydney. Smith later worked in housing and always made sure he followed the Saints.

Smith, George

Half-back

Born: *1919 Portsmouth* **Died:** *2001*
Playing career: *Huddersfield Town, Southampton, Crystal Palace (1936-1951)*

Like so many players of his era, Smith "lost" four years of his career as war broke out, and he settled for a combination of military service and "unofficial" wartime football. Nicknamed the Guernsey Terrier due to his tenacity and hard-working style, he started out in the Reserves before replacing Frank Hill and becoming virtual ever present in Tom Parker's evolving Saints side. During the War he saw active service as a rear gunner on the Lancaster bomber and then a PTE instructor, before resuming his football career at The Dell. Smith went on to play over 100 games before retiring in 1950. Coached at Braintree before emigrating to Australia where he worked as an ambulance driver and for a gas company.

Smith, Paul

Goalkeeper

Born: *1979 Epsom*
Playing career: *Charlton Athletic, Brentford, Southampton, Nottingham Forest, Middlesbrough, Southend United (1997-2016)*

With Antti Niemi firmly installed as Southampton's first choice, Smith had to settle for the role of back up stand in. He would play in the cups when Niemi was given a breather, or unavailable through injury. When Niemi left newly relegated Saints, Smith - whom had waited patiently - got his chance. Dropped to third choice after the signings of Bartosz Bialkowski and Kevin Miller, so he moved on to Nottingham Forest. Made history by scoring after 15 seconds in a game with local rivals Leicester. The unusual goal happened in a replayed match - with the initial League Cup abandoned after Clive Clarke collapsed when Forest led 1-0. Leicester allowed Forest to walk the ball in unchallenged, thereby restoring their previous advantage, in a wonderful piece of sportsmanship that dominated the headlines throughout the world. Later played for Southend and Smith is currently Colchester United's goalkeeping coach.

Smith, Stanley

Outside-right

Born: *1884 Southampton*
Died: *1956*
Playing career: *Southampton Cambridge, Ryde, Bitterne Guild, Southampton (1908-1911)*

Described as a "small but plucky winger," he earned a reputation for crossing accurately from seemingly impossible and awkward situations. Yet in his three seasons at The Dell, Smith was a man on the peripheral fringes of the first team and was shuffled around the forward positions during his nine appearances in the senior side, deputising for the likes of John Bainbridge and Harry Brown. Smith left Saints after three years having become a regular at Reserve team level and attracted interest from several Scottish clubs. He would reject each offer, though, to retire from the game and joined the 18th Queen Mary Hussars during WW1.

Smith, Thomas

Outside-right

Born: *1877 Ashton-in-Makerfield*
Died: *1953*
Playing career: *Ashton Town, Preston North End, Southampton, QPR, Preston North End, Ashton Athletic (1893-1901)*

Preston North End already had a player by the name of Tom Smith when this Smith arrived at the Lancashire club. The 'Lilywhites' would make both players available for transfer after only a season, and whilst one Smith moved to Spurs, his less experienced namesake headed for The Dell. There was some confusion at the club, with the board believing they had signed the Spurs Smith, not the one they actually got! Nevertheless, he scored on his Saints debut in the first match at The Dell, a 4-1 win over Brighton. Yet he would find indifferent form, despite becoming a virtual ever present in Saints Southern League side for the remainder of the 1898-99 season. Southampton would win the league that season, but Smith wouldn't stay beyond it, moving to QPR and then dropping into non league with Ashton. He played 24 times for the club and later became a builder.

Smith, William
Centre-forward
Born: *1885 Denaby Main* **Died:** *1933*
Career: *Brentford, Southampton (1912-1915)*
Initially a pony-driver in Yorkshire, Smith's change of career direction took him to Southern league Brentford where he did enough to catch the eye of divisional rivals Southampton. He slotted straight into the side but struggled to recreate the form that had persuaded Saints to sign him. Scored four times in 20 appearances but quickly moved on to join non League Halifax. Served as a PTE during the War before taking up a job as a teacher.

Smithson, Albert
Striker/inside right
Born: *Blackhall, Co Durham*
Playing career: *Horden Colliery Welfare, Southampton, Aldershot, Scarborough, Scunthorpe & Lindsey United (1931-1936)*
Smithson was a regular at Reserve team level but never played for the first team and was released at the end of the 1931-32 season. Later played for Aldershot, Lincoln and Scunthorpe. Smithson served in the Army during the War before retiring to Medway where he worked for the council.

Smoker, Henry
Outside-left
Born: *1881 Hinton Ampner, Hampshire* **Died:** *1966*
Playing career: *Southampton (1900-1904)*
Following in his father's footsteps, Henry Smoker played cricket for Hampshire. A talented, all round, multi functional sportsman, Smoker also played football for Southampton. Initially taken on trial, he spent most of his stay in the Reserves. He would be drafted in to the first team on two occasions but four years apart. He would leave Saints to focus on cricket, taking 7-35 against the touring South Africans in 1907 and playing 31 times for Hampshire at first class level. Served with the Royal Field Artillery in France during the War, rising to the role of Sergeant, before resuming his cricket career. Later joined the staff of Birkenhead School as a groundsman and caretaker, also coaching cricket to the students.

Soltvedt, Trond Egil
Midfielder
Born: *1967 Voss, Norway*
Playing career: *Ny-Krohnborg, Viking, Brann, Rosenborg, Coventry City, Southampton, Sheffield Wednesday (1985-2003)*
A tall, rangy, box-to-box midfielder, Soltvedt - capped four times by Norway - was signed for Southampton by Dave Jones £300,000. Described as an "elegant midfielder with an air of calm" and quickly became a regular, playing just behind Marian Pahars and Matt Le Tissier at the apex of the engine room. He would become dogged by injuries and then ultimately wasn't favoured by Jones successor, Glenn Hoddle. Scored at Liverpool - one of only two league goals - before being released. Soltvedt joined Sheffield Wednesday and went on to captain the Owls, playing 74 times for the club before returning to his native Norway. After retirement, Soldvedt has coached in his native homeland, becoming a PE teacher and has done media and television punditry.

Soye, Jimmy

Inside-forward
Born: *1885 Govan, Scotland*
Died: *1975*
Playing career: *Rutherglen Glencairn, Distillery, Southampton, Newcastle U, Aberdeen (1904-1915)*

An inside-forward with a "good distribution ability," Soye had played in his native Scotland and Northern Ireland - winning the treble with Distillery - before being plucked from the Irish league to join Southampton. He would struggle during his first foray in England, with Soye in and out of the side, playing in seven different positions and only scoring five goals. Lost his place to Frank Jefferis as Saints missed out on a third successive title, with Soye moving north to Newcastle after only one season at Saints. Played 18 times for the club and would hardly fare better at Newcastle, playing only seven times in three seasons, with the club winning the league in two of those. Soye returned to Scotland to Aberdeen, scoring on his debut and going on to play over 200 times for the Dons. Served as an engineer during WWII, playing part time in Northern Ireland after the conflict, later becoming a farmer.

Spedding, Duncan

Midfielder
Born: *1977 Camberley*
Playing career: *Southampton, Northampton Town (1994-2003)*

A blink and you miss it Saints career, Spedding was signed by Saints as a schoolboy and rose through the ranks to get an opportunity under Dave Jones. It would be a chance he'd miss though, playing only seven times and failing to make an impact. A tall, left-sided wing-back, Spedding would move on to Northampton Town and had five years there, playing over 100 games and helping the club to promotion. Released in 2003, Spedding went on to become the manager of a health spa in Derby and then a co-director of a health and fitness company - *Serious about Fitness* - in Wootton. Ultimately, the Duncan Spedding story is the tale of the one who got away.

Speedie, David

Striker
Born: *1960 Glenrothes, Scotland*
Playing career: *Barnsley, Darlington, Chelsea, Coventry City, Liverpool, Blackburn Rovers, Southampton, Leicester City (1978-2007)*

Since retirement, Speedie - a former coal miner - has coached at non-league level, worked as a player agent and scouted for Chelsea - the club with which he is most associated. He currently lives in Ireland where he regularly features on radio and on television for RTE and ESPN providing commentary and analysis for Premier League matches. In 2018, Speedie was given €85,000 (£75,000) in damages after the Sunday World newspaper accused him of alleged criminal activity - allegations which were proven to be defamatory by a High Court. Speedie has continued to work at Chelsea, hosting hospitality events and working for their Media channels. He has represented the Blues in ex-Legends events and had a stint on the board of the Scottish FA. Speedie had the nickname of "pocket battleship" during his career.

Spence, George

Half-back/Inside-forward
Born: *1877 Rothesay, Argyll and Bute, Scotland*
Playing career: *St Mirren, Derby County, Gainsborough T, Reading, Preston NE, Southampton, Hull C, Clyde, Cowdenbeath (1897-1907)*

A "fast and tricky winger who loved working hard." Spence spent all of his playing days alternating between the Anglo-Scottish border. He would spend eight years in England, helping Southampton to their sixth and final Southern League title during his solitary season on the south coast (1903/04). One of the most notable things about Spence was his versatility - in his 14 games for Saints, manager Ernest Arnfield deployed his charge in seven different positions. Briefly made the left-half position his own, but moved on to Hull having helped Saints to the league championship. Had two seasons on Humberside before returning to his native Scotland where he played for Clyde and Cowdenbeath. Spence later became a masseur in the salt water swimming baths back in his native Rothesay.

Spencer, Tommy

Striker/Central defender
Born: *1945 Glasgow, Scotland*
Playing career: *Southampton, York City, Workington, Lincoln City, Rotherham. (1965-1977).*
A burly centre-forward plucked from the backwaters of his native Scotland, Spencer's Southampton days saw play three times as the Saints earned promotion into the top flight. After hanging up his boots, Spencer moved in coaching, taking charge of Nuneaton and serving as assistant at Boston United.

Sperring, Alistair

Goalkeeper
Born: *1963 Hayling Island*
Playing career: *Southampton, Swindon Town, Bognor Regis Town, Hayling United (1980-1986)*
There was a certain irony that Alistair Sperring's path to stardom was blocked by the man Sperring described as his "boyhood idol" in Peter Shilton. He would never make a league appearance for the club, playing once in a League Cup tie at Rotherham in 1983. Six minutes into his debut, Sperring was injured in a collision with team-mate Mark Wright who suffered a broken nose in the incident. Had stints at Swindon and non league Bognor and Hayling, before setting up his own car business. Became the managing director at Havant Motors and then worked for Ford.

Stage, William

Inside-forward
Born: *1893 Whitby* **Died:** *1957*
Playing career: *Middlesbrough, Hibernian, St Bernard's, Bury, Burnley, Southampton, Darwen, Rossendale United , Fleetwood (1913-1931)*
In the twilight of his career at 37 by the time he arrived at The Dell, Stage joined Southampton in 1930 and spent much of his time there in the Reserve team, also coaching the second string. An archetypal "fetcher and forager" despite his advancing years, Stage would find first team game time hard to come by, playing only four times and scoring once (in his last appearances against Charlton). Later played in non league in Lancashire until his mid 40s and then became licensee of the *Stanley Arms* in Bury.

Stansbridge, Leonard

Goalkeeper
Born: *1919 Southampton* **Died:** *1986*
Playing career: *Southampton, Basingstoke Town , Southampton Schools (1936-1953)*
A winner of the national schools trophy with Southampton, Stansbridge - a local lad - joined as an amateur before signing pro a few months later. He would go on to feature in every peace-time season until 1952, accumulating games in goal mainly as trusty, reliable back up. Served at Dunkirk during WW2 before being captured and made a prisoner of war. Guested for Saints before serving as first choice until the arrival of George Ephgrave, and eventually moved to non league Basingstoke. Served Saints for 17 years, including the is years he spent at war, making 52 appearances but staying loyal and proving an able deputy when needed. Worked at Southampton Sports Centre as a groundsman, eventually returning to The Dell in the same role before retiring. Died 1986 aged 67.

Statham, Derek

Full-back
Born: *1959 Wolverhampton*
Playing career: *West Bromwich Albion, Southampton, Stoke City, Walsall. (1976-1991)*
An agile, athletic and lightning quick full-back and fierce in the tackle, Derek Statham burst onto the scene as a 19-year-old at West Brom. Regarded as a solid, classy defender with excellent distribution, he made over 350 appearances for the Black Country side in Ron Atkinson's impressive side with the likes of Bryan Robson, Cyrille Regis and Laurie Cunningham. Moved to Saints and was voted Player of the Season in his debut campaign under Chris Nicholl. Statham featured 80 times for the club in two seasons, before moving to Stoke. Also played for Walsall in his native west Midlands and had a stint with non league Telford. Capped three times by Bobby Robson's England, Statham would almost certainly have added to that tally if not for Kenny Sansom. Later sold spas and hot tubs in Spain, working in corporate hospitality whilst strutting his stuff on the Costa del Sol golf courses.

Stead, William

Goalkeeper
Born: *1887 Portsmouth* **Died:** *1939*
Playing career: *Southampton, Aberdeen, Salisbury City, Clapton Orient, Salisbury City (1905-1920)*
Portsmouth born but signed to Southampton as a teenager, Bill Stead initially found himself as third choice but played in six games in the Southern League, its Western equivalent and the FA Cup. He played in the first ever meeting between the two fierce rivals, his current employers winning against the city of his birth 5-1 in front of a capacity crowd at The Dell with Stead showing "nerves of steel and great confidence" during the game. After WWI, he served as a seaman on the *Mauritania* and then worked for the *Union Castle* line with the *Durban Castle*.

Steele, James "Jim"

Centre-back
Born: *1950 Edinburgh, Scotland*
Playing career: *Heart of Midlothian, Dundee, Southampton, Rangers, Washington Diplomats, Pittsburgh Spirit, Memphis Rogues, Chicago Sting, (1965-1981)*
Moved to the USA where he played at semi-professional level for a while before injury forced the 76' FA Cup winner to hang up his boots. He found work in Washington, operating HGVs before becoming a foreman at an electrical plant and running a bar in the capital. He would return 'home' to Edinburgh in 1995 before Steele moved back to Southampton where he ran a number of pubs including the *White Horse* in the New Forest and *Black Bear* in Moreton-in-Marsh with both becoming popular with Saints fans. He was also the manager and proprietor of the Hampshire Irish nightclub and bar in Eastleigh. After a decade there, Steele left hospitality for the holiday sector, running a caravan site near Lymington and also working for Saints as an after dinner speaker, a hospitality host and for their media channels as a match summariser. Steele was, memorably, man of the match in the Wembley win over United, at the heart of the Southampton defence alongside Mel Blyth. He lives in retirement in Hedge End.

Stekelenburg, Maarten

Goalkeeper
Born: *1982 Haarlem, Netherlands*
Playing career: *Ajax, Roma, Fulham, Monaco, Southampton, Everton (1997-Still Playing)*
A Dutch international with 58 caps for his country, Stekelenburg linked up with compatriot Ronald Koeman at St Mary's. Spent the 2015-16 season on loan at Saints from Fulham, making 17 appearances and playing in Europe, before following his fellow Dutchman to Merseyside when Koeman took over at Everton. As of 2020, the goalkeeper is back in his native homeland with his first club, Ajax, having won two league titles and three domestic cups during his first stint with the Amsterdam giants. World Cup runner up in 2010 and played at Euro 2012.

Stensgaard, Michael

Goalkeeper
Born: *1974 Copenhagen, Denmark*
Playing career: *Hvidovre, Liverpool, Copenhagen, Southampton, Copenhagen (1993-2001)*
Danish Under 21 international with eight caps, he spent five years in English football without ever playing. He was signed by Liverpool as understudy David James, in the absence of the recently departed Bruce Grobbelaar. He would never break into the first team, his chances hampered by a bizarre dislocated shoulder sustained by an ironing board! Aged 21, he would have two surgeries before returning to Denmark for rehabilitation. Coached at FC Hvidore, he rejoined Copenhagen and was able to resume his career. Ended up at Southampton as back up cover for Paul Jones, but would drop to third choice and returned once again to Copenhagen having never played for Saints. Retired at 26 through injury to work as a business conflict mediator. Lectured at the University of Copenhagen and is also employed as a players' agent.

"DID YOU KNOW?"

"Peter Osgood was alleged to have taken the FA cup home and slept with it after the 1976 victory!"

Steven, David

Inside-forward
Born: *1878 Dundee, Scotland* **Died:** *1903*
Playing career: *Dundee Violet, Dundee, Bury, Southampton (1896-1903)*

Spent most of his career in Scotland with hometown team Dundee, with two spells across the border in England sandwiched in between. Struggled to break into the Bury side ahead of established England man Jack Plant, eventually falling out with club's powers that be and returning north of the border. After another brief stint with Dundee, Steven was on the move again, this time to Southern League Southampton. Steven's "fearless, dashing forward play" instantly endeared him to team-mates, supporters and coaches alike. He did enough to collect two league title medals though, alternating with Harry Wood in the Saints first season at The Dell to help them to a third consecutive Southern League championship. He returned to Dundee in search of regular first team game time, but would die of a heart attack aged only 25 in 1903.

Stevens, Samuel

Wing-half
Born: *1935 Rutherglen, Scotland*
Playing career: *Queen's Park, Airdrieonians, Southampton (1956-1989)*

Scottish winger, started out as an amateur with Queen's Park before serving in the Royal Corps of Scotland as a PTE. Caught the eye of Ted Bates during a guest appearance for Southampton and the Saints manager watched his progress carefully. Described as a good sportsman and a "committed, whole-hearted left back," Stevens initially played for the Reserves before breaking into the senior side and going on to impress during a run of games linking up with Charlie Livesey, alternating with Bobby McLaughlin before being released in 1959. Moved to Poole Town under former Saints manager Mike Keeping, before turning out for several local non clubs and a spell at Swaythling as player-manager. Coached the Saints youth team, combining this role with a job as a PE teacher in Winchester and also later worked for the Hampshire FA.

Stevenson, Ernie

Inside-forward
Born: *1923 Rotherham*
Died: *1970*
Playing career: *Wolverhampton Wanderers, Cardiff City, Southampton, Leeds United (1946-1952)*

Had his early career disrupted by the outbreak of the scond world war, having started out as a teenage trainee with Wolverhampton Wanderers. He moved on to Cardiff City, top scoring for the Welsh side in the first post-War season before Southampton manager Sid Cann - impressed by his performance for the visiting Bluebirds at the Dell - fought off the interest of several top flight teams to bring the Rotherham born Yorkshireman to the south coast. Wilf Grant moved the other way in an exchange deal but Stevenson was never able to fully establish himself and left for Leeds United after less than a year having made only 24 appearances for the club, scoring eight goals. Later became a non league referee. The former inside forward died back in his home town in October 1970. He was only 46 at the time.

Steventon, Edwin

Goalkeeper
Born: *1891 Nantwich*
Died: *1961*
Playing career: *Walsall, Wednesbury Old Athletic, Southampton, Aston Villa, Nantwich Victoria, Stoke, Nantwich Victoria, Wolverhampton W (1914-1922)*

Midlands born, 'Ted' Steventon had an illustrious career as a cricketing amateur alongside less well known playing days as a goalkeeper. Steventon dismissed 1,554 batsmen as a reputable fast bowler playing for Nantwich, Crewe, Cheshire and Staffordshire. After playing for Nantwich FC, he joined Shrewsbury - winning the Shropshire Cup - and had trials with Villa without success. Played for Stourbridge and then joined Stoke, deputising for Percy Knott for three games in the 1920-21 season. Served Southampton and Wolves as back up keeper without getting a game in goal before retiring in 1940. Steventon ran a Nantwich footwear business and served as chairman of the Midland Cricket League for many years. Died in 1971 aged 70.

Stoddart, William
Centre-half
Born: *1907 Leadgate, County Durham*
Died: *1972*
Playing career: *West Stanley, Manchester City, Coventry City, Southampton, Bristol Rovers, Accrington Stanley, Annfield Plain (1926-1934)*
Despite being with struggling third tier Coventry, a series of fine individual performances earned him a chance with Second Division Saints, having impressed Southampton manager Arthur Chadwick. So much so, that Chadwick was willing to sell Tom Allen and Bill Henderson to bring Stoddart to The Dell. He would never fully establish himself, despite becoming a regular at reserve team level. He would feature over 100 times for the second string, but he played only 12 times for the first team in three years, mainly due to the consistency of George Harkus. Latterly played for Bristol Rovers, Accrington and non-league Annfield Plain based in Durham. In retirement, Stoddart coached at Accrington Stanley and worked as a mechanic during and after WW2.

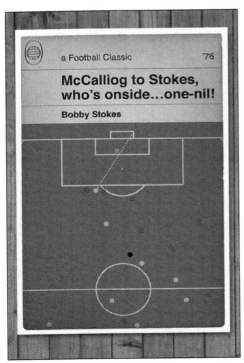

Poster available from https://www.etsy.com

Stokes, Bobby
Forward
Born: *1951 Portsmouth* **Died:** *1995*
Career: *Southampton, Portsmouth. (1968-1977)*
The scorer of the most iconic goal in Southampton history wrote himself into Saints folklore with the 83rd minute winner in 76'. Mick Channon's flick to Jim McCalliog to hit Stokes clean through - with a low finish past Alex Stepney, is a sequence that has been replayed hundreds of times everywhere. It is ironic that he was transfer-listed throughout the season that would end in FA Cup glory, playing in every round prior to his Wembley heroics. Stokes played over 200 games before moving to join his hometown team Portsmouth. Had a solitary season with them before jetting across to the 'States to play for Washington Diplomats. Later turned out in non league for Havant and Cheltenham. In retirement, Stokes ran a pub in Pompey and also worked in his cousin's cafe on the harbour. Stokes has a suite named after him at St Mary's as well as Stokes Court, a block of flats on the site of Saints former home.

Stride, William
Half-back
Born: *1865 Southampton* **Died:** *1942*
Playing career: *Freemantle, Southampton Harriers, Southampton St. Mary's (1887-1894)*
Stride had won sprint titles at both national and regional level as an amateur and played for Freemantle as a formidable half-back and then for Southampton Harriers. Joined "The Saints" when the Harriers disbanded. His time at the club pre-dated St Mary's days as a league club, so Stride would feature in a team which only played in FA Cup, Hampshire Junior Cup and its senior equivalent. He would go on to play over 100 times although the vast majority of these came in non-competitive friendly fixtures. Southampton would become founding members of the newly formed Southern League - a division giving clubs outside the league system a chance to play competitive professional league football. Stride, not wanting to commit to the new venture, remained in Southampton to work for the council as an engineer.

Stroud, William
Wing-half
Born: *1919 London* **Died:** *2006*
Playing career: *Southampton, Leyton Orient, Newport County , Hastings United (1938-1954)*
Despite his lengthy career with the Saints, Bill Stroud only had one season as an established first teamer. A combative and hard working Saint, his career was interrupted by the outbreak of WWII, but he played almost 200 games in non competitive wartime fixtures for Saints and Chelsea - only Albie Roles and Ted Bates played more. Initially a forward, Stroud converted to a wing-half and moved on to Leyton Orient, in exchange for Ted Ballard, having played 29 games for the Saints. Later turned out for Newport and wound up back in the Southern League with Sussex club Hastings. After retiring, Stroud went back to Newport as reserve team coach and then returned to Southampton, too, where he served as youth team assistant boss. Stroud helped to develop the likes of Mick Channon, Matt Le Tissier and Alan Shearer before retiring in 1987. He also briefly worked for the Hampshire FA.

Summers, John
Outside-forward
Born: 1915 Chorlton, Manchester **Died:** *1991*
Playing career: *Manchester North End, Burnley, Fleetwood, Preston North End, Leicester City, Derby County, Southampton (1931-1938)*
Rose left local non league football to join top flight Burnley as a trainee. Never played for their first team but attracted interest from Manchester United only for the Clarets hierarchy to veto the move. Turned out fo Lancashire rivals Preston and then went to Leicester and Derby before arriving at Southampton for £250. Striking up a partnership with Dick Neal, Summers became first choice at outside forward, playing 30-odd games before injury stopped him in his tracks. Lost his place to Bill Bevis and retired soon after. Summers became a full time member of the police force until 1968, winning the Police Cup with several other ex Saints men. Later became chairman of the Southampton Police football committee until his dying day aged 76 in 1991.

Svensson, Anders
Midfielder
Born: *1976 Gothenburg, Sweden*
Playing career: *Guldhedens IK, Hestrafors IF, Elfsborg, Southampton, (1980-2015)*
The Swedish Beckham, the eldest of Southampton's two (unrelated) Svenssons, is the most capped player for his country and was renowned for his dead eye set piece abilities, his passing range and playmaking role. Svensson captained Southampton and played in the 2003 FA Cup final also featuring in the UEFA Cup for the club. Played 140 times for Southampton, silencing his critics who dismissed him as something of a show pony. Svensson would also captain Sweden and played in five major tournaments - three Euros (2004, 2008 and 2012) and two World Cup finals (2002 and 2006) - scoring a 30 yard free kick against Argentina in the former. Played 148 times for Sweden and is the eighth most capped European player in history. Returning to Elfsborg, Svensson would play for another decade in his native homeland before retiring and has since launched a media career on Swedish radio and television. Twitter: https://twitter.com/anders8svensson

Svensson, Michael

Centre-back
Born: *1975 Varnamo, Sweden*
Playing career: *Halmstads BK, Troyes, Southampton, Halmstads BK (1993-2013)*
Swedish international centre-back with 25 caps whom rose to prominence with Halmstads BK in his homeland. Svensson was snapped up by Saints for £2m from the French club Troyes and slotted straight into the centre of defence alongside Scandinavian colleague Claus Lundekvam, helping the club to the FA Cup final in his debut season. Having been a virtual ever present, an injury sustained in the warm up meant he missed the best part of two years. Svensson would endure a injury ravaged four seasons but, having worked his way back to full fitness, was made Saints skipper. Svensson played 85 times for Saints and later worked on the coaching staff under Mark Wotte. Represented Sweden at the 2002 World Cup during his playing days. Latterly served as assistant manager, coach and head of Academy at former club Halmstads.

Swinden, James

Inside-forward
Born: *1905 Fulham* **Died:** *1971*
Playing career: *Southampton, (1922-1929)*
Worked as a fitter on the railways at Eastleigh whilst playing part time for their works team. Turned out in non league with Winchester and Salisbury before earning a trial at Saints. Scored twice on his Reserves team debut and duly signed pro, quickly earning a reputation as a "small and tricky" winger. What he lacked in size he more than made up for in pace and trickery, playing three games for the Saints first team, deputising for the injured Bill Rawlings and Jerry Mackie respectively but, despite staying at the club for the next three years, he would never play for Southampton again. Swinden returned to his original trade as a railway worker, staying involved in local football with Newport IoW and Pirelli General, coaching both clubs and also working for the Hampshire FA.

Sydenham, John

Forward
Born: *1939 Southampton*
Playing career: *Southampton, Aldershot (1956-1971).*
Having become an eye-catching and stylish member of Southampton's exclusive 400-club, Sydenham wound down at Aldershot before he emigrated to Australia. Played for Perth Glory before Sydenham hung up his boots, going on to set up an insurance company which he ran with his wife. Coached the State side and became player-coach of Athena, before working as Southampton's official Australian-based scout. Two of his recommendations, Brett Emerton and Chris Herd, went on to make it at professional and both played in the Premier League. Sydenham set up a coaching academy, nurturing any young talent coming through, but his soccer school folded in 2014, and since then Sydenham has been the Vice-President and Chairman of the ex-Saints Association, organising legends events and ex-player representation for the club. He continues to live Down Under in retirement, residing in Melbourne.

Tankard, Allen

Left-back
Born: *1969 Islington*
Playing career: *Southampton, Wigan Athletic, Port Vale, Mansfield Town (1985-2003)*

Despite going on to play over 500 professional games, Allen Tankard - an attacking, London-born left-back - never cut it at Saints. He only featured five times for the club and was then released, being signed by emerging force Wigan Athletic. Racked up a half century of games for the Lancashire Latics, moving on again when they were relegated. Tankard joined divisional rivals Port Vale for a record £87,500 under John Rudge, helping them to promotion to the top flight for the first time in their history. Played for Mansfield and wound down in non league locally, before retiring. Tankard - voted Vale's greatest ever left-back, retired and briefly coached at Vale before setting up a minibus and coach hire company.

Taylor, Ernie

Half-back
Born: *1871 Liverpool* **Died:** *1944*
Playing career: *St. Cuthberts, Stanley, Everton, Southampton St. Mary's, Freemantle (1892-1896)*

Set sail for Southampton through his work with Philadelphia Shipping company *American Line*. Transferring its mail service from New York to the south coast, Taylor came with them in time for the football club's inaugural season in the Southern League. Even when the side was sprinkled with professionals, amateur Taylor managed to hold his own. A versatile player equally as adept at attacking as he was defensively, he would only play intermittently due to work commitments. Taylor would feature 19 times for Saints in three seasons whilst remaining an amateur before moving into non-league with Southampton's local rivals Freemantle. Taylor played as a cricketer with Hamble and Deanery and represented Hampshire in three different sports. Worked as head of operations and then as chief cashier for the infamous *White Star Line* and also ran their Sports Association, with Taylor responsible for setting up the annual football match for the seaman's orphanage in 1899.

Taylor, Frederick

Inside-forward
Born: 1890 *Halesowen* **Died:** *1970*
Playing career: *Stourbridge, Hull City, Wellington Town , Southampton, Barrow (1910-1915)*

Employed as a tool-maker, Fred Taylor was plucked from the obscurity of the Midlands League by Southampton's coach (soon to be manager) Jim McIntyre. A forward with an impressive reputation, Taylor had failed to fulfil his potential at Hull but was drafted straight into the side at inside right. He would only score once in his first twelve games and, although Southampton collectively struggled, Taylor was seen as something of a scapegoat for their shortcoming. Taylor's appearances would be few and far between and he moved to Lancashire side Barrow in 1913 after only one campaign at The Dell. Played 15 times for Southampton, scoring twice. Taylor worked in a factory during WW1 and then found employment as an electrician.

Taylor, Gareth

Forward
Born: *1973 Weston-super-Mare*
Playing career: *Southampton, Bristol Rovers, Crystal Palace, Sheffield United, Manchester City, Port Vale (loan), QPR (loan) , Burnley (loan), Nottingham Forest, Crewe Alexandra (loan), Tranmere Rovers, Doncaster Rovers, Carlisle United (loan), Wrexham (1990-2011)*

Having left the Southampton youth system without ever playing for the club at any level, Taylor began a career which would see him with 15 different clubs. A holding midfielder by trade, he developed into a striker and played for Palace after stints in non league with Gloucester City and Weymouth. Taylor went on to play for Sheffield United, Manchester City, QPR, Burnley, Forest, Crewe, Tranmere, Doncaster, Carlisle and Wrexham - earning 15 caps for Wales in the process, despite being born in England (Taylor's father was born in Wales, making Taylor eligibile to play for the country). Played 500 games in an 18-year league career, earning a reputation as a selfless and hard-working - rather than a prolific - striker. As of 2020, Taylor is currently head coach of the women's side at his former club Manchester City.

Taylor, Maik
Goalkeeper
Born: *1971 Hildesheim, West Germany*
Playing career: *Barnet, Southampton, Fulham, Birmingham City, Leeds U, Millwall (1985-2013)*

Northern Ireland international goalkeeper with 88 caps, best known for his time in the Premier League with Fulham and Birmingham. His time at Southampton may seem merely a footnote but for Taylor - a boyhood Saints fan - despite his German roots, it was the realisation of a dream. Played 18 times under Graeme Souness at The Dell, signed on the recommendation of Taylor's Barnet manager, former England no.1 Ray Clemence. Kept a clean sheet on debut, and became a regular for the remainder of that 1996-97 season. When Souness successor Dave Jones signed another Jones - goalkeeper Paul - Taylor was out of favour. Signed for Fulham working under boyhood idol Kevin Keegan who described the keeper as the "best taker of a cross you could find." Went on to play for Birmingham, Leeds and Millwall before retirement. Taylor had the choice to represent any of the four home nations having been born overseas, but he chose Northern Ireland. Taylor has also worked as goalkeeping coach at Bradford. The former keeper is currently helping the next generation of shot-stoppers as he reprises his role as goalkeeping mentor at Walsall.

Maik Taylor

Taylor, Samuel
Inside-forward
Born: *1893 Sheffield* **Died:** *1973*
Playing career: *Huddersfield Town, Sheffield Wed, Mansfield, Southampton, Halifax Town (1919-1930)*

A late developer thanks to the intervention of Adolf Hitler, Taylor was 26 before he made an impact in top level football. Played in the FA Cup final for Huddersfield before moving to Mansfield and Sheffield Wednesday. Joined Saints for £300 and instantly slotted into an attacking quartet with Bill Rawlings, Stan Woodhouse and Billy Murphy. Taylor would immediately endear himself to the Southampton faithful with a goal on his debut against Portsmouth. The four men would become arguably Saints finest pre-War attack, in which Taylor would prove equally adept at finding the net as he would running the channel and working as a decoy for the others to shine. Went on to play almost 80 times in two seasons. After leaving Saints he dropped down to non league level with Halifax and Chesterfield before running a pub in his native Sheffield. He also became an organiser of snooker tournaments and was an accomplished pianist.

Taylor, Thomas
Inside-forward
Born: *1903 Wavertree* **Died:** *1978*
Playing career: *Rhos, Manchester City, Southampton (1925-1929)*

Taylor impressed in the Welsh non league system and earned a crack at the Second Division with Manchester City. He would never play for the club and moved to divisional rivals Southampton in 1927. Due to the exploits of namesake Sammy and Saints impressive four-fold attack, Taylor would never fully establish himself in the side, playing only eight times in four seasons. Despite first team game time being few and far between, Taylor scored four times in those eight games but his contract was terminated at the player's request. After which, he drifted from the banks of the Mersey to the Welsh foothills - and back - for a string of clubs in the lower and non leagues. Taylor would late scout for Tranmere and Liverpool whilst working in a petroleum factory in St Helen's.

Tejera Battagliesi, Marcos

Attacking midfielder
Born: *1973 Montevideo, Uruguay*
Playing career: *Defensor Sporting , Cagliari, Boca Juniors, Tecos UAG, Southampton, Penarol, Nacional, Millonarios, Liverpool (1989-2009)*

Uruguayan midfielder with five caps. Spent the majority of his career in his native South America with nine different clubs before signing for Southampton on trial in 2005. Tejera would join the club at the same time as fellow midfielder and Polish international Kamil Kosowski. Whilst the latter would get 18 games for second tier Saints on loan, Tejera never played for the club at any level and returned to his native Uruguay after only two months at Saints. It never worked out for him at St Mary's. Played for Liverpool (the Uruguayan one, not the Premier League club) and coached at former club Boca Juniors. Tejera has also worked as a player agent in South America.

Telfer, Paul

Right-back
Born: *1971 Edinburgh, Scotland*
Playing career: *Luton Town, Coventry City, Southampton, Celtic, AFC Bournemouth, Leeds United, Slough Town (1988-2010)*

Arrived at St Mary's from Coventry along with newly appointed Saints manager Gordon Strachan. A versatile player capable of playing in either full-back position or in midfield, Telfer was never spectacular but was considered a solid and reliable hard working squad player capable of doing a job wherever and whenever needed. Capped once by Scotland in 2000 and played on the right of midfield in the 2003 FA Cup final in which Saints lost 1-0 to Arsenal. Featured 127 times for Saints, scoring once, and was popular with his managers, his team mates and the fans alike. Went on to win two SPL titles and the domestic cup during his two seasons at Celtic, also turning out for AFC Bournemouth, Leeds and Slough. Had a stint as player-coach of Sutton United and gained an Open University degree in psychology.

Tessem, Jo

Midfielder
Born: *1972 Arland, Norway*
Playing career: *Orland, Lyn, Molde, Southampton, Lyn, Millwall, Bournemouth, Eastleigh, Totton & Eling (1994-Still Playing)*

There are many interesting things about Jo Tessem - with his versatility on the field matched by his life away from football. Whilst rising through the ranks with his first club, BK Orland in his native Norway, Tessem served in the Norwegian Air Force as an engineer. He worked at Vaernes Air Base, loading and unloading aircraft including USAF C-5 Galaxy cargo planes and Chinook helicopters. He combined playing for Lyn with working as a fully qualified police officer, also taking up a job as a security officer and, later, a social services manager. Tessem went on to earn nine caps for Norway and came on as sub in the 2003 FA Cup final. Tessem coached at non-league level at Totton & Eling and has done some media work, appearing on BBC Solent. In 2019-20, he was signed on with ninth tier non league side Hythe & Dibden as player-coach and continued to play in his 50th year!

Thomas, Edwin
Goalkeeper
Born: *1931 Swindon*
Playing career: *Southampton (1949-1956)*

A Swindon born goalkeeper, Thomas worked as a trainee apprentice for British Rail, turning out for their works side. His dad happened to be 'in' with one of the directors of Southampton Football Club whilst another former keeper (turned scout) Ted Nash recommended the young custodian to Saints manager Sid Cann. Thomas became Saints youngest-ever first team goalie, until Bob Charles usurped him in that respect a decade later. Went on to play another nine games for the club before being released. Thomas later reportedly represented Wiltshire in water polo. He also worked as a secretary for the Swindon & District Football League, ran a couple of pubs in the area, and was employed as a draughtsman for the council.

Thomas, Martin
Midfielder
Born: *1973 Lyndhurst*
Playing career: *Southampton, Leyton Orient, Fulham, Swansea City, Brighton & Hove Albion, Oxford United, Exeter City (1992-2004)*

A former trainee with Southampton, Thomas signed pro in 1992 but never played for the club at any level. His Football League debut came with the O's of Leyton Orient, signing at Brisbane Road after six unsuccessful months on the south coast. He failed to establish himself at Orient and became best known for his time at Fulham and Swansea, playing over 200 times combined for those two clubs as a cultured, box-to-box midfielder. Went on to Brighton, Oxford and Exeter in the Football League before dropping into non-league with Eastleigh, Winchester and AFC Totton. He coached at the latter and latterly worked for the Hampshire FA whilst also employed as an insurance salesman.

Thomas, Reginald
Full-back
Born: *1912 Weymouth, Dorset* **Died:** *1983*
Playing career: *Weymouth Central School, Weymouth Wolves, Weymouth, Southampton, Folkestone, Bath City, Guildford City , Sittingbourne, Ashford Town, Dartford, Margate (1930-1939)*

A full-back who had four seasons with Saints, he would only play eight times for the first team - in part due to the longevity and consistency of established right-back Bill Adams. Curiously, both his first and last appearances in the Saints senior side came against south coast rivals Portsmouth. He failed to ever really stand out, breaking a leg in a friendly that forced the end of his professional career. Thomas went on to play for a string of non league clubs but he drifted out of the game and went on to become a policeman. Died in 1983.

Thomas, Wayne
Defender
Born: *1979 Gloucester*
Playing career: *Torquay United, Stoke City, Burnley, Southampton, Doncaster Rovers, Atromitos, Veria, Luton Town, Rochdale, (1995-date)*

Having written to all 92 professional league clubs in request of an opportunity, striker Thomas was signed by Torquay- one of only two clubs to reply. Filling the void left by the Southampton-bound Garry Monk, Thomas went on to play over 100 games at Plainmoor before getting promoted with Stoke. George Burley twice tried to sign him, before finally getting his man having taken over at Saints. Thomas instantly became first choice at the back, with Chris Baird and Pele having left, Alan Bennett out of form and Claus Lundekvam injured. Offering a physical presence, Thomas played 50-odd games for the Saints in the Championship (scoring twice) and stayed with them as the club dropped into the third tier. A series of injuries held him back and he eventually fell out of favour with new manager Alan Pardew. Had a spell in Greece before returning to England and ground-hopping around the lower leagues before moving into coaching. Managed New York Red Bulls Academy side in the MLS, also coaching at Kidderminster and with Rushall Olympic.

Thompson, Dave

Right winger
Born: *1945 Catterick Camp*
Playing career: *Wolverhampton Wanderers , Southampton, Mansfield T, Chesterfield (1962-1974)*

Having made his name at Wolves, Thompson was ready for a "new challenge" and so signed for Second Division Southampton on the word of Saint and next door neighbour Jimmy Melia. With John Sydenham and Terry Paine tearing it up and keeping Thompson out the team, his pass-and-move style seemed a better fit than Wolves more direct, robust approach. Ted Bates tended to use Thompson as a grafting spoiler rather than a creative string-puller, but shuffled him around to such an extent that Thompson never properly settled. He would captain the Reserves and played 24 games for the first team, but later admitted to have "found his level" with lower division Mansfield and then fourth tier Chesterfield. Retiring with injury, Thompson worked for his brother's haulage business, latterly inspecting roads for the council in Leeds.

Thompson, George

Goalkeeper
Born: *1900 Treeton* **Died:** *1968*
Playing career: *York City, Southampton, Dinnington Miners' Welfare (1927-1930)*

Yorkshire-born keeper who had three seasons at Saints, but only played sixteen times as cover for Tommy Allen or Willie White. Spent most of his Saints career with the Reserves, going to play over 100 games at that level and captaining the second string. Kept a clean sheet on his first team debut at Notts County but then ingloriously had a nightmare on his first FA Cup appearance, making two costly errors in a 1-4 Third Round defeat at Bradford. Thompson was eventually demoted to third choice behind White and new arrival Bert Scriven, being placed on the transfer list by Arthur Chadwick. No offers were forthcoming and so he returned to his native Yorkshire, playing locally whilst working in the mines. He later became a foreman. Both of Thompson son's, George Jr, and Des, became professional goalkeepers.

Thomson, William

Full-back
Born: *1873 Chatham, Kent* **Died:** *1940*
Playing career: *Strathmore , Stoke, Southampton St Mary's , Cowes (1892-1900)*

Part of a mass influx of Stoke players, "Lachie" Thomson arrived at Saints in time for their inaugural Southern League campaign in 1884. Alf Littlehales and Charles Baker also arrived from the Potteries, with the three new recruits thrown straight into the side as manager Cecil Knight built a side good enough to compete in league football. Described as "strong with plenty of pluck" Thomson often played with "judgement and plenty of energy" and went on to feature 27 times in the league (another ten matches coming in FA Cup ties). Saints would finish in third place for two successive seasons, but there was always simmering tensions with the board and he left the club, moving to Eastleigh and Cowes. Later coached at that club whilst working on the island as a marine engine fitter. Killed in an air raid on Southampton in 1940.

Thorpe, Frank

Centre-half
Born: *1879 Hayfield, Derbyshire* **Died:** *1928*
Playing career: *Stalybridge Rovers , Newton Heath, Bury, Plymouth Argyle, Southampton (1897-1910)*

A 1903 FA Cup winner with Bury, Thorpe became a mainstay of the Shakers defence for the best part of five years, before moving to Southampton where he played 65 times. Started out at Newton Heath - the club known today as Manchester United - but failed to establish himself, moving to Lancashire rivals Bury. Their 6-0 win over Derby still stands as the record final win (jointly with Manchester City), with Thorpe at the centre of the backline helping to ensure a clean sheet in every round. Moved to Plymouth then moved along the coast to Saints where he would be appointed team captain. Linking up with former Bury team-mate John Johnston, they finished third in hid debut 1907-08 season, before he returned to his beloved Bury at the end of the following season. He coached the club, managing the reserve team and serving as first team assistant.

Tilford, Arthur

Left-back
Born: *1903 Ilkeston* **Died:** *1993*
Playing career: *Trowell St Helens, Nottingham Forest , Blackpool, Coventry City, Fulham, Southampton, Walsall (1924-1935)*

It was personal tragedy that took Fulham's Arthur Tilford to Southampton. When his young daughter died in 1932, the Cottagers manager - former Saints boss Jimmy McIntyre - signed Mike Keeping from Saints and suggested a move to The Dell to help Tilford recover. He played only ten times for Southampton and eventually re-joined Fulham. Also played for Nottingham Forest, Blackpool, Coventry and Walsall thereby featuring in all four professional divisions in England. He returned to his native Derbyshire to play non league before running a fish and chip shop in retirement. Tilford worked in a bakery and as a library cleaner in later life. died in 1993.

Tisdale, Paul

Midfielder
Born: *1973 Valletta, Malta*
Playing career: *Southampton, Northampton Town, Huddersfield Town, Bristol City, Exeter City, Dundee United (1991-2010)*

Born in Malta, but moved to England where he rose through the youth system at Saints, signing for the club as a nine year old and going on to play for them at first team level. Due to their familiar high turnover of managers Tisdale never fully established himself and was loaned out to Huddersfield having played 17 games. Had trials as a cricketer for Somerset but decided to focus on football. Went on to Bristol City and the club he would later become synonymous with, Exeter City. Tisdale moved into management, taking up a position with the University of Bath. Took the club into the first round proper of the FA Cup and led the club to four promotions before being appointed at former side Exeter. He would become both their longest serving and most successful manager ever. After over 600 games in charge and three promotions Tisdale managed MK Dons between 2018-19. Agreed to help Colchester United in advisory capacity in April 2021.

Titmuss, Fred

Full-back
Born: *1898 Pirton, Hertfordshire*
Died: *1966*
Playing career: *Pirton United, Hitchin Town, Southampton, Plymouth Argyle (1919-1923)*

Served in the Lancashire Fusiliers as a gunner during WW1, keeping in contact with Southampton coach Bert Lee throughout the hostilities. He would arrive at the Saints in time for the first post-War season, linking up with future manager Tom Parker in an outstanding left-hand side pairing, described by boss Jimmy McIntyre as the "best pair of backs in the South". Titmuss was an ever-present as Saints won promotion to the Second Division in 1922, with the man himself described as an "expert tackler, although his sound positional play meant this skillset was hardly ever needed." Both Titmuss and Parker would go on to be capped by England, with Fred earning two caps and Parker just the one. Titmuss played 250 times for Southampton before being suddenly frozen out and sold. Played and coached at Plymouth Argyle, working as a mechanic and a licensee until the outbreak of another war. Died in 1966.

Todd, Lee

Defender
Born: *1972 Hartlepool*
Playing career: *Hartlepool United, Stockport County, Southampton, Bradford City, Walsall, Rochdale, Mossley, Stalybridge Celtic (1989-2004)*

Hartlepool born defender, who started out at his hometown club but made his name at Stockport County with 226 league appearances where he played under Dave Jones who then brought him to Southampton in 1997 for a fee of £85,000 along with teammate Paul Jones, but he failed to establish himself at Premier League level. After 10 games, Todd moved onto Bradford City in search of regular football again but again only managed fifteen games in two seasons. Later re-established himself at Rochdale before dropping into non league. Played into his 40s with Stockport-based Fingerpost Flyers FC, later becoming their assistant manager and secretary.

Toman, Wilfred

Centre-forward
Born: *1874 Bishop Auckland* **Died:** *1917*
Playing career: *Dundee, Victoria United, Burnley, Everton, Southampton, Everton, Stockport County, Oldham Athletic, Newcastle United (1896-1907)*
An established Football League forward, Wilf Toman had played for Burnley and Everton when he was scouted and signed by Saints as a replacement for the departed Roddy McLeod. Toman would form an attack alongside Alf Milward and Edgar Chadwick to help Saints to the Southern League title in his debut campaign at The Dell. He returned to Everton after only one season, though, seeing his career wrecked by injury problems. Played for Stockport and briefly had a stints at Oldham, Newcastle and then in Scotland, failing to settle anywhere. Toman was killed in action in France during WW1.

Tomlinson, Isaac

Outside-right
Born: *1880 Chesterfield* **Died:** *1970*
Playing career: *Chesterfield, Arsenal, Chesterfield, Southampton, Portsmouth, Heart of Midlothian, Clay Cross works (1899-1908)*
Played parks football in Derbyshire before joining Second Division Chesterfield, before going to have a season with Arsenal without breaking into their first team. Returned to Saltergate and impressed during an FA Cup tie with Portsmouth, catching the eye of Southampton manager Ernest Arnfield.

Tomlinson played 29 times (eight goals) in his solitary season at the club. Saints finished second in the league and had a good FA Cup run including a 9-1 win over Northampton in which Tomlinson impressed. Moved down the Solent to join Portsmouth but never established himself and had a stint in Scotland with Hearts. Managed a hotel and ran a pub in retirement, also working for Bournemouth & Boscombe Athletic as a scout.

Tomlinson, Reginald

Centre-forward
Born: *1914 Sleaford*
Died: *1971*
Playing career: *Horncastle Town, Grimsby Town, Southampton (1935-1939)*
As manager Tom Parker shuffled seven different players in a bid to find consistency at centre-forward, he turned to Grimsby for the answer. Reg Tomlinson - no relation to Isaac (above) - was "hefty, strapping man" but, despite his apparent size, he was quick and lithe up front, and possessed a "fierce" shot. Slotting into a new-look Saints attack alongside fellow new arrival Fred Briggs in a "useful" pairing. He would hit double figures in what turned out to be his only season at the club, 1938-39, before war broke out and he served in the police, guesting for several clubs including Portsmouth. Later became a full-time police officer whilst regularly turning out for a strong Metropolitan Police side. Died in 1971.

Toomer, Walter

Right-half/Outside-right
Born: 1883 Southampton
Died: 1962
Career: *Fulham, Chelsea, Southampton (1905-1914)*
Amateur player who worked as a teacher and an outfitter whilst playing for Southern League sides Fulham and Chelsea and at The Dell for almost a decade. Toomer would make sporadic appearances for the first team, ten in total. He later enlisted in the Royal Artillery and served in France during WW1. He returned to Southampton and resumed his teaching career, before working in his family's sportswear business just off London Road. Toomer was later a director and a scout at The Dell. Died in 1962.

Townsend, Andy

Midfielder
Born: 1963 Maidstone
Playing career: *Welling United, Weymouth, Southampton, Norwich City, Chelsea, Aston Villa, Middlesbrough, West Bromwich Albion (1980-2000)*
Eligible to play for the Republic through family ancestry, Townsend was capped 70 times by Ireland (seven goals) and played in the 1990 and 1994 World Cups, captaining the country in the latter. Plucked from non league by Lawrie McMenemy and signed for Southampton for £35,000, helping the Saints into Europe only for the events at Heysel to scupper the dream. A solid if unspectacular player, Townsend was "had working and tough tackling," and made a place in the Saints midfield his own, along with Jimmy Case and Glenn Cockerill. Played 83 games for Saints before moving to divisional rivals Norwich.

Chelsea then paid £1.2 million to take the Kent born Irishman to Stamford Bridge. Later played for Aston Villa (where he would win two League Cups), Middlesbrough (helping them to promotion) and West Brom. Currently a co-commentator for Premier League Productions and CBS Sports, Townsend has also worked for ITV, Five Live and BT Sport as a pundit and commentator.

Traynor, Tommy

Left-back
Born: 1933 Dundalk, Ireland
Died: 2006
Playing career: *Dundalk, Southampton (1950-1966,*
A one club man and an institution, left-back Traynor became a key cog for another legendary figure, Ted Bates, as the manager built the nucleus of two great Saints sides around him. Capped eight times by Ireland, he had a "superb football brain and a great left foot," despite not being the greatest of natural athletes, racking up almost 500 games and helping the Saints to two promotions. Fourth on the all time list of Southampton appearances, he had arrived from Ireland as cover for Peter Sillett. But Sillett would be sold in 1952 and Traynor would make the left-back position his own, playing in an exciting, free-scoring team with the likes of John Sydenham, Terry Paine and Derek Reeves. Traynor later became an influential figure at the club, even after he stopped playing. Traynor served on the board, helped with coaching and did some scouting. Away from football, he ran an off licence and then took up a job on the Docks.

Andy Townsend

Triggs, Walter

Full-back
Born: *1880 Southampton* **Died:** *1904*
Playing career: *Southampton (1897-1902)*

Southampton-born, Triggs was plucked joined Saints from local league football and soon made his name as a player with all the attributes of a "brilliant" full-back. Unfortunately, an even better one, namely George Molyneux, was ahead of him in the pecking order. When the latter received his England call up, international duty freed up the position and Triggs was drafted in for two games, missing out on a place in the Cup final team when Molyneux returned to resume his role. Triggs briefly captained the Reserves but never got his place back and left football. Triggs would die and only 24 from a lung complication having only picked up a cold.

Trueman, Albert

Left-half
Born: *1882 Leicester* **Died:** *1961*
Playing career: *Southampton, Sheffield United, Darlington (1899-1915)*

Signed by local professional side Leicester Fosse after catching the eye in amateur football in the area. Played 47 times in three seasons with the Second Division side before joining Southampton despite their Southern League status. With Harry Hadley having retired, Trueman became a regular at the back despite his diminutive size. His judgement, positioning and skill more than made up for his lack of height (a mere 5ft 6) with Trueman also described as "quick, resourceful and decisive." Trueman turned out for the Southern League Representative XI and had a trial with England, but he was never called up. He would make the left-half position his own, forming a formidable defensive trio with John Johnston and either Sam Jepp or Frank Thorpe. Trueman played 87 times in three years at The Dell before Sheffield United paid £350 to take him to Bramall Lane. He would finish his career with United, save for a brief stint at Darlington, guesting for several clubs during the war. In later life, Trueman worked as a labourer and a taxi driver.

Tully, Fred

Winger
Born: *1907 St Pancras, London*
Died: *1969*
Playing career: *Rosehill Villa, Preston Colliery, Chaddleston Mental Hospital, Aston Villa, Southampton, Clapton Orient (1926-1939)*

A winger of "thrust and enterprise" and a busy player capable of playing anywhere across the front, Tully's pairing with Dick Neal became a familiar sight for the Southampton faithful in the mid to late 30s. After three seasons of regular first team football, Tully fell out of favour and moved to Saints divisional rivals Clapton Orient only for his playing days to be interrupted by the war. Having retired from playing, Tully joined his father's carpentry business. Played 107 times for Southampton, scoring ten goals. Died in 1969.

Turnbull, Fred

Inside-forward
Born: *1888 Wallsend*
Died: *1959*
Playing career: *Newcastle United, Coventry City, Southampton, North Shields Athletic (1909-1913)*

Another product of the Wallsend Boys Club, Fred Turnbull trod a familiar path as he broke through at Newcastle before moving to Southern League Coventry. When the club's coach, Jimmy McIntyre, moved to divisional rivals Southampton under secretary/manager Ernest Arnfield, McIntyre returned to his former club to bring in a forward. Shot-shy Southampton turned to Turnbull, and the move paid instant dividends when he scored on his Southern League debut, keeping his place for the rest of the campaign. Turnbull was not prolific and did not solves Saints problems in front of goal, but he endeared himself to the fans through his bustling nature and high energy style. Turnbull scored twice in 23 appearances before returning to his native North East to play at non league level and work as a blacksmith. Served in France during WW1, later working in the quarries on Tyneside having been demobbed.

Turner, Arthur 'Archie'

Outside-right
Born: 1877 Hartley Wintney
Died: 1925
Playing career: Southampton, Derby County, Newcastle United, Tottenham Hotspur, Bristol City, Southampton (1892-1914)

Played in two FA Cup finals for Saints and was capped twice by England - becoming the first Hampshire-born player to earn that honour. It was a meteoric rise for the a man who played exclusively in non-league before being snapped up by all-conquering Southampton. Saints had won the Southern League for three successive seasons when they moved for Turner, a played capable of "dazzling" wing play, but a style that also made his an easy target for rough treatment from opponents. Turner would help the side to yet another title in his second season at The Dell, with his accurate crossing and "fine" distribution a key cog in Southampton's dominance of the league. Later played for Derby and Newcastle before returning to Saints - via Spurs and Bristol City - but never recaptured the form that made him a household name. Turner would go on to work in his family's cloth business in Farnborough where he died in 1925.

Turner, Ernest

Forward
Born: 1898 Brithdir, Caerphilly, Wales **Died:** 1951
Playing career: Bargoed, Caerphilly, Merthyr Town, Southampton (1922-1926)

Had a low key career in the backwaters of the Welsh league before joining Southampton where he served as back up to established strike force Arthur Dominy and Bill Rawlings. Served in the Machine Corps Gun Battalion during the war and also represented the Welsh FA whilst a regular at Merthyr during their Football League heyday. Turner would spend only one season at The Dell, during which he played 16 times and scored three. He failed to hold down a regular role in the team and was deployed in five different positions, before leaving football and emigrating to Canada. He soon returned to England but never played again and later worked for the coal board in his native Wales.

Turner, Frederick

Full-back
Born: 1930 Southampton **Died:** 1955
Playing career: Bitterne Nomads, Southampton, Torquay United (1948-1953)

Born in Southampton as the son of one of the football club's directors, there perhaps seemed an inevitability that Frederick Turner would play for his hometown team. A "quiet but thoughtful full-back with good positional sense," he signed for Saints as an amateur and then joined pro two years later. He played regularly for the Reserves before briefly turning out for Torquay having completed his National Service. He would go to play 19 teams for the first team, slotting in at right-back next to Len Wilkins. Turner became a regular, playing 17 games in a row before being struck down with illness and quit the game in 1955. Five months later Turner was dead through leukaemia aged only 25.

Turner, Harry

Outside-right
Born: 1882 Farnborough **Died:** 1967
Playing career: South Farnborough, Southampton, Farnborough, Reading, Farnborough (1900-1908)

Working as an ironmonger's assistant in Farnborough, Turner looked to follow in his brother Archie's footsteps when he was scouted and signed by Southampton having impressed in local non league football. Although he would never be capped for England like his brother, Turner would vie for the outside-right position with another Turner, unrelated namesake Joe. He would prove reasonably successful, being described by the Echo as "being able to centre the ball with great judgement" and a forward with a "powerful shot and an eye for goal" but lacking the game-changing skill and trickery of his elder sibling. Won the Hampshire Senior Cup with the Reserves before he returned to Farnborough. He would re-try his hand at Saints, rekindling his partnership with Archie. He did create a unique piece of history in a game against Swindon in 1904 when he and Archie became the first - and so far - only pair of brothers to score in a game for Saints. Turner later became a painter and decorator.

Turner, Joe

Outside-forward
Born: *1872 Burslem* **Died:** *1950*
Playing career: *Southampton St. Mary's, Stoke, Everton, Southampton, Northampton (1893-1908)f*

When club secretary Charles Robson and director (later manager) Alfred McMinn visited Stoke looking to strengthen Southampton St Mary's, they returned south having signed six players. The two men had procured the best Staffordshire had to offer with Turner among the new arrivals. He would dovetail nicely with Watty Keay, scoring 18 goals from wide on the left in tandem with Keay and another Stoke-based import Jack Farrell. Turner would be part of the Saints sides that won four Southern League titles, also playing the FA Cup final of 1902 and going on to feature over 200 times for the club across two spells on the south coast. Later worked in a brewery and also a library before he died in 1950 aged 78.

Turner, William

Half-back
Born: *1894 South Moor, Co Durham*
Died: *1970*
Playing career: *Dipton United, Scotswood, Leadgate Park, Southampton, Bury, QPR (1919-1928)*

Born and raised in the football hotbed of the North East, Bill Turner started out in local non league until W1 interrupted his career. After the conflict, he joined Southern League Saints and instantly slotted into the side at left-back, initially in place of Fred Titmuss. Later settling at left-half, Turner possessed a strong tackle, quick feet and an "impressive" heading ability. Helping the Saints to promotion, Turner became n ever-present part of a formidable half-back line next to Bert Shelley and Alec Campbell as Saints won Division Three in 1922-23. Turner spent five seasons at The Dell, playing 186 league and cup games (scoring once) until he lost his place and moved to Bury. Later played for QPR before retiring. Turner briefly returned to Saints as a coach but eventually drifted out of the game and became a blacksmith. Died in 1970.

Turner, Ian

Goalkeeper
Born: *1953 Middlesbrough*
Playing career: *Grimsby Town, Walsall, Southampton, Newport County, Lincoln City & Halifax Town*

A goalkeeper big both in heart and stature, Turner was best known for his part in the team of 76', ensuring a shutout in the Wembley final to help Saints to their finest hour. A brave and reliable shot-stopper, Turner made key saves from Gerry Daly and Gordon McQueen to put his name among the annals as one of the twelve men to go down in Saints folklore. Turner ground-hopped around Hampshire on the non-league scene, where he took charge as manager of Romsey, Brockenhurst and Totton, coaching at Horndean and working for Saints as mentor to the keepers in their Academy under Alan Ball. Later reprised that role at Luton and Millwall, combining his work as a shot-stopping coach with employment as a plumber and pipe fitter for BP - a role he eventually took up full time. His work in the oil industry later took him to Asia, working in Pakistan, Oman and Libya as an engineer and project manager, as well as several other British oil and gas refineries. He has taken part in many ex-Saints reunion events as an after-dinner speaker and continues to serve the club in the match day hospitality sector.

Tyson, Charles

Centre-half
Born: *1885 Liverpool* **Died:** *1964*
Playing career: *Crystal Palace, Dulwich Hamlet, Southampton (1908-1913)*

A south London schoolteacher before being capped by England at amateur level and earning a move to Southern League Southampton. Bert Lee, captain and a regular member of the Saints defence, had been dropped and so Tyson slotted straight into the heart of the defence. Played 14 games in succession before losing his place to Ted Salway. Commanding and more robust than the average amateur, he could be "trusted to keep a grip on opposing forwards." He served in the War as part of the Army Medical Corps, becoming quartermaster with the 105th Ambulance Corps. After the war was over, Tyson's playing days were over and he returned to his full-time job as a teacher.

Van Damme, Jelle

Defender/Left midfielder
Born: *1983 Lokeren, Belgium*
Playing career: *Ajax, Southampton, Werder Bremen, Anderlecht, Wolverhampton Wanderers, Standard Liège, LA Galaxy, Royal Antwerp (2001-)*

Versatile Belgian with 31 caps still playing for Lokeren in his native homeland. Van Damme has played in the Netherlands, Germany and England during his career, turning out for Wolves as well as Southampton. He would make little impact on the south coast though, playing only six times in 2004-05 as the Saints were relegated. A big signing in more ways than one, at 6ft 4 and over £2m, Van Damme was gone almost as quickly as he arrived, moving to Germany after only one season amidst turmoil, Championship football and a merry go round of Southampton managers. He moved back to Belgium and carved out a reputable career with Anderlecht and Standard Liege, winning two league titles and a domestic cup with the former. He failed to shine at Wolves, too, again only playing six times, and marking considerable under-achievement on these shores for a player regarded as ideal for the English game.

Veck, Robert

Outside-left
Born: *1920 Titchfield*
Playing career: *Southampton, Gillingham, Chelmsford City (1938-1952)*

Rose through the ranks as a goalscoring winger, until war intervened. Served with the RAF during the conflict and was posted overseas before resuming his career with Southampton after the end of WW2. Made his debut in the first post-War campaign when only FA Cup fixtures were played, before slotting in to Saints new-look Second Division side as one of eight players handed a debut, and scored. Veck would keep his place for most of the rest of the campaign before being displaced by Wilf Grant as Bill Dodgin looked to assemble a team capable of promotion. Veck would be in and out of the side as his manager tried several different players in many positions, eventually joining Gillingham after four seasons and 27 games for Saints - with the side in third place on three successive occasions. Veck finished his playing days in non league and later worked as a taxi driver.

Barry Venison

Venison, Barry

Defender
Born: *1964 Consett, County Durham*
Playing career: *Sunderland, Liverpool, Newcastle United, Galatasaray, Southampton (1981-1997)*
Won two FA Cups with Liverpool and helped Newcastle to the newly formed Premier League, earning two caps for England before he arrived at Southampton. Venison, a cultured midfielder with a penchant for the spectacular, had already played for Graeme Souness twice at Liverpool and Galatasaray, before the pair linked up again when Souness succeeded Dave Merrington at Saints. Venison would never fully establish himself at The Dell, playing as a deep lying playmaker and also at full-back, before his notoriously bad back finally gave in and he retired aged 32 in 1996. Venison featured 28 times for Saints. After hanging up his boots, Venison worked as a pundit for ITV and Sky Sports before he set up his own online sports memorabilia auction business bid4sport. com with the help of friend and fellow professional player Brad Friedel. Worked in property development both in the UK and across the pond, before he returned to football as Technical Director - and later head coach - of USL Pro side Orange County Blues. Venison continues to live Stateside where he has set up and run his own furniture, fitting and equipment business, *Premier Install,* supplying hotels, holiday resorts, motels and luxury residences across the US. https://twitter. com/BarryVenison

Verney, William

Half-back
Born: *1871 Aldershot*
Died: *1950*
Playing career: *Southampton St. Mary's , Cranbury Avenue (1888-1898)*
As you'd perhaps expect from the son of a Sergeant Major, William "George" Verney was a well-disciplined and tenacious defender who would "uncompromisingly challenge for every ball" during his time with Saints. Verney joined the fledgling St Mary's club three years after inception, helping the side to win the Hampshire Junior Cup.

He linked up to "good effect" with Bill Stride and Charlie Deacon as the Saints retained the trophy the following season of 1890-91. Verney played for the Hampshire FA Representative team and stayed with the club after they became founding members of the new Southern League. Verney would never feature in the new competition, though, playing in the Reserves and serving as assistant coach at that level. He would play in local non league football for the rest of his career, going on to become a mercantile clerk and later a land salesman.

Vernon, Douglas

Centre-forward
Born: *1905 Devonport*
Died: *1979*
Playing career: *Royal Air Force, Southampton, Wycombe Wanderers , Leyton (1929-1931)*
Served in the RAF as a gunner post-World War 1, before he saw action of a slightly more tranquil nature in the front line of the Southampton attack after the conflict. With injury-hit Saints missing top marksman Willie Haines, manager Arthur Chadwick had struggled to find a centre-forward to solve his side's goalscoring issues. Vernon had no previous football experience to call upon, apart from brief cup action with the Air Force, but this did not stop Chadwick from taking a punt on the wily, rangy striker. He would prove a stopgap signing until the arrival of Archie Waterston, playing five games up top having been thrown straight into the side by Chadwick. He was then recalled by the RAF and served overseas, but resumed his career with non league Wycombe. Won an Amateur FA Cup with the club and briefly turned out for non league Leyton before leaving the RAF and served in the Metropolitan Police until the outbreak of WW2.

"DID YOU KNOW?"

"Saints won the Daily Express National Five-a-Sides tournament in 1971 and 1983."

BBC NEWS

Home Brexit Coronavirus UK World Business Politics Tech Science Health Family & Education

World | Africa | Asia | Australia | Europe | Latin America | Middle East | US & Canada

Jhon Viáfara: Colombia extradites ex-footballer to US on drugs charges

⟳ 24 January 2020

Jhon Viáfara was arrested in Cali, Colombia, in March last year

Viafara, Jhon
Midfielder
Born: *1978 Robles, Colombia*
Playing career: *Deportivo Pasto, America de Cali, Deportivo Pasto, Once Caldas, Portsmouth, Real Sociedad, Southampton, Once Caldas, La Equidad, Atletico Junior, Deportivo Pereira, La Equidad, Independiente Medellin, Deportivo Cali, Rionegro Aguilas (1999-2015)*

A well travelled, mobile, box-to-box midfielder with 34 Colombia caps. A series of fine performances in his native homeland led to a move to England with Premier League Portsmouth, where he would link up with returning manager Harry Redknapp. Played in Spain on loan before signing for his former side's fierce south coast rivals, Southampton, re-uniting with his former manager up the Solent. Viafara's style was well suited to the recently relegated Saints, scoring twice in the ultimately unsuccessful Championship play-offs against Derby and he would be a virtual ever-present in 2007-08 as the club narrowly avoided another demotion. Viafara would be a victim of circumstances, playing for the club during a turbulent time and a high turnover of managers, players and board members. Fell out with Jan Poortvliet and returned to Colombia where he finished his playing career. in April 2021, Viafara was sentenced to 11 years' imprisonment by a Texas jury for drug trafficking and the importation of two tonnes of cocaine worth $21 million.

Vignal, Gregory
Defender
Born: *1981 Montpellier, France*
Playing career: *Castelnau Le Cres FC, Montpellier, Liverpool, Bastia, Rennes , Espanyol, Rangers, Portsmouth, Lens, Kaiserslautern , Southampton, Birmingham City, Atromitos, Dundee United, AS Beziers (1997-2013)*

Another well-travelled defender, Vignal turned out for fourteen different clubs in nine different countries including Germany, Greece, France, Spain and in England. As his tour of Europe would suggest, though, Vignal never settled anywhere, never playing more than 30 games for any one of his clubs. Had five years at Liverpool - featuring in their 2001 'treble' season and then winning the League Cup and the SPL with Rangers north of the border. His time at Southampton was a loan deal in the 2007-08 campaign having impressed George Burley on a pre-season tour of Norway. He would feature sporadically for second tier Saints, mainly at left-back as the club avoided relegation on the final day. Nigel Pearson came in and Vignal moved on, finishing his career in France - via Bimingham, Atromitos and Dundee United - and earning four caps for France at Under 21 level. Vignal moved into coaching, taking charge of the Rangers Women's team and he is currently first team at Marseille in his native France.

Waigo N'Diaye, Papa
Winger/Striker
Born: *1984 Saint-Louis, Senegal*
Playing career: *Verona, Cesena, Genoa, Fiorentina, Lecce, Southampton, Grosseto , Ascoli, Al-Wahda, Al-Ettifaq, Al-Raed, Ittihad Kalba, Al Urooba, Al-Thaid (2002-Still Playing)*

A mercurial striker who was either unplayable or anonymous and very rarely anything in between. A Senegalese striker with 15 caps for the African nation, his unorthodox running style, pace, trickery and "off the cuff" approach made him a handful for even the most miserly of defences at his best. Sadly for the Saints faithful who witnessed his 40-odd games on loan from Fiorentina, Papa Waigo was also inconsistent and seemed to be caught offside too often.

He scored on his second game and Gillingham - one of five goals for Saints - including two on the road to Wembley as Southampton won the Johnstone's Paint Trophy in 2010 and one in the final itself making him the tournament's top scorer. Saints had the option to make his move permanent but they opted not to and so he returned to Italy. Waigo is currently without a club having left Emirati club Masafi in 2019.

Waldron, Malcolm

Defender
Born: *1956 Emsworth*
Playing career: *Southampton, Burnley, Portsmouth. (1974-1984)*

From shoring up defences to providing cover for others, Waldron has moved into investment and insurance since retiring as a player. After retiring, he worked as a double glazing salesman and marketing with *Abbey Life* before being scouted and signed by Norwich - Norwich Union that is. He specialised in private financial advice and was employed as divisional manager. Waldron set up his own private business, MW Sales & Marketing Ltd, prioritising in brokering private medical insurance. He is also a partner for the Health Insurance Group in Bournemouth, and Waldron is currently employed by Christchurch-based Carleton Associates Management as Management Consultant Director, where he divides his time between the south coast and Texas in the US, where he works in real estate services, and property management finances.

Walker, David

Central defender
Born: *1941 Colne* **Died:** *2015*
Playing career: *Burnley, Southampton , Cape Town 1960-1975)*

Broke through with his local professional side, Burnley, but was never able to establish himself in the Clarets formidable half-back line. For the sake of career and in search of regular football, Walker moved to Southampton, despite interest from Bill Shankly's Liverpool. Ted Bates swooped for the young defender and he instantly became a regular.

Walker would go on to feature over 200 times for the Saints in only nine years, illustrating his consistency and ability to stay fit. Despite the arrivals of Jimmy Gabriel and John McGrath, Walker would often shield the defence, breaking up play with his tough tackling style and starting attacks with his "dangerous" range of passing. He would find regular game time few and far between in the latter days of Bates' tenure and then fell our favour completely under Lawrie McMenemy. Briefly played and coached in South Africa before returning to Hampshire. Walker worked in an antiques shop near his old stamping ground at The Dell, and then ran a B&B in the New Forest in later life.

Walker, John

Inside-forward
Born: *1928 Glasgow, Scotland* **Died:** *2019*
Playing career: *Wolverhampton Wanderers , Southampton, Reading (1944-1964)*

Walker - plucked from parks football in his native Scotland - was scouted and signed by Wolves and broke through at Molineux as a fresh faced 18 year old. An unpolished diamond in a galaxy of stars, Walker spent five years with the Black Country side but despite not playing regularly he plundered 21 goals in 38 games. He led the scoring charts as Stan Cullis men reached the FA Cup semi finals in 1951, but he fell out of favour and moved to division-lower Southampton for £12,000 a year later. Signing for an ageing and struggling Saints side, Walker was described as a "hard working forager" and became a fans favourite for his energy and unconventional style. He would stay on the south coast for six seasons, scoring 52 goals in nearly 200 games and linking with the likes of Derek Reeves, Tommy Mulgrew, Don Roper and - latterly - the emerging talents of John Sydenham and Terry Paine. Walker moved to divisional rivals Reading where he wound down his career, later serving as the Royals reserve team coach before leaving football. Walker later continued to deliver as a postman and also continued to partake in Saints hospitality events as a guest speaker. Died in January 2019 at the age of 90.

Wallace, Adam

Forward
Born: *1981 Ashford*
Playing career: *Southampton, Salisbury City, Southend United , Basingstoke Town , Windsor & Eton, Slough Town, Fleet Town, (2002-2008)*

Adam Wallace signed for Southampton as a thirteen year old, and was tipped as one for the future by several illustrious Saints at the time including Matt Le Tissier after impressing on trial. Despite these lofty proclamations, Wallace - a nippy, fleet-footed forward - never made his long-awaited breakthrough, although he did manage a handful of outings at Reserve team level.After six years at the club, Wallace was released back into the system and would never play for a top level side again. He would go on to turn out for a number of lower and non league clubs, including two spells at Salisbury, Southend United, Basingstoke, Windsor & Eton and Fleet Town. Now aged 39, he has coached at Eastleigh and former club Salisbury.

Wallace, Danny

Striker/Winger
Born: *1964 Greenwich*
Playing career: *Southampton, Manchester United, Millwall (loan), Birmingham City, Wycombe Wanderers (1977-1995)*

The eldest of the three Wallace brothers, all of whom played for Southampton, with a tragic backstory. David, aka "Danny" Wallace, became the Saints youngest ever debutant aged 16 years and 313 days in 1980, a record that he held until Theo Walcott burst on to the scene a quarter of a century later. Not only that, but this Wallace would make his debut on one of English football's biggest stages when he was given his chance against Manchester United at Old Trafford. Small, skilful and explosive, Wallace would often delight the Southampton faithful with a penchant for the spectacular and became known as a scorer of great goals, rather than a great goalscorer (as highlighted by his winning the 1983/84 Match of the Day goal of the season award, a 25-yard overhead scissor kick against title chasing Liverpool). History was made in 1988 when his brothers Ray and Rod linked up alongside

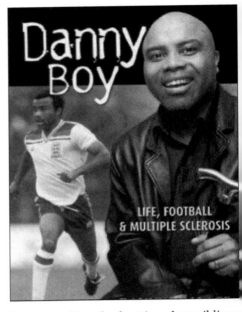

Danny, marking the first time three siblings had appeared together for the same club in the English game since 1920. Danny would go to join Manchester United, winning the FA Cup and the Cup Winners Cup and earning one cap for England (scoring on his one and only appearance for his country, against Egypt). Wallace retired after a series of niggling injuries, after spells with Birmingham and Wycombe, later being diagnosed with multiple sclerosis. Wallace has learned to live with his condition, completing several marathons and triathlons to raise money and awareness for his condition. Danny accumulated over 300 games for Saints during his decade long association with the club.

Wallace, Lawrence

Outside-left
Born: *1917 Sandown* **Died:** *1978*
Playing career: *Southampton (1939-)*

An international standard sprinter, Lawrence Wallace had represented England at the 1938 Empire Games (now known as the Commonwealth Games). He won the silver medal in the 4x100m relay and represented his country at both individual events (100m and 200m) before he was selected to turn out for University Athletic XI against the Amateurs, a football match to be played at The Dell. Unsurprisingly, pace was his greatest asset and he caught the eye of Southampton, signing on amateur terms. This promo failed to transcend into any meaningful impact, however, with Wallace said to be "overwhelmed" and "out of sorts" on his debut at Manchester City in 1939. He would never play for the first team again, playing occasionally at Reserve team level before returning to athletics. Served in the Royal Artillery during the War and then took up a job as a teacher after the conflict.

Wallace, Ray
Full-back
Born: *1969 Lewisham*
Playing career: *Southampton, Leeds United, Swansea City, Reading, Stoke City, Hull City, Airdrieonians, Altrincham, Winsford United, Drogheda United, Witton Albion (1986-2002)*
His brothers Danny and Rod were known as speedy, explosive and tricky wingers, but Ray - perhaps not as naturally gifted - carved out a niche for himself as a tough and combative right-back. Joined Southampton as an apprentice at the same time as Rod, going on to play four times for England at Under 21 level but never getting a call up for the full senior side. Wallace's debut would bring it a piece of history as he joined Danny and Rod on the field at the same time - the first instance of Southampton having three brothers in the same team in the same time, and the first time this had happened anywhere since 1920. He would be a virtual ever present until the arrival of Jason Dodd, eventually moving on to Leeds, Stoke and Hull City. After football, Wallace worked in a *Fitness First* gym and then as manager of a health club in Manchester. Played almost 50 games for Saints in three years at the club.

Wallace, Rod
Striker
Born: *1969 Lewisham, London*
Playing career: *Southampton, Leeds United, Rangers, Bolton Wanderers, Gillingham (1988-2004)*
Relying on strength and crossing rather than the raw pace and flair of his brother Danny, Rod arrived at Saints with his twin Ray with the other aforementioned

Wallace, Danny, already an established Saint. Picking out the other forwards with pinpoint precision soon became Rod's trademark, a quality no doubt embellished by the presence of Matt Le Tissier and an emerging Alan Shearer. All three attracted interest from bigger clubs, but Rod stayed loyal to the Saints and went on to feature 151 times for them, scoring an impressive 56 goals. He later followed his brother to Leeds, and also played for Rangers, Bolton and Gillingham. In 2016, Wallace co-founded PSM (Phoenix Sport and Media Group) along with fellow formers pros Brian Deane, Andy Cole, Michael Thomas, Paul Williams and Mark McGhee. PSM are a collection of individual companies helping sports and media personalities in a variety of issues such as sports coaching, media training, legal advice and business affairs, safeguarding players and coaches during their careers whilst also preparing for life after football.

Waller, Wilf
Goalkeeper
Born: *1877 South Africa*
Playing career: *Vampires, Corinthian, Richmond Association, Tottenham Hotspur, Bolton Wanderers, QPR, Southampton, Watford, Aylesbury United (1899-1901)*
One of the finest amateur shot stoppers of his day, Wilf Waller had become the first player from South Africa to feature in English football. Featured for an FA Representative XI and had a brief stint with Spurs before arriving at Southampton via Bolton and QPR. At a time when a foreign player was almost alien to the British domestic game, Waller proved to be something of a pioneer. Although dual-signed with amateur side Richmond, the rules allowed Waller to play in the Football or Southern Leagues and so he featured for Saints, deputising for the unavailable England international keeper, Jack Robinson. Southampton went on to win the title for the fourth time in five seasons but Waller only played once more. After spells with Watford and Aylesbury, Waller returned to his native South Africa where he later worked as a farmer.

Walters, Mark

Midfielder/Winger
Born: *1964 Birmingham*
Playing career: *Aston Villa, Rangers, Liverpool, Stoke City, Wolverhampton W, Southampton, Swindon Town, Bristol Rovers (1981-2002)*

Capped once by England, Mark Walters has been a man of talents since retiring as a player in 2002. He initially moved into coaching, working with five to eleven year olds at a school in Coventry, becoming a permanent member of staff and going on to set up a pathway between the school and Coventry City in which club scouts would come and watch the best young talents and sign them for City. Walters worked as head coach of the under 14s at Aston Villa's Academy, also serving his former club as chief scout and as Head of Languages. Later spent five years running coaching workshops in Midlands-based schools on behalf of the FA but was never given the chance to coach or manage at senior first team level. Walters has also been heavily involved in football's anti-racism campaigns and has represented Rangers in Masters tournaments and legend events. He has since dabbled in the property market and done media work for the Glasgow giants. Walters released his autobiography "Wingin' It" in 2018. Twitter: https://twitter.com/mew1934

Ward, Alfred

Outside-forward
Born: *1883 Eastwood, Nottinghamshire*
Died: *1926*
Playing career: *Clowne White Star, Notts County, Brighton & Hove Albion , Aberdeen, Bradford Park Avenue, Southampton (1903-1909)*

Played for his two local village sides before Ward - an "intelligent" inside forward, was scouted and signed by top flight Notts County in 1903. Ward went on to make a handful of appearances for them before a stint at Brighton and Aberdeen. Spent two seasons at Pittodrie before returning to England - somewhat bizarrely playing in the Southern League with Yorkshire-based Bradford PA (defying geography in the process). Ward joined divisional rivals Southampton after one season and signed in time to go on the club's first "overseas" tour as Saints sent a side to Austria, Germany and Belgium. He would pick up an injury whilst on the tour, though, having three operations on a knee before finally getting his chance. Briefly displaced Frank Jefferis to score on his debut but would only make three further appearances and eventually failed to recover sufficiently from his injury problems. Later worked as a general carter in his hometown of Nottingham.

Ward, Frank

Full-back
Born: *1902 Leigh, Lancashire*
Playing career: *Walshaw United, Bury, Preston North End , Southampton, Folkestone (1923-1935)*

Made his name at Bury in his native Lancashire alongside future Saints Stan Woodhouse and John Gallagher, helping the Quakers into the top flight for they first time in their history. Ward had played over 50 games for the quaint Lancashire club before opting to link up with former team-mate Woodhouse in the Southampton side. Ward was not a flashy or brilliantly eye-catching addition to the struggling Saints, but his experience, nous and versatility enabled him to do a solid job in a backline badly in need of consistency. Despite only being at The Dell for two seasons, Ward was deployed in six different positions, playing in both full-back positions, right-half, left-half, centre-back and even inside left. Ironically, he would be displaced in the team by old team-mate Woodhouse, and would be given a free transfer to another Southern League club, Folkestone, after 28 games for Saints. Ward later found work as an engineer.

Ward, Herbert

Forward
Born: *1873 Hammersmith* **Died:** *1897*
Career: *Southampton St Mary's (1893-1895)*

A teacher and a multi-talented sportsman whom excelled at both cricket and football, there were many strings to Herbert Ward's bow. Scored on his debut for the fledgling St Mary's side in the FA Cup, making the left wing spot his own before switching to centre-forward. Scored a hat-trick in the 14-0 FA Cup win over Newbury, a result that remains Southampton's biggest ever competitive victory. Ward quit football in 1895 to focus on cricket, joining Hampshire and scoring a half century on his debut. Played 33 first class games for the county and took best bowling figures of 5-17 against Sussex. A mere 17 days after the last of his matches for the county, he died from typhoid aged only 24.

Warhurst, Samuel

Goalkeeper
Born: *1907 Nelson* **Died:** *1981*
Playing career: *Nelson, Stalybridge Celtic , Bradford City, Southampton (1926-1939)*

Began his career with his hometown team Nelson during their Football League heyday before stepping up to second tier Bradford. Never fully established himself with the Valley Parade Bantams and left to join Southampton, shortly after City's relegation from the Second Division. He would replace the recently retired Bert Scriven as Southampton's no.1, becoming a familiar figure between the posts, going on to play 81 times for the club in total. He almost certainly would have featured in many more, if not for the outbreak of WW2. It not only stopped the professional game in its tracks, but also ended the careers of many players including Warhurst although he did play as a guest for Saints during the conflict . A keeper on the "small side" but with "a fine reputation for agility, good sportsmanship and comradeship", he stayed with Saints in a coaching role, working both with the reserves and the first team before leaving football. He would continue to live in Southampton, becoming a hotelier in the city in later life.

Warner, John

Full-back
Born: *1883 Preston* **Died:** *1948*
Playing career: *St Michaels, Preston North End , Southampton, Portsmouth (1902-1915)*

John "Jack" Warner, a bricklayer by trade broke through at his hometown team, Second Division Preston. He made sporadic appearances for them but was demoted to the Reserves after North End's promotion in 1904. Moving to the south coast and Southampton, Warner was dubbed as a "speedy full-back and more than a match for any forward". His Saints career would be abruptly and harshly cut short after the board mistakenly felt one of his knees wasn't up to scratch. They were to be proved woefully wrong when Warner joined south coast rivals Portsmouth and went on to feature over 200 times at Fratton Park. After the war he coached at Pompey and later became a mechanic. Died in 1948.

Warner, Philip

Utility player
Born: *1979 Southampton*
Playing career: *Southampton , Brentford, Cambridge United, Eastleigh, Aldershot Town, Eastbourne Borough, Havant & Waterlooville, Bognor Regis Town, Totton, Heidelberg United, Poole Town (1997-2011)*

A local lad rising through the ranks to the Premier League, Warner made six appearances at that level for Saints. His first and last games for Southampton came against the two major north London clubs, coming on for Jason Dodd to make his debut in a draw with Spurs and culminating in another 1-1, at Arsenal. Warner - playing at right-back - was given the runaround by Marc Overmars and never played for the club again. Warner, a versatile utility man capable of playing anywhere in defence, dropped two divisions to Brentford but failed to re-ignite his career and ended up in the non league game. Played at Anfield as Havant & Waterlooville gave Liverpool an FA Cup scare in 2008, but then played in Australia before returning to these shores. Warner latterly found work as a van driver and property developer before taking up a job as a sports massage therapist.

Warren, Christer
Midfielder
Born: *1974 Weymouth*
Playing career: *Cheltenham Town, Southampton, Brighton & Hove Albion, Fulham, AFC Bournemouth, QPR, Bristol Rovers (1993-2008)*

Alan Ball took, by his own admission, a huge risk when he paid £40,000 to pluck Christer Warren from Southern League Cheltenham to top flight Southampton. Warren became Cheltenham's record sale and it soon became clear that Ball's gamble was one that had failed to pay off. Warren - a left-sided midfielder - made no impact at Southampton, playing only nine times (two starts, seven from the bench) in his two seasons at the club. After two loan spells, Warren moved across the New Forest to Bournemouth, then in the second tier for three years before going on to QPR and Bristol Rovers and a stint in non league. Managed at Wimborne Town for the 2007-08 season before drifting out of the game and taking up a job with an industrial stationery company back in Southampton.

Warren, Ernest
Inside-left
Born: *1910 Sunderland, Tyne and Wear*
Playing career: *Usworth Colliery, Southampton, Burton Town, Northampton Town, Hartlepools United, South Shields (1929-1936)*

Scouted and signed by Southampton, plucked from the works team of Usworth Colliery in his native North East. Warren would play only once for Saints and it proved a baptism of fire with the "lively" forward "marked out of the game" as West Brom prevailed 5-1 on the final day of the 1929-30 season. He would remain at The Dell for another year but never played for the club again at any level and played for Burton Town in the Birmingham & District League before moving to Northampton. He would become a man-for-one-season player at Northampton, Hartlepool and South Shields back in his native north East. Warren remained in the area after retiring as a player, working for the coal board, as a surveyor for the council and on the docks at Gateshead.

Waterston, Archibald
Centre-forward
Born: *1902 Musselburgh, Scotland* **Died:** *1982*
Playing career: *Leicester City, Cowdenbeath, Newport County, Southampton, Tranmere Rovers , Southport, Doncaster Rovers (1922-1935)*

A prolific net busting striker in the lower echelons of the English game, Waterston racked up 36 goals in 44 games for Newport to attract the attentions of a Southampton side in need of re-inforcements. Making the step up from the third tier to the Second Division, Waterston would he only play six times in as many months, scoring one against Hull City. He returned to the Third Division with Tranmere and Southport and would score 31 in 29 for the Merseyside. After retirement as a player, Waterston worked as a foreman in the dye department of the wool mill in Musselburgh. Died in 1982.

Watkinson, Russell
Winger
Born: *1977 Epsom*
Playing career: *Woking, Southampton, Millwall, Aldershot Town, Farnborough Town (1994-1999)*

Although the Saints faithful have long since forgotten Russell Watkinson, his rise from non league to the top flight within a month will live long in the player's memory, He only played twice in the Premier League in a fortnight, before going out on loan and disappearing from the spotlight just as quickly as he'd arrived. Watkinson had started out in the non league game with Woking and Fleet before being signed on trial by Saints having impressed Saints coach Ray Clarke in a pre-season friendly between the clubs. Despite an expensive influx of foreign imports, Saints manager Graeme Souness handed Watkinson his chance in games against Spurs and Middlesbrough in which the player showed "flashes of pace and potential." That was the zenith of his incredible fairytale rise and Watkinson ground-hopped at a several minor clubs before playing at The Dell once again in 1999 when winning the Hampshire Senior Cup with Aldershot. In later life, Watkinson set up and ran his own youth coaching academy, RAW Skills, based in Wiltshire

Watson, Dave

Central defender
Born: *1946 Stapleford, Nottinghamshire*
Playing career: *Notts County, Rotherham United, Sunderland, Manchester City, Werder Bremen, Southampton, Stoke City, Vancouver Whitecaps, Derby County, Fort Lauderdale Sun, Notts County, Kettering Town (1966-1986)*

Watson - the proud owner of 65 England caps - started out as a striker before converting to the centre of defence under Bob Stokoe at Sunderland, where he won the FA Cup - keeping Allan Clarke and Mick Jones of Leeds quiet in the process. Went on to Manchester City where he won the League Cup and spent four seasons at Maine Road. Had a stint in Germany before signing for Lawrie McMenemy's Southampton, where he struck up a "grit and guile" partnership with Chris Nicholl. Watson played 83 times across three seasons for the club before going on to Stoke, Vancouver Whitecaps, Derby, Fort Lauderdale and Notts County. Captained England on three occasions and played for the country at the 1980 European championships, but Watson remains the most capped player never to feature in a World Cup tournament. He has continued to live in Nottingham, and set up *DWI Ltd*, an agency for former international players across the world. It creates opportunities for players such as media appearances, photo shoots, after dinner speaking and sponsorship events, working with the FA, UEFA and amor brands including MacDonald's, Nike, American Express and Sky. In 2020, Watson was diagnosed with a neurodegenerative disease linked to years of headed clearances.

Watson, Gordon

Forward
Born: *1971 Sidcup*
Playing career: *Charlton Athletic, Sheffield Wednesday, Southampton, Bradford City, AFC Bournemouth, Hartlepool United (1989-2003)*

Gordon "Flash" Watson may not have been the most stylish of forwards but he instantly endeared himself to the Southampton faithful as an "effervescent, never-say-die and unstinting" player of the sort fans love, the style of player to unsettle even the most miserly of opposition.

This mutual affection only grew when he scored on his home debut against Newcastle to turn a 1-0 deficit into a 2-1 lead to spark a late-season revival that saw the club safe. Watson scored thrice in his first nine games but was used less frequently by Dave Merrington and eventually moved to Bradford City, going on to turn out for AFC Bournemouth and Hartlepool. Watson featured 52 times for Saints and would later receive £96,000 in damages after Kevin Gray of Huddersfield broke Watson's leg in a tackle during a match Bradford. Trained with Portsmouth but never played for the club and retired in 2004. Having hung up his boots, Watson became involved in property renovation and worked for *BBC Solent*, *Radio Hampshire* and the club's own radio station *The Saint* as a co-commentator and match summariser. Scouted for Leicester and became a director for Eastleigh-based sportswear company *Kicker Sports Ltd.*
https://twitter.com/Flash_37

Watson, Reginald

Outside-forward
Born: *1900 Thelwall* **Died:** *1971*
Playing career: *Thelwall, Arpley Street, Grappon Hall, Fairfield United, Monks Hall, Witton Albion, Oldham A , Southampton, Rochdale (1921-1932)*

A "great trier," Watson was taken on trial by Man United but failed to make the grade, instead going on to Lancashire rivals Oldham where he would play for eight seasons. Featured over 233 times (64 goals) for the Latics, before moving to the south coast as a "makeweight" in the transfer of Billy Murphy, whom moved the other way. He would struggle to acclimatise to life at Southampton, and never fully established himself in the first team. Watson was directly involved in four goals in his first six games (scoring two himself) but was displaced in the side by Stan Cribb and the emergence of John Arnold. Watson would only feature sporadically at first team level in his two seasons at the club but contributed regularly for the Reserves as a goalscoring winger, earning a move back to the third tier with Rochdale before retirement. Watson later worked as a labourer.

Watson, Vic

Centre-forward
Born: *1897 Girton, Cambridgeshire*
Died: *1988*
Playing career: *Wellingborough Town, West Ham United, Southampton (1920-1930)*

The word 'legend' is often overused when it comes to football, but no other description can do Watson's West Ham career justice. The club's all time record goalscorer with 326 in 505 games, Watson scored thirteen hat-tricks with the east London side, scoring four goals in a game twice, five once and even, on one occasion, six goals in a single game. He was capped five times by England, scoring four goals, and played in the 1923 FA Cup final for the Hammers, the first showpiece to be held at Wembley. They beat Southampton en route to the final and when the captain that day, George Kay, recently appointed as Saints manager, went in search of re-inforcements, he turned to the ageing, 37-year-old Watson. Both parties still felt he had one more season left in him and os its proved. Watson top scored for Southampton, as he plundered 15 goals in 35 games, including a hat-trick, the Saints oldest ever scorer of a treble. Watson netted on both his debut and last appearance for Saints, retiring at the end of 1935-36 and going on to become a market-gardener in his native Cambridgeshire.

Wayman, Charlie

Centre-forward
Born: *1922 Bishop Auckland*
Died: *2006*
Playing career: *Newcastle United, Southampton, Preston North End, Middlesbrough, Darlington. (1946-1957)*

A free-scoring striker, Charlie Wayman was the archetypal no.9 and formed a revered and legendary partnership with the great Ted Bates during his time at Southampton. Having become Saints record signing at the time for £10,000 from Newcastle - where he would also regularly find the net - Wayman more than repaid that fee when he plundered 77 goals in 105 games during three seasons on the south coast. Bill Dodgin would build his emerging side around the net-busting exploits of

Wayman, but whilst his team-mates Alf Ramsey and Bill Ellerington would earn full recognition with England, Wayman would be afforded no such luxury - although, in mitigation, England had the likes of Nat Lofthouse, Tommy Lawton, Jackie Milburn and Stan Mortensen leading the country's line when Wayman was at the peak of his considerable powers. Wayman, described as an "elusive, nippy" little forward with a "ferocious" shot, would leave Southampton after his wife became unhappy but he still continued to score with ease, with an extraordinary strike rate of 105 in 157 games for Preston, scoring in every round of the FA Cup in 1954, although his goal in the final was not enough to prevent North End's defeat to West Brom. Wayman hit 31 in 55 for Middlesbrough and 17 in 24 for Darlington before having to retire through injury. In later life, Wayman coached and managed at non league Evenwood Town, later becoming a salesman for the *Scottish & Newcastle Breweries*. Wayman died in 2006 at the age of 83. His brother Frank was also a professional player with Preston and Chester.

CHARLIE WAYMAN SOUTHAMPTON

Weale, Bobby
Outside-right
Born: *1905 Troed-y-rhiw, Wales* **Died:** *1952*
Playing career: *West Ham United, Swindon Town, Southampton, Cardiff City, Boston Town, Guildford City, Newport County, Wrexham, Glentoran, Cheltenham Town, Bath City (1925-1936)*

Weale was plucked from the backwaters of Welsh amateur football to earn a crack at the big time with West Ham. He only played three times in two years in east London, though, before signing for Swindon. Southampton had been keeping tabs on his rapid rise for some time and paid £1,000 to bring him to The Dell. He made the no.7 shirt his own, displacing Bert Jepson and caching the eye with his skilful and technical wing play. Weale scored a hat-trick in his third outing for the club, but would often be the main provider of goals for strikers Willie Haines and Dick Rowley. A combination of injury and a loss of form saw Weale fall down the pecking order and Jepson get his place back. Moved back to Wales and played for Cardiff before a nomadic, ground hopping existence in the non league game. Weale later found employment at a car assembly plant in Coventry. Played 48 times (ten goals) for Saints in two and a bit seasons at the club.

Webb, Charles
Outside-right
Born: *1879 Higham Ferrers* **Died:** *1939*
Playing career: *Chesham Grenadiers, Higham Ferrers, Rushden, Kettering, Leicester Fosse Wellingborough , Southampton, Dundee, Manchester City , Airdrieonians (1898-1909)*

A harness maker by trade, Webb scored twice for giant-killing Kettering to knock second tier Chesterfield out of the FA Cup and spark his rise to prominence. His exploits attracted the attentions of Chesterfield's divisional rivals Leicester Fosse, eventually signing for Southampton after a stint back at Kettering - where he would link up with former Fosse team-mate Bert Dainty, replacing Dick Evans at The Dell and joining the Southern League Saints in 1904. A "brilliant wing man with turn of speed, notable for his centres nd long shots", vying with the returning Archie Turner for Southampton's right ank berth.

The two could not be accommodated in the same side and so Webb was in and out of the team, playing 19 times (five goals) in his solitary season on the south coast before moving to Scotland. He and Dundee would finish second in the league before Webb returned to England with Manchester City, staying until they were relegated in 1909. After hanging up his boots, Webb managed a bakery business in his native Northamptonshire.

Webb, Danny
Defender
Born: *1983 Poole*
Playing career: *Southampton, Southend United, Brighton & Hove Albion , Hull City, Lincoln City, Cambridge United , Yeovil Town, (2000-2014)*

Webb began his career in the youth ranks at Southampton but failed to break into the first team squad after a handful of games at Reserve team level. He was eventually signed by his old man, the aforementioned Dave, Southend's manager at the time. Went on to become a first team regular but lost his place upon his dad's resignation and went on to turn out for Brighton and a number of clubs in the Football League and at non league level. Webb played for seventeen clubs during a 14-year career as a playing over 300 games in total, before he hung up his boots in 2014. In later life, he coached at AFC Totton and worked at Leyton Orient, taking charge of the Under 14s, U16s and Under 18s before eventually being appointed as boss of the first team in 2017 but left the position after only twelve games in the hotseat. He has since worked as youth team coach of the O's.

Webb, David

Defender
Born: *1946 Stratford, Essex*
Playing career: *Leyton Orient, Southampton, Chelsea, Leicester City, QPR, Leicester City, Derby County, Bournemouth, Torquay U. (1964-1984).*

Scored on his debut at Wolves - with an overhead kick no less - having signed for Southampton from Leyton Orient at the expense of George O'Brien. Known for his heading ability and set piece prowess, his goal at Molineux kick-started a sequence that would see Saints promoted. Playing primarily at right-back but also at centre-half as deputy for the injured or unavailable Tony Knapp. He would later make that no.4 shirt his own, partnering new signing Jimmy Gabriel, until he left for Chelsea after two seasons and 75 games. Webb would make his name with the Stamford Bridge side, winning the FA Cup in 1970 (Webb scored the extra-time winner in the replay) and the Cup Winners Cup the following year as Dave Sexton's "team of the decade" rose to prominence with a stylish swagger. Webb played in every position for Chelsea, including in goal - keeping a clean sheet in the process against Ipswich - then scoring a hat-trick as a stand-in striker in the return match! Voted Chelsea's Player of the Season in his debut campaign at the Bridge, and featured over 200 times in west London. Son of another ex-Saint, Danny Webb (above), David Webb went on to become a manager having retired from playing. He served Bournemouth and Torquay as player-boss, had three spells at Southend, and also took charge of Brentford, Yeovil and his beloved Chelsea. Latterly, Webb has worked in property development and management. Having worked behind the scenes at Bournemouth and Spurs, Webb served as technical director of Swedish club Ostersunds before being appointed at Huddersfield Town in 2019, as head of football operations.

"DID YOU KNOW?"

"Hollowbread Gardens, Bursledon is named after Saints 'keeper John."

Webber, Eric

Centre-half
Born: *1919 Shoreham-by-Sea* **Died:** *1996*
Playing career: *Norwich City, Southampton, Torquay United (1937-1956)*

Webber had a trial at Portsmouth but wasn't deemed good enough. Former Saints player turned scout, Jim Angell, was clearly impressed though, and recommended him to future Southampton manager Tom Parker. He would spend most of his first year at The Dell in the Reserves, but would get a first team debut - in 1939 - before WWII intervened. Served in the RAF during the War before returning to The Dell. He would become an ever-present at the back and a rock at the heart of the Saints defence, playing 137 games in succession and stacking up 200 appearances in total. Later served as player-manager at Torquay United. He took charge of Poole Town in 1965 before retiring five years later to run the *Manor House* pub in Woolston for many years. Died in 1996.

Eric webber 943.

Wells, Peter

Goalkeeper
Born: *1956 Nottingham*
Playing career: *Nottingham Forest, Southampton, Millwall, Leyton Orient (1971-1989)*

Broke through with his hometown team Nottingham Forest, preceding their glory days by three years, before he joined Lawrie McMenemy's Southampton for £8,000 to displace Cup-winning incumbent Ian Turner. Saints were building a side capable of Second Division promotion, with Wells one of five keepers to feature in 1976-77. Saints would return to the top flight the following season by which time Terry Gennoe had arrived and made the no.1 jersey his own, playing in the 79' League Cup final. But Wells would finally get his chance, usurping first Gennoe and then Ivan Katalinic, playing in excess of 100 games before the arrival of Peter Shilton - ironically from Wells' former club Nottingham Forest. Wells turned out 160 times for Saints in five and a half seasons but left the club upon the signing of Shilton. Later returned to Nottingham where he worked as a taxi driver.

Wheatley, Roland

Wing-half
Born: *1924 Radford, Notts* **Died:** *2003*
Playing career: *Nottingham Forest, Southampton, Grimsby Town. (1947-1951)*

A pit worker turned paratrooper, football must have seemed easy for Wheatley - a man accustomed to the school of hard knocks. Saints manager Bill Dodgin saw something in Wheatley and signed him from Forest, but Sid Cann would replace Dodgin before the player had been able to show what he could do. A heart defect caused him to miss six months and by the time he returned, Ted Bates and Jack Edwards had become Saints regular wing-half pairing. Wheatley was player-coach of the Reserves whilst sporadically filling in at senior level. He had been advised to retire but defied medical advice to play twelve games for Saints, before moving to Grimsby. In retirement, and licking his wounds, Wheatley continued to serve Saints as Bates chief Midlands scout throughout the his 18 years in charge.

Wheeler, Alfred

Inside-forward/Centre-forward
Born: *1910 Bilston* **Died:** *1978*
Playing career: *Walsall, Mossley, Brentford, Northampton Town , Southampton, Barnsley, Norwich City, Gillingham (1931-1936)*

Arrived at Saints as a "well recommended" striker from Northampton, but despite an "outstanding" 24-minute hat-trick in his second game, Wheeler struggled for consistency. He would score six times in his eleven games for the club, but had to make do with sporadic game time as back up to the established and experienced Arthur Holt. He would be dropped in favour of new signing Walter Pollard, and left for Barnsley after only a single season at The Dell. Wheeler went on to Barnsley, Norwich and Gillingham before dropping into non league. Wheeler later worked as a mechanic.

Whiston, Peter

Central defender
Born: *1968 Widnes*
Playing career: *Plymouth Argyle, Torquay United, Exeter City, Southampton, Shrewsbury Town, Stafford Rangers (1987-2006)*

Despite being born in the north west town of Widnes, Peter Whiston played most of his football at the other end of the country, turning out for Devonian trio Plymouth, Torquay and Exeter as a "classy and cultured" centre-back, catching the eye of Southampton on his travails. So much so, that incoming Saints manager Alan Ball shelved out £30,000 to sign Whiston for his Premier League side. The World Cup winner was well known for his slightly left field approach to the transfer market, and the step up proved too steep for the player. Whiston would only play once for Southampton, against Newcastle at St James Park in a 1-5 loss. Loaned out to a third division club - Shrewsbury - Whiston would never feature again for Saints at any level and ended his career in non league. Managed Witton Albion and Northwich Victoria before he drifted out of the game and took up a job as a financial advisor, later becoming a director of Blackburn-based GPSE Consultancy.

White, Ian
Half-back
Born: *1935 Glasgow, Scotland*
Playing career: *Celtic, Leicester City, Southampton, Hibs (1954-1972)*

Played four times for Scotland at junior level but found his path to stardom with hometown team Celtic barred by Paddy Crerand. Described as "ball-player," White moved to England where he helped the club to the FA Cup final in 1961, although he would not play at Wembley. A move to Chelsea fell through and so joined Southampton, slotting into the side at centre-half alongside former Leicester team mate Tony Knapp. He would become a regular for Saints over the next four years, occasionally playing in midfield and even at inside forward as Ted Bates led the club to promotion. He eventually lost his place and - following the arrival of compatriot Hugh Fisher - White was let go by the club. Went on to play non-league and managed Hampshire-based clubs Portals and Swaythling, opening a sports shop in Totton with ex-Saint Ron Davies.

White, William
Goalkeeper
Born: *1895 Scotland*
Playing career: *Hamilton Academical , Heart of Midlothian, Southampton, Aldershot (1923-1933)*

A "student of the game," White moved from the Scottish League to the south coast and signed for Saints as replacement for Tommy Allen. With £375 of his £800 fee paid for by the club's fans, he would become a virtual ever-present, and missed only two games in his first two seasons. White and his defence helped ensure the club a fourth placed Second Division finish, a placing they would not better for over two decades. White would lose his place to an emerging Bert Scriven. That prompted a move for White as he moved on to Football League rookies Aldershot, but White would never turn out for the Shots with his role restricted to that of a non-playing goalkeeping mentor. He later returned to Southampton to run a pub and then moved back to his native Scotland where White took up a job as a foreman in a tube steel factory in Glasgow.

Whitelaw, Robert
Half-back
Born: *1907 Stonehouse, South Lanarkshire, Scotland*
Playing career: *Doncaster Rovers, Celtic, Albion Rovers, Bournemouth & Boscombe Athletic , Glentoran, Queen of the South, Cowdenbeath, Albion Rovers, Southampton (1926-1937)*

Spent the majority of his career in his native Scotland, occasionally crossing the border to turn out for Doncaster, Southampton and Kidderminster as well as two stints in northern Ireland with Glentoran. Whitelaw was 33 by the time he arrived on the south coast, signed by newly appointed manager George Goss to replace the retired Stan Woodhouse. He would become a settle member of the Saints backline, slotting in alongside the Bills - Kennedy and Kingdon - and played 19 times in succession until he was displaced by Cyril King. A "strong and reliable" defender, he would not be offered a new contract at the end of his only season with the club, going on to Kidderminster Harriers before retirement. Whitelaw worked in intelligence and served in the Army before he became a hotelier in Kidderminster.

Whiting, William
Half-back
Born: *1882 Southampton* **Died:** *1973*
Playing career: *Southampton, Salisbury City, Eastleigh, Southampton Wanderers (1901-1910)*

Despite spending six years at Southampton and playing over 200 games for the Reserves, Whiting only turned out four times for Saints at senior first team level. Won the Hampshire Senior Cup with the second string and filled in for Sam Meston in the first team on three occasions during the 1902-03 season. Played his last game two years later before Whiting - a "committed half-back not lacking skill" left the club in search of regular first team football. He was even prepared to drop into non league to get it, turning out for Salisbury and Eastleigh in the Southern and Hampshire Leagues respectively, before retiring from the game. Whiting later became a chimney sweep and also worked as a referee at Southern League level. He also ran a clothes shop in Southampton for many years.

Whitlock, Mark
Centre-back
Born: *1961 Portsmouth*
Playing career: *Sarisbury Sparks, Southampton, Grimsby Town, Aldershot, Bournemouth, Reading, Aldershot, Aerostructures S & S (1975-1992)*

Rising through the ranks at Saints, Whitlock - a centre-back - began as a schoolboy, going on to become an apprentice and signing as a professional in 1979. His breakthrough would coincide with the greatest period in Saints history, with a side containing Channon, Boyer, Ball, George and Holmes, later rising to the top of the First Division with Kevin Keegan now in tow. Whitlock made his debut in the season that Southampton sat on the summit of the top flight for the first time in their history, with Whitlock's only goal for the club, against Stoke City, sending them there. He would occasionally be deployed in midfield, before being transferred to Bournemouth after 65 appearances. Whitlock would win a Third Division title medal with the Cherries under Harry Redknapp, going on to Reading and Aldershot before retirement. In later life, Whitlock worked a security officer, then as an HGV driver in Southampton.

Widdrington, Tommy
Midfielder
Born: *1971 Newcastle upon Tyne*
Playing career: *Southampton, Wigan Athletic, Grimsby Town, Port Vale, Hartlepool United, Macclesfield Town, Port Vale (1990-2010)*

Not flashy nor stylish, rather tough and combative, Widdrington joined Southampton at 15 and spent six years racking up 81 appearances in five different positions. Developed by Dave Merrington in the youth setup, and signing pro under Chris Nicholl, Widdrington would survive the cull of three further Saints managers to carve out a solid - if unspectacular - career with the Premier League Saints. A hard-worker with great energy, Widdrington scored three times before joining Grimsby following the arrival of yet another new manager at The Dell, Graeme Souness. He would help "The Mariners" to promotion and an Auto Windscreens Shield win for good measure.

Also played for Port Vale (twice), Hartlepool, Macclesfield and Salisbury through a nomadic career in the lower leagues before Widdrington retired. After the end of his playing days, Widdrington moved into coaching, serving his last club Salisbury as player-manager and then Southend as assistant to Paul Sturrock (another former Saints boss). Having briefly taken charge of National League club Hemel Hempstead Town, Widdrington returned to that level in 2012 when he was appointed as boss of east Sussex side Eastbourne Borough. Widdrington played at all 92 league grounds - and turned out in all four divisions of English football - during his playing career. After one game as Bristol Rovers caretaker manager, Widdrington moved "upstairs" at the Memorial Ground, working as head of recruitment and, as of 2020, he is currently Director of Football at the Pirates. Twitter: https://twitter.com/tommywidd

Wilcock, George
Goalkeeper
Born: *1890 Edinburgh, Scotland* **Died:** *1962*
Playing career: *Bradford Park Avenue, Barnsley, Goole Town , Brighton & Hove Albion , Southampton, Preston North End (1909-1921)*

A law stationer from Scotland turned goalkeeper, Wilcock failed to break through at Barnsley and Yorkshire rivals Bradford PA, before a handful of appearances for Brighton shortly before the outbreak of WW1. During the conflict, he joined military unit the *Royal Field Artillery* and was mortally wounded in Loos, France, in 1915. Working as a army-trainer, he slowly recovered from his injuries and represented the Army against the Navy when he was scouted and signed by Southampton. Wilcock joined the club in time for the first post-War season of 1919-20. A "very able custodian," Wilcock displaced Arthur Wood between the sticks for Saints, going on to play 22 times for the club before Saints relutanctsy released him. Wilcock later played for Preston, albeit briefly, dipping into the Welsh league before taking up a job on the Docks upon returning to Southampton.

Wilcox, Joe
Outside-right
Born: *1886 Stourbridge*
Died: *1940*
Playing career: *Stourbridge Standard, Cradley St Luke's, Dudley, Aston Villa, Birmingham, Southampton , Wellington Town (1906-1916)*

A winger, at his best when "beating opponent defenders," Wilcox was the archetypal creator of goals rather than a prolific scorer himself. Signed by Southampton as new manager George Swift embarked on a radical spending spree, Wilcox turned out to be one of Swift's better buys, becoming established on the right with his speed, crossing ability and capacity to "manoeuvre astutely" his best assets. Wilcox played 32 times for the club and scored five goals in his first ten games before form, individually and collectively, dipped and Wilcox was displaced by another new arrival Sid Kimpton. He would spend only the one season at The Dell, eventually dropping into non league football with Stourbridge and Wellington Town, later serving with the Royal Field Artillery during WW1. Posted to Canada with the Royal Gun Artillery, Wilcox became an engineer after the conflict.

Wilkins, Leonard
Half-back
Born: *1925 Southampton* **Died:** *2003*
Playing career: *Southampton*

A one club man and local boy made good, Wilkins - aka "Spud" or "Dusty," Wilkins had his limitations but was universally appreciated by the Southampton faithful for his versatility, commitment and unstinting determination to the cause. Toured Brazil in 1948 and returned to make his debut in Alf Ramsey's last appearance for Southampton. Wilkins played anywhere across the defence, even playing in midfield and up front on several occasions. Wilkins donned every jersey from 2 to 11 at The Dell, and turned out almost 300 times for the club during a decade's service to Southampton. Captained the Reserves to league and cup glory in 1952, and then skippered the senior side during an ever-present season - mainly at right-

back - two seasons later. When retirement finally came, Wilkins emigrated to Canada, occasionally playing locally and had a stint in Los Angeles, staying for 45 years across the pond, occasionally returning to attend Saints testimonial events and benefits.

Wilkinson, Charlie
Full-back
Born: *1907 Medomsley*
Died: *1975*
Playing career: *Leeds United, Sheffield United, Southampton, Bournemouth (1928-1939)*

An FA Cup finalist with Sheffield United during his time at Bramall Lane, before joining divisional rivals Southampton in 1938. Wilkinson would go straight into the team at right-back, only to be struck down by a chronic keen injury that would need two operations on a damaged cartilage. Wilkinson would recover, but Saints had brought in Tom Emanuel as their new left back. He would only play once more for Saints, with Emanuel's consistency and longevity blocking his path. Wilkinson would drop down the divisions to join Bournemouth as player-coach, before the outbreak of war ended his career as a pro. Wilkinson later worked in construction and also as a factory worker.

Williams, Andrew
Defender
Born: *1977 Bristol*
Playing career: *Southampton, Swindon Town, Bath City (1992-2004)*

Capped twice by Wales, Williams was the youngest Saint to earn international recognition when he play against Brazil and Malta in 1997 and 1998. His time at Saints would mirror his Welsh career however - short and unfulfilling. He spent three years at Saints but started only three Premier League games, being restricted to substitute appearances and fleeting cameos in his other 18 games. Loaned out to Swindon, the Wilshire side signed him permanently and he would play just shy of 47 times for Swindon, but - dogged by injuries - Williams would be lost to the game at the age of only 24. He quit in 2001 after becoming disillusioned and took up a career in the police.

Williams, Ernest

Outside-left
Born: 1882 Ryde
Died: 1943
Playing career: Ryde, Portsmouth, Chelsea, Portsmouth, Southampton (1906-1913)

A teacher by trade, amateur player Ernie represented Hampshire at both cricket and football, and attracted interest from all-conquering Arsenal before signing for Pompey. He would spend three years at Fratton Park, playing sporadically at no.11, before moving to Chelsea where he earned two caps for England at amateur level. Played 32 times for Portsmouth before making the journey only the foolhardy dare go - as an ex-Pompey player signing for the Saints. He would make only a single appearance for Southampton though, in place of the injured Len Andrews in 1912, before retiring at the end of the 1912-13 season to focus on teaching. Williams died in 1943 during the war as, when on duty as a fire warden, he fell from a moving bus and struck his head on the kerb.

Williams, Frederick

Full-back
Born: 1918 Hucknall
Died: 1994
Playing career: Hucknall Colts, Southampton, Mansfield Town, Liverpool, Stockport County, Linby Colliery (1937-1959)

Williams, a coal miner by trade and a "tough tackling defender" on the field, joined Southampton's Academy in 1937, signing pro the following year and going on to make the right-back position his own for the 1938-39 campaign. Injury - and the outbreak of WW2, hindered him, and he guested for Saints - as well as Mansfield and Liverpool - in unofficial wartime football before returning to his native Nottinghamshire. Later played for Stockport before returning to his roots as a coal miner, playing for Linby Colliery's works side and helping them to the FA Cup first round proper in 1950. Williams played 22 times for Southampton during his solitary season at The Dell.

Williams, George

Inside-forward
Born: 1897 Ventnor **Died:** 1957
Playing career: Southampton, Exeter City, Netley Sports, Cowes, Salisbury City (1919-1926)

Joined Saints as an amateur after he had served in the Hampshire Regiment during WW1. Williams first and last games for Southampton came against Portsmouth, briefly filling in for the injured Arthur Dominy at centre-forward for three games in the 1920-21 season and scoring on his debut. Williams struggled to adapt to the demands of the Football League. His career would be ended by injury and ultimately a case of what might have been. Williams took up employment as a painter and decorator. Died in 1957 aged 59.

Williams, Oshor

Midfielder /Forward
Born: 1958 Stockton-on-Tees
Playing career: Manchester United, Southampton, Exeter City, Stockport County, Port Vale, Preston North End. (1976-1987)

Williams had spent a year as a youngster with Manchester United before Lawrie McMenemy snapped him up for a modest £4,000 fee. He showed flashes of what he could do but ultimately only played 7 times for the first team. After he retired in 1989, Williams became the Community Development Officer for Preston and worked on the coaching staff at Aberdeen. Williams returned to full time study, gaining a BA Honours in Politics and History from Salford University and went on to become head lecturer on the Sports Studies course. Williams joined the PFA in 1996, initially as a player liaison officer and later as the organisation's Assistant Director of Education. Williams role is to ensure that players and PFA members past and present have access to education, and opportunities. He heads up the "Making the Transition" project which enables players to plan for the future and explore options for when they retire. Williams sits on the committee of the General Federation of Trade Unions and is a driving force behind the PFA's "Achieving through Sport" project, aiming to spearhead the organisation's learning activities.

Williams, Paul

Centre-back/midfielder
Born: *1971 Burton upon Trent*
Playing career: *Derby County, Lincoln City, Coventry City, Southampton, Stoke City, Richmond Kickers (1989-2005)*

Started out as a striker and in midfield for Derby, a stone's throw away from his native Burton upon Trent. Williams played almost 200 games for the Rams, before joining Saints - via a stint at Premier League Coventry. When the Sky Blues manager was appointed at Southampton, Williams would go with him, initially on a short term deal. Replacing cult hero Dean Richards, the 30-year-old became a solid ever-present and the club finished in mid-table. Williams would miss most of the 2002-03 season in which the club reached the FA Cup final and qualified for Europe, being released soon after having made almost 50 appearances. Went on to Stoke and Richmond Kickers across the pond before moving into coaching and management. Took charge of Nottingham Forest on a caretaker basis in 2016 and had a spell as interim boss of England's U20 side the same year. Having worked under another ex-Saint, Jason Dodd, as no.2 at Aldershot, Williams was Head of Youth at Saints, and also worked at Team Solent and Eastleigh. Became first team coach at Sheffield Wednesday in March 2021.

Williams, Royston 'Roy'

Inside-forward
Born: *1932 Hereford* **Died:** *2011*
Playing career: *Hereford Lads' Club, Thynnes Athletic, Hereford United, Southampton, Worcester City, Cinderford Town (1947-1963)*

A diminutive inside-forward, Royston Williams aka Roy - at a mere 5ft 4 - will be remembered as one of the smallest Saints ever. Despite his size, Williams stocky build enabled him to "mix it" with the other forwards and he was able to trouble even the most miserly of defences thanks to his pace. He would become a first team regular, stepping in to the significant shoes of Ted Bates to score on his debut, ending up with seven goals in his 41 appearances which were spread across three years on the payroll.

Williams returned to where it all began for him at Hereford, going on to become the second highest goalscorer in the now defunct club's history, with 154 in 357 games for the club. He later played for Worcester and Cinderford and had a benefit match with Saints. After retirement, Williams worked as a window cleaner and as a labourer. Died back in his hometown Hereford in 2011.

Williams, Steve

Midfielder
Born: *1958 Romford*
Playing career: *Southampton, Arsenal, Luton, Exeter, Derry (1975-1985)*

Williams dabbled in several ventures having hung up his boots. Moved into coaching initially, working under Alan Ball at Stoke City and former side Exeter. He would move to Devon permanent, working for a successful and award winning magazine publishers alongside another ex pro and former Grecian Alan Trump. Williams worked as chief executive and secretary at LCD Publishing Ltd, a company still in existence to this day although Williams left n 2003. The firm have produced titles including *Action GTX* and *Pony World* aimed at younger audiences. Southampton's Player of the Year 1976-77 has also worked as a surveyor and property developer, turning his hand to the building trade for an Exeter-based construction company. He continues to reside in Devon and still appears at St Mary's occasionally as a guest of honour in their hospitality suits and corporate events.

Williams, Stuart

Full-back
Born: *1930 Wrexham, Wales* **Died:** *2013*
Playing career: *Grove Park Grammar School, Victoria Youth Club, Wrexham, West Bromwich Albion, Southampton (1948-1966)*

A 43-cap Wales international defender with "a fine temperament, excellent positional sense and a sure kick," Williams started out at Wrexham but made his name and reputation with West Bromwich Albion. In partnership with Don Howe at full-back, Williams played over 200 times for the Baggies during his 12-year stay.

Represented Wales at the 1958 World Cup tournament, before joining Ted Bates' Southampton as the Saints manager looked to strengthen his squad with experience. He would become a virtual ever-present during his four year stint with the club, occasionally playing at left-back, and helped the club into Division One for the first time in their history before the arrival of David Webb brought his days at The Dell to an end. Williams turned out 167 times for Saints before retiring from the game. Williams would hold several coaching and managerial roles including assistant to Bates at Southampton. Worked as a coach at Aston Villa, former club West Brom and took charge of Paykan in Iran and Viking FK of Norway. After leaving football, he worked as a tyre salesman and then head of finance at a Hampshire transport business.

Williamson, Herbert

Goalkeeper
Born: *1871 Manchester*
Died: *1946*
Playing career: *Southampton St. Mary's, Royal Ordnance Factories (1894-1896)*

Manchester-born Williamson, an agile and alert shot stopper, joined Ardwick (the club known today as Manchester City) as a schoolboy but he never played for the club at any level. Moving to Southampton in time for the south coast side's inaugural league season, and despite conceding a goal within two minutes of his debut, he would settle as St Mary's no.1. He would only remain at the Antelope Ground for a single season, playing twelve games, before leaving for Eastleigh, combining playing with a job on the railways. He moved to London and briefly returned to football with the Royal Ordnance Factories, conceding 46 goals in only seven games, including a 10-0 thumping by former side Southampton at the aforementioned Antelope Ground. The club would disband after some heavy losses, collapsing under financial constraints. Williamson returned to his native Manchester where he worked as a cotton merchant.

Williamson, Mike

Defender
Born: *1983 Stoke-on-Trent*
Playing career: *Torquay United, Southampton, Torquay United, Doncaster Rovers , Wycombe Wanderers, Watford, Portsmouth, Newcastle United, Wolverhampton W, Oxford United (2001-date)*

Strong in the tackle and a threat from set pieces given his 6ft 4 frame, Williamson was on the books at Southampton, with his time at the club sandwiched between two stints with Torquay. Williamson would never break into the first team at Saints, however, returning to Plainmoor after two appearances for the Reserves. Played for Doncaster and Wycombe on loan before moving to Watford, where he was signed by Paul Hart at Portsmouth for £2m. It would be at Newcastle where Williamson would become best known, however, earning Man of the Match on his debut for the Toon, striking up a solid and reliable pairing with Fabricio Coloccini at the heart of the Newcastle defence. He played 150 times for the SJP side, winning the Championship in record-breaking style in 2009-10 to propel the club back to the top flight. He has since played for Wolves and Gateshead, where he became the club's player-manager.

Mike Williamson

Wilson, Arthur

Half-back/Inside-forward
Born: *1908 Newcastle upon Tyne*
Died: *2000*
Playing career: *Southampton, West Ham United, Chester, Wolves, Torquay United (1926-1940)*
Wilson was scouted and signed up by Southampton when still only 18. He would have to wait two years for his first team breakthrough but went on to play 66 times. Strapped for cash, the club accepted the £500 offered by West Ham for Wilson. He returned to his native Tyneside after the WWI where he worked in the brewery trade. Died in 2000 at the age of 92.

Wilson, Barry

Midfielder
Born: *1972 Kirkcaldy, Scotland*
Playing career: *Southampton, Ross County, Raith Rovers, Inverness CT, Livingston, St Johnstone , Queen of the South, Peterhead, Elgin City, Wick Academy (1992-2013)*
A creative, box-to-box player, Wilson has spent his entire career in his native Scotland having started out at Southampton. Wilson never played for the Saints first team. Heholds a unique claim to fame, being the last goalscorer of the old millennium and the first goalscorer of the new one, whilst at Caley Thistle. Since retiring, Wilson has held a variety of coaching and managerial roles, notably as manager of Wick Academy and Elgin City. He is currently first team coach at former side Inverness CT.

Wilson, Thomas

Full-back
Born: *1930 Southampton*
Died: *2010*
Playing career: *Southampton, Fulham, Brentford, Folkestone Town (1947-1962)*
Wilson was on the books but without a first team appearance to his name before following manager Bill Dodgin to Fulham. After he hung up his boots, Wilson remained involved in football as a director of Fulham from the last 1980s until the sleepy capital club was purchased by Mohamed Al Fayed. He later worked as a quantity surveyor and in the property statement. Died in 2010

Wimshurst, Ken

Right-half
Born: *1938 South Shields*
Died: *2017*
Playing career: *Newcastle United, Gateshead, Wolverhampton Wanderers, Southampton, Bristol City (1957-1971)*
Having failed to make the grade at Newcastle and Wolves, Wimshurst was spotted for ex Saints-turned-scout Bill Rochford whilst playing for the RAF. Having signed for a then record fee of £1,500, Wimshurst slotted straight into the team on the right wing, going on to strike up a formidable triumvirate with Terry Paine and Stuart Williams - a partnership that would remain unchanged for the best part of four years. A "great passer of the ball with good vision," Wimshurst - despite being called up to England's Under 21 side, was considered unfortunate never to get capped by his country. Wimshurst also has the claim to fame of being Southampton's first ever substitute, helping the side climb from the this tier to the top flight before losing his place to Hugh Fisher. Wimshurst played 167 times for Saints, moving on to Bristol City in a player-coach capacity and then staying on as assistant to John Sillett (another former Saint) at City after retiring as a player. Coached at Dundee and in Egypt, also had a job with a sports shop in Bristol and later ran Southampton's Centre of Excellence. Wimshurst also scouted at Leeds and Aston Villa.

Dennis Wise

W

Wise, Dennis
Midfielder
Born: *1966 Kensington*
Playing career: *Wimbledon, Chelsea, Leicester City, Millwall, Southampton, Coventry City (1985-2006)*

One of the beautiful game's most infamous hard men, Dennis Wise kicked anything that moved and picked fights almost as often as he would collect medals. Wise had been signed by Southampton aged eight, but he failed to breakthrough having fallen out with Lawrie McMenemy. Wise would have to wait two decades to finally make headway on the south coast, going on to become synonymous with the FA Cup. Wise won the trophy thrice, captaining Chelsea to their FA Cup wins in 1997 and 2000, and was one of Wimbledon's "Crazy Gang" to shock Liverpool in the 88' showpiece. Wise returned to Saints on a free transfer in 2005 and played 12 times under Harry Redknapp, later taking over as joint caretaker-manager after Redknapp's departure. After retirement, Wise has remained heavily involved in football. He managed Leeds and Swindon and last served Newcastle in an executive role. He has also done commentary on Five Live and TalkSport and has appeared on Sky Sports. He finished fifth on I'm a Celebrity in 2017, proving a popular member of the camp in the Australian jungle. He continues to work in the media as an analyst.

Withers, Edward
Inside-forward
Born: *1915 Ower* **Died:** *1994*
Career: *Southampton, Bristol Rovers, (1933-1939)*

Joined Southampton as an amateur groundsman but was soon rewarded with a crack at first team football. Withers would never fully establish himself in the Southampton side. Having played six times for Saints, Withers departed in 1937 en route to Second Division Bristol Rovers where he turned out 17 times, before moving back to the south coast. Worked as a masseur in London and then took up employment with *de Havilland* working in aircraft manufacturing. Withers later worked as an accountant and was a regular spectator at The Dell.

Womack, Tim
Outside-left
Born: *1934 Denaby* **Died:** *2010*
Playing career: *Denaby United , Derby County, Southampton, Workington (1957-1961)*

Having failed to establish himself at Derby Womack moved to the south coast to gain regular football but would again find himself on the periphery thanks to the sustained consistency of John Sydenham Saints had a settled side in the Third Division and so Womack would remain predominantly in the Reserves. Southampton would win the league and earn promotion to the second tier but Womack played no part in their triumph and was released, dropping down two divisions to sign for Workington. He had little success, there, too scoring once in nine games before retiring from the game - disillusioned with life as a professional player - and later worked as a carpenter.

Wood, Arthur
Goalkeeper
Born: *1894 Walsall* **Died:** *1941*
Playing career: *Southampton, Clapton Orient, Ryde Sports, Newport (1914-1931)*

Followed in his father Harry Wood's footsteps by going on to become a regular in the Southampton team, having watched his old man from the terraces at The Dell. Wood joined Saints as a fresh-faced 19 year old amateur. Described as agile and commanding, Wood displaced Ernie Steventon within six months of his arrival at the club, sharing the work between the sticks when Steventon, the regular keeper, returned. Wood served during the First World War in the Royal Engineers, resuming his career after the conflict instilled as the Saints no.1. George Wilcox later took over and Wood played only twice more before moving to divisional rivals Clapton Orient. He became ever-present in his eight seasons there, playing almost 400 games in a decade with the club. He later returned to the south coast and player for Ryde and Newport on the Isle of Wight before working as an insurance worker in Portsmouth. Died in Portsmouth in April 1941 at the age of 47.

Wood, Harry
Inside-forward
Born: 1868 Walsall
Died: 1951
Playing career: Walsall Swifts, Wolverhampton Wanderers, Walsall, Southampton (1887-1905)
Already a prolific net buster a both local and national level, Harry Wood (father of Arthur, above), had won the FA Cup and racked up 109 goals in 241 games for Wolves when he arrived at Saints. Wood had played in three FA Cup finals (winning it in 1893) and had earned three caps for England when he moved to The Dell. Joining the two-time defending Southern League champions, Wood signed for £70 at Birmingham New Street Station and was immediately made captain. He would lead the side to one of the most trophy-laden eras in their history, winning four Southern Leagues in five seasons. Wood went on to feature 158 times for the club, hitting 62 goals as their string-pulling talisman. Later worked as a coach at Portsmouth whilst seeing his son Arthur make the grade as a Saints keeper. Wood retired from football to work as the licensee of the *Milton Arms* pub in close proximity to Fratton Park.

Wood, Steve
Central defender
Born: 1963 Bracknell
Playing career: Reading, Millwall, Southampton, Oxford United. (1981-1996).
An elegant and ball-playing centre-back, Wood was on the books at Arsenal before becoming a regular in Ian Branfoot's promotion winning Reading side. He spent eight years with the Royals as they rose to the Second Divisionand then helped Millwall reach the top flight during his debut season as something of a promotion specialist before moving to the south coast and signing for Southampton's newly appointed manager Branfoot. Almost 50 games later, Wood - now out of favour under Alan Ball - joined third tier Oxford, yet again helping them to go up. Having retired from the game, Wood worked for a coaching academy in Farnham and later became a player agent, setting up *Midas Sports Management*, an advisory organisation for professional players.

Woodford, George
Full-back
Born: 1915 Lymington **Died:** 1966
Playing career: Lymington, Norwich City, Southampton (1934-1939)
Having followed manager Tom Parker from east Anglia back to Hampshire, Woodford was unable to establish himself as first choice and played only seven games in two years between 1937 and 1939. Having been released by the club prior to WW2, Woodford played for non league Lymington and served in the Marine Corps during the conflict. He later worked as an engineer on the railways at Eastleigh.

Woodhouse, Stanley
Inside-forward/Half-back
Born: 1899 Warrington **Died:** 1977
Playing career: Bury, Southampton (1921-1937)
Started out at Bury and helped the Shakers into the top flight for the first time in their history. In a bid to bolster their ranks for the First Division, Southampton's Bill Turner moved to Gigg Lane with Woodhouse moving the other way. He soon became a virtual ever present and made the left-half spot his own. Despite the emergence of Bill Luckett, Woohouse played 366 games in over a decade at The Dell, with those games coming under four different Saints managers. He later worked as a labourer and licensee of the *Bricklayers Arms* in Millbrook. Coached Saints youth sides and took up a job as chief steward at a golf club in Romsey. Died in 1977.

Woods, Chris
Goalkeeper
Born: 1959 Swineshead, Lincolnshire
Playing career: Nottingham Forest, QPR, Norwich City, Rangers, Sheffield Wednesday, Reading, Southampton, Sunderland, Burnley. (1976-1998)
A much travelled goalkeeper with 43 England caps, Woods won a League Cup winners medal with Forest as an 18-year-old stand-in, with Peter Shilton unavailable. He would never truly usurp Shilton, and had was regularly loaned out including a four match spell with Saints. Woods later had a career as a goalkeeping coach with David Moyes at Everton, Manchester United and West Ham.

Woolf, Levi

inside-right

Born: *1916 Johannesburg, South Africa* **Died:** *2003*
Playing career: *Southampton (1937-1939)*

Levi Woolf's path from South African junior to England's Second Division was a very unusual one. He had played for Transvaal and Orange Railways as a junior but his dream lay in playing in the promised land of Blighty. Living and working on board the *Balmoral Castle* ship, Woolf was introduced via satellite to Tom Parker - the manager of Southampton whom duly arranged for Woolf to be met by a Saints coach upon arrival on the dockside in Southampton. He was signed by the club and achieved his dream of first team football, albeit only for one match. In a match at Coventry, Woolf - playing at right-half was the game's "outstanding player" but the fixture was called off at half time due to heavy snow. He would make his official debut the following week in a match with Spurs but proved less of a success and his career was over almost before it had truly begun. Later turned out for Guildford City in the Southern League and served in Bangalore with the Royal Engineers during WW2. Returned to South Africa after the War and worked in retail.

Worthington, Frank

Forward

Born: *1948 Halifax*
Playing career: *Huddersfield Town, Leicester City, Bolton, Birmingham City, Leeds United, Sunderland, Southampton, Brighton, Tranmere Rovers, Preston North End, Stockport County. (1966-1987).*

A maverick talent who mixed work and pleasure - perhaps the latter more so - Frank Worthington played into his 40s, earned eight caps for England and stacked up over 700 games in the Football League. 'Worthy' never stayed at most of his 24 clubs for long. He was 34 and in the twilight of his career when he signed for Lawrie McMenemy's Southampton. He would stay for less than a year but won the fans over with his extravagant party tricks in an eye-catching Saints side. His Saints career would end in ignominy when he fell out with McMenemy, with the manager refusing to believe that Worthington was merely "having a chat" with two female Saints fan in a hotel room before an away match at Stoke. Whilst at Huddersfield, Worthington had been caught red handed with a couple of dancers and later released an autobiography entitled "One Hump of Two." Died on 22nd March 2021 after a lengthy illness. He was 72.

Frank Worthington and Peter Shilton

Wotton, Paul
Defender/Midfielder
Born: *1977 Plymouth*
Playing career: *Plymouth Argyle, Southampton, Oxford United, Yeovil Town (1994-2015)*
A member of Southampton's Football League Trophy winning side in 2010, Wotton signed for Saints as much-needed experience either in defence or midfield for the young squad assembled by Dutch duo Jan Poortvliet and Mark Wotte. Capable of playing in either of those roles, Wotton had been released by Plymouth after Argyle's relegation after over 400 games. Went on to feature over 50 times for Saints before moving to Oxford having failed to disrupt the emerging Morgan Schneiderlin and Dean Hammond midfield pairing, despite that appearance at Wembley. Later played for Yeovil and had a spell back at Plymouth, playing another half century of games whilst helping coach their reserves. Became manager of Southern League Premier side Truro City in July 2019.

Wrigglesworth, Billy
Outside-forward
Born: *1912 South Elmsall* **Died:** *1980*
Playing career: *Chesterfield, Wolves, Manchester United, Bolton Wanderers, Southampton, Reading, Burton Albion, Scarborough (1932-1948)*
A diminutive, pint sized winger, Wrigglesworth made his name with Wolves before playing for Manchester United in their infamous relegation of 1937. He played 37 games in ten years at United, as his career was disrupted by the outbreak of WW2. Served in the Merchant Navy during the conflict before moving on to bolton and then signing for Second Division Southampton, in exchange for Jack Bradley. Described as a "clever, dribbler with a deceptive body swerve." Despite the addition of an ageing Wrigglesworth, 35 by the time he moved to The Dell, he proved to be a crowd pleaser and a box of tricks, displacing Bobby Veck and featuring 14 times (four goals) in the 1947-48 season. Later moved on to Reading and Burton Albion before winding down in non league with Scarborough. Settled in Lancashire in later life where he coached at Accrington and Bury.

Wright, Frank
Outside-right
Born: *1898 Birmingham* **Died:** *1987*
Playing career: *Southampton (1920-1921)*
Spotted by a Southampton scout whilst playing for the works side of Hampton Colliery, arriving at The Dell ahead of the club's inaugural season in the Football League. Wright would go straight into the Reserve team in midfield, later switching to the right flank where he would make his first team debut at Grimsby in December 1930. Wright - a midfielder of "skill and pace" had a disappointing debut as the game "passed him by," and that would prove his one and only foray at senior first team level for the club. Wright returned to the Reserves, but never fully rediscovered the form that earned him his first team chance. Released at the end of the 1920-21 campaign, Wright returned to his native Staffordshire, playing in the Birmingham League and later rejoining Hampstead Colliery. He later worked as an engineer for the post office. Died in 1987 aged 89.

Wright, Jermaine
Midfielder/Defender
Born: *1975 Greenwich*
Playing career: *Millwall, Wolves , Doncaster Rovers, Crewe Alexandra, Ipswich Town, Leeds United, Southampton, Blackpool (1992-2011)*
Peaked at Ipswich under George Burley, and featured almost 200 times across three seasons as the club went up to the Premiership and then down again. With Burley recently installed in the Saints dugout in 2006, Wright's former manager took him on loan from Leeds - signing him permanently in a summer that ended in play-off heartache. Wright would be the given captain's armband with Claus Lundekvam injured and became a virtual ever present. The Londoner played just short of a century of games at Saints but - now 32, he was released by Saints under the new youth-based experiment of Dutch managers Jan Poortvliet and Mark Wotte. Had a brief stint at Blackpool and then retired after a short time in non league with Croydon Athletic and Lewes. Wright has since coached at Ipswich and has worked for the PFA.

Wright, Mark

Defender
Born: *1963 Dorchester on Thames*
Playing career: *Oxford United, Southampton Derby County, Liverpool (1980-1998)*

The future England international defender joined Saints as a fresh faced 18 year old from Oxford in 1982 and became a permenant fixture in the heart of a very strong defence. Played 170 games before Derby offered £760,000, a record at the time for a defender, to take him to the Baseball Ground. Again, the 6ft 2in defender helped his employers with a series of eye catching performances. Ultimately, they led to interest from Liverpool and another move. Since retirement, Wright moved into coaching, managing Oxford, Southport twice, Peterborough and Chester where he had three spells as boss. Later returned to Southport to serve on the board as scout, director and Head of Club Development before being dismissed in 2017. He now appears as pundit on BT Sport and for Liverpool's internal TV station LFCTV. Wright is also one of the founders of a company called Premier Legends.

Mark Wright (on left!)

This is a scheme designed for members of the public to join a football celebrity for stadium tours, Q&A sessions, corporate football tournaments, golf days, charity galas and personal appearances such as book and shirt signings. The venture ceased in 2018. Along with Michael Owen, he set up Red Sports - as the name suggests, a Liverpool based academy specialising in school and education training and coaching courses across the world, notably in the UK, US and China. As an ambassador of Foster Care Associates, Wright and his wife regularly help with national campaigns to highlight major issues and raise awareness about adoption. Twitter: *https://twitter.com/ mark5wright*

Wright, Richard

Goalkeeper
Born: *1977 Ipswich*
Playing career: *Ipswich Town, Arsenal, Everton, West Ham United, Southampton, Sheffield United, Preston North End, Manchester City (1995-2016)*

Rose to prominence with hometown team Ipswich and played over 300 times for the Suffolk club before earning a dream move to Premier League giants Arsenal. Wright would be back up to David Seaman,. Saved a penalty on his Champions League debut and deputised for Seaman enough to earn a league winners medal in 2001-02. Played 22 times for the Gunners but eventually became third choice behind Seaman and Stuart Taylor and so he moved to Everton where he would spend five years and made 60 appearances. An agile keeper and keeper with good distribution who read the game well, Wright played twice for England in friendlies against Malta and Netherlands. Loaned to Southampton in the 2007-08 season in the midst of a goalkeeping crisis with Kelvin Davis, Bartosz Bialkowski and Michael Poke all sidelined through injury. Wright played seven games for Saints, conceding only six goals, but did not sign permanently. Had a second, and indeed a third, coming at Ipswich and also played for Sheffield United and Preston, later moving to Manchester City where he never featured. He currently works under Pep Guardiola at the Etihad as City's goalkeeping coach.

Yahia, Alaeddine

Central defender

Born: *1981 Colombes, Hauts-de-Seine, France*
Playing career: *Louhans-Cuiseaux, Guingamp, Southampton, Saint-Etienne, Sedan, Nice, Lens , Caen, AS Nancy (2000-Still Playing)*

Tunisian centre-back with 21 caps for the north African nation. Yahia spent almost all of his playing career across the Channel in France and had a brief spell at Southampton although he never played for the club. A tall, cultured and ball playing centre-back, Yahia joined Saints from French club Guingamp ahead of the 2004-05 campaign as a triahlidt, but he failed to impress and never turned out at St Mary's at any level, moving back to France where he played for Sedan, Nice, Lens, Caen and AS Nancy. Represented Tunisia at the 2004 Athens Olympics and won the AFCON tournament in the same year. Yahia is currently a free agent having left Nancy in 2019.

Yates, Jimmy

Outside-righ

Born: *1869 Tunstall, Stafordshire*
Died: *1922*
Playing career: *Kelvinhaugh, Burnley, Ardwick, Sheffield United, Southampton, Gravesend United, Southampton, Hastings & St Leonards , Southampton, Gravesend United, Salisbury City (1891-1909)*

With the exception of Sheffield United, Jimmy Yates - a ground hopping winger - never stayed at any of his eleven clubs for long than two seasons. He spent four years at Bramall Lane, helping the Blades to the runners up position in the top flight before dropping into the Southern League to join Southampton. The St Mary's club were putting together an all conquering team consisting mainly of experienced players from higher leagues with Yates - described as a "dapper, clever forward virtually unstoppable at his best" - immediately becoming a first team regular as an established member of Saints forward line-up. He would go on to win three Southern League titles on the south coast as Southampton lived up to their billing, also reaching the FA Cup final in 1900, where they would lose 4-0 to Bury. Yates had three spells with the Saints, flitting to Gravesend and turning out for Hastings as player-coach in between his time with the club. He would play only once in his final swansong with the club, before finishing in non league with Salisbury City. In later life, Yates worked as a stevedore on Sotuthampton Docks. Forced to quit his job through ill-health, Yates took his own life on Southampton Common in 1922, aged 52.

Yeomans, Harry

Goalkeeper

Born: *1901 Farnborough*
Died: *1965*
Playing career: *Camberley & Yorktown, Southampton (1922-1926)*

Ironically known as "Tiny", Yeomans, along with goalkeeping compatriot George Ephgrave, holds the record as the tallest keeper ever to play for Saints (6ft 4). Farnborough-born, Yeomans played for Camberley as an amateur whilst representing Hampshire. He would serve as back-up throughout his four years at Saints, initially as cover to Tommy Allen, and played only twelve games for the club (four in 1924-25 and eight the following season), before becoming disillusioned with life as second choice. Yeomans would drift out of the game altogether and never worked in football again, going on to become a Constable with the Southampton Police, occasionally turning out for their works side.

Thankyou

The following photos are used courtesy of their owners and all copyrights are acknowledged and respected. CC BY-SA 4.0 *https://creativecommons.org/licenses/by-sa/4.0*, via Wikimedia Commons unless otherwise stated.

Chris Baird: *Mikhail Slain*
Dave Beasant: *Holdenbuckley*
James Beattie: *Add92*
Dexter Blackstock: *TuborgLight*
Boa Morte: *East Ham Bull*
Wayne Bridge: *Rybakova Elena*
Colin Clarke: *Runningboards*
Andy Cook: *Jeremy68*
Stephen Crainey: *Ronnie Macdonald*
Peter Crouch: *Agnieszka Mieszczak*
Christian Dailly: *Egghead06*
Andrew Davies: *Add92*
Kevin Davies: *Free-ers*
Rory Delap: *Wonker*
Richard Dryden: *Jonesy702*
Jason Euell: *Wonker*
Tim Flowers: *Jonesy702*
Martin Foyle: *Mattythewhite*
Ricardo Fuller: *Add92*
Bruce Grbbelar: *Jarle Vines*
Fitz Hall: *Peter McNally*
Danny Higginbottom: *Add92*
Mark Hughes: *Oyvind Vik*
Inigo Idiakez: *TuborgLight*
Stern John: *Struway*
Kenwyne Jones: *Lynchg*
Kachloul, Hassan: *Jonesy702*
Kanchelskis Andrei: *Self photographed*
Kevin Keegan: *scartinho*
Kasey Keller: *Borusse86*
Tony Knapp: *Jarvin*
Alan Knill: *ingythewingy*
Kamil Kosowski: *Slawek*
Ollie Lancashire: *FishyPhotos*
Graeme Le Saux: *Benny Glowinsky*
Sammy Lee: *Flums*
Chris Lucketti: *ingythewingy*
Scott McDonald: *Camw*
David McGoldrick: *Jon Candy*
Im Magilton: *Nick*
Mick Mills: *Nick*
Garry Monk: *Rhysowainwilliams*
Graeme Murty: *Robwingfield*

Neilson, Alan: *Jonesy702*
Antti Niemi: *Tomkeene*
Oakley, Matt: *Stew jones*
Brett Ormerod: *Jon Candy*
Egil Ostenstad: *Jarvin*
Marians Pahars: *Papuass*
Alex Pearce: *Robwingfield*
Dan Petrescu: *John Dobbo*
Kevin Phillips: *Jameboy*
Darren Potter: *Jon Candy*
Jason Puncheon: *BillyBatty*
Grzegorz Rasiak: *Slawek*
Redknapp, Jamie: *Will Palmer*
Peter Reid: *Philip Dews*
Graham Roberts: *Bully Wee*
Uwe Rösler: *Kjetil Ree*
MarekSaganowski: *Jdowling7*
Alan Shearer: *carltonreid*
Peter Shilton: *Joebloggsy*
Robbie Slater: *Camw*
Trond Egil Soltvedt: *Jarle Vines*
David Speedie: *Mark Freeman*
Anders Svensson: *Skistar*
Michael Svensson: *Halmstad*
Maik Taylor: *Struway*
Jo Tessem: *Kjetil Ree*
Wayne Thomas: *BigDom*
Andy Townsend: *Marion O'Sullivan*
Ian Turner: *Trevor John Faulkner*
TheoWalcott: *Gjt6*
Mark Walters: *Jarvin*
Webb, Daniel: *Jonesy702*
Mike Williamson: *mickyb59*
Paul Wotton: *Alan Head*
MarkWright: *TuborgLight*
Bradley Wright-Phillips: *Argyle 4 Life*

Audi- quattro-Cup: *Werner100359*
Shirt: *Werner100359*
CF Tyson: *Unknown author*
1899-1900: *Unknown author*
1904: *Unknown author*
1904.2: *Unknown author*
Fans' flag: *Werner100359*

Bus: *Colin Smith*
The Dell: *Steve Daniels*
Both courtesy of *geograph.co.uk*

You can read more and add your own comments/memories at:
www.where-are-they-now.co.uk/club/southampton

Home   Clubs   Latest   Books   Can You Help?   About Us   Contact

Search Player (by surname)

Southampton

Home / Southampton

Where Are They Now? - Southampton

Request a Twilio Flex Demo
Twilio

We hope that this collection of former players will bring back some happy memories of watching Southampton over the years.

The list is by no means exhaustive but is being added to all the time so please do check back from time to time. The current list of players can be found a little further down this page and this section is broken down by the first letter of their surname.

We are keen to include as many Southampton footballers as possible. If you know what has happened to any former players not listed here, please do let us know - thanks.

START

Easily Convert Doc to PDF,
Merge PDF, Compress PDF
& More!

Southampton Memorabilia and Books

If you like this site then we would recommend that you have a look at Amazon's latest collection of **Southampton items for sale** (often at a discounted price!). Although best known for selling books, they now have expanded their range to include all sorts of goodies - you never know what you might find!

Southampton Book

Have you ever wondered what happened to all of those players that you have seen come and go over the years?

The old belief was that ex-footballers became publicans or publicans or TV pundits. However, we hope that you will be interested, and in some cases amused, to find out that this is no longer the case. The characters featured are now scattered around the globe and have provided plenty of colourful stories!

Relive memories of all of your favourite stars of yesteryear in this fascinating insight into life after Southampton.

Features over 450 former Southampton players and lots of recent photographs.

Coming Soon - Find Out More

Printed in Great Britain
by Amazon